The Roman Emperor and His Court c. 30 BC–c. AD 300

Volume 2: A Sourcebook

At the centre of the Roman empire stood the emperor and the court surrounding him. The systematic investigation of this court in its own right, however, has been a relatively late development in the field of Roman history, and previous studies have focused on narrowly defined aspects or on particular periods of Roman history. This book makes a major contribution to understanding the history of the Roman imperial court. The first volume presents nineteen original essays covering all the major dimensions of the court from the age of Augustus to the threshold of Late Antiquity. The second volume is a collection of the ancient sources that are central to studying that court. The collection includes: translations of literary sources, inscriptions, and papyri; plans and computer visualizations of archaeological remains; and photographs of archaeological sites and artworks depicting the emperor and his court.

BENJAMIN KELLY is an associate professor in the Department of History at York University, Toronto. He is the author of *Petitions, Litigation, and Social Control in Roman Egypt* (2011).

ANGELA HUG teaches at York University, Toronto, in the Departments of History and Humanities, and at Glendon College. She is a Roman historian whose research interests focus on women, the family, and the cultural politics of fertility and reproduction during the Principate.

The Roman Emperor and His Court c. 30 BC–c. AD 300

VOLUME 2

A Sourcebook

Edited by

BENJAMIN KELLY
York University, Toronto

ANGELA HUG
York University, Toronto

CAMBRIDGE
UNIVERSITY PRESS

CAMBRIDGE
UNIVERSITY PRESS

University Printing House, Cambridge CB2 8BS, United Kingdom

One Liberty Plaza, 20th Floor, New York, NY 10006, USA

477 Williamstown Road, Port Melbourne, VIC 3207, Australia

314–321, 3rd Floor, Plot 3, Splendor Forum, Jasola District Centre, New Delhi – 110025, India

103 Penang Road, #05–06/07, Visioncrest Commercial, Singapore 238467

Cambridge University Press is part of the University of Cambridge.

It furthers the University's mission by disseminating knowledge in the pursuit of education, learning, and research at the highest international levels of excellence.

www.cambridge.org
Information on this title: www.cambridge.org/9781316513231
DOI: 10.1017/9781009063814

© Cambridge University Press 2022

First published 2022

Printed in the United Kingdom by TJ Books Limited, Padstow Cornwall

A catalogue record for this publication is available from the British Library.

ISBN – 2 Volume Set 978-1-108-42361-8 Hardback
ISBN – Volume I 978-1-316-51321-7 Hardback
ISBN – Volume II 978-1-316-51323-1 Hardback

FOR OUR MOTHERS
Anne Louise Kelly
and
Frances Anne Burton

Contents

Figures

Contributors

NEIL W. BERNSTEIN, Department of Classics and World Religions, Ohio University, Athens, Ohio.

CAILLAN DAVENPORT, Centre for Classical Studies, Australian National University, Canberra.

FANNY DOLANSKY, Department of Classics and Archaeology, Brock University, St Catharines, Ont.

MICHELE GEORGE, Department of Classics, McMaster University, Hamilton, Ont.

ROBYN GILLAM, Department of Humanities, York University, Toronto, Ont.

OLIVIER HEKSTER, Radboud Institute for Culture and History, Radboud University, Nijmegen.

ANGELA HUG, Department of History and Glendon College, York University, Toronto, Ont.

BENJAMIN KELLY, Department of History, York University, Toronto, Ont.

DOMINIK LENGYEL, Department of Architecture, Brandenburg University of Technology, Cottbus, and Lengyel Toulouse Architekten.

KELLY OLSON, Department of Classical Studies, University of Western Ontario, London, Ont.

JENS PFLUG, Architecture Department, German Archaeological Institute, Berlin.

MATTHEW B. ROLLER, Department of Classics, Johns Hopkins University, Baltimore, Md.

Contributions

While most chapters of this book were collaborative enterprises, individuals took initial responsibility for authoring the chapter introductions, as well as the translations, introductions, and commentaries for each source. The sections for which each individual had primary responsibility are listed below; sections in relation to which two individuals played a substantial role are attributed to both.

NB: **3** 16–26
CD: **1** 23; **4** Intro., 1–21; **5** 16
FD: **4** 32–5; **5** 13
MG: **2** 9b, 11, 17–23
RG: **5** 14
OH: **5** Intro., 2, 3, 5a–b, 10, 11, 12, 14, 15, 17, 18, 19, 23
AH: **3** Intro., 27–55; **5** Intro., 2, 5a–c, 6, 9, 22; **6.**1–2
BK: **1** Intro., 1–26; **2** Intro., 1–9a, 9c–10, 12–16, 24–5; **3** 1–15, 38 (c), 50 (b); **4** 3b, 6b–c, 6f; **5** 11; **6** Intro., 3–4
DL: **2** Intro.
KO: **5** 1, 4, 7, 8, 13, 20, 21, 24–5
MR: **4** 22–31

Acknowledgements

Given the nature of this project, many of the acknowledgements made in Volume 1 apply equally to this volume. Here we have confined ourselves to acknowledging those who made specific contributions to this second volume, beginning with our contributors. Their willingness to embrace the challenge of this second, very different approach to the court and their continuing tolerance for our (many) editorial interventions were very much appreciated. The majority of contributions to this second volume were finalized in early 2020, so the reader will find that works published later than 2018 are referred to only sporadically.

We are very grateful to the Social Sciences and Humanities Research Council of Canada for the award of an Insight Grant. This allowed us to run a second workshop in February 2018, at which this sourcebook volume began to take shape. The grant also allowed us to employ several research assistants, two of whom worked on this volume: Chris Dawson, who helped with the bibliography and with securing image permissions, and Samantha Rohrig, who compiled the indices and assisted with editing the translations and checking the bibliography.

We are also thankful for the generosity of colleagues who assisted us in obtaining images and permissions relating to archaeological sites and items of material culture. The creators of the images are acknowledged in the list of images above. In addition, we thank the colleagues who gave advice about images and facilitated the process of obtaining permissions: Heinz-Jürgen Beste; Maria Carmen D'Onza; Elizabeth Fentress; Marko Kiessel; Ann Kuttner; Daria Lanzuolo; Karl-Uwe Mahler; Goran Nikšić; Katja Piesker; Christian Rollinger; and Elena Stolyarik. Special thanks are also due to Jens Pflug, who not only helped us obtain permissions for most of the images in Chapter 2 relating to the imperial palaces in Rome, but also spent significant time updating some of these to ensure they reflect the latest archaeological findings.

At an early stage, our York colleagues Sarah Blake, Jonathan Edmondson, Rob Tordoff, and Ryan Wei gave invaluable advice about the structure and format of this sourcebook. Benjamin Kelly also profited from discussions with Jaclyn Neel, Jens Pflug, and Rolf Strootman about the appropriate combination of sources for Chapter 2. We would like to express our deepest thanks to one of the Press's anonymous referees, who gave sympathetic and constructive advice about the structure of the source-book, encouraging us to avoid making it a mirror image of Volume 1, and to instead use it as an opportunity to draw out themes that cut across the chapters of the first volume. The process of peer review can be imperfect, but this was a genuinely fruitful interaction.

We would like to dedicate this volume to our mothers, Anne Kelly and Frances Burton. Both spent their careers teaching in schools in Australia and Canada respectively; Anne Kelly in fact found herself teaching Ancient History in her first post – much to her surprise. Since we have designed this book partly with pedagogical uses in mind, it seemed appropriate to dedicate it to the first teachers in our lives.

Conventions

All translations are the authors' own and dates are AD unless otherwise marked. We have not striven to be hypercorrect with names. Where English place names exist, we use these. Otherwise, we tend to use Roman place names, but we also mention the modern name the first time a place is mentioned in a chapter, so that the location may be found easily using mapping applications. All places are in Italy, unless otherwise indicated. With personal names, we have used anglicized versions where they are conventional (e.g. Julia Domna, Pliny the Younger); otherwise, we use Latin spellings (e.g. Iulius Montanus, *PIR*^{2} I 434).

Figures in **bold** type refer to other sources within this volume (e.g. **3.21**) or pages in Vol. 1 of this work (e.g. **Vol. 1, 123–4**).

( )	enclose words added by the translator to clarify the author's meaning; we have avoided using round brackets to enclose parenthetical statements by the ancient author.
< >	enclose words conjectured by a modern editor when text is clearly missing from an extant manuscript due to a scribal error.
[ ]	enclose words that are missing due to damage to the extant manuscript or inscription and that have been reconstructed by a modern editor.
[---]	mark a gap in the manuscript or inscription that cannot be reconstructed; we have not attempted to provide estimates of the number of letters missing.
. . .	mark points where the ancient text in a passage continues, but we do not translate it because it is not relevant to the issue at hand.
Italics	have been used for Latin and transliterated Greek words; these are either translated or glossed where they stand, or explained in the Glossary (in the case of words appearing repeatedly).

When ancient texts have been excerpted, we have added a summary of the material that was excised, if this is necessary to allow the reader to follow the thread of the narrative. We have set those summaries in italics and enclosed them in round brackets.

Abbreviations

Journal titles are abbreviated according to the system in *L'Année philologique* and authors of ancient literary works and titles of their books are abbreviated using the conventions of the *Oxford Classical Dictionary*. Epigraphic publications are abbreviated using the system of *L'Année épigraphique* and abbreviations for papyrological publications follow the conventions of the *Checklist of Editions of Greek, Latin, Demotic, and Coptic Papyri, Ostraca, and Tablets* (available at https://papyri.info/docs/checklist).

In addition, we have used the following abbreviations in this volume:

ANRW   Temporini, H. and Haase, W. (eds.) (1972–92) *Aufstieg und Niedergang der römischen Welt*. Berlin: de Gruyter.

BL   Preisigke, F. et al. (eds.) (1922–) *Berichtigungsliste der griechischen Papyrusurkunden aus Ägypten*.

BNP   Cancik, H. et al. (eds.) (2002–10) *Brill's New Pauly: Encyclopaedia of the Ancient World. Antiquity* (22 vols.). Leiden and Boston, Mass.: Brill. [Ger. orig. (1996–2003) *Der Neue Pauly: Enzyklopädie der Antike* (16 vols.). Stuttgart: J. B. Metzler.]

EU   *Excerpta Ursiniana*

EV   *Excerpta Valesiana*

Haines Haines, C. R. (1928–9) *Fronto: Correspondence*, rev. ed. (2 vols.). Loeb. Cambridge, Mass. and London: Harvard University Press.

JA   Joannes Antiochenus

LIMC   Ackermann, H. C. and Gisler, J.-R. (eds.) (1981) *Lexicon iconographicum mythologiae classicae*. Zurich: Artemis.

LTUR   Steinby, E. M. (ed.) (1993–9) *Lexicon Topographicum Urbis Romae* (6 vols.). Rome: Edizioni Quasar.

OLD   Glare, P. G. W. (ed.) (1982) *Oxford Latin Dictionary*. Oxford: Clarendon.

PIR^2 Groag, E. et al. (1933–2015) *Prosopographia Imperii Romani saec. I. II. III.* (8 vols.), 2nd ed. Berlin, Leipzig, and New York: de Gruyter.

PLRE   Jones, A. H. M., Martindale, J. R., and Morris, J. (1971–92) *The Prosopography of the Later Roman Empire* (3 vols.). Cambridge: Cambridge University Press.

PP   Petrus Patricius, *Excerpta Vaticana*
RE   Pauly, A. et al. (eds.) (1893–1980) *Paulys Realencyclopadie der classischen Altertumswissenschaft*. Stuttgart: A. Druckenmuller.
RIC   Mattingly, H. et al. (eds.) (1923–) *Roman Imperial Coinage* (10 vols.). London: Spink.
SCPP   *Senatus Consultum de Pisone Patre*
ShB   Shackleton Bailey, D. R. (1977) *Epistulae ad familiares* (2 vols.). Cambridge Classical Texts and Commentaries, 16–17. Cambridge: Cambridge University Press.
vdH   van den Hout, M. P. J. (1988) *M. Cornelii Frontonis Epistulae*. Bibliotheca Teubneriana. Leipzig: Teubner.
Xiph.   Xiphilinus

List of Roman Emperors to c. AD 300

27 BC–AD 14	AUGUSTUS	*PIR*² I 215; *BNP* Augustus 1
14–37	TIBERIUS	*PIR*² C 941; *BNP* Tiberius II 1
37–41	CALIGULA (GAIUS)	*PIR*² I 217; *BNP* Caligula
41–54	CLAUDIUS	*PIR*² C 942; *BNP* Claudius III 1
54–68	NERO	*PIR*² D 129; *BNP* Nero 1
68–9	GALBA	*PIR*² S 1003; *BNP* Galba 2
69	OTHO	*PIR*² S 143; *BNP* Otho
69	VITELLIUS	*PIR*² V 740; *BNP* Vitellius II 2
69–79	VESPASIAN	*PIR*² F 398; *BNP* Vespasianus
79–81	TITUS	*PIR*² F 399; *BNP* Titus II 1
81–96	DOMITIAN	*PIR*² F 259; *BNP* Domitianus 1
96–8	NERVA	*PIR*² C 1227; *BNP* Nerva 2
98–117	TRAJAN	*PIR*² V 865; *BNP* Traianus 1
117–38	HADRIAN	*PIR*² A 184; *BNP* Hadrianus II
138–61	ANTONINUS PIUS	*PIR*² A 1513; *BNP* Antoninus 1
161–80	MARCUS AURELIUS	*PIR*² A 697; *BNP* Marcus II 2
161–9	LUCIUS VERUS	*PIR*² C 606; *BNP* Verus
177–92	COMMODUS	*PIR*² A 1482; *BNP* Commodus
193	PERTINAX	*PIR*² H 73; *BNP* Pertinax
193	DIDIUS IULIANUS	*PIR*² D 77; *BNP* Didius II 6
193–211	SEPTIMIUS SEVERUS	*PIR*² S 487; *BNP* Septimius II 7
197–217	CARACALLA	*PIR*² S 446; *BNP* Caracalla
209–11	GETA	*PIR*² S 454; *BNP* Geta 2
217–18	MACRINUS	*PIR*² O 108; *BNP* Macrinus
218–22	ELAGABALUS	*PIR*² V 273; *BNP* Elagabalus 2
222–35	SEVERUS ALEXANDER	*PIR*² A 1610; *BNP* Severus II 2
235–8	MAXIMINUS THRAX	*PIR*² I 619; *BNP* Maximinus 2
238	GORDIAN I	*PIR*² A 833; *BNP* Gordianus 1
238	GORDIAN II	*PIR*² A 834; *BNP* Gordianus 2
238	PUPIENUS	*PIR*² C 1179; *BNP* Pupienus
238	BALBINUS	*PIR*² C 126; *BNP* Balbinus 1
238–44	GORDIAN III	*PIR*² A 835; *BNP* Gordianus 3

244–9	PHILIPPUS ARABS	PIR^2 I 461; *BNP* Philippus II 2
249–51	DECIUS	PIR^2 M 520; *BNP* Decius II 1
251–3	TREBONIANUS GALLUS	PIR^2 V 579; *BNP* Trebonianus Gallus
253	AEMILIUS AEMILIANUS	PIR^2 A 330; *BNP* Aemilianus II 1
253–60	VALERIAN	PIR^2 L 258; *BNP* Valerianus 2
253–68	GALLIENUS	PIR^2 L 197; *BNP* Gallienus
268–70	CLAUDIUS II GOTHICUS	PIR^2 A 1626; *BNP* Claudius III 2
270	QUINTILLUS	PIR^2 A 1480; *BNP* Quintillus
270–5	AURELIAN	PIR^2 D 135; *BNP* Aurelianus 3
275–6	TACITUS	PIR^2 C 1036; *BNP* Tacitus 2
276	FLORIANUS	PIR^2 A 649; *BNP* Annius II 4
276–82	PROBUS	PIR^2 A 1583; *BNP* Probus 1
282–3	CARUS	PIR^2 A 1475; *BNP* Carus 4
283–5	CARINUS	PIR^2 A 1473; *BNP* Carinus
283–4	NUMERIANUS	PIR^2 A 1564; *BNP* Numerianus 2
284–305	DIOCLETIAN	PIR^2 A 1627; *BNP* Diocletianus
286–310	MAXIMIAN (Caesar 285)	PIR^2 A 1628; *BNP* Maximianus 1
305–6	CONSTANTIUS I (Caesar 293–305)	PIR^2 F 390; *BNP* Constantius 1
305–311	GALERIUS (Caesar 293–305)	PIR^2 V 126; *BNP* Galerius 5

Register of Prominent Courtiers

We include in this list prominent courtiers who are mentioned repeatedly in one or both volumes using the customary short forms of their names. When describing relationships, we give emperors' names in capitals.

Acte   Claudia Acte. Freedwoman mistress of NERO. *PIR*[2] C 1067; *BNP* Claudia II 4.

Agrippa   M. Vipsanius Agrippa (64/3–12 BC). *Cos. ord.* I 37 BC, II 28 BC, III 27 BC. Close supporter of Octavian/AUGUSTUS; married to Julia, daughter of AUGUSTUS, 21–12 BC. *PIR*[2] V 674; *BNP* Agrippa 1.

Agrippa Postumus   Agrippa Iulius Caesar [originally: M. Vipsanius Agrippa Postumus] (12 BC–AD 14). Son of Agrippa and Julia; adopted as son by AUGUSTUS (AD 4), then exiled (AD 6). *PIR*[2] I 214; *BNP* Agrippa 2.

Agrippina the Elder   Vipsania Agrippina (c. 14 BC–AD 33). Daughter of Agrippa and Julia; married to Germanicus (c. AD 5–19). *PIR*[2] V 682; *BNP* Agrippina 2.

Agrippina the Younger   Iulia Agrippina (AD 15–59). Daughter of Germanicus and Agrippina the Elder; wife of CLAUDIUS (49–54); mother of NERO. *PIR*[2] I 641; *BNP* Agrippina 3.

Antinous   (d. 130). A Bithynian youth who was the lover of HADRIAN. He mysteriously drowned in the Nile, provoking extravagant demonstrations of grief by HADRIAN. *PIR*[2] A 737; *BNP* Antinous 2.

Antonia the Elder Antonia (maior) (b. 39 BC). Elder daughter of Mark Antony and Octavia. *PIR*[2] A 884; *BNP* Antonia 3

Antonia the Younger	Antonia (minor) [later: Antonia Augusta] (36 BC–AD 37). Younger daughter of Mark Antony and Octavia; wife of Drusus the Elder; mother of Germanicus and CLAUDIUS; grandmother of CALIGULA. *PIR*² A 885; *BNP* Antonia 4.
Berenice	Iulia Berenice (b. c. 28). Daughter of Herod Agrippa I. Mistress of TITUS before he became emperor. *PIR*² I 651; *BNP* Berenice 7b.
Britannicus	Ti. Claudius Caesar Britannicus [earlier: Ti. Claudius Caesar Germanicus] (41–54/5). Son of CLAUDIUS; brother by adoption of NERO, who allegedly murdered him. *PIR*² C 820; *BNP* Britannicus.
Burrus	Sex. Afranius Burrus (d. 62). Influential praetorian prefect of NERO (51–62). *PIR*² A 441; *BNP* Afranius 3.
Caenis	Antonia Caenis. Freedwoman of Antonia the Younger. Concubine of VESPASIAN. *PIR*² A 888; *BNP* Antonia 6.
Callistus	C. Iulius Callistus. Reportedly powerful at the courts of CALIGULA and CLAUDIUS; freedman *a libellis* of the latter. *PIR*² I 229; *BNP* Iulius II 36.
Cleander	M. Aurelius Cleander. Influential freedman at the court of COMMODUS. *PIR*² A 1481; *BNP* Aurelius II 10.
Cocceius Nerva	M. Cocceius Nerva (d. 33). *Cos. suff.* 21 or 22. A distinguished jurist and close associate of TIBERIUS, who sojourned with that emperor on Capreae. *PIR*² C 1225; *BNP* Cocceius 5.
Domitia Lucilla	Domitia Lucilla (minor) (d. 155–61). The mother of MARCUS AURELIUS. *PIR*² D 183; *BNP* Domitia 8.
Drusus the Elder	D. Claudius Drusus [later: Nero Claudius Drusus Germanicus] (38–9 BC). Son of Livia; stepson of AUGUSTUS; brother of TIBERIUS. *PIR*² C 857; *BNP* Claudius II 24.
Drusus the Younger	Nero Claudius Drusus [later: Drusus Iulius Caesar] (c. 15–14 BC–AD 23). Son of the emperor TIBERIUS. *PIR*² I 219; *BNP* Drusus II 1.

Eclectus	(d. 193). The *a cubiculo* of COMMODUS, who was allegedly involved in that emperor's murder. *PIR*² E 3; *BNP* Eclectus.
Faustina the Elder	Annia Galeria Faustina (d. 140). Wife of ANTONINUS PIUS and mother of Faustina the Younger. *PIR*² A 715; *BNP* Faustina 2.
Faustina the Younger	Annia Galeria Faustina (c. 130–175/6). Daughter of ANTONINUS PIUS, wife of MARCUS AURELIUS (145–175/6), mother of COMMODUS. *PIR*² A 716; *BNP* Faustina 3.
Fronto	M. Cornelius Fronto (c. 110–after 176). *Cos. suff.* 143. Tutor of MARCUS AURELIUS and LUCIUS VERUS, and influential at their courts. A corpus of letters to and from Fronto survives. His correspondents included ANTONINUS PIUS, MARCUS AURELIUS, and LUCIUS VERUS, as well as several important courtiers. *PIR*² C 1364; *BNP* Fronto 6.
Gaius (Caesar)	C. Iulius Caesar (20 BC–AD 4). Grandson, and later adoptive son, of AUGUSTUS. Until his early death, the presumptive successor to AUGUSTUS' position, along with his brother, Lucius Caesar. *PIR*² I 216; *BNP* Iulius II 32.
Ti. Gemellus	Ti. Iulius Caesar Nero (19 or 20–37). The natural grandson of TIBERIUS. Despite his grandfather's wishes, CALIGULA excluded him as successor and later allegedly had him murdered. *PIR*² I 226.
Germanicus	Germanicus Iulius Caesar [originally: Nero Claudius Drusus] (15 BC–AD 19). Son of Drusus the Elder and Antonia the Younger; adoptive son of TIBERIUS. *PIR*² I 221; *BNP* Germanicus 2.
Herod Agrippa	M. Iulius Agrippa (I) (10 BC–AD 44). Grandson of Herod the Great (king of Judaea); moved in Roman court circles in his youth; eventually ruled his grandfather's kingdom. *PIR*² I 131; *BNP* Herodes 8.

Julia Domna	Iulia Domna (d. c. 217). Wife of SEPTIMIUS SEVERUS and mother of CARACALLA and GETA. *PIR*² I 663; *BNP* Iulia 12.
Julia Maesa	Iulia Maesa (d. 226). Sister of Julia Domna; mother of Julia Mamaea and Julia Soaemias; grandmother of ELAGABALUS and SEVERUS ALEXANDER. *PIR*² I 678; *BNP* Iulia 17.
Julia Mamaea	Iulia Avita Mamaea (d. 235). Mother of SEVERUS ALEXANDER; niece of Julia Domna. *PIR*² I 649; *BNP* Iulia 9.
Julia Soaemias	Iulia Soaemias Bassiana (d. 222). Mother of ELAGABALUS; niece of Julia Domna. *PIR*² I 704; *BNP* Iulia 22.
Livia	Livia Drusilla [later: Iulia Augusta] (58 BC–AD 29). Wife of Octavian/AUGUSTUS; mother of TIBERIUS. *PIR*² L 301; *BNP* Livia 2.
Livilla	(Claudia) Livia Iulia (c. 14–11 BC–AD 31). Daughter of Drusus the Elder; wife (AD 4–23) of Drusus the Younger; niece and daughter-in-law of TIBERIUS. *PIR*² L 303; *BNP* Livilla 1.
Lollia Paulina	(d. 49). The third of CALIGULA's four wives. She suvived his reign, but was exiled then murdered as a potential rival to CLAUDIUS' wife, Agrippina the Younger. *PIR*² L 328; *BNP* Lollia 1.
Lucius (Caesar)	L. Iulius Caesar (17 BC–AD 2). Grandson, and later adoptive son, of AUGUSTUS. Until his early death, the presumptive successor to AUGUSTUS' position, along with his brother, Gaius Caesar. *PIR*² I 222; *BNP* Iulius II 33.
Macro	Q. Naevius Cordus Sutorius Macro (d. 38). Praetorian prefect (31–8); influential at the courts of TIBERIUS and CALIGULA. *PIR*² N 12; *BNP* Naevius II 3.
Maecenas	C. Maecenas (c. 70–8 BC). A close friend of AUGUSTUS and a patron of literature. *PIR*² M 37; *BNP* Maecenas 2.
Marcellus	M. Claudius Marcellus (42–23 BC). The son of Octavia the Younger and nephew of AUGUSTUS. *PIR*² C 925; *BNP* Claudius II 42.

Marcia	Concubine of COMMODUS. *PIR*² M 261; *BNP* Marcia 7; Flexsenhar 2016.
Messalina	Valeria Messalina (b. 20–5, d. 48). Wife of CLAUDIUS (c. 38/9–48). *PIR*² V 241; *BNP* Messalina 2.
Narcissus	(d. 54). Freedman *ab epistulis* of CLAUDIUS, and reportedly a powerful figure at his court. *PIR*² N 23; *BNP* Narcissus II 1.
Octavia	Claudia Octavia (c. 40–62). Daughter of CLAUDIUS; wife of NERO (53–62). *PIR*² C 1110; *BNP* Octavia 3.
Octavia the Younger	Octavia (minor) (69–10/11 BC). The sister of Octavian/AUGUSTUS. *PIR*² O 66; *BNP* Octavia 2.
Pallas	M. Antonius Pallas (d. 62). Freedman of Antonia the Younger. *A rationibus* under CLAUDIUS. Reportedly powerful at the courts of CLAUDIUS and NERO. *PIR*² A 858; *BNP* Antonius II 10.
Paris	(d. 83). Pantomime actor influential at the court of DOMITIAN, and allegedly a lover of the emperor's wife, Domitia Longina. *PIR*² P 128; *BNP* Paris 3.
Parthenius	Ti. Claudius Parthenius (d. 97). Influential *a cubiculo* of DOMITIAN. *PIR*² C 951a; *BNP* Claudius II 51.
C. Piso	C. Calpurnius Piso (d. 65). *Cos. suff.* under CLAUDIUS. Figurehead of the failed conspiracy to assassinate NERO in 65. *PIR*² C 284; *BNP* Calpurnius II 13.
Cn. Piso	Cn. Calpurnius Piso (c. 42 BC–AD 20). *Cos. ord.* 7 BC; governor of Syria AD 17–19. Confidant of the emperor TIBERIUS. Tried in the Senate in connection with events surrounding Germanicus' death in 19, he pre-empted the verdict with suicide. *PIR*² C 287; *BNP* Calpurnius II 16.
Plautianus	M. Fulvius Plautianus (d. 205). Close friend and praetorian prefect (197–205) of SEPTIMIUS SEVERUS. *PIR*² F 554; *BNP* Fulvius II 10.

Plautilla	Publia Fulvia Plautilla (d. 212). Daughter of Plautianus and wife (202–5) of CARACALLA. *PIR*² F 564; *BNP* Fulvia 3.
Pliny the Younger	C. Plinius Caecilius Secundus (c. 61/2–112), from Novum Comum (modern Como), nephew of Pliny the Elder. *Cos. suff.* 100, and holder of multiple administrative positions, including governor of Bithynia-Pontus. A collection of his letters and his panegyric for TRAJAN have survived. *PIR*² P 490; *BNP* Plinius 2.
Plotina	Pompeia Plotina (b. 62–72, d. 123). Wife of TRAJAN and adoptive mother of HADRIAN. *PIR*² P 679; *BNP* Plotina.
Poppaea	Poppaea Sabina (31–65). Wife of NERO (62–5). *PIR*² P 850; *BNP* Poppaea 2.
Sabina	Vibia Sabina (c. 85–c. 137). Wife of HADRIAN. *PIR*² V 600; *BNP* Sabina.
Sejanus	L. Aelius Seianus (b. c. 23–20 BC, d. AD 31). Influential praetorian prefect (14–31) of TIBERIUS. *PIR*² A 255; *BNP* Aelius II 19.
Seneca the Younger	L. Annaeus Seneca (c. 1–65). *Cos. suff.* 56. Close adviser of NERO. Author of works of drama, philosophy, natural history, and satire. *PIR*² A 617; *BNP* Seneca 2.
C. Silius	(d. 48). *Cos. design.* 49 (?). A lover of Messalina, wife of CLAUDIUS. Reportedly Silius married her in CLAUDIUS' absence, perhaps planning usurpation, and was executed. *PIR*² S 714; *BNP* Silius II 1.
Sporus	(d. 69). A favourite eunuch catamite of NERO and (briefly) OTHO. *PIR*² S 805; *BNP* Sporus 2.
C. Stertinius Xenophon	The influential personal physician of CLAUDIUS. *PIR*² S 913; *BNP* Stertinius 4.
Sura	L. Licinius Sura (c. 56–c. 108). *Cos.* I *suff.* c. 93, II *ord.* 102, III *ord.* 107. A close friend of the emperor TRAJAN. *PIR*² L 253; *BNP* Licinius II 25.
Thrasyllus	(d. 36). Astrologer. Reportedly influential at the court of TIBERIUS. *PIR*² T 190; *BNP* Thrasyllus 2.

Tigellinus	Ofonius Tigellinus. Influential praetorian prefect of NERO (62–8). *PIR*² O 91; *BNP* Ofonius Tigellinus.
L. Vitellius	L. Vitellius (c. 10 BC–c. AD 51). *Cos. ord.* I 34, II 43, III 47. Father of VITELLIUS. Important figure in the courts of CALIGULA and CLAUDIUS. *PIR*² V 741; *BNP* Vitellius II 3.

Major Authors and Literary Works Translated in this Volume

Arrian L. Flavius Arrianus (b. 85–90, d. 160). *Cos. suff.* 129 or 130 and a friend of HADRIAN. Originally from Nicomedia (Bithynia; modern İzmit, Turkey), Arrian studied under the philosopher Epictetus, whose thought he has preserved (in Greek) in his *Discourses of Epictetus* and the *Encheiridion*. Also an author of works on a variety of other topics, including biography and history, many of which survive. *PIR*^{2} F 219; *BNP* Arrianus 2.

Aulus Gellius A. Gellius (b. 125–8). A miscellanist who lived in Rome and in c. 180 published his *Attic Nights*. The work collects assorted information on topics including grammar, literature, law, history, and philosophy, and quotes many passages from now-lost works. *PIR*^{2} G 124; *BNP* Gellius 6.

Aurelius Victor Sex. Aurelius Victor (b. c. 320), from Africa. Governor of Pannonia Secunda (361) and urban prefect (c. 389). He published his series of short imperial biographies, *On the Caesars*, in c. 361. His sources included a lost series of mid-fourth-century imperial biographies, called the *Kaisergeschichte* by modern scholars. *PLRE* 1.960; *BNP* Victor 7.

Cassius Dio L. Cl. (?) Cassius Dio Cocceianus (?) (c. 164–after 229), from Nicaea (Bithynia; modern İznik, Turkey). *Cos.* I *suff. c.* 204, *cos.* II *ord.* 229; enjoyed a distinguished senatorial career. Wrote the *Roman History* (in Greek), which records events from the foundation of the city to AD 229 in annalistic form. Of the original 80 books, Bks. 46–60 are extant; for the rest we rely on later epitomes and excerpts, especially those of Xiphilinus for the later books. *PIR*^{2} C 492; *BNP* Cassius III 1.

Cicero	M. Tullius Cicero (106–43 BC), from Arpinum (Italy). *Cos. ord.* 63 BC, and an important late Republican statesman. Very many of his letters and works on rhetoric and philosophy (including *On Laws* and *On Duties*) survive, as do numerous written versions of his speeches. *RE* 29; *BNP* Cicero.
Fronto	See above, xxiii.
Historia Augusta	A collection of biographies of the emperors (and usurpers) from HADRIAN to CARINUS and NUMERIANUS. The collection presents as the work of six authors in the era from DIOCLETIAN to CONSTANTINE I, but was likely written by a single author c. 400. Reliable sources lie behind parts of some of the biographies, but they contain many inaccuracies and outright fabrications.
Josephus	Flavius Iosephus (37/8–100), from Jerusalem (Judaea). Initially a general on the Judaean side in the war of 66–72/3 against Rome, he was captured but spared, and moved to Rome in 71. His extensive surviving works (all in Greek) include his autobiographical *Life*, and the *Jewish Antiquities*, which covers Jewish history from Creation to AD 66. PIR^2 F 293; *BNP* Iosephus 4.
Juvenal	D. Iunius Iuvenalis (b. c. 67), probably from Aquinum (modern Aquino). Little is known about his biography; he wrote in the early second century. Sixteen of his *Satires* survive, attacking the corruption and hypocrisy of contemporary society. PIR^2 I 765; *BNP* Iuvenalis, D. Iunius.
Lactantius	L. Caelius Firmianus Lactantius (c. 250–325), from Africa. A teacher of rhetoric at Nicomedia (Bithynia, modern İzmit, Turkey), where he converted to Christianity. Eventually he became tutor to the emperor CONSTANTINE'S son, Crispus (c. 317). His surviving works include *On the Deaths of the Persecutors*, which takes as its theme God's vengeance on persecutors of Christians – and in the process preserves significant historical information about the poorly documented Tetrarchic period. *PLRE* 1.338; *BNP* Lactantius 1.

Latin Panegyrics	*XII Panegyrici Latini*. A collection of orations given before emperors, consisting of Pliny's *Panegyric* for TRAJAN (AD 100), and then eleven orations delivered to emperors in Gaul from 289 to 389. Some of the orators are identified by name, others are not.
Marcus Aurelius	M. Aurelius Antoninus (121–80), Rome. Emperor 161–80. His *Meditations*, which are a collection of his philosophical reflections (in Greek), contain some hints of his thoughts on the court and the imperial family. *PIR*^{2} A 697; *BNP* Marcus II 2.
Martial	M. Valerius Martialis (b. 38–41, d. 101–4), from Bilbilis (Hispania Tarraconensis, near modern Calatayud, Spain). He had relationships of literary patronage with DOMITIAN and various members of his court. Many of his epigrams survive, often giving witty insights into contemporary society and (sometimes) the court. *PIR*^{2} V 123; *BNP* Martialis 1.
Ovid	P. Ovidius Naso (43 BC–AD 17), from Sulmo (modern Sulmona). Held some minor judicial offices at Rome, but mostly devoted himself to poetry, leaving behind a large corpus of work, much of it extant. Exiled in AD 8 by AUGUSTUS to Tomi (modern Constanța, Romania), where he continued to write works, including the *Tristia* and *Letters from Pontus*. *PIR*^{2} O 180; *BNP* Ovidius Naso, Publius.
Philo	Philo of Alexandria/Philo Iudaeus (c. 15 BC–c. AD 50). Member of a distinguished Jewish family in Alexandria (Egypt). Led an embassy of Alexandrian Jews to CALIGULA in AD 39. An extensive corpus of his works (all in Greek) survives; there are philosophical, exegetic, and historical/apologetic works, including the *Embassy to Gaius*. *PIR*^{2} P 370; *BNP* Philo I 12.
Philostratus	L. Flavius Philostratus (b. c. 170), from Athens. Moved in court circles under SEPTIMIUS SEVERUS, having close contact with Julia Domna.

	His surviving works (all in Greek) include the biography-cum-historical novel *The Life of Apollonius of Tyana* (published after 217), and the *Lives of the Sophists* (completed c. 242). *PIR*² F 332; *BNP* Philostratus 5.
Pliny the Elder	C. Plinius Secundus (23/4–79), from Comum (modern Como), uncle of Pliny the Younger. An *amicus* of VESPASIAN and TITUS, he had a distinguished equestrian career, ending as the commander of the fleet at Misenum (modern Miseno). A prolific author in several genres, his encyclopaedic *Natural History* has survived. *PIR*² P 493; *BNP* Plinius 1.
Pliny the Younger	See above, xxvi.
Seneca the Younger	See above, xxvi.
Statius	P. Papinius Statius (b. c. 40–50, d. c. 96), from Naples. A professional poet, his surviving works include epics on mythological themes (the *Thebaid* and the unfinished *Achilleid*), and the thirty-two shorter *Silvae*, which touch on aspects of society under DOMITIAN, including the court. *PIR*² P 104; *BNP* Plinius 2.
Strabo	Strabo of Amaseia (c. 64 BC–c. AD 24), from Amaseia, Pontus (modern Amasya, Turkey). Lived in both Rome and Alexandria. Historical and geographical writer (in Greek); only his *Geography* has survived. *PIR*² S 922; *BNP* Strabo 1.
Suetonius	C. Suetonius Tranquillus (b. c. 70). Had a distinguished equestrian career, culminating in tenure of the post of *ab epistulis* under HADRIAN. A prolific writer of antiquarian and biographical works. His *Lives* of Julius Caesar and the emperors from AUGUSTUS to DOMITIAN survive, as do some of his *Lives* of prominent grammarians and literary figures. *PIR*² S 959; *BNP* Suetonius 2.
Tacitus	P.(?) Cornelius Tacitus (c. 55–c. 120). *Cos. suff.* 97, he had a distinguished senatorial career. Author of works on history, biography, ethnography, and rhetoric. His *Annals*, some parts of which are lost,

covered Roman history from AD 14 to 68; his *Histories* covered the period 69 to 96, but only the parts dealing with 69 to mid-70 survive. *PIR*^{2} C 1467; *BNP* Tacitus 1.

Valerius Maximus   Author of a book of *Memorable Deeds and Sayings*, written c. AD 27–31, which collected historical examples (*exempla*). Apparently a close associate of Sex. Pompeius (*cos.* 14; *PIR*^{2} P 584). *PIR*^{2} V 127; *BNP* Valerius III 5.

Glossary

ab admissione The head of the department (*ratio*) of admissions in the imperial household, which controlled access to the emperor.

ab epistulis An imperial secretary whose responsibilities related to the drafting of the emperor's letters. At various times there was both an *ab epistulis Latinis* (for letters in Latin) and an *ab epistulis Graecis* (for letters in Greek).

a cubiculo The emperor's chief bedroom attendant, whose constant access to the emperor often made him influential. Typically an imperial freedman.

adoratio An act of obeisance performed before a god or ruler. In the Roman court of the Tetrarchic period and later, it involved lowering oneself before the emperor and kissing his purple robe.

adventus The emperor's ceremonial entry into a city.

a libellis An imperial secretary whose responsibilities related to the drafting of the emperor's responses to petitions.

a rationibus An imperial secretary who oversaw the imperial financial administration.

amicus, amicitia 'Friend, friendship'. Used of genuine friends of the emperor, but also (in certain contexts) in relation to men of high rank with whom the emperor was interacting.

atrium A large, open space near the entrance in an elite Roman house. Typically used as the setting for the morning **salutatio** ritual, amongst other functions. See **2.3**, **fig. 2.2.1**, Room B.

auctoritas 'Authority' that did not necessarily rest on a formal position or office.

aula Latin loan word from the Greek *aulē*, which originally meant 'courtyard'. *Aula* came to refer to a palace, but also to the circle of people around a monarch – the court.

civilis princeps	The ideal emperor (in the eyes of the aristocracy), who behaved with *civilitas*.
civilitas	The unassuming behaviour expected of an ordinary citizen, when interacting with other citizens. Emperors in the Principate who showed such behaviour are much praised in the sources.
cliens	'Client'. The subordinate party in a relationship of patronage.
comitatus	Originally the group of people who travelled with the emperor. In the third century, it came to refer to the court in general, even when stationary.
comites	The members of the emperor's *comitatus*. Singular: *comes*.
consilium	A council that gave advice to the emperor.
consistorium	The late-antique descendant of the *consilium*. Its membership and proceedings were more formalized than those of its predecessor.
consul ordinarius	*(Cos. ord.)* One of the two consuls who took office at the start of a year. The consul had been the highest regular magistrate under the Republic. Under the Principate, the consulship entailed much less real power, but was still a very important honour in the career of a senator.
consul suffectus	*(Cos. suff.)* A consul appointed to come into office later in a year, after one or both of the *consules ordinarii* had stepped down. A suffect consulship was a lesser honour than an ordinary consulship, but still very prestigious.
convivium	A banquet.
corona civica	A crown of oak leaves, traditionally awarded for saving the life of a citizen in battle.
cubicularius	A bedroom attendant in an elite house or the imperial court.
damnatio memoriae	'Condemnation of memory'. A modern coinage referring to the process of damning the memory of prominent individuals who had fallen from grace, which could include the destruction of their images and removal of their names from inscriptions and coins.
domus	Can refer to the house as a building, and also to a person's 'house' in the sense of their relatives, slaves, and freedmen and -women.

equites	Members of the equestrian order, the stratum of society below senators. They were not necessarily as wealthy as senators and did not sit in the Senate, but were eligible for important administrative and military posts.
familia	'Family'. A flexible word that could cover a group of relatives related by blood and (occasionally) marriage, as well the slaves of a particular household, or the slaves, freedmen, and freedwomen of a single owner in a particular place.
fiscus	Originally the private funds and property of the emperor, the *fiscus* came to operate as a central imperial treasury. Its relationship to the *aerarium*, the treasury that had existed since the Republic, is unclear and much debated.
fratres arvales	'The Arval Brethren'. A college of twelve priests mainly concerned with worshipping the Dea Dia. The college included the emperor, men of the imperial family, and other courtiers.
gens	An extended kinship group or clan.
grammaticus	A teacher of literature and philology.
imperator	A title originally given to a successful general by his soldiers. Under the Principate, it came to be a title used by emperors. The earlier custom also continued, since emperors were saluted as *imperatores* after victories.
imperium	The legal power to give orders and be obeyed inherent in the positions of some magistrates, of provincial governors, or of emperors.
lares	The gods deemed important to the household and worshipped in a household shrine (the *lararium*).
nomenclator	A freedman or slave tasked with reminding a householder or emperor of the names of people, for instance at the **salutatio**.
ornamenta triumphalia	Insignia awarded to successful generals, who could no longer celebrate a triumphal procession in the Principate unless they were members of the emperor's family.
otium	'Active leisure'. In Roman elite culture, this entailed withdrawal from daily business (*negotium*) to engage in contemplation, philosophical discussion, writing, and the enjoyment of nature.
paedagogiani	Servile 'page boys' who worked as domestic servants in the imperial house.

paedagogium	An establishment for training **paedagogiani**.
palatium	Originally referred to the Palatine Hill in Rome. In time, the word came to refer to the imperial palace complex on the hill, and also the court within it.
paterfamilias	The head of a family, who had certain legal powers over those under his control.
pater patriae	'Father of the Fatherland'. An honorific title given to emperors.
philos	(Greek) 'Friend'. Plural: *philoi*.
pontifices	A college of priests at Rome. The emperor typically held the position of chief pontiff (*pontifex maximus*).
princeps	'The first man'. Under the Principate, it came to be used to describe the emperor.
proskynēsis	(Greek) An act of obeisance to a god or a ruler.
pulvinar	The imperial box reserved for the emperor and members of his court in the Circus Maximus.
recusatio	The semi-ritualized refusal of a position or honour. In the case of writers, *recusatio* involved refusing a request from a prominent person (such as the emperor) to write a work.
res publica	The body politic or state. It can refer to the 'Republic' that existed before the Principate, but not necessarily.
salutatio	The morning greeting ritual. At the house of a Roman aristocrat, clients would greet their patron. At the emperor's court morning greeters (*salutatores*) would include senators and high-ranking equestrians.
tab(u)linum	A room in a Roman elite house between the **atrium** and the peristyle courtyard behind it. See **2.3**, **fig. 2.2.1**, Room D.
toga virilis	'The toga of manhood', the assumption of which marked a boy's transition to manhood.
triclinium	A dining room.
Vestal Virgins	*Sacerdotes vestales*. Priesthood of six (usually aristocratic) women, expected to remain chaste during their thirty years of service. Devoted to the goddess Vesta, their duties included tending the goddess' sacred fire.

Introduction: The Sources for the Roman Court

BENJAMIN KELLY, *WITH CONTRIBUTIONS FROM* JENS PFLUG

In this volume, we present a selection of the most important sources for the Roman imperial court. We have been guided by two criteria in choosing them. Some of the sources – which almost select themselves – are *the* central pieces of evidence on a particular point and have been repeatedly discussed in the modern scholarship (e.g. **1.8 [g]**, **2.9 [b]**, **3.6**, **4.16**). On other issues, the evidence is more plentiful and historical knowledge rests on the patient accumulation of data. In these cases, we have aimed to provide at least a representative sample, with the full awareness that we are omitting other texts which also illustrate the same points. We have exercised such selectivity, for instance, with anecdotes in literary sources showing the (alleged) power of imperial women and freedmen (see **3.30, 37, 39–40, 43**) and with the many inscriptions that evidence the job titles and hierarchy of court domestic servants (see **3.41, 4.5, 5.11**).

As with the first volume of this book, the period covered runs from Augustus to the end of the third century AD, and we continue to use 'court' as an etic category that refers to the social circle surrounding the emperor.[1] However, as Chapter 2 shows, the study of space is essential to understanding social interactions, and we have also included a selection of sources illustrating the language that the Romans themselves used to describe the court surrounding their emperor (**1.7–16**).

The writing of history is a process invariably shaped by the types of sources at our disposal. It is therefore worth reflecting on what kinds of evidence have survived, and on how the genres of that evidence predetermine what we can know about the Roman court. Such reflection should be conducted in a comparative spirit, with an eye to the sort of evidence available for monarchical courts in more recent periods, so as to highlight the particularities of the Roman evidence. The goal is not to complain about how little evidence Roman historians have in comparison to historians of early modern or modern courts – this would be churlish, given that the Roman court is so much more richly documented than most other ancient courts. Rather, we anticipate that many users of this volume will not be professional historians of ancient Rome, so it is worth explaining what is distinctive about the Roman sources, since this is not self-evident.

---

[1] See **Vol. 1, 5–8**.

Documentary Sources

For the courts of some historical societies, we possess archival material that allows us to peer into the inner workings of the royal household. Thus, for example, extensive financial accounts survive relating to the courts of many late-medieval kingdoms and principalities of north-west Europe. These allow us to recover details about the physical realities of court life (food, drink, clothing, etc.) and about aspects of court culture such as patronage of music, literature, and the visual arts.[2] In the Roman case, a mass of ephemeral paperwork relating to the running of the emperor's household must have been generated.[3] None of this has survived the intervening two millennia.

In the case of late medieval Europe, we also have household ordinances, which fall somewhere between being descriptions of the royal household as it was, and the household as the king wished it to be, since they often represent attempts to control expenditure.[4] Also mingling the descriptive and the prescriptive are ceremonial manuals. For instance, the Byzantine *De ceremoniis* preserves details of ceremonial practice at the court in Constantinople. At the same time, it is also an attempt by its compiler, the emperor Constantine VII Porphyrogenitus, to revive rituals that had fallen into desuetude, thereby creating a sense of order and reinforcing his dynasty's position.[5] As far as we know, there were no similar attempts to regulate in writing the operation of the Roman emperor's household or his court ceremonial, and certainly no such texts have come down to us.

Courts in literate societies also produce masses of paperwork relating to the monarch's political and administrative duties. Some documentary material of this kind does survive from the Roman world. By and large, it does not allow us to see in detail the processes of deliberation that led to the emperor's decisions. Rather, what we possess in large quantities are documents communicating the emperor's decisions: his edicts, his letters to communities and individuals, and his written responses to petitions. These have not survived in public archives. Rather, a few hundred survive on inscriptions and on papyri preserved in the dry sands of Egypt; several thousand more that had legal relevance were incorporated into late-antique law codes, which have come down to us through the manuscript tradition. These texts were the products of interactions between the emperor, his advisory councils (*consilia*), his various secretaries (especially the *ab epistulis* and *a libellis*), and sometimes other courtiers. Generally these interactions are not recorded in the document, but occasionally they are, and we have included several that explicitly show the influence of mothers and wives on the emperor's decisions (**3.27, 29, 32, 34**), as well as documents that

---

[2] Vale 2001: 9–10, 69–135.

[3] On the *ratio castrensis*, the office administering the emperor's household finances, see Davenport and Kelly, **Vol. 1, 134–5**, and Edmondson, **Vol. 1, 172**.

[4] Vale 2001: 9, 42–56.

[5] Cameron 1987; see Moffatt and Tall (2012) for text and translation.

give fragments of information about the composition and workings of advisory *consilia* (**3.7–8, 4.6 [f]**).

Rather more plentiful than inscribed examples of the emperor's official communications is another genre of inscription, namely funerary epitaphs. Some thousands of these epitaphs, most discovered in and around the city of Rome, record the job titles and family relationships of imperial slaves and freedmen. These give vital data about the organization of labour amongst domestic servants at court, and about the social world of these workers.[6] Somewhat fewer but still very plentiful are epitaphs and other inscriptions that tell us about the careers of the senators and equestrians who came into contact with the court (**4.6 [b–c]**). In this book, we have given a selection of relevant epitaphs and career inscriptions, but they represent a mere fraction of what survives. It is only by combining hundreds of these inscriptions that we can build up a picture of the groups working in administrative, political, and domestic roles at court.

Eyewitness Accounts

There are some eyewitness accounts of life at the Roman court, but again they are quite different from those that exist for many more recent courts. There are no Roman equivalents to the *Mémoires* of the Duc de Saint-Simon (1675–1755), that give such an important perspective on the court of Louis XIV,[7] or of the court memoir of Lord Hervey (1696–1743), a favourite of Caroline of Ansbach, the wife of George II of England.[8] There are, however, letters written by Roman aristocrats that give details about the emperor's court. The correspondence of Pliny the Younger occasionally touches on matters relevant to the court (**2.20, 3.5, 4.30**), although he was never an important courtier, as much as he wished to be. More important is the corpus of letters written by and to Fronto, who was a leading courtier for part of the Antonine period. These letters, which survived through the manuscript tradition (like those of Pliny),[9] are rich with important details about court ceremonial and etiquette (**4.3 [b], 4 [d], 14**), about the physical spaces of court life (**2.17, 22 [a], 23**), and about how Fronto negotiated his relationships with emperors and fellow courtiers (**4.10**). The Fronto letters are not, however, analogous to some of the famous early modern corpora of correspondence by courtiers, such as the letters of Madame de Sévigné (1626–96), another shrewd observer of the court of the Sun King.[10] The letters in the Fronto corpus rarely

---

[6] For fundamental treatments of these texts, see Boulvert 1970, 1974; Weaver 1972. See too Edmondson, **Vol. 1, Chapter 8**.

[7] Sainte-Simon 1983–8.   [8] Hervey 1931.

[9] On the transmission of classical manuscripts from Antiquity to the Renaissance, Reynolds and Wilson (2013) and Wilson (2017) provide fundamental surveys.

[10] Sévigné 1972–8.

relate detailed sequences of court events, so they do not permit us to reconstruct a narrative history of the court, not even for the period in which Fronto's influence was at its zenith.

In the Roman case, some important eyewitness testimony also comes from an unexpected quarter: philosophical treatises. A number of surviving philosophical works from the first and second centuries were written by people who belonged to or were close observers of the imperial court. Because of the importance of practical ethics in Roman philosophy, these authors at times reflect on the real conditions and events of the social world surrounding them. Thus, Seneca the Younger, an important courtier under Claudius and (especially) Nero, discusses individuals and specific events at court (**1.4, 18; 4.12 [a], 22**) and the aulic milieu more generally (**1.8 [a], 19**). The *Meditations* of the emperor Marcus Aurelius also include generalized reflections on court life (**1.8 [g], 23, 26; 3.11**).

Also intriguing is the philosopher Epictetus, whose lectures (as recorded by his pupil Arrian) recount what seem to be anecdotes concerning real events at the court of the mid-first century (**1.22, 3.39–40**). Epictetus tells us that he had been the slave of a certain Epaphroditus, who is often taken to be the man of this name who was Nero's secretary for petitions (*a libellis*), in which case Epictetus offers the perspective of someone very close to the centre of the court.[11] On the other hand, doubts have been cast on whether this courtier was his master.[12] In any case, Epictetus offers well informed reflections on the court, and, unusually, these come from somebody of servile rather than senatorial or equestrian status. Indeed, we must always be aware that, with the exception of the tombstones relating to domestic servants, sources relevant to the court generated at a sub-elite level are vanishingly rare.[13]

Another kind of eyewitness testimony comes from surviving poetic works. A number of poets were in patronal relationships with the emperor and individual courtiers;[14] indeed, these court connections are perhaps part of the reason why their works were preserved and eventually made their way into the medieval manuscript tradition. The poems of such authors give a general sense of the literary tastes prevailing in court circles during particular periods. More specifically, Ovid gives vital eyewitness testimony about Augustus' residence (**1.3 [a], 2.9 [a]**). Writing in the late first century AD, Martial and Statius refer in their poems to physical characteristics of the Flavian Palace (**1.10, 2.15, 2.16 [a],**

---

[11] Millar 1965; cf. Starr 1949.   [12] Weaver 1994.

[13] The paradoxographer Phlegon of Tralles (*PIR*² P 389), a freedman of Hadrian, records seeing human and animal curiosities that had been displayed at the court of Hadrian (*Mir.* 34.3–35, 97), but does not offer any profound insights into the court; the rumour that Hadrian ghostwrote Phlegon's works is unlikely: SHA *Hadr.* 16.1. Phaedrus (*PIR*² P 338), some of whose *Fables* comment directly (2.5) or indirectly (e.g. 1.2, 4.13, 14, 5.1) on the Roman court, is often described as an imperial freedman, but there are now significant doubts about his servile status: Champlin 2005: 98–101.

[14] See Bernstein, **Vol. 1, Chapter 18**.

4.29 [a]), and discuss their relationships with the emperor (**3.20–2**) and individual courtiers (**1.24–5**), as well as the social rituals of the court (**4.29 [a], 33 [c]**). As one would expect of poets who were (or wanted to be) close to the emperor, these works paint a flattering picture. But writings that reproduce the ideology of the regime are still historically important for this reason; we just need to see them for what they are.

Literary Histories and Biographies

Some of the most useful and vivid evidence for the Roman imperial court comes from literary histories and biographies.[15] The coverage provided by such sources is uneven, since there are more dealing with the first century than there are for the second and early third, and very few of good quality give accounts of the period after the Severan emperors. This uneven coverage necessarily unbalances our knowledge of the court in favour of the earlier period. These works, which have all come down through manuscript tradition, are literary in the sense that they are not bare chronicles of deeds and events, but are self-consciously artistic works. Tacitus, Cassius Dio, and Herodian, the historians who feature most frequently in this sourcebook, use the full battery of rhetorical and dramatic techniques to craft interesting narratives. They supplement their factual narratives with speeches that are (at best) imaginative reconstructions of what was said on an occasion;[16] they indulge in forceful authorial judgements; they attribute interior mental and emotional states to the major figures in their narratives. Their choices about which events to report and their decisions about emphasis are driven by their wider thematic concerns. They stand, in other words, in the grand tradition of Graeco-Roman history writing, which sought to produce works of history that were entertaining to read and morally edifying.[17]

The tradition within which these authors worked has implications for how useful they are for understanding the court. Warfare and high politics were considered in Antiquity to be the proper subject of historical works. As a result, no historian set out to write a history of the Roman court per se; rather, events at court are mostly narrated at length only when they have a direct impact on high politics. These narratives naturally tend to relate to acute crises at court, such as the fall of a powerful courtier (**6.1–2**) or the murder of an emperor in a palace conspiracy (**6.3–4**) – hence the focus of Chapter 6 of this book. We should be wary of taking these court narratives at face value, since our authors

---

[15] Matthews (2007: 269–76) surveys the historical and biographical works (both extant and lost) that recorded the history of the Principate.

[16] On speeches in ancient historiography, see Marincola 2007b.

[17] Mellor (1999: 185–200) provides a convenient overview of Roman ideas about the function of historical writing and the tensions between factual accuracy and literary artistry in Roman historiography.

would have had genuine difficulty finding reliable information about what happened in the inner recesses of the palace.[18] This problem was even worse when authors were discussing events that took place decades or even centuries before they were writing, as is often the case. The suspicion is that the surviving historical works (or the now-lost literary histories they were using) creatively embellished what would have been a very slender frame of hard historical data to make a more readable story.

As well as extended narratives, there are many smaller anecdotes about the court in works of Roman historiography, just as there are in works of philosophy. These accounts of what was said or done on a particular occasion add splashes of colour to narratives, and can be used by the author to make moral points or to illustrate the character of key figures such as emperors. Such anecdotes presumably circulated orally in Roman upper-class culture (and perhaps sometimes in society more generally) before being recorded in writing.[19] One can see the impact of this process of transmission in the cases where the same anecdote appears in two or more sources, reported differently each time. Thus, for example, Tacitus, Cassius Dio, and the biographer Suetonius all record a story about the future emperor Vespasian being banned from court for being insufficiently enthusiastic about one of Nero's artistic performances.[20] Tacitus sets the episode in Italy, whereas Dio and Suetonius claim it happened during Nero's Greek tour. The authors also vary on the question of precisely what Vespasian had done during the performance to provoke the crisis, and Suetonius evidently was aware that different answers to this question were in circulation.

In works of biography such as Suetonius' *Lives* of the emperors from Augustus to Domitian, these kinds of anecdotes are commonly deployed. The ancient biographers of the emperors were not as concerned as history writers about producing chronologically coherent narratives. Rather, their concern was with the characters of their subjects, and so anecdotes about the private behaviour of emperors are frequently reproduced in service of this aim, along with more general discussions about the lifestyles and habits of emperors.[21] As a result, the pages of Suetonius are a fertile source for the early Roman court, and we have included many Suetonian passages in this book. On the other hand, we have been sparing in reproducing material from the other main collection of imperial biographies, the *Historia Augusta*. This collection of biographies of emperors from Hadrian to the late third century presents as the work of multiple authors writing in the Tetrarchic period, but is generally agreed to be the work of one author writing c. AD 400. While some of the early biographies in the collection seem to be based on sound sources, much of the collection is

---

[18] Cassius Dio (53.19, cf. 54.15.1–3) admits this explicitly; cf. Tac. *Ann.* 1.6.3.
[19] On anecdotes as sources for the history of the Principate, see Saller 1980.
[20] Suet. *Vesp.* 4.4, 14 (= **3.13**); Tac. *Ann.* 16.5.3; Dio Cass. 65(66).11.2 (Xiph.).
[21] See especially Wallace-Hadrill 1995.

inaccurate and borders on the fraudulent.[22] The few passages from this work that we have included tend to be those that, for good or ill, are heavily discussed in the modern scholarship, or that can be confirmed by reliable evidence.

Given that most ancient writers of history and biography embellished their narratives and included anecdotes of dubious accuracy, it is tempting to give them the same treatment as the *Historia Augusta* and keep them at arm's length. This would be an easy way to deal with a complex source problem, but in our view it would be too crude. Factually inaccurate sources are still useful if one asks the right sort of questions of them. It is important to realize that Tacitus, Cassius Dio, and Suetonius all had direct experience of the imperial court of their own days. In cases where they pass moral judgement on what happens in an anecdote – as they often do – they are also giving precious information about how people connected with the court believed the emperor and his courtiers should conduct themselves. Moreover, when they chose to include an anecdote or embellish a report in a particular way, they did so because what they were writing accorded with their general sense of what was likely at the Roman court. Thus, their works are evidence for general patterns of behaviour and material realities at court.[23] For instance, every version of the story of Vespasian's banishment from Nero's court emphasizes the dangerous and frightening position that Vespasian was in as a courtier who had lost the emperor's favour. They also hint that even senators like Vespasian were at the mercy of the slaves and freedmen who regulated access to the emperor, since in the stories it is a member of Nero's admissions staff who rudely turns Vespasian away from Nero's morning *salutatio*. Other sources repeatedly confirm the general truth of these details, even if we cannot be confident about precisely what happened on this specific occasion. Thus, in many cases, historians should read anecdotes and more extended narratives about the court in the same way as they do Apuleius' Latin novel, *The Golden Ass* – not as a source for actual events (since men do not turn into asses) but for its rich collection of realistic background details about rural life, about social and economic relations, and about being a subject in the Roman empire.[24]

Material Culture

In this book, we have included a selection of material evidence relating to the Roman court. Aside from the inscriptions discussed above, which are material artefacts as well as texts (see **3.50 [b]**), the material sources fall into two basic

---

[22] Syme (1971) is a classic work in the massive bibliography on this problematic source; see too Thomson (2012) for a survey of scholarship on key issues.

[23] Cf. Lendon 1997: 27–9.

[24] This is, of course, the argument of Millar's (1981) classic study on the world of *The Golden Ass*.

categories: artistic representations of court groupings, and remains of palaces and other court spaces. With the first category of material evidence, we must again be judicious about the questions we ask. A group of statues of the imperial family (**5.7**), or a relief depicting the emperor and select courtiers at a hunt (**5.13**), or a coin depicting the emperor with his bodyguards (**5.6**) are not direct reflections of events on a particular occasion. They should not be read in the same way that we might read a photograph from the late nineteenth century, for example – which is not to imply that photographs are always artless reflections of reality either. Instead, artistic depictions of court groupings should be recognized as idealized representations of what the court should be like. Viewed in this way, they are immensely useful sources, since ideology is a historical fact too.

With the archaeological remains of court spaces, we obtain what is, in a sense, the most unmediated access to the court. No ancient author or artist stands between us and the ancient remains. There are other difficulties, however. Since the Roman palaces stand in the heart of a city that has been inhabited since Antiquity, much of the stone has been robbed out for reuse. Likewise with the Tetrarchic palaces in Augusta Treverorum (modern Trier, Germany) and Spalatum (modern Split, Croatia) (**2.24–5**) and the imperial villas in Italy that are known archaeologically (**2.18, 21–2**). We cannot experience these palaces in the same way that we can relatively intact palaces from more recent monarchies, such as the Residenz in Munich, the Winter Palace in St Petersburg, or the Forbidden City in Beijing. Moreover, what does remain of the Roman imperial residences can be devilishly complex. The site of the imperial palaces on the Palatine in Rome is 300 by 500 metres in size, and has up to six different storeys or levels of use. There are as many as eighteen different building stages preserved in the archaeology. An additional sort of complexity is introduced by the fact that these are important sites which are mentioned in ancient texts. Sometimes the texts and the archaeological remains match very well, such as with the winery at the Villa Magna at Anagnia (modern Anagni) (**2.22**). With other sites, such as the so-called House of Augustus on the Palatine (**2.9**) and Hadrian's Villa at Tibur (**2.21**), squaring the texts with the archaeological remains is much more problematic.

Archaeological remains do not, of course, speak for themselves; they need us to interpret them. The analysis of the Roman palaces in the first volume of this book[25] stands within the German tradition of historical *Bauforschung* ('building research'). This involves as a first step the painstaking documentation, using drawings and written lists, of the remains of a structure and the small finds from the site. The construction phases are then identified and separated to build up a sense of the evolution of the building over time. The end goal of the process is to connect the structure to its broader historical and social context.

---

[25] Pflug and Wulf-Rheidt, **Vol. 1, Chapter 9**.

Although it is impossible in a sourcebook to reproduce all of the documentation produced by this process, Chapter 2 contains some of the plans of the Flavian Palace that have been generated by this interpretative approach, and it highlights what is known of particular phases of the palace and how they connect with historical realities.

Continuity and Change

The nature of our evidence for the imperial court allows us to write only certain kinds of history. We cannot write true narratives of court events over the course of months or years; at best, ancient historians such as Tacitus give us narratives of crises at court that ran for a few days or weeks. On some issues, we can put together rather more abstract narratives of change over time. We have the evidence to reconstruct the broad developments in the language the Romans used to describe their court (**1.7–16**), in the palace precinct in Rome (**2.9–16**), and in the ceremonial forms of greeting accorded to the emperor (**4.11–18**). On many issues, however, we have just a few data points that allow us to see examples of specific behaviours, relationships, and discourses separated by decades or centuries, without having the evidence to tease out subtle changes with time. Such is often the case with ancient social history.

1 | Conceptualizing the Roman Court

BENJAMIN KELLY

Introduction

This sourcebook and its companion volume explore the Roman manifestation of a particular transhistorical social configuration – the monarchical court. In doing so, we use an etic concept: that is, a modern category of analysis that has emerged from historians' studies of many different monarchical societies: cf. **Vol. 1, 5–8**. Our choice of this method for analysing Roman society does not mean, however, that the Romans were unaware that there was a court surrounding their emperor. On the contrary, there are several Latin terms that roughly correlated with our concept of the court, and Roman authors were capable of making generalizations about their court as an entity. The Roman ability to conceptualize their own court in this way reassures us that we are not being anachronistic when applying the etic concept of the monarchical court to the Roman Principate. But it is also an important cultural fact that is worth exploring in its own right.

My analysis of Latin terminology begins with a negative point (**1.3–6**). From the start of the Principate, one finds literary sources and some official documents talking about the *domus* ('house') of the emperor, often with an added epithet such as *Augusta*, *Caesaris*, or *principalis* to emphasize its special status. However, terms like *domus Augusta* do not correlate well with our concept of the court: they refer only to the emperor's relatives and his slaves and freedmen; there is nothing to suggest that the *domus* was considered to include other important groups who surrounded the emperor, such as his friends and his bodyguards. The *domus* of the emperor was therefore the kernel of the imperial court, but not the whole court.

Rather, the Latin word *aula* came closer to what we would call the court; the use of this word in reference to the Roman court is documented from the reign of Claudius onward. The *aula* was thought to include a range of people beyond the emperor's family and servants, including aristocrats, bodyguards, entertainers, and religious specialists (**1.8**). It could also refer to the physical building in which such people would meet – the palace (**1.9**). Once the Flavian Palace came to dominate the whole of the Palatine Hill in the 90s AD, *palatium* also came to be applied to this building (**1.10–11**) and the people within it (**1.12**), and later to any palatial building in which the emperor sojourned (**1.13**). The mobility of the court during the mid- and late third century sparked another telling change: the term *comitatus*, which originally referred to the elite companions who accompanied the travelling emperor (**1.14 [a]**), came to refer to the whole court as an institution (**1.15–16**).

It is striking that when one finds reference to the Roman *aula* in literary sources, the context often – albeit not always (cf. **1.24–6**) – is pejorative (**1.17–23**). It is also interesting that, unlike *domus Augusta* and other '*domus*-phrases*', *aula* tends not to be used in public documents such as senatorial decrees. Further, the thousands of tombstones from Rome commemorating emperors' slave and freed domestic servants do not refer to the deceased as having worked in the *aula*: when their place of work is mentioned, it is said to be the *domus* (often with a qualifier, such as *domus Augustana*): see Edmondson, **Vol. 1, 173** for examples. The lack of clear language to describe the *aula* in documents intended for public consumption does not mean that there was no *aula* in Rome during the Principate. Rather, this absence was a product of the deep ambivalence that Romans felt about the court and the moral standards of its denizens, an ambivalence they inherited from the Hellenistic world (**1.2**). The moralizing stereotypes that attached to court life are a recurring theme in the subsequent chapters of this sourcebook.

I | The Concept of 'Court' in the Hellenistic World

Roman political thought and language were often influenced by that of the Greek world, and this certainly applied to the Roman conception of the court, since the Latin word *aula* was borrowed from the Greek *aulē*. As Athenaeus (writing c. 200) discusses in a learned passage below (**1.1**), the Greek word originally meant 'courtyard', but by the Hellenistic period had come to refer to royal palaces, presumably because of the prominence of courtyards in Hellenistic palace architecture. *Aulē* was by no means the most common Greek word for 'palace': *basileion/basileia* are more frequent. *Aulē* tends not to refer to the people of the palace – the court in the social sense; instead, one more often finds the circumlocution *hoi peri tēn aulēn* (lit. 'those around the courtyard') (**1.2**). One does also find *aulikos* used as a substantive to mean 'courtier' (e.g. Polyb. 16.22.8), and the Latin adjective *aulicus* came to be used in an identical way (**1.8 [f]**). On Hellenistic Greek language for palaces and courtiers, see Tamm 1968: 135–68; Strootman 2014: 38–9.

1.1 *Aulē* in Homeric and Hellenistic Greek

Athenaeus 5.189e–190a

But these days they call royal residences *aulai*, just like in Menander:[1] 'to attend palaces (*aulai*) and satraps'.[2] So too in Diphilus: 'It seems to me that to attend palaces (*aulai*) is characteristic of the fugitive or the destitute man or the rogue in need of a whipping.'[3] (They are so called) either because they have large, open-air spaces in front of the dwellings, or because the bodyguards sleep near (*paraulizesthai*) and keep watch beside the royal residences. Homer, however, always employs *aula* for open-air spaces, where the altar of Zeus Herkeios[4] was found. For example, Peleus is found 'in the part of the courtyard (*aulē*) used for feeding animals; he held a gold cup, pouring a libation of glistening wine on blazing offerings'.[5] And Priam: 'wallowing in the droppings in the parts of the courtyard (*aulē*) used for feeding animals'.[6] Further, Odysseus commands Phemius and those around him: 'But go out of the well-situated house to the courtyard (*aulē*), away from the carnage.'[7]

1 A comic playwright of the Hellenistic period, 342/1–291/0 BC. This is Menander, frag. 436 (ed. Kassel and Austin 1998: 259).
2 Satraps were governors in the Achaemenid Persian Empire.
3 Diphilus was also a Hellenistic comic playwright; his exact birth and death dates are unknown. This is Diphilus, frag. 97 (ed. Kassel and Austin 1986: 109).
4 Zeus Herkeios was Zeus in his capacity as protector of the domestic courtyard.
5 Hom. *Il.* 11.774–5.
6 Hom. *Il.* 24.640.
7 Hom. *Od.* 22.375–6. The text here deviates from the standard text of Homer.

1.2 Hellenistic courtiers: *hoi peri tēn aulēn*

Polybius 5.40.1–3

In this part of his *Histories*, Polybius is narrating the events leading up to the Fourth Syrian War (219–217 BC) between the Hellenistic kingdoms of Ptolemaic Egypt and Seleucid Syria. For the general background, see Hölbl 2001: 127–32.

Not long after this, Theodotus,[1] an Aetolian by origin, who had been given charge of Coele Syria,[2] took it upon himself to communicate with Antiochus[3] and hand over the cities in Coele Syria. The reason was partly that he despised the king[4] because of the licentiousness of his lifestyle and his entire conduct, and partly that he distrusted the courtiers (*hoi peri tēn aulēn*). For shortly before, he had given notable service to the king in relation to several things, including the first assault by Antiochus on Coele Syria.[5] Not only did he fail to receive any gratitude for these services, but on the contrary, he was recalled to Alexandria and was almost in danger of his life.

1 For Theodotus, see Peremans and van't Dack 1950–81: no. 15045.
2 Coele Syria (lit. 'Hollow' Syria) is here used to refer to the area of south-west Syria under Ptolemaic control at this point.
3 Antiochus III, king of Syria.
4 Ptolemy IV Philopator, king of Egypt.
5 In 221 BC, Seleucid forces had attempted to seize Coele Syria, but were repelled by Theodotus.

II │ The *domus* of the Emperor

From the earliest stages of the Principate, the sources show a clear sense that there was something exceptional about the domestic milieu of the emperor.

Whilst sometimes the sources speak plainly of the emperor's *domus* ('house') as they would of that of any Roman aristocrat (e.g. Sen. *Ad Polybium de consolatione* 12.5; Tac. *Ann.* 1.4.1, 1.6.3, 3.17.2, 6.24.2, 13.4.2, *Hist.* 1.15.2, 1.29.2), a custom grew up of adding special epithets to the word *domus* to mark out the imperial house as special.

Most common in the sources are *domus Augusta*, *domus principalis* (and the closely related *domus principis/principum*), and *domus divina*. One also finds a variety of other formulations, each attested only a handful of times. These include *domus regnatrix* (Tac. *Ann.* 1.4.4); *domus Caesaris/Caesarum* (Tac. *Ann.* 1.10.6, 2.34.2, *Hist.* 2.92.3; Suet. *Galb.* 2); *domus sacra* (Ov. *Pont.* 4.6.20; Stat. *Silv.* 5.1.85–6); *domus imperatoria* (SHA *Verus* 2.11, cf. *Marc.* 3.1). There was not, therefore, a fixed formulation that was used for the emperor's *domus*, and even *domus Augusta*, which appears in official documents, coexisted with other related phrases.

Although this terminology for the imperial house is rich, and shows an awareness of its special status, none of these '*domus*-phrases' in sources from the Principate can be seen as referring to the imperial court as a whole; they refer only to an important subset of people within the court. Only with the late-antique *Historia Augusta* is the boundary between *domus* and *aula* blurred with the confused *domus aulica*: SHA *Hadr.* 11.3, *Marc.* 5.7. In sources from the first three centuries, neither *domus Augusta* nor any of these other terms for the imperial house can be shown to refer to a group wider than the emperor's relatives and freedmen. It has been suggested that aside from referring to relatives and freedmen of the emperor, these terms might refer to 'other people who formed the imperial "House"' (Winterling 1999: 196), but none of the passages in which these terms appear clearly refer to individuals who were not freedmen of the emperor or persons related to him. These '*domus*-phrases' are therefore no wider in the group of people they include than is the word *domus* when used of aristocratic houses and households: Saller 1984: 342–9, 1994: 80–8; Rilinger 1997: 76.

1.3 The *domus Augusta*

(a) Ovid, *Letters from Pontus* 2.2.67–74

This passage is from a poem celebrating the triumph of Tiberius in AD 12, following his campaign in Illyricum. It provides the earliest occurrence of the phrase *domus Augusta*. It makes it clear that relatives of Augustus (including relatives by adoption and marriage) were considered part of this *domus*. On the poem and its historical context, see Millar 1993: 12–13. The term *domus Augusta* is also attested in senatorial decrees from the principate of Tiberius that have been preserved on inscriptions: *SCPP* l. 33; *Tabula Siarensis* l. 17 = **5.3**. On the *domus Augusta* generally, see Winterling 1999: 21–2, 196; Corbier 2001; Pani 2003: 18–20; Moreau 2005: 8; Michel 2015: 122–7.

The appropriate time has come for entreaties: he[1] flourishes, and he sees that your strength, which he built up, is flourishing, O Rome. His wife,[2] who is in unimpaired health, looks after the divine couch. His son[3] expands Ausonia's empire.[4] Germanicus himself surpasses his years in courage, and Drusus'[5] vigour does not fall short of his high birth. Add to this the fact that his dutiful daughters-in-law and granddaughters,[6] his grandsons' sons,[7] and the other members of the House of Augustus (*domus Augusta*) are all flourishing.

1 Augustus.
2 Livia.
3 Tiberius, who was the adoptive son of Augustus.
4 The Roman empire; 'Ausonia' was a poetic term for Italy.
5 More likely Drusus the Younger, the son of Tiberius, rather than the long-dead Drusus the Elder, but cf. Helzle 2003: 283.
6 Here we translate *nurus* and *neptesque*; for the textual issue and a discussion of the individuals to whom Ovid refers, see Helzle 2003: 283.
7 The sons of Germanicus: Nero Iulius Caesar (*PIR*[2] I 223), Drusus Iulius Caesar the Younger (*PIR*[2] I 220), and Caligula. The infant son of Drusus the Younger was possibly also born at this point: Millar 1993: 13.

(b) Valerius Maximus, *Memorable Doings and Sayings* 2.8.7

Aside from referring to a group of people, *domus Augusta* could also refer to the physical House of Augustus, as is clear from this passage, which is part of a discussion of the customs surrounding triumphs, and the fact that they were not awarded for victories in civil wars. Valerius Maximus uses the same phrase elsewhere (8.15 praef.), interestingly signalling the special status of the building by also calling it a *templum* ('temple') (cf. below **2.2 [b]**). Some of the variant formulations used to refer to the *domus* of the emperor are also used to refer to the emperor's physical house: Plin. *Pan.* 47.6 (*domus principis*); Tac. *Ann.* 2.34.2 (*domus Caesaris*).

It is irksome and tiring to go on writing about the wounds of the state any further.[1] The Senate did not give a laurel to anyone, and nobody wanted one to be given to him with part of the community weeping. But hands are held out for the oak, when a crown ought to be awarded because citizens have been saved. With this crown, the doorposts of the House of Augustus (*domus Augusta*) exult with perpetual glory.[2]

1 I.e. inflicted by civil wars.
2 On this honour, see below, **1.13, 2.9 (a)**.

1.4 The *domus principalis*

Seneca the Younger, *To Polybius, On Consolation* 2.4

The emperor's *domus* is referred to in various other verbal formulations aside from *domus Augusta*; most frequent amongst these alternatives are *domus principalis*, *domus principis*, and *domus principum*, which can all be rendered 'the emperor's (or emperors') household'. In this passage and elsewhere (Sen. *Ben.* 6.32.1), Seneca the Younger prefers the first formulation. This passage comes from Seneca's letter of consolation to C. Iulius Polybius, an imperial freedman, on the death of his brother, who was also apparently an imperial freedman. At this point in the letter, Seneca argues that aside from death, there

was nothing truly harmful that could have been inflicted by Fate on Polybius' brother –
not even the loss of friends. The passage makes it clear that *domus principalis* could
include imperial freedmen; for freedmen as part of the emperor's *domus*, see too Tac.
Ann. 11.28.1, 12.1.1, *Hist.* 2.92. This is not, however, different from the way in which
domus was used of ordinary aristocratic houses, since the word could embrace an
aristocrat's slaves and freedmen.

But you knew that he was so loveable that he could easily replace with others
those (friends) he had lost. For out of all those whom I have seen in influential
positions in the emperor's household (*principalis domus*), I seem to have
recognized this in him alone: although it was useful for everyone to have him
as a friend, it was, to an even greater extent, agreeable.

1.5 Tacitus on the *domus principis*

Tacitus, *Annals* 2.40.3

Tacitus presents a slight variation on Seneca's *domus principalis*, referring to the
emperor's house as *domus principis/principum* on multiple occasions: Tac. *Ann.*
4.52.1, 11.28.1, 12.1.1, 13.47.1. *Annals* 2.40.3 is especially interesting from a linguistic
point of view because Tacitus explicitly contrasts the *domus principis* with the senatorial
and equestrian orders, underlining the fact that this term does not embrace courtiers
outside the imperial family. The passage is part of Tacitus' account of the affair of
Clemens, the slave of Agrippa Postumus. In AD 16, Clemens apparently attempted to
impersonate his master and pretend that he was still alive, which prompted Tiberius to
have him captured, interrogated, and murdered.

Tiberius interrogated him about how he had been turned into Agrippa, and he
is said to have replied: 'In the same way you were turned into Caesar.' He could
not be compelled to disclose his collaborators. Tiberius did not dare to punish
him publicly, but ordered that he be killed in a secluded part of the palace
(*palatium*),[1] and the corpse secretly carried away. There was no enquiry at all,
even though many people from the emperor's household (*domus principis*), as
well as equestrians and senators, were rumoured to have supported him with
resources and aided him with advice.

1 For the anachronistic use by second-century AD authors of *palatium* to mean 'palace', see
below, **2.9 (c)**.

1.6 The *domus divina*

Roman Inscriptions of Britain 897 (AD 242; Old Carlisle, Britain)

The term *domus divina* ('Divine House') is heavily attested on inscriptions relating to
the imperial cult: Fishwick 1987–2005: 2.1.423–35. The term appears first in inscriptions
from the principate of Tiberius (*CIL* 13.4635; *AE* 1978.295); it also occasionally crops up
in literary sources (Phaedrus 5.7.38; Stat. *Silv.* 5 praef.). There is no reason to think that
the semantic range of the word is any wider than *domus Augusta*: Fishwick 1987–2005:
2.1.423–4. Statius (*loc. cit.*) calls the imperial freedman Abscantus a *latus … divinae*

domus, which could be read to imply that he counted as a part of the *domus divina*. The text below illustrates a fairly late example of the phrase, which occurs on an altar dedicated to Jupiter for the welfare of the emperor Gordian III and his wife. For the inscription and its protagonists, see Birley 2005: 259–60.

To Jupiter, the Best and Greatest, for the well-being of the emperor M. Antonius Gordianus P(ius) [F(elix)] Invictus Augustus and Sab[in]ia Furia Tranquil(lin)a, his wife, and for their entire Divine House (*domus divina*). The cavalry squadron Augusta, so-called because of its valour, Gordian's own, set this up. Aemilius Crispinus, cavalry prefect, born in the province of Africa, originally from Thysdrus, is in command of them. Under the administration of Nonius Philippus, proprae[torian] legate of the emperor. In the consulship of [At]ticus and Praetextatus.

III | The Roman Court as *aula*

At least by the mid-first century BC, the Romans had apparently borrowed the Greek *aulē* and formed a Latin equivalent: *aula*. In the earliest attestations, we find *aula* applied in foreign and zoological contexts: Cic. *Fam.* 15.4.6 (= ShB 110); Hor. *Carm.* 4.14.36 = **1.7**; Verg. *G.* 4.90 (of beehives, ruled by kings [sic]). At this early stage, *aula* certainly could mean a royal palace; whether it should be taken to mean 'court' in the sense of the society surrounding the monarch is less clear.

By the mid-first century AD, one finds Latin sources applying *aula* to the Roman court, with the earliest references coming from Seneca the Younger (**1.8 [a]**, **1.18–19**). By this stage, the word clearly could mean either the social circles surrounding the monarch (**1.8**) or the physical palace in which he dwelt (cf. **1.9**): Pani 2003: 20–2. In some contexts, of course, the precise connotations are unclear, and the word could be read as having physical and social dimensions simultaneously: Winterling 1999: 201–2. In Greek works from the Roman Principate, with one clear exception (**1.8 [g]**), one does not find *aulē* used of a social circle: it continues to mean 'palace' (e.g. **1.22**).

1.7 *Aula* applied to foreign kingdoms

Horace, *Odes* 4.14.34–40

In this *Ode*, Horace is praising the military accomplishments of Augustus' stepsons, Drusus the Elder and Tiberius, against Alpine tribes. He draws attention to the coincidence of dates between the Alpine victory (in 15 BC) and Octavian's entry into Alexandria in 30 BC, following his defeat of Antony and Cleopatra.

Fifteen years from the day[1] when Alexandria as suppliant opened her ports and her deserted palace (*vacua aula*),[2] favourable Fortune has again granted a successful conclusion to a war. She has attributed renown and the desired honour to completed campaigns.

1 1 August 30 BC, according to the Roman calendar.

2 The royal palace in Alexandria was literally empty of its queen when Octavian entered, since
   Cleopatra had sought refuge in her mausoleum: Plut. *Ant.* 76–80; Dio Cass. 51.10–11. For
   vacua aula, see too Verg. *G.* 4.90; [Sen.] *Oct.* 161–2.

1.8 *Aula* as a circle of people

Once it came to be applied to the Roman court, *aula* began to refer to the
society of people around a monarch, and not just to a palace building. This
sense continued into late-antique Latin: e.g. *Pan. Lat.* 2(12).13.4 (AD 389). *Aula*
could include not just members of the imperial family (**1.8 [g]**) and imperial
slaves and freedmen (**1.8 [b]**), but also members of the aristocracy (**1.8 [g]**,
cf. **3.1**); bodyguards (**1.8 [c]**); diviners, physicians, and philosophers (**1.8 [g]**);
and actors, eunuchs, and buffoons (**1.8 [d], [e]**).

(a) Seneca the Younger, *On Tranquillity of Mind* 6.2

This passage is generally seen as one of the earliest references to the Roman court as an
aula: Winterling 1999: 197.

The diffidence of certain people makes them unsuitable for political affairs,
which need a firm demeanour. The defiance of others is not effective at the
court (*aula*).[1] Some do not have their anger under control, and the slightest
indignation leads them to reckless words. Some do not know how to curb
their refined wit and do not desist from dangerous jokes. For all such people, a
quiet life is more profitable than one of public engagement: a fierce and
intolerant temperament should avoid provocations to free speech likely to
be harmful.

1 It has been suggested that *aula* should be translated as 'atrium' here, and that Seneca actually
   has in mind the *atria* of aristocratic houses and the subservient mien that clients must adopt
   there when they visit their patrons: Schumacher 2001: 332–3. But Seneca's advice does not
   look like it is directed at those of low social station, who were unlikely to have had the luxury
   of withdrawing from the client–patron system to a life of seclusion.

(b) Suetonius, *Life of Otho* 2.2

Suetonius here narrates the early life of the future emperor Otho. Aside from displaying
the perception that entry into court circles and influence with the emperor could be
procured by sexual favours, the passage shows that imperial freedmen and freedwomen
were conceived of as part of the *aula*. See too SHA *Comm.* 7.2.

Following the death of his father, Otho even pretended to love an influential
court freedwoman (*libertina aulica*) – despite the fact she was elderly and
almost decrepit – so that he could cultivate her favour more effectively.
Through her, he easily got on intimate terms with Nero and held the highest
position amongst his friends (*amici*), thanks to the similarity of their characters and – as some people in fact say – to their habit of fornicating with
each other.

(c) Tacitus, *Annals* 1.7.3–5

Tacitus here narrates the events surrounding the death of Augustus and the accession of Tiberius in 14. Tiberius initially showed an unwillingness to become *princeps*. Tacitus believes this unwillingness was feigned, Tiberius' disingenuousness partly being revealed by the fact that he began to use bodyguards (from the praetorian cohorts, and perhaps also the *Germani custodes*), which Tacitus sees as part of the trappings of the court – thus revealing the assumption that security personnel were part of the *aula*. The same assumption would seem to lie behind Plutarch's (*Galb.* 2.2) description of praetorian guardsmen as *aulikoi* ('courtiers').

For Tiberius began all things at the initiative of the consuls, just as if the old Republic were in existence and he were undecided about exercising power. He even issued the edict by which he summoned the senators to the Senate house under the title of the tribunician power[1] he received under Augustus. The words of the edict were few and their sense very modest: that he was going to consult the Senate about the honours for his father, that he was not deserting Augustus' body, and that he was taking upon himself this one part of the public obsequies. With Augustus dead, however, he had given the password to the praetorian cohorts just like an emperor; he had sentries, troops, and the other trappings of a court (*aula*); soldiers escorted him into the forum and the Senate house. He sent letters to the armies just as if he had obtained the position of emperor, and he was never hesitant except when he was speaking in the Senate.

1 Tiberius was granted tribunician power in 6 BC. This power, which was modelled on that of tribunes of the plebs under the Republic, was granted to Augustus to give some legal basis for his extraordinary position. Its grant to Tiberius marked him as Augustus' intended successor as *princeps*.

(d) Tacitus, *Histories* 2.71.1

Tacitus here narrates Vitellius' march on Rome in the civil war of AD 69, mentioning that actors, eunuchs, and other lowlife from Nero's *aula* attached themselves to Vitellius. For entertainers as members of the *aula*, see too Suet. *Ner.* 45.1 (*luctatores aulici*: 'court wrestlers'); SHA *Hadr.* 19.6 (*histriones aulici*: 'court actors').

The closer Vitellius' march drew (to Rome), the more corrupt it became, with actors, mobs of eunuchs, and everything else typical of the Neronian court (*Neroniana aula*) being mingled in. For Vitellius used to talk about Nero himself with admiration, and habitually tagged along on his singing tours, not out of compulsion, as was the case with all the most respectable men, but because he was a slave to indulgence and gluttony.

(e) Tacitus, *Annals* 15.34.2

As Tacitus' description of Vatinius makes evident, wits and buffoons could also be seen as members of the *aula* – and even as influential and powerful members.

Vatinius[1] was amongst the foulest monstrosities of Nero's court (*aula*), the son of a cobbler's shop, with a twisted body and a jester's wit. He was originally taken on as a target for insults. Then, by laying charges against every decent man, he became so powerful that because of his favour (with Nero), his money, and his capacity to inflict harm he surpassed even villains.

1 *PIR²* V 307.

(f) Suetonius, *Life of Caligula* 19.3

This passage is part of Suetonius' account of how Caligula bridged the Bay of Naples in AD 39; cf. Dio Cass. 59.17. In reporting a family tradition about the emperor's motivations, Suetonius shows how the adjective *aulicus* could be used as a substantive to mean 'courtier', and also implies that different courtiers had different degrees of access to the emperor.

I know that many people have thought that Caligula came up with the idea of such a bridge out of rivalry with Xerxes, who bridged the Hellespont[1] – which is considerably narrower – and provoked a certain amount of astonishment. Others, I know, have thought that he did so to frighten Germany and Britain, which he was threatening (to attack), with a rumour about a massive exploit. But as a boy I used to hear my grandfather relating the reason for the exploit, which was revealed by Caligula's more intimate courtiers (*interiores aulici*): that when Tiberius was anxious about his successor and was leaning towards his natural grandson,[2] the astrologer Thrasyllus[3] assured him that Caligula was no more going to be emperor than he was going to drive about on the Gulf of Baiae with horses.

1 The Persian king Xerxes bridged the Hellespont in 480 BC in the lead-up to the Second Persian War: Hdt. 7.54–7. On Caligula's reasons for building the bridge, see especially Malloch 2001.
2 Ti. Gemellus.
3 On Thrasyllus (*PIR²* T 190), see **3.44** and Dolansky, **Vol. 1, 413–14**.

(g) Marcus Aurelius, *Meditations* 8.31

This passage comes in the context of the emperor Marcus Aurelius' reflections on the transience not just of individuals but also of groups, specifically families (*genē*) and courts. It offers a very rare example of an author writing in Greek using *aulē* to refer to a circle of people rather than a physical palace. This is probably because Marcus' Greek was influenced by his Latin-speaking milieu, so he gave the Greek word the semantic range of the Latin *aula*: Winterling 1999: 203. The passage is therefore evidence of the sorts of people a Roman would consider to be part of the *aula*: the emperor's relatives and friends; physicians; and even experts in divination.

The court of Augustus: his wife, daughter, grandsons, stepsons, sister, Agrippa, kinsfolk, household (*oikeioi*), friends, Areus,[1] Maecenas, physicians, diviners[2] – the whole court, dead.

1 Areus (*PIR²* A 1035), an Alexandrian philosopher, was a teacher of Augustus (Octavian) in his youth, and later a friend and confidant.
2 The Greek word here – *thytai* – could also refer to the personnel who carried out sacrifices.

1.9 *Aula* as a physical place

Alongside the meaning of *aula* as a group of people – the 'court' in the social sense – the word continued to refer to physical structures, just like its Greek prototype *aulē*. In the next three passages, all from the late first and early second centuries AD, the *aula* is treated more as a physical structure, not a group of people. It can be covered in marble and gold, as Nero's Golden House was (**1.9 [a]**), it has a physical footprint, part of which can be later covered by other public buildings, again like Nero's Golden House (**1.9 [b]**), and it has furnishings that can be auctioned (**1.9 [c]**). *Aula* continued to be used in this sense well into Late Antiquity: e.g. *Pan. Lat.* 2(12).12.1, 2(12).16.2 (AD 389).

(a) [Seneca] *Octavia* 624–31

Let the arrogant Nero construct a palace (*aula*) out of marble and sheathe it with gold.[1] Let armed cohorts (*armatae cohortes*) watch over their leader's doorway. Let a depleted world send vast resources. Let Parthians grasp at his bloody right hand as suppliants, and kingdoms bring their riches. Yet the day and the hour will come when he will surrender his guilty soul because of his crimes and present his throat to his enemies (to be cut) – solitary, ruined, and bereft of everything.

1 Elsewhere in the *Octavia*, the playwright similarly uses *aula* to refer to Nero's physical palace structures: [Sen.] *Oct.* 162, 285, 668, 689 (= **5.9 [a]**), 699, 781.

(b) Martial, *On the Spectacles* 2

Here, where the starry colossus[1] gazes at the stars at closer range and high scaffolding[2] rises in the middle of the road, the odious halls of a savage king used to shine, and in the entire city only one house stood.[3] Here, where the hallowed bulk of a remarkable amphitheatre is erected, were Nero's lakes.[4] Here, where we marvel at the baths – a swift benefaction – a haughty estate had deprived the poor of their houses. Where the Claudian portico stretches out its expansive shadows, there was the final part of the palace (*aula*).[5] Rome has been restored to herself, and with you as custodian, Caesar, the pleasures that belonged to a master now belong to the people.

1 This refers to the colossus (with a blaze of rays around the head) originally set up as part of Nero's Domus Aurea complex, and later moved to be beside the Flavian Amphitheatre – hence its later name, the Colosseum.
2 *Pegmata*. For the involved debate on the meaning of this word, see Coleman 2006: 22–7.
3 Nero's Domus Aurea.
4 The Flavian Amphitheatre was built partly where the lake in the Domus Aurea complex once lay. Suetonius (*Ner.* 31.1 = **2.11 [a]**) mentions only a single lake.
5 Martial uses *aula* to refer to palace structures in a physical sense elsewhere in his surviving works: Mart. 5.6.8 (= **3.21 [b]**), 9.11.8, 9.36.10.

(c) Suetonius, *Life of Caligula* 39.1

In Gaul also, since Caligula had sold at immense prices the jewellery, furniture, slaves, and even freedmen of his sisters after they had been convicted,[1] attracted by profit, he ordered from the city all the moveables from the old palace (*vetus aula*).[2] To transport them, hired wagons and draught animals from mills were also requisitioned – to such an extent that bread was often lacking in Rome and many litigants lost their cases because they were absent and unable to appear in court at the appointed time.

1 Caligula's sisters Iulia Livilla (*PIR*[2] I 674) and Agrippina the Younger were exiled as a result of their alleged connection with a conspiracy against Caligula in 39; it is unclear whether they were formally tried before the Senate: Barrett 2015: 144–5.

2 Caligula carried out building and renovation works in the imperial complex on the Palatine (see **2.8, 10**), so Suetonius must refer here to the furnishings of the original parts inhabited by Augustus and Tiberius. For a similar auction of palace furnishings (*res aulicae*) under Marcus Aurelius, see Davenport and Kelly, **Vol. 1, 143**.

IV | *Palatium* and *comitatus*

Aula was not the only Latin word that roughly corresponded to the English 'court'. During the course of the Principate, *palatium* went from meaning the Palatine Hill in Rome, to the imperial palace on that hill (**1.10–11**), to any palace where the emperor sojourned (**1.13**). By metonymy, the *palatium* could also sometimes mean the people inside the palace – i.e. the members of the court (**1.12**). For the development of the word *palatium*, see Millar 1992: 41–2; Winterling 1999: 209–17.

In Late Antiquity, another Latin word for 'court' emerged: *comitatus*. In earlier periods, the word simply referred to the retinue of *comites* – close friends and aristocratic associates with whom an emperor might travel: **1.14 [a]**; cf. Halfmann 1986: 92–103; Eck 2000a: 206–7. By the Tetrarchic period, *comitatus* came to refer to a fixed, stable institution, rather than an emperor's ad hoc group of travelling companions (**1.15–16**). In other words, it came to mean 'court' in the fullest sense. This development is a reflection of the fact that during the crisis period of the third century, and even during the Tetrarchic period, emperors travelled very frequently, so the emperor's travelling retinue effectively was the court. On the history of *comitatus*, see *TLL* 3.1796, s.v. *comitatus* III; Millar 1992: 42–3; Schlinkert 1996.

1.10 *Palatium* as palace

Statius, *Silvae* 1.1.32–6

This passage from Statius, written around 91 to commemorate the dedication of an equestrian statue of Domitian, provides one of the earliest cases of *palatium* meaning not the Palatine Hill, but rather the palace complex that came to dominate it. In the works of historians of the second century, *palatium* is used sometimes to refer to the emperor's house in pre-Flavian times, but this is strictly anachronistic: see Winterling 1999: 212–13.

But you yourself[1] shine down upon the temples, your high head surrounded by clean air. You seem to look in front of you. Does the new palace (*palatium*) rise up more handsome than before, disdaining the flames? Does the Trojan fire with its silent torch keep a vigil and Vesta praise her attendants, now tried and true?[2]

1 I.e. the head of the statue of Domitian.
2 This is a reference to the fact that the Vestal Virgins kept alight a sacred fire, allegedly brought from Troy at the foundation of Rome, and to the fact that Domitian had recently executed four Vestals for unchastity.

1.11 A conversation *in vestibulo palatii*

Aulus Gellius 19.13

In this passage, Gellius recounts a learned conversation that he overheard about Latin and Greek words for 'dwarf'. Importantly for our purposes, he locates the scene *in vestibulo palatii* ('in the forecourt of the palace'), illustrating again how *palatium* came to refer to the palace building following the construction of the Flavian Palace.

Cornelius Fronto,[1] Postumius Festus,[2] and Sulpicius Apollinaris[3] happened to be standing together chatting in the forecourt of the palace (*in vestibulo palatii*). I was standing nearby with certain other people and eavesdropping rather curiously on the conversations that they were having on literary topics.

1 The orator and teacher of Marcus Aurelius; see above, xxiii.
2 M. Postumius Festus, a senator from Africa and *cos. suff.* 160; *PIR*[2] P 886.
3 C. Sulpicius Apollinaris, a distinguished grammarian: *PIR*[2] S 984.

1.12 *Palatium* as court (in a social sense)

Martial, *Epigrams* 7.28

Very soon after *palatium* came to refer to the Flavian Palace, its potential meanings further expanded to include the people who inhabited or frequented that structure – i.e. members of the court in the social sense. This social meaning is evident in this poem. Martial asks Fuscus (*PIR*[2] F 599) to read and evaluate some of his epigrams during the Saturnalia holidays in December; he prefaces his request with reference to Fuscus' usually busy life, which includes the management of his estate at Tibur (modern Tivoli), successful work as an advocate, and engagement with the *palatium* liable to excite praise. Buildings obviously cannot sing praises; Martial means those who inhabit or frequent the building – the members of the court society. Martial uses *palatium* in a similar way elsewhere: Mart. 9.42.5, 12.21.3.

So may the woods of Diana of Tibur grow up for you, and may the grove that has often been cut down come back quickly. May your olives, Fuscus, not give in to (competition from) olive presses in Tartesus[1] and your vast wine vats give good must. So may the fora marvel at you, so may the palace (*palatia*) extol you and may many palms adorn your double doors.[2] But while the middle of December gives you a bit of leisure, examine the trifles (of mine) that you read and with unerring judgement. (You say,) 'Do you want to know the truth? It's a difficult thing!' But you can tell me what *you* want to be told![3]

1 A region of southern Spain.
2 Palms were used to decorate advocates' houses after successful cases: *Laus Pisonis* 31; Juv.
  7.106–18.
3 I.e. if Fuscus is frank about Martial's poems, Martial will likewise give an honest verdict on
  Fuscus'. On the other hand, Martial will requite flattery with flattery.

1.13 The 'palatium' moves with the emperor

Cassius Dio 53.16.4–6

According to Cassius Dio, the word *palatium* (and its Greek transliteration *palation*)
underwent a further development with time, and came to refer to any building in which
an emperor resided. On the passage, see Winterling 1999: 214, 216; Haensch 2012: 272.
This development in meaning is also seen in **4.17**, where the imperial residence at
Mediolanum (modern Milan) is called the *palatium* by an orator of the Tetrarchic period.

Anyhow, Caesar[1] received many honours even previously, when the issues of
his turning down a monarchical position and of the distribution of the provinces were discussed.[2] For the entitlement both to plant laurel trees in front of
his imperial residence (*basileia*) and to hang the oak crown over (the doorway
of) the residence was voted to him at that time, on the grounds that he was
always victorious over enemies and that he saved citizens.[3] The imperial
residence (*basileia*) is called the *palatium* (*palation*), not because it was ever
resolved that it should be so called, but because Caesar used to live on the
Palatine (*Palation*) and had his headquarters (*stratēgion*)[4] there, and his house
also received a certain renown from the whole hill, in view of the fact that
Romulus dwelt there previously. For this reason, even if the emperor lodges
somewhere else, the stopping-place keeps the title of *palatium* (*palation*).

1 Octavian, the future Augustus.
2 Dio Cassius here alludes to the meeting of the Senate on 13 January 27 BC, when Augustus
  relinquished control of his provinces to the Roman people – and then had control over some
  of them immediately returned to him: *Mon. Anc.* 34; Dio Cass. 53.12–16; Suet. *Aug.* 47.
3 See **1.3 (b)**.
4 Winterling (1999: 214) takes *stratēgion* as the equivalent of *praetorium* (a military
  commander's headquarters) here. However, Haensch (2012: 272) argues that the word should
  mean 'administrative headquarters', just as it was used for the administrative headquarters of
  civilian officials in Greek cities.

1.14 *Comitatus*: the emperor's travelling retinue

(a) Tacitus, *Histories* 2.87

In this passage from the *Histories*, Tacitus describes the march of Vitellius on Rome in
AD 69. Tacitus assumes that a *comitatus* was likely to consist of military officers and
friends of the emperor, and to be distinct from the general military forces with which an
emperor might travel.

While Vespasian and the generals of his party were doing these things throughout the provinces, Vitellius, who each day was more despicable and slothful,

made for Rome with a ponderous horde, pausing at all the charming towns and villas. Sixty thousand soldiers, spoilt by lax discipline, were following him. There was an even greater number of soldiers' attendants, together with camp followers, who were especially uncontrollable, even by the standards of slaves. A retinue of this many military officers and friends (*tot legatorum amicorumque comitatus*) would not have been inclined to obedience, even if they had been controlled with the utmost discipline. Senators and equestrians who came from the city to meet Vitellius further weighed down the throng. Some came because of fear, others out of flattery, and others – and gradually everyone – so that they would not themselves be staying behind when the others were setting out. From the plebs, buffoons, actors, and charioteers flocked together – all known to Vitellius through their disgraceful services. He took astonishing joy in these degrading friendships.

(b) *Digest* 49.16.13.3 (from Macer, *On Military Law* Book 2)

By the later Severan period, we find the jurist Aemilius Macer (*PIR*^{2} A 379) regarding *comitatus* as a term official enough to use in legal handbooks. This passage has been seen as illustrating how the word was heading in an 'impersonal' direction (Millar 1992: 43); Macer certainly gives no hint that he has in mind only officers who were dishonourably discharged: it seems to be any soldier suffering this disgrace who is barred from the *comitatus*.

There are three general grounds for discharge: honourable discharge, discharge for health reasons, and dishonourable discharge. A discharge which is given after the period of military service is complete is honourable. A discharge is for health grounds when a man is declared unfit for military service because of some defect of his mind or body. The ground for discharge is dishonourable when a man is released from his military oath because of a crime. Someone who is dishonourably discharged is not able to spend time either in Rome or in the imperial retinue (*sacer comitatus*).

1.15 *Comitatus* as a centre for legal administration

The Code of Justinian 7.67.1

The text below, preserved in a sixth-century legal code, is a rescript – i.e. a response from the emperors to a petition from a litigant asking for a ruling on a point of law. The language of the rescript treats *comitatus* as a place where routine administration of justice might take place. During the period when the rescript was issued, Diocletian was engaged in a multi-year tour of the lower Danubian provinces (AD 293–4); from the sheer quantity of rescripts from this period, it has been deduced that the emperor must have travelled with his *scrinium libellorum* ('office of petitions'), whose lawyers composed rescripts in response to petitions: Connolly 2010: 55–62.

The emperors Diocletian and Maximian Augusti and the Caesars to Diophanes. If a judicial ruling was made against you and no appeal was lodged, you realize that you ought to be satisfied with what has been settled. For you could have feared nothing in our imperial court (*sacer comitatus*).[1] Written on 17 June at Philippolis, when the Augusti were consuls.

1 I.e. if he was dissatisfied with the ruling, Diphanes should have appealed promptly to the emperors.

1.16 *Comitatus* as a fixed centre for legal administration and record keeping

Année épigraphique 1996.1498 ll. 12–22 (= *CIL* 3.12134)

This decree of the Tetrarchs Constantius I and Galerius dates to AD 305/6, and concerns people who owe money to the *fiscus* (the imperial treasury), and the fact that unscrupulous officials of the *fiscus* (the *Caesariani*) have been pursuing false claims against such debtors. The salient fact for present purposes is that the *comitatus* of the emperor (presumably Galerius) is seen as a place to which documentation can be sent for archiving and examination. The passage is often taken as the earliest clear case of *comitatus* meaning 'court' in an impersonal sense – the centre of government: *TLL* 3.1796, s.v. 'comitatus' III 2; Millar 1992: 43. The word has no real connotations of travel in the decree. A large fragment of the original Latin of the decree survives from Tlos, with smaller fragments from Ephesus. There is also a Greek translation from Athens: *IG* 2^2.1121 (= *AE* 1996.1403). Here we translate the original Latin, with the lacunae restored from the Greek translation. For the decree and its various texts, see Feissel 1996; Corcoran 2007.

So that the legal basis for harassment of this kind [may be cut off at the roots and forever put to sleep], know that the directives of our decree have sprung forth. (These directives are) [that absolutely all *adnotatio*]*nes*[1] that on the aforementioned day (were) in the possession of the bureaux of the *fiscus* and [remained in the register – whether on parchment or] even papyrus or on documents of whatever kind – should be sent [immediately to our court (*comitatus noster*)]. Naturally, if even after this [benefaction from Our Piety] such documents [remain] in the possession of the bureaux [aforementioned, so that no opportunity may be] presented to the Caesariani [for robbing] our provincials [in their customary way, henceforth nobody is to be summoned before a fiscal tribunal unless on the basis of manifest] proof and properly drafted undertakings. [Orders have even been given, by the instruction] of our ordinance, [that henceforth if] *adnotationes* [are supplied] to the accounts of our *fiscus* in a similar case, [nobody should be sued on the basis of them], but the *adnotationes* should all be referred immediately to our court (*comitatus noster*).

1 *Adnotationes* in this context would appear to have been documents of some kind that authorized the seizure of property on the grounds of an unpaid fiscal debt: Corcoran 2007: 227.

V | The Court as a Target for Moralists

The histories of words such as *aula*, *palatium*, and *comitatus* show that the Romans had a clear idea that what we would call a monarchical court existed during the Principate. What did they think about this institution at a general, abstract level? Some writers of a moralizing bent made the court and courtiers a target of virulent moral condemnation – an attitude that is already visible in accounts of Hellenistic courts from writers of the Hellenistic period (e.g. Polybius, **1.2** above). The following selection of passages highlights some of the themes one finds in Roman moralists' condemnations of court society.

1.17 The worries of life at court

Valerius Maximus, *Memorable Doings and Sayings* 7.1.2

Valerius Maximus records an anecdote in which the mythical king of Lydia, Gyges, consulted the oracle of Apollo at Delphi about whether any mortal was more fortunate than him. Apollo's answer – that the impoverished Aglaus of Psophis was the happiest mortal – is seen by Valerius as an endorsement of Aglaus' hut (*tugurium*) over Gyges' palace (*aula*), with all its cares and anxieties. The passage therefore provides an early example of moralists' reservations about court life – albeit in relation to a non-Roman court. The anecdote was known to Pliny the Elder (*HN* 7.151), and the second-century AD Greek author Pausanius apparently alludes to it as well (Paus. 8.24.13). Valerius therefore perhaps found it in a Greek source, in which case it provides an example of how Greek moralizing about court life was taken over by Romans of the early Principate.

Gyges, conceited because of the kingdom of Lydia, which was most abundant in arms and riches, had come to Pythian Apollo to inquire whether any mortal was more blessed than him. The god sent his voice forth from the concealed cave of his shrine and ranked Aglaus of Psophis in front of Gyges. Aglaus was the most impoverished of the Arcadians, and, already of advanced years, he had never left the boundaries of his small plot of land, satisfied with the produce of his tiny estate. But assuredly Apollo, with the acuteness of an oracle, understood the goal of a blessed life, and not just in a shadowy way. On account of which he replied to Gyges, who was arrogantly boasting about the splendour of his fortune, that he approved of a shack smiling in safety more than a palace (*aula*)[1] unhappy because of cares and worries, and of a few clods of soil immune from terror more than the richest fields of Lydia loaded with fear, and of one or two pairs of oxen easy to maintain more than armies and weapons and cavalry onerous with insatiable expenses, and of a small storehouse for essential use that would not attract too much attention more than treasuries vulnerable to the plots and avarice of everyone. Thus Gyges, when he longed to have the god as a supporter of his groundless belief, learnt where firm and genuine good fortune was to be found.

1 *Aula* here has been taken as meaning 'court life' (Winterling 1999: 197), but the contrast in Valerius' Latin between the *tugurium* of Aglaus and the *aula* of Gyges suggests that the author has the physical dwellings of the two men in mind.

1.18 The court as a place of humiliation

Seneca the Younger, *On Anger* 2.33

Some scholars have seen this passage as the first example of *aula* being used to refer specifically to the Roman court (Winterling 1999: 197; Michel 2015: 11), since the aphorism about how to survive in the *aula* is then illustrated with an anecdote concerning the court of Caligula. It cannot, however, be excluded that Seneca is thinking generically about courts, and that the aphorism originally belonged to a courtier in a Hellenistic kingdom. Either way, it shows one sort of negative connotation that courts in general could have in the mind of a Roman writing in the age of Claudius.

Wrongs committed by the more powerful must be endured not only with tolerance but with a cheerful face, for they will do it again if they believe they have succeeded once. People who are haughty because of their good fortune have the worst mental trait: they hate those whom they harm. Well known is the dictum of a man who had grown old doing homage to kings: when someone asked him how he had achieved that rarest distinction in a court (*aula*), namely old age,[1] he replied: 'By accepting wrongs and giving thanks for them.' Often it is so inexpedient to avenge a wrong that it is not even profitable to acknowledge it. *(Seneca then recounts a lengthy anecdote in which Caligula executed a man, then invited his father to dinner; the father managed to get through the banquet without displaying signs of grief liable to inflame the murderous emperor.)*

1 On the *topos* that courtiers rarely were allowed to grow old, see **3.6**.

1.19 The moral turpitude of the court lifestyle

Seneca the Younger, *Letters* 29.4–6

In this somewhat playful passage, Seneca assumes that being involved with the *aula* could be used as a reproach against a philosopher, just as sexual immorality and dining in cheap eating houses could be grounds for criticism. One perhaps detects a hint of Seneca's inner disquiet at the fact that he was a philosopher who spent much of his life at court.

I do not yet despair of our friend Marcellinus.[1] Even now he can be saved, if a helping hand is extended to him quickly. Indeed, there is a risk that he may drag down the person offering him the hand. He had great strength of character – but his character is already becoming warped. Nevertheless, I shall undergo this danger and I shall dare to show him the error of his ways. He will do what he usually does: he will resort to his notorious wit, which can pry laughter from those in mourning. He will joke first at his own expense, and then at mine. He will twist to his own advantage everything that I am going to say. He will probe our philosophical schools and charge philosophers with accepting imperial handouts, keeping mistresses, and having an appetite. He will show me one philosopher committing adultery, another dining in a greasy spoon, another at court (*in aula*); he will show me the charming philosopher Aristo, who used to discourse while being carried in a litter – for he had seized on this time for broadcasting his works.

1 Nothing is known of Marcellinus (*PIR*² M 182), beyond the inference from this letter that he was a mutual friend of Seneca and his correspondent, Lucilius. The Tullius Marcellinus whose death is mentioned in Sen. *Ep.* 77.5 may or may not be the same man.

1.20 The court as a place of luxury and dissolute living

Tacitus, *Histories* 1.22.1

At this point in Tacitus' *Histories*, Otho is contemplating whether to attempt to usurp the emperor Galba, who has recently become emperor following the suicide of Nero. The passage clearly connects Nero's *aula* with a string of 'royal' vices. The context of *aula* in this passage could perhaps lead one to translate the word as 'court lifestyle' – i.e. to refer to court activities rather than a circle of people or a place; thus Winterling 1999: 201. However, it may be simpler to assume that Tacitus meant to say that Otho's unscrupulous slaves and freedmen used the prospect of becoming master of Nero's Domus Aurea as an enticement to usurp Galba.

The mind of Otho was not soft as his body was. His closest slaves and freedmen, who were subject to looser discipline than their counterparts in private houses, showed to the eager Otho the palace of Nero (*aula Neronis*) and the luxury, the adultery, the serial marriages, and the other desires entertained by kings of like character – all his, if he dared. But they reproached him for being inactive as though these things belonged to others. Even the astrologers put pressure on him, since by watching the stars they confirmed that there would be a change in government and an illustrious year for Otho. They are a breed of men treacherous for the powerful and deceptive to the hopeful; in our state, they will always be both forbidden and retained.

1.21 Courtiers use unscrupulous methods to gain the emperor's favour

Tacitus, *Histories* 2.95.2

The complaint that courtiers were wont to gain the monarch's favour through gifts, flattery, and other unscrupulous methods was a *topos* inherited from the Greek world, and had a long history at Rome, surviving into Late Antiquity (e.g. *Pan. Lat.* 3[11].19.4; cf. Curt. 8.8.22). In this passage, Tacitus claims that at the court of Vitellius, courtiers gained the emperor's favour by putting on lavish dinner parties.

Nobody in that court (*aula*) competed in honesty and hard work; there was one path to power: to satisfy the insatiable appetites of Vitellius with extravagant banquets, expenditure, and gluttony. He himself thought that it was sufficient if he was enjoying his present activities without making longer-term plans; he is believed to have squandered 900 million sesterces[1] in just a few months.

1 For such moralizing claims about the cost of court banquets, see Davenport and Kelly, **Vol. 1, 139**.

1.22 Life at court as unquiet – yet seductive

Arrian, *The Discourses of Epictetus* 1.10.2–6

I know a man[1] older than me who is now the Prefect of the Grain Supply in Rome. When he passed by here returning from exile, what things he said to me! He inveighed against his earlier life and proclaimed that in the future, after he had returned to Rome, he would be eager for nothing else except to live out the rest of his life in peace and quiet, 'For how much time is left to me?' And I said to him, 'You will not do this, but when you have merely caught the smell of Rome, you will forget all these things.' I added that should some kind of access to the palace (*aulē*) be given, he would barge his way in, rejoicing and thanking god. He said, 'If you discover me, Epictetus, putting one foot in the palace (*aulē*), you can think what you like about me.' Now then, what did he do? Before he entered Rome, letters from Caesar came to him. He took them and utterly forgot all the things that he had said, and henceforth he has accumulated one thing after another. I used to wish that I could stand beside him now and make mention of the words which he said as he passed by, and that I could say, 'How much cleverer am I than you as a prophet!'

1 Identity unknown; possibly M. Rutilius Lupus (*PIR*² R 252) or Ser. Sulpicius Similis (*PIR*² S 1021), both of whom are known to have been *praefectus annonae* in the same general period that Epictetus delivered his discourses: Millar 1965: 145–6.

1.23 The unnecessary pomp of court life

Marcus Aurelius, *Meditations* 1.17.5

In this part of the *Meditations*, Marcus Aurelius lists the many things for which he is grateful to the gods. There is an interesting tension here between Marcus' distaste for the pomp and luxury usually associated with courts, and the acknowledgement that some things still need to be done with a certain grandeur, in a fashion befitting a ruler (*hēgemonikōs*).

For the fact that I was under the power of an emperor and a father[1] who was to take away all my arrogance and lead me to the realization that one can live in a court (*aulē*) without the need for guards, conspicuous clothing, torches and statues, and[2] all aspects of ceremony of these kinds,[3] but that it is possible to lower oneself almost to the condition of a private individual and not as a result to be too humble or perfunctory in relation to the things that have to be done for the public good in a fashion befitting a ruler.

1 Antoninus Pius, Marcus' adoptive father.
2 Here we follow the emended Greek word order suggested by Farquharson (1944: 2.481).
3 The *Historia Augusta*, for what it is worth, reports that Antoninus Pius reduced the level of imperial pomp at court, much to the horror of the court attendants (*aulici ministri*) (*Ant. Pius* 6.4) – although the same work has Antoninus Pius forcing courtly distinction (*aulicum fastigium*) on the resistant Marcus Aurelius when he was still Caesar (*Marc.* 6.3).

VI | The Court and Courtiers in Panegyrical Contexts

In spite of the strong condemnation of the court and courtiers in the writings of moralists, it would be a mistake to see the court as always prompting negative associations in the minds of Romans. As the following passages illustrate, the court could have quite positive associations in some contexts.

1.24 The father of Claudius Etruscus at the *aula*

Ti. Iulius Aug. l. [- - -], a high-ranking imperial freedman whose full name is not known, was the father of Claudius Etruscus (*PIR*² C 860). He was the subject of poetic eulogies from both Statius and Martial. For both, the dead man's association with the *aula* was a circumstance attracting praise. For the man and his career, see Weaver 1972: 284–94 = Weaver 1965.

(a) Statius, *Silvae* 3.3.59–78

But you were not sent over to Latium from barbaric shores: your native earth was Smyrna, and your drink was the awesome spring of the Meles, and Hermus' waters,[1] where Lydian Bacchus enters and restores his drinking horns with golden silt. After this there was a happy sequence and your esteem was made greater with different posts held successively, and you were allowed to always walk near deities, to always serve at Caesar's side and hold on tightly to the holy secrets of the gods. Firstly, the Tiberian palace (*aula*) was opened up to you when new manhood was barely changing your face. Here manumission came your way, given to you for free, for your talent far outstripped your years. Nor did the next imperial successor send you away, even though he was harsh and harried by the Furies.[2] So next as his youthful companion (you travelled) as far as the Arctic frosts, tolerating a tyrant dreadful in word and appearance and brutal to his own. You were like those who domesticate the terrifying hearts of wild animals and order them to release hands already placed in their jaws, even though they have already tasted blood, and live without prey. But Claudius, an old man not yet sent off to the star-studded sky, raised you to exceptional duties because of your deserts and transferred you to his successor after long service.[3]

1 Both rivers in western Asia Minor, near Smyrna (modern İzmir, Turkey); the Hermus was gold-bearing.
2 Caligula. The Furies were goddesses of vengeance.
3 The manuscript tradition has transmitted this last clause corruptly; here we translate Shackleton Bailey's conjecture of *longo transmittit ab aere nepoti*. The word *nepos* (lit. 'grandson' or 'nephew') is still odd, since neither Nero nor any of his successors was the nephew or grandson of Claudius. The poet could be alluding to the fact that Nero was Claudius' grand-nephew, or using *nepos* very loosely to mean 'successor'. For the passage, see Weaver 1965: 147 n. 3, 1972: 287; Shackleton Bailey 2015: 378–9.

(b) Martial, *Epigrams* 7.40

Here rests an old man, well known in the Augustan court (*aula*), who endured both moods of the god[1] with unsubmissive heart. His pious children mixed him with his wife's holy shade; the grove of Elysium[2] holds them both. She passed away first, defrauded of the bloom of youth; he lived almost three times six Olympiads.[3] But anyone who caught sight of your tears, Etruscus, believed that he was seized from you after the years had been hurried along.

1 *utrumque deum*: i.e. Domitian in both an angry and a calm mood: Friedländer 1886: 1.494.
2 A paradise for deceased heroes and the righteous dead.
3 He died at around age 90.

1.25 Courtiers behaving well (according to Martial)

Martial, *Epigrams* 9.79

Rome previously hated the servants of its leaders – the former mob of attendants and the Palatine haughtiness (*Palatinum supercilium*). But now, Augustus,[1] your retinue is so beloved by all that for each man, care for his own household is secondary. So tranquil are their minds, so great is their deference to us, so peaceful is their serenity, so great is the modesty on their faces. No imperial servants have their own manners, but rather they have their master's – this is a characteristic of a mighty court (*aula*).

1 The emperor Domitian.

1.26 The court as cyclical drama

Marcus Aurelius, *Meditations* 10.27

Marcus Aurelius, in reflecting on the cyclical nature of history, repeats a *topos* already well established: courts as theatrical performances: Philo *Leg.* 351, 359, 368; Plut. *Demetr.* 18.3, 34.3; cf. Diod. Sic. 31.16.1. That he sees the *aulē* of his revered father and predecessor Antoninus Pius as fundamentally the same as that of previous Roman, Macedonian, and Lydian courts suggests the associations of *aulai* were not unequivocally negative in Marcus' mind.

Think continuously about how all things that now happen both happened previously and will happen in the future. Place before your eyes the entire dramas and their backdrops, all alike in form, of the sort that you came to know from your own experience or from earlier history: for example, the whole court (*aulē*) of Hadrian, and the whole court (*aulē*) of Antoninus, and the whole court (*aulē*) of Philip,[1] of Alexander,[2] of Croesus.[3] For all these dramas were the same (as the ones that happen now), only with different players.

1 Philip II of Macedon, the father of Alexander the Great.
2 Alexander the Great, king of Macedon.
3 Croesus was king of Lydia in the mid-sixth century BC.

2 | Court Spaces

MICHELE GEORGE AND BENJAMIN KELLY

Introduction

Roman Court Spaces and their Predecessors

At the beginning of the Roman Principate, there was no self-evident model to which the residence of the Roman emperor could conform: Wulf-Rheidt 2012a: 33. What resulted was a long period of experimentation, as different emperors and their architects attempted to fashion spaces appropriate both to the ceremonies and social rituals of their courts, and to the general self-image they aimed to project. In the 30s and 20s BC, Octavian/Augustus created a kind of imperial complex that included temples, libraries, and pre-existing aristocratic houses (**2.9**). In the 60s AD, Nero built his vast Domus Aurea, with spaces for *otium* reminiscent of those in aristocratic villas outside of Rome (**2.11**). Eventually in the early 90s, Domitian completed the first phase of an enormous palace on the Palatine Hill, which included spaces where the social rituals of the court could be performed on a grand scale, as well as more intimate spaces for *otium* (**2.12–15**). This Flavian Palace continued to be the imperial residence in Rome for centuries without fundamental alterations and, in the late third and early fourth centuries, it provided the model for Tetrarchic palaces outside Rome (**2.24–5**). However, space in the Flavian Palace was still sufficiently flexible to allow different emperors to pursue diverse styles of court life and ceremony.

With imperial villas (**2.17–23**), there was even greater scope for diversity. No single 'villa model' ever emerged; rather, different emperors created different villa complexes to suit their tastes. This said, the archaeological remains of imperial villas are consistent to the extent that all have spaces appropriate for social rituals such as dining, for secluded *otium*, and for at least some level of governmental activity. Many imperial villas also played a role in projecting imperial power, since they were architecturally impressive and often dominated the surrounding landscape.

The palaces and villas of the Roman emperors therefore were constructed with an eye to the needs of the court life that took place within them. But architects and their patrons would inevitably meet their design goals by drawing on the precedents provided by earlier buildings. The case has been made for Hellenistic palaces influencing the general layout and location of Roman palace complexes, e.g. Meyboom 2005: 242, 247; Wulf-Rheidt 2012a: 37; Raimondi

Cominesi 2018: 720, 728; cf **2.2–3**. There is also reason to think that there was Hellenistic influence (probably indirect) on the configuration and decoration of particular rooms (see **2.1**). At the same time, the elite houses of the late Republic, which themselves had become increasingly palatial, provided a model of space that was configured to suit specifically Roman forms of social relationships and rituals. Features of Republican aristocratic houses came to be reflected in emperors' residences (**2.3–8**), where traditional social rituals formed the backbone of court life.

Virtual Photography: Computer Visualizations as Architectural Hypotheses

While this volume is mostly concerned with collecting sources for the imperial court, this chapter includes a number of computer visualizations of court spaces (**2.13 [a]**, **[b]**, **2.22 [b]**; see too **Vol. 1, figs. 9.5, 9.7, 10.3**). Unlike, say, an ancient text or the remains on an archaeological site, computer visualizations are not 'sources'. Nor are they like archaeological plans, which are direct – albeit schematic – representations of archaeological remains. Rather, computer visualizations are representations of architectural hypotheses.

We often use language to represent such hypotheses. When archaeologists say (or write) they have discovered a 'house', they rely on both the audience's experience of other structures that are so labelled and its knowledge of the specific physical and cultural context in order to generate a sense of what the specific building was once like. But words have an openness to them; 'house' refers to a category of buildings with a wide range of characteristic properties, only some of which will be found in a specific structure. Hearing an archaeological find described as a 'house' will therefore lead different people to imagine the original structure somewhat differently. This is the classic dilemma of communication, one that can never be completely solved.

In generating computer visualizations, we attempt to translate a hypothesis from a linguistic to a pictorial statement, albeit one that is still inherently uncertain. Specific archaeological findings are combined with analogy and abstraction to create a spatial model that, depending on the quantity of data, is a more or less abstract generalization. This in turn raises the importance of the photographic composition – the 'constructed view' (cf. Rosa 1994) – given of a space or structure in a visualization, since it attempts to reflect the ancient viewer's spatial perception of the architecture, as seen from a specific point. Alongside the shape, surface texture and colour are also hypothetical and abstract in computer models of structures. Over time, the original condition of structures changes irreversibly. Weather erodes; human habitation and use cause wear and tear; structural elements can be destroyed or even lost. A computer model, being a static abstraction, must necessarily ignore how the fabric of buildings changed with time. Traditional model-making used in archaeological design is the inspiration for this whole process (cf. **2.18 [b]**), but now the resources of computer science can also be used to help viewers explore hypotheses in their imaginations.

Dominik Lengyel and Benjamin Kelly

I | Hellenistic Court Spaces

Some of the royal residences of the Hellenistic kingdoms are known archaeologically (especially Augai [modern Vergina, Greece] and Pergamon [modern Bergama, Turkey]), and this knowledge can be supplemented with literary sources (especially for Ptolemaic Egypt); see Strootman (2014: 54–90) for a recent synthesis and Morgan (2017: 32–5) on the danger of anachronism in speaking of Hellenistic court spaces as 'palaces'. Three points relevant to understanding Roman palaces emerge. Firstly, many Hellenistic royal precincts were not simply large residences for the monarch, but complexes that included sacred spaces, libraries, and places for assembly and entertainment such as stadia, hippodromes, and theatres. Secondly, these complexes were generally in cities (or on their edges), but also were separated from the rest of their cities by natural features (e.g. hills, waterways). Thirdly, elements of design and interior decoration attested for Hellenistic court spaces were paralleled in Roman palaces, with elite Republican houses and villas serving as intermediaries in the process of transmission (see below, **2.3–8**).

2.1 The river ship of Ptolemy IV Philopator

Callixeinus *FGrH* 627 F 1 (ap. Athenaeus 5.204f–206a)

No detailed descriptions of the interior layout and decoration of Hellenistic royal residences survive, but two fragments of the *On Alexandria* of Callixeinus of Rhodes, who probably wrote in the second century BC, describe a temporary dining pavilion of Ptolemy II of Egypt (*FGrH* 627 F 2 ap. Athenaeus 5.196a–197c) and a river-boat of Ptolemy IV (translated below). These descriptions provide some of the best evidence available of royal interior design in the Hellenistic world: Fittschen 1976; Nielsen 1999: 20–3, 133–8; Strootman 2014: 78–9. They show, for example, the use of columns within rooms and the extensive use of peristyles, elements originally adopted from Greek public architecture. These were to become a feature of elite domestic architecture at Rome: Wallace-Hadrill 1994: 20–3. The references to shrines also show the intermingling of the sacred and the profane in Hellenistic court space. On the river ship of Ptolemy IV Philopator (r. 221–204 BC), see especially Caspari 1916; Janni 1996: 425–48; Thompson 2013: 189–92. For a Roman imperial parallel, see below, **2.19**.

(Having described the external appearance and dimensions of the ship, Callixeinus turns to its interior layout and furnishings.)

In the middle, its hold was equipped with dining-rooms, bedchambers, and the other things useful for daily life. Around the ship on three sides there was a pair of covered walkways (*peripatoi*). The perimeter of one of these was not less than five *plethra*,[1] while the arrangement of the other, which was below deck, was very similar to that of a peristyle (*peristylon*); the upper one was like a cryptoportico (*kryptē*), surrounded on all sides by screens and windows.

As one boarded from the stern, the first vestibule was open in front, with a row of columns around it. In the part of the vestibule towards the bow, an entrance was constructed from ivory and the most costly wood. Once one passed through this, there was a sort of proscenium,[2] furnished with a roof. Similarly, there was again on the middle side another vestibule at the back, and a gateway with four openings led into it. Low windows were installed on the left and right, providing ventilation.

The largest room was connected to these vestibules. It had a row of columns around it and could fit twenty dining couches. Most of the room was constructed from Syrian[3] cedar and Milesian cypress. There were twenty doors in the room's portico, and they had been glued together from citron-wood panels and had ivory decorations. The ornamental studs on the front of the doors and the knockers were made from a ruddy copper and had received their gilded appearance from (being treated with) fire. The bodies of the columns were cypress-wood; their capitals were Corinthian in style, and had been decorated with ivory and gold. The whole architrave was made from gold, and a frieze was affixed to it containing highly visible ivory figures more than a cubit[4] high, ordinary enough in its technical execution, but worthy of wonder for its sumptuousness. There was a beautiful ceiling with square coffering in cypress-wood over the dining-room; its decorations were carved and gilded. Beside this dining-room there was a bedroom with seven beds. Connected to this room was a narrow corridor that ran across the breadth of the hold, separating off the women's quarters. In these, there was a dining-room with nine couches, almost equal in extravagance to the large one, and a bedroom with five beds. Such, then, were the structures on the first deck.

When one ascended the stairs located near the bedroom I previously mentioned, there was another room with five couches which had a ceiling with lozenge-shaped coffering. Near it was a shrine to Aphrodite that was like a rotunda, in which there was a marble statue of the goddess. Opposite this there was another extravagant dining-room with a row of columns around it. Its columns were made of Indian marble. Next to this dining-room were bedrooms, fitted out just like the ones I have already described. As one moved forward towards the bow, there was a room devoted to Bacchus with thirteen couches and a row of columns around it, with the cornice gilded as far as the architrave running around the room. The ceiling was fitting for the characteristics of the god. In this room, a grotto had been built on the right side. Its façade had stonework that had been fabricated from genuine precious stones and gold. Statues of the royal family were set up in it, made from translucent marble. There was another pleasing enough dining-room, with the structure of a tent, on the roof above the biggest room. It did not have a roof, but bow-shaped rods had been stretched at a certain distance from each other, on which purple curtains were draped when the ship was underway. Next an open courtyard took the same position above as the vestibule that lay below. Beside this was a spiral staircase leading to the covered walkway (*peripatos*) and a dining-room with nine couches, built in the Egyptian style . . . (*Callixeinus then describes in some detail the construction of the columns in the room, which were stylistically Egyptian, and then finally the ship's mast and sails.*)

1 A *plethron* was 100 feet, and therefore varied between c. 27 and 35 m, depending on the particular Greek measurement standard.
2 A proscenium formed part of the stage of a Greek theatre.
3 The manuscripts have ἀπὸ κέδρου σχιστῆς ('from split cedar'); for the emendation of σχιστῆς to Συριακῆς, see Burzacchini 2017: 208 n. 533.
4 *Circa* 45 cm.

2.2 The Ptolemaic royal district at Alexandria

(a) Strabo 17.1.8–9 (excerpts)

The geographer Strabo, who sojourned in Alexandria in the 20s BC, provides an invaluable eyewitness account of the royal precinct soon after the Roman conquest. The complex included not only residences built for the Ptolemaic kings, but also a temple of Poseidon, gardens, a theatre, and the Museum (which included the great Library of Alexandria). Even though located in a populous city, some areas were secluded using features of the harbour. Nielsen (1999: 18–25, 130–3), Strootman (2014: 74–81), and Morgan (2017: 46–50) provide general analysis of the Alexandrian royal district, citing additional ancient textual evidence.

The city has very beautiful public temple precincts and royal districts (*basileia*), which comprise a quarter or even a third of the whole city. Each of the kings, just as they used to add some embellishment to the public buildings through a love of splendour, would also privately build a dwelling in addition to the existing ones, with the result that now, as Homer says, 'there is building upon building'.[1] All are connected, however, with each other, with the harbour, and with the spaces situated outside it.[2] The Museum forms part of the royal district (*basileia*). It has a covered walkway, an *exedra*,[3] and a large house in which the association of scholars connected with the Museum has its dining hall. This association not only has common property but also a priest overseeing the Museum, who was once appointed by the kings, but now by the emperor. Also part of the royal district (*basileia*) is the so-called Sema, the precinct in which the tombs of the kings and of Alexander were located. . . . (*Strabo here digresses, discussing the confused situation following Alexander the Great's death, which saw his body brought to Alexandria.*)

In the Great Harbour, to the right of the entrance is the island and tower of Pharos,[4] and on the left are reefs and the promontory of Lochias, which has a royal district (*basileia*). As one sails into the harbour, to the left is the inner royal district (*basileia*), connected to that on Lochias, which has many multicoloured buildings and groves. Lying beneath these is the artificially excavated harbour that can be closed off – the private harbour of the kings – and also Antirhodos, an islet situated in front of the artificial harbour, with a royal building (*basileion*) and a small harbour; Antirhodos is so called because it supposedly contends with Rhodes. Above this lies the theatre, then the Posideion, a curved spit of land projecting from what is called the Emporion, on which there is a temple to Poseidon. Mark Antony added to this spit another projecting still further into the middle of the harbour and built on its tip a royal dwelling (*diaita basilikē*), which he called the Timoneion. This he did as his last act, when, abandoned by his friends, he sailed off to Alexandria after the fiasco at Actium, choosing the lifestyle of Timon[5] for his remaining days, which he was destined to spend without all those friends. Next comes the Caesareion[6] and the Emporion and storehouses together with dockyards as far as the Heptastadion.[7] These, then, are the things around the Great Harbour.

1 This line of Homer (*Od.* 17.266) describes the palace of Odysseus on Ithaca.
2 I.e. the royal district is connected to the rest of the city as well as the harbour.
3 A semi-circular recess in a wall, often with a domed roof.
4 The famous lighthouse.
5 An Athenian misanthrope: cf. Plut. *Ant.* 69.4–70.4.
6 The temple to the Roman imperial cult.
7 The causeway connecting the island of Pharos to the mainland.

(b) Lucan 10.111–26

The description of the residence of Cleopatra VII provided by the poet Lucan (cf. **3.19**) should by no means be taken as literally true. This passage from his epic poem has extensive intertextual dependence on earlier poetry and a complex literary role in Lucan's work: see Schmidt 1986: 190–7. Nevertheless, it provides important evidence of how a Roman of the Neronian age could imagine a Hellenistic court space; for Lucan, Cleopatra's residence was not just staggeringly luxurious, but its design also evoked temple architecture. It is also suspected that the passage implicitly critiques Nero's Hellenistic tastes in building, as manifested in the Domus Transitoria and in the plans for the Domus Aurea, which was still unfinished when Lucan died: Bastet 1970: 140; Voisin 2015: 540.

The place itself was like a temple of a sort that a more degenerate era could scarcely construct.[1] The panelled ceilings bore riches, and a thick layer of gold covered the beams. The House (*domus*) shone and not with a mere veneer of marble slabs,[2] and agate stood there useful in its own right; so too porphyry.[3] Alabaster, spread through the whole palace (*aula*), was trod upon.[4] Ebony from Meroe[5] did not cover huge doors but stood in for ordinary wood – a support, not an adornment, of the House (*domus*). Ivory covered the entrance hall, and on the doors there were artificially coloured Indian tortoise shells,[6] their spots densely embellished with emerald. Gems glittered on the couches and the tableware made of tawny jasper <weighed down the tables, and dining couches with multicoloured>[7] coverlets gleamed. Most of the coverlets had been long steeped in Tyrian dye and in more than one vat;[8] some sparkled with gold embroidery in a feathered pattern; some were fiery with scarlet dye, as there is a custom of mixing the warp-threads in Egyptian cloth.[9]

1 In a more degenerate era, resources would be lacking to build such a lavish structure.
2 Rather, the walls were made of solid marble.
3 Agate (a multicoloured stone) and porphyry (a purple stone) served a structural function; they were not merely ornamental.
4 It was used as flooring.
5 A city in Nubia, in what is now Sudan.
6 The artificial tinting of tortoise shells was seen as an example of extreme luxury: Sen. *Ben.* 7.9.2; Plin. *HN* 16.233.
7 The manuscripts are missing a line here; we translate Houseman's hypothetical reconstruction.
8 The city of Tyre (in what is now Lebanon) was famed for the production of purple dye. The poet refers here to the steeping of textiles in multiple batches of purple dye to give them an especially vivid hue.
9 The cloth would have multicoloured warp threads. On the weaving process, see Walbank 1940: 98; Schmidt 1986: 209.

II | Republican *domus* and *villae*

The continuous habitation of the city of Rome has all but deleted remains of elite houses from the Republican period. One must therefore look to literary discussions of Republican houses and to the remains of older houses in Pompeii and Herculaneum. Caution is needed: domestic spaces in the regional (and originally Samnite) town of Pompeii may not perfectly reflect conditions in the capital, and the literary sources provide an idealized and often moralizing picture of elite housing in Rome. Nevertheless, we have enough to form a picture of Republican housing, at least in broad outline. The moralizing bent of the literary sources is historically important, since the criticisms of grandeur and luxury applied to Republican houses were later directed towards imperial residences: Hales 2003: 61.

2.3 Republican elite housing: the House of the Faun at Pompeii

The House of the Faun at Pompeii dates mostly to the second century BC. Covering 3,050 m^2 and taking up a full city block, it provides a classic example of the spatial arrangement of the elite Roman *atrium* house. The western *atrium* (B) and *tablinum* (D) provided spaces that could be used, inter alia, for the social ritual of the *salutatio*. The two large peristyle gardens (F) and the three dining rooms (*triclinia*) with views into the gardens, provided spaces for *otium* that the master of the house, his family, and his invited guests could enjoy. Although visitors at the *salutatio* would not necessarily be invited into the house's inner recesses, upon entering they could gaze across the rainwater pool (*impluvium*) in the *atrium*, into the *tablinum* (where the master of the house might be positioned), and then through a large window to the southern peristyle garden and the chamber at its rear. Such sight-lines hinting at the expanse of the house were

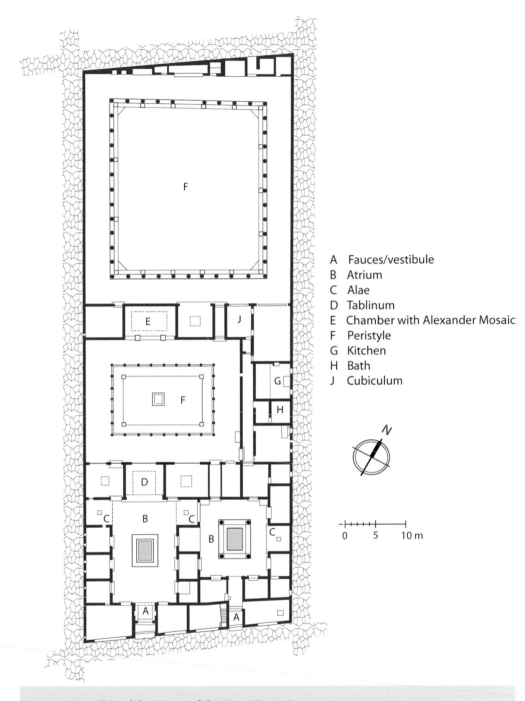

A   Fauces/vestibule
B   Atrium
C   Alae
D   Tablinum
E   Chamber with Alexander Mosaic
F   Peristyle
G   Kitchen
H   Bath
J   Cubiculum

Figure 2.2.1 Plan of the House of the Faun, Pompeii.
Courtesy of F. Yegül, D. Favro, and G. Varinlioglu.

a common feature of Roman elite houses: Drerup 1959; Bek 1980: 181–6; Clarke 1991: 2–6, 14–16; Wallace-Hadrill 1994: 44–5; Hales 2003: 107–17; Hartnett 2017: 189–92. The service areas of the house, including the kitchen (G), were tucked away, out of the sight of visitors. Somewhat unusually, the House of the Faun has a second, less elaborate *atrium* in the south-east of the house; there is debate over its function: Yegül and Favro 2019: 254–5. The house also shows traces of how Roman aristocrats adopted elements of a 'globalized', Mediterranean elite culture with roots in Hellenistic court culture: cf. Strootman, **Vol. 1, Chapter 2**. The mosaic in chamber (E) is the celebrated depiction of Alexander the Great at the Battle of Issus, probably a copy of a Hellenistic original. More generally, the introduction of peristyle gardens in Roman houses has been seen as the product of influence from Hellenistic, and ultimately palace, buildings: Clarke 1991: 12; Hales 2003: 99, 2013: 56.

2.4 Visibility and Republican Housing

Velleius Paterculus 2.14.3

This anecdote is used by the early imperial historian Velleius Paterculus to illustrate the character of M. Livius Drusus (*tr. pleb.* 91 BC; *RE* 18). His house was located on the Palatine, in view of the whole city, as we hear from Cicero, a later occupant: Cic. *Dom.* 100; see too Krause 2004: 39–45; Coarelli 2012: 303–36 on the precise location. Drusus also wanted the house's interior to be visible. As tribune of the plebs he needed to be accessible to the people; moreover, closed, inaccessible houses evoked the stereotypical tyrant's citadel, and could also be suspected to be hotbeds of rebellion: Hales 2003: 38; Beck 2009: 362–3, 367.

He was building a house on the Palatine on the site where there is now the house that was once owned by Cicero, later by Censorinus,[1] and these days by Statilius Sisenna.[2] His architect promised that he was going to build it in such a way that he would be free from the public gaze and immune from all judgements, and that nobody would be able to look down into it. But Drusus replied: 'If you indeed have any skill, build my house in such a way that whatever I do can be seen by everyone.'

1 Probably L. Marcius Censorinus (*PIR*[2] M 223), *cos.* 39 BC, or his son, C. Marcius Censorinus (*PIR*[2] M 222), *cos. suff.* 8 BC.
2 Sisenna Statilius Taurus (*PIR*[2] S 851), *cos.* AD 16.

2.5 Cicero reflects – and moralizes – on magnificent aristocratic houses

Cicero, *On Duties* 1.138–40

Elite houses were often targets for moralists in the Republic, so it is no surprise that the topic comes up in *On Duties*, one of Cicero's philosophical works. At their simplest, moralizing discourses could involve the condemnation of excessive expense and splendour, as Cicero does in the case of L. Licinius Lucullus (*cos.* 74 BC; *RE* 104), who was notorious for lavish villa construction: Hales 2003: 20–3; see too **2.6** below. Cicero's assessment of the house of Cn. Octavius (*cos.* 165 BC; *RE* 17) on the north-east side of the Palatine, later annexed to the House of Scaurus (see Papi, *LTUR* 2.26), is rather more nuanced. For Cicero, a house's use is critical: if used for crowded social rituals, a grand house is acceptable; if its owner rattles around in it alone, not so much. Thus, for the Republican elite, a grand house was ideally not a place of private retreat, but of social interaction: Wallace-Hadrill 1994: 44.

We have heard that for Cn. Octavius, who was the first person from his family to be made consul, the fact that he built a magnificent and impressive house on the Palatine was a source of esteem.[1] When it was seen by the masses, the house was thought to have canvassed for the consulship on behalf of its master, a 'new man'.[2] Scaurus[3] demolished this house and added an appendage to his own. Thus, Octavius first brought the consulship to his house; Scaurus, the son of a most distinguished and illustrious man,[4] brought to his enlarged house not only electoral defeat but even disgrace and disaster. For esteem may be enhanced by a house, but it ought not be sought entirely from a house; a master ought not be honoured by a house but a house by its master. And just as in other matters one should give consideration not only to one's own interests but also to those of others, so too with the house of an illustrious man, in which many guests must be received and a multitude of men of every kind must be admitted: attention ought to be given to spaciousness. On the other hand, a large house is often a discredit to its owner, if it is empty, and especially if once, under another owner, it was constantly liable to be crowded. For it is disagreeable when passers-by say:

O ancient house! How different a master now rules you![5]

One may, indeed, say this of many houses these days.

Especially if you yourself are building a house, you should beware of going over the top with expense and splendour; in this kind of thing there is much harm even in the example it sets. For many people zealously copy the deeds of the leading men especially on this point. Take, for instance, the deeds of L. Lucullus, a most distinguished man: who imitates his virtues? But how many people have copied the sumptuousness of his villas! A limit must assuredly be imposed on these and that limit must be brought back to a more moderate level. This same moderation should be applied to each practice and mode of living.

1 On the house and what might have distinguished it, see Welch 2006: 122–3.
2 As the first of his family to be elected to the consulship, Octavius was a *novus homo* ('new man').
3 M. Aemilius Scaurus (*praetor* 56 BC; *RE* 141). He was tried and acquitted of charges of provincial extortion in 54 BC, and then tried again for electoral bribery and forced into exile.
4 M. Aemilius Scaurus (*RE* 140), *cos.* 115 BC and *princeps senatus* (the senior senator, who spoke first on any senatorial motion).
5 A fragment from an unknown play, possibly Accius' *Erigona*: Dyck 1996: 317–18.

2.6 The villas and gardens of Lucullus

Attacks on the luxuriousness of the villas of L. Licinius Lucullus are also found in Cicero's *On Laws* (another philosophical work), and in Lucullus' second-century

AD biographer, Plutarch. The quip that Lucullus was 'Xerxes in a toga' illustrates a general anxiety that the feats of landscape modification involved in villa building smacked of eastern despotism: cf. Purcell 1987: 190–4; Hales 2003: 22–3, 30. Lucullus' defence of his Tusculan villa (near modern Frascati) reflects the role of competition in inflating luxury (Wallace-Hadrill 1994: 4–5, 143–7), and Plutarch hints at the role of plunder from military campaigns in financing it.

(a) Cicero, *On Laws* 3.30–1

L. Lucullus, a great man and a friend of all of us here, was felt to have replied appropriately – more or less – when the splendour of his Tusculan villa had been criticized. He said that he had two neighbours – a Roman equestrian above him and a freedman below[1] – and since their villas were splendid, he ought to be permitted what people of a lower order were allowed. Do you not see, Lucullus, you are responsible for the very fact that these people desire splendour – people who would not be allowed splendour if you did not behave as you do? For who could have tolerated these men when he saw their villas crammed with sculptures and paintings, some public property, others sacred and meant for religious use? Everyone would have cracked down on their desires, except that the very people who were meant to do this[2] were seized by the same desires.

1 These neighbouring villas were situated on higher and lower ground respectively.
2 Members of the senatorial order, who were meant to set the moral tone.

(b) Plutarch, *Life of Lucullus* 39.2–4

I regard as frivolities the pricey buildings, the covered walkways (*peripatoi*), and the baths, and even more so the pictures and statues – and Lucullus' zeal concerning these works of art, which he used to collect at great expense. On these, he lavishly spent the large and splendid fortune that he had amassed from his campaigns. For even now, although luxury has grown so much, the Gardens of Lucullus are reckoned to be amongst the most expensive of the imperial gardens. But regarding his works by the sea and around Naples – where he hung ridges above huge underground galleries, and constructed around his houses circuits of sea and streams full of fish, and erected buildings in the sea – when the Stoic Tubero beheld them, he called Lucullus 'Xerxes in a toga'.[1] He had a country house near Tusculum, fitted out with belvederes, open-air dining-rooms, and covered walkways (*peripatoi*). When he was there, Pompey had once reproached Lucullus that although he set it up in the optimal way for summer, he made the country house uninhabitable in the winter. Laughing, Lucullus said, 'Do I seem to you to have less sense than the cranes and storks, and not change my abode with the season?'[2]

1 The Persian king Xerxes notoriously bridged the Hellespont and dug a canal through the Athos peninsula in the late 480s BC in preparation for his invasion of Greece. It is unclear which of the multiple Aelii Tuberones known from the late Republic was responsible for the quip.
2 Lucullus had multiple villas and migrated amongst them as the seasons changed.

2.7 Vitruvius on elite *domus* architecture

Vitruvius 6.5

The architectural writer Vitruvius, writing in the Augustan era but reflecting a late-Republican mindset, provides an idealized description of how elite houses should be designed and used. Like Cicero (**2.5** above), he assesses the appropriateness of houses by the social uses to which they were put. His comment about the need for spaces for public councils, lawsuits, and arbitrations also shows that 'state' functions were being carried out in noble houses even before the advent of an imperial court. Vitruvius' statement that noble houses need tall, kingly forecourts (*vestibula regalia alta*) acknowledges the architectural debt elite houses owed to Hellenistic palaces. On the passage, see further: Wallace-Hadrill 1994: 10–12; Hales 2003: 3–6, 27–9; Hartnett 2017: 117–19.

Once the rooms have been laid out with regard to the regions of the sky,[1] then one must consider the principles according to which rooms exclusively for householders should be built in private dwellings, and how rooms shared with outsiders should be built. Included amongst the exclusive rooms, which nobody can enter unless invited, are, for example, bedrooms, dining rooms, baths, and other rooms which have the same sort of functions. Shared rooms are those which even uninvited members of the general public can enter by right – i.e. forecourts, inner courtyards, peristyles, and spaces that can have the same functions. Thus, splendid forecourts, *tablina*, and *atria* are not necessary for people of ordinary social position, because they fulfil their duties by going around to visit others, and other people do not come around to visit them.

In the forecourts of those whose occupation is agricultural production, stables and shops should be built, and in their houses cellars, granaries, store-rooms, and other spaces that are more useful for conserving produce than for giving an appearance of refinement.

Likewise, for bankers and tax farmers, more agreeable and attractive rooms that are safe from burglaries should be built; for advocates and orators, more refined and ample rooms to accommodate meetings. And for nobles, who, because they hold offices and magistracies, have duties to their fellow-citizens to fulfil, should be constructed tall, kingly forecourts, and very sizeable *atria* and peristyles, as well as groves and quite spacious walkways appropriate to their dignity. Moreover, they need libraries, picture-galleries, and basilicas set up with a splendour not dissimilar to that of public buildings, since in their houses both public councils and private lawsuits and arbitrations are carried out rather often.

Thus, if buildings are laid out according to these principles to suit the roles of each kind of person, as is discussed in Book One under the rubric of decorum,[2] there cannot be any complaints. For they will have plans that are agreeable and perfect for every purpose. But the principles on these matters will apply not just to buildings in the city, but also in the country, except that in the city, *atria* are usually near the doors, but in the country, houses imitating the urban style have peristyles first, and then *atria* with paved porticoes around them that are oriented towards *palaestrae* and walkways.

1 Vitruvius has just discussed how different kinds of rooms should be oriented in relation to the sun.

2 Vitr. *De arch.* 1.2.5–7.

2.8 Pliny the Elder on the houses of the Republican nobility

Pliny the Elder, *Natural History* 36.109–12

As we can see from this passage, the moralizing critique of excessively grand elite houses survived into the Principate, and then came to be applied to imperial palaces: cf. Hales 2003: 61. At the same time, Pliny makes the important assumption that Julio-Claudian palaces were not standard elite houses: the palaces of Caligula and Nero were of unprecedented scale.

As is apparent in (the writings of) the most careful authors, in the consulship of M. Lepidus and Q. Catulus,[1] no house at Rome was more beautiful than that of Lepidus himself. But, by Hercules, within thirty-five years, the same house was not in the top hundred. Include in the reckoning, if you like, the mass of marble, the paintings, the kingly expenditures, and the hundred houses contending with the most beautiful and esteemed house[2] – a hundred houses later outdone by countless others up until today. Assuredly, fires punish luxury; however, fashions cannot be made to understand that there is something more mortal than humans themselves.

But two houses (*domus*) outdid all these. Twice we have seen the whole city surrounded by the houses of the emperors Caligula and Nero; the house of the latter, indeed, was golden[3] – just to make sure nothing was missing! Presumably those who made this empire so great dwelt just like this,[4] setting out to conquer peoples and obtain triumphs from the plough or hearth – men whose farms were also smaller than the sitting-rooms (*sellaria*)[5] of Caligula and Nero!

To be honest, it sets you thinking about how much smaller than these houses were the plots given by decree at public expense to undefeated generals for building their homes. The greatest distinction enjoyed by the latter homes was for a provision to be added to the decree saying that their doors should open outwards and be flung back into the streets. So it was in the case of P. Valerius Publicola, the first consul together with L. Brutus,[6] after so many meritorious services, and in the case of Publicola's brother, who had defeated the Sabines twice, also as consul.[7] This was the most illustrious distinction even for houses belonging to men who had celebrated triumphs.

1 Q. Lutatius Catulus (*RE* 8) and M. Aemilius Lepidus (*RE* 72), *coss.* 78 BC.

2 The House of Lepidus.

3 On Nero's Domus Aurea, see below, **2.11**.

4 This is ironic; moralists conventionally stressed the modesty of the dwellings and lifestyles of aristocrats of the Early and Middle Republic.

5 Or perhaps mock-brothels: Champlin 2011: 318–22.

6 P. Valerius Publicola (*RE* 302) and M. Iunius Brutus (*RE* 46a), who, according to tradition, were respectively *cos. suff.* and *cos. ord.* in 509 BC. Publicola (or Poplicola) supposedly demolished the splendid house he had begun to build on the Velia, fearing public disapproval;

the people then voted him a house at public expense; see Beck 2009: 361–5 for references and analysis.

7 M. Valerius (*RE* 74), supposedly *cos.* 505 BC.

III | Imperial Residences in Rome

2.9 The House of Augustus

There has been extensive – and sometimes heated – debate about how we should imagine the dwelling place of the emperor Augustus: Carettoni 1983; Iacopi and Tedone 2005–6: 363–77; Carandini and Bruno 2008; Wiseman 2009, 2013b, 2019; Coarelli 2012: 347–420; Wulf-Rheidt 2012a. The quality of the available evidence is largely to blame for the lack of consensus. The building activities of subsequent emperors erased much of the Augustan phase on the Palatine, and the archaeological remains that do exist do not easily align with the textual evidence, which itself is not very extensive. Below we present the three texts that have been central in the discussion, and also a plan of the archaeological remains; we do not aim to resolve the debate, but in comments to individual passages we do identify some of the major issues. It is also worth stating what is relatively uncontroversial. Firstly, Augustus' residence was not a single palace building but more a compound – an ensemble of buildings, some of them built by Augustus and some of them pre-existing structures that came into imperial ownership: Wulf-Rheidt 2012a: 37, 39; Wiseman 2013b: 258–60; Hall 2014: 182. Secondly, there were distinct echos of Hellenistic royal complexes. As in the royal district of Alexandria (**2.2**), Augustus' living quarters were juxtaposed with temples (Apollo, Victoria, and the Magna Mater) and were located quite close to public entertainment space (the Circus Maximus). Moreover, parts of the complex (especially the Temple of Apollo and associated libraries) were used for public functions such as Senate meetings and the reception of embassies, much as Hellenistic monarchs intermingled their domestic life and public duties in their residences: Meyboom 2005: 242, 247; Wulf-Rheidt 2012a: 39. Thirdly, the concerns found in Republican sources about excessively luxurious houses are visible in discussions of the House of Augustus, especially that of Suetonius (**2.9 [b]**). It could be that at least Augustus' living quarters were configured to project an image of moderation – even if the rest of the complex was rather grand.

(a) Ovid, *Tristia* 3.1.31–48, 59–68

The exiled Ovid imagines one of his books of poetry going to Rome in search of a library, and being given a guided tour of the city by a helpful stranger. The tour includes the western side of the Palatine, providing a contemporary, eyewitness account of Augustus' residence. On the poem, see Huskey 2006; Wiseman 2015, both citing further literature. Ovid also alludes to the Augustan Palatine elsewhere: Ov. *Fast.* 4.949–54, *Pont.* 2.8.17–18 (= **5.2**).

From there he turned right. 'This is the gate to the Palatine,' he said. 'This is (the Temple of Jupiter) Stator. Rome was first founded in this place.'[1]

While I was admiring each thing individually, I saw doorposts distinguished by gleaming weapons and an abode worthy of a god, and I said, 'Is this Jupiter's house?', for I thought it was: an oak wreath put this guess in my head.[2] When I heard who its master was, I said, 'I am not wrong! This truly is the house of mighty Jupiter. But why is the doorway concealed with laurels placed in front of it? Why do shady trees surround the august doors? Is it because this house has deserved continual triumphs? Or because it has always been loved by the god of Leucas?[3] Is it because the house itself is festive or because it makes everything festive? Or is this a sign of the peace that the house has given to the world? And just as the laurel is always verdant and does not need to have withered leaves plucked off, does this house also have eternal glory?'

'The rationale for the wreath placed on top of the door is declared in writing: it proclaims that by his help citizens were saved.' ... *(Ovid's poem then makes an extended plea to Augustus to save him from exile.)*

From there I was led in a similar direction up steep steps to the lofty, gleaming white temple of the unshorn god.[4] There, alternating with columns of foreign marble, are statues: the Belides and their barbarian father[5] with sword drawn. And there the books which ancient and contemporary men have created[6] with their learned minds are available for examination to those who want to read them.[7]

1 Roman legend apparently had Romulus founding the city on a site at the summit of the Palatine: Wiseman 2019: 82–102.
2 A *corona civica* was hung above Augustus' doorway and a pair of laurel trees flanked it on either side: Ov. *Met.* 1.562–3; *Mon. Anc.* 34.2; Val. Max. 2.8.7 (= **1.3 [b]**); Dio Cass. 53.16.4 (= **1.13**). Oak wreaths also were traditionally associated with Jupiter: Phaedrus 3.17.2.
3 Apollo, who had a temple on the island of Leucas, near Actium.
4 Apollo was typically depicted with long hair.
5 The mythological Danaus, son of Belus, and his fifty daughters (often known as the Danaids). On the location and archaeology of the Portico of the Danaids, see Iacopi and Tedone 2005–6: 358–63; Wiseman 2019: 132–9.
6 Here we translate Ellis' (1890: 197) conjecture of *peperere* instead of *cepere*, which appears in most manuscripts.
7 There was a library complex with Latin and Greek sections in the Temple of Apollo precinct. On the location and remains of the library complex, see Iacopi and Tedone 2005–6: 351–8; Wiseman 2019: 135–8.

(b) Suetonius, *Life of Augustus* 72

In other aspects of life, it is agreed that he was most abstemious and free from suspicion of any vice. At first he lived beside the (Roman) Forum above the Stairs of the Ring-makers in a house that had once belonged to the orator Calvus.[1] Later he lived on the Palatine Hill in a house of Hortensius[2] that was no less modest, being exceptional neither in size nor decoration, with simple colonnades of Alban stone[3] and rooms without any marble or fine pavements. For more than forty years he used the same bedroom in winter and summer, and he habitually spent winter in the city even though he knew that the city was no good for his health at that time of year. If he ever planned to do anything discreetly or without interruption, there was a solitary upper quarter which he called his 'Syracuse'[4] and 'workshop' (*technyphion*),[5] where he used to go, either there or to a villa belonging to one of his freedmen in the suburbs; when he was ill, however, he slept at Maecenas' house.[6] Of all the places for solitude he chiefly visited the coast and the islands of Campania or towns near Rome such as Lanuvium, Praeneste, and Tibur,[7] where he often even gave judgements in the porticos of the Temple of Hercules.[8] He particularly disapproved of spacious and elaborately decorated country estates, and he even demolished some that his granddaughter Julia had built at great expense. His own villas were of moderate dimensions and were decorated not with sculpture and paintings but with shady terraces, groves, and artefacts notable for their antiquity or rarity. On Capreae,[9] for example, there were huge limbs of monstrous whales and wild animals, which some call the bones of giants, as well as the weapons of heroes.

1 C. Licinius Calvus (82–47 BC; *RE* 113), poet and orator.
2 Q. Hortensius Hortulus (114–50 BC; *RE* 13), orator and *cos.* 69 BC.
3 Peperino stone from the nearby Alban Hills – and therefore fairly cheap in Rome.
4 Syracuse, a Greek city on the island of Sicily, was the birthplace of the mathematician and inventor Archimedes, who was killed in the Roman siege of the city, but who enjoyed a posthumous reputation at Rome as a thinker happily engaged with his creations; see Jaeger 2008; Gowers 2010.
5 Alternatively, Suetonius perhaps wrote *tegyphion* ('cubby hole'): see Kaster 2016: 118.
6 Maecenas' luxurious estate on the Esquiline Hill, the Gardens of Maecenas (Horti Maecenatis), comprised a multi-storey house, orchards, vineyards, promenades, statuary, and an elaborate fountain structure. Built atop a pauper's cemetery (Hor. *Sat.* 1.8), the Gardens passed into imperial ownership after Maecenas' death. The emperor Tiberius lived here briefly (Suet. *Tib.* 15), and Nero built the Domus Transitoria to connect this estate with other imperial holdings on the Palatine Hill. See too **2.11**.
7 Three locations of imperial villas (modern Lanuvio, Palestrina, Tivoli), all in the countryside near Rome.
8 An extensive sanctuary dedicated to Hercules Victor at Tibur, 25 km from Rome.
9 On the imperial villas on Capreae (modern Capri), cf. **2.18** and George, **Vol. 1, 242–5**.

(c) Suetonius, *Lives of the Grammarians* 17.1–2

Aside from the House of Hortensius, Augustus' Palatine complex included the houses of other late-Republican aristocrats that he had acquired: Vell. Pat. 2.81.3. The passage below provides evidence that the house of Q. Lutatius Catulus (*cos.* 102; *RE* 7) was one such house, and was used by the imperial family, even if it was not part of the emperor's actual residence.

M. Verrius Flaccus,[1] a freedman, became famous especially because of his teaching method. For, to arouse the intellects of the students, he used to pit contemporaries against each other, not only setting the topic on which they had to write but also offering a prize that the winner would collect. The prize was always some antique book that was beautiful or rather rare. For this reason, Flaccus was also chosen by Augustus as his grandsons'[2] teacher and he moved to the palace (*palatium*) with his entire school – but with the proviso that he not take on any more pupils thereafter. He taught in the *atrium* of the House of Catulus, which was then part of the palace (*palatium*),[3] and received 100,000 sesterces per year.

1 *PIR*[2] V 422.
2 Gaius (b. 20 BC) and Lucius (b. 17 BC); the House of Catulus was therefore being used as a school c. 10 BC.
3 The house was destroyed in subsequent redevelopments of the Palatine, so it was not there in Suetonius' day. The biographer's use of *palatium* to refer to the complex is anachronistic: in Augustus' day, this was purely the name of the hill: Winterling 1999: 209–17, esp. 213.

(d) The 'Carettoni House' on the Palatine Hill

In the 1950s and 60s, the archaeologist Gianfilippo Carettoni excavated a site on the western side of the Palatine, to the immediate north-west of the Temple of Apollo:

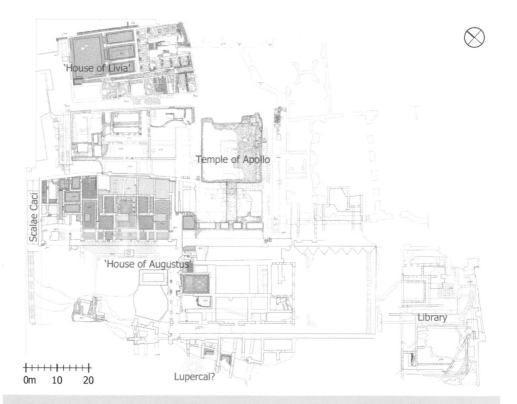

Figure 2.3.1 Plan of the 'Carettoni House' and surrounds, Palatine Hill, Rome.
Plan by Jens Pflug, after an original plan by Monica Cola.

Carettoni 1983. The excavations revealed the remains of an elite house that he suggested was the House of Augustus, an identification that has attracted considerable support. However, the identification faces several problems. Firstly, Suetonius (**2.9 [b]** above) says Augustus' residence had columns of Alban stone but no marble or fine pavements, but the 'Carettoni House' has marble decoration and some elaborate mosaic pavements: Hall 2014: 181; Wardle 2014: 454–5; Raimondi Cominesi 2018: 722. Secondly, Ovid (**2.9 [a]** above) assumes that a visitor coming via the Roman Forum from the north-east along the Clivus Palatinus would first see the entrance to Augustus' residence, and then continue straight on to the Temple of Apollo; Ovid's description is difficult to understand if Augustus lived in the 'Carettoni House', west of the temple: Meyboom 2005: 255–6; Claridge, Toms, and Cubberley 2010: 141; Wiseman 2013b: 260, 2019: 128. Thirdly, subsequent investigations of the 'Carettoni House' have suggested multiple stages of renovation and reconstruction ending in c. 30 BC, when a sizeable section of the house was demolished and buried as part of the building of the Temple of Apollo: Iacopi and Tedone 2005–6: 367–71. One could suggest that c. 30 BC Octavian moved from the 'Carettoni House' to another (cf. Pensabene and Gallocchio 2011: 484) or that he simultaneously had two houses, one 'private' and one 'public'. Suetonius (**2.9 [b]** above), however, knows of Octavian/ Augustus residing in only one Palatine house, not two (Hall 2014: 181), and there is no sure sign in the archaeology of a second residence. Considerable ingenuity is required to deal with these problems, and debate is ongoing.

2.10 The imperial residence from Tiberius to Claudius

Several campaigns of archaeological investigations on the Palatine Hill have revealed traces of significant building work in the period from Tiberius to Claudius, especially in the area of the Domus Tiberiana on the north-west of the hill: Krause 2004: 47; Tomei and Filetici 2011; cf. Michel 2015: 39–58 for synthesis. The area was heavily modified in subsequent periods, so the finds have consisted of cryptoporticos, decorative features, and isolated architectural elements; the reconstruction of coherent building plans is impossible. There was possibly building work in this zone of the Palatine under Tiberius (Tomei 2011a: 12, 2011b: 68, 2011c: 162–3, 2011d: 225–7) and there is secure archaeological evidence for a Claudian phase of construction (Tomei 2011d: 224–8; Coarelli 2012: 463). The textual sources relating to the imperial residence in this period are few, but they give some faint hints of amplification and monumentalization under Claudius (Winterling 1999: 60–5), which may be consistent with the recent archaeological investigations. But the most explicit literary evidence comes from the passages below relating to the brief reign of Caligula; cf. **2.8** above.

(a) Suetonius, *Life of Caligula* 22.2, 22.4

If there is truth in Suetonius' claim (repeated by Dio Cass. 59.28.5 [Xiph.; *EV*]) that Caligula extended 'the palace' into the Forum, then this would have been some kind of appendage to the Domus Tiberiana running down the north-west slope of the Palatine. No credible archaeological remains have been found of a bridge to the Capitoline Hill, or of a House of Caligula there; Suetonius' moralizing agenda does not inspire confidence in these tales. See Tomei 2011b: 68; Coarelli 2012: 454–65 on Caligula's residence.

But when he was warned that he had gone beyond the level of emperors (*principes*) and kings, he began to claim divine majesty for himself from then on. He gave the order that deities' statues outstanding in their numinousness and artistic value – including the statue of Jupiter at Olympia[1] – should be brought from Greece so that he could remove their heads and replace them with his own. He then extended part of the palace (*palatium*) as far as the Forum. Having transformed the Temple of Castor and Pollux into a forecourt, he used to display himself standing between the divine brothers so that those who approached could do homage to him. Some greeted him as Jupiter Latiaris. . . .

By night, he regularly used to invite the moon for embraces and sex when it was full and shining. Moreover, in the daytime, he would converse privately with Capitoline Jupiter, now whispering and offering his ear in turn,[2] now more loudly and not without abuse. For he was heard to threaten: 'Either lift me up or I shall lift you.'[3] Finally, he was persuaded – so he used to relate – and spontaneously invited (by the god) to live in close association (*contubernium*). He therefore connected the Palatine and the Capitoline with a bridge built over the Temple of the Deified Augustus. A little later, he laid the foundations of a new house in the Area Capitolina,[4] so as to be closer.

1 Cf. below, **2.15 (a)**.
2 That is, to the mouth of the cult statue of the god.
3 Hom. *Il*. 23.724, spoken by Ajax to Odysseus during a wrestling bout.
4 The flat, open space around the Temple of Jupiter Optimus Maximus on the Capitoline.

(b) Josephus, *Jewish Antiquities* 19.117

When describing how Caligula's assassins fled from the scene of the crime, Josephus includes this digression about the nature of the imperial residence on the Palatine in AD 41. The passage has been seen as evidence that even then, the imperial residence was still a complex of distinct buildings that had grown up organically, rather than a unitary 'palace': Winterling 1999: 58; Wiseman 2009: 535, 2019: 32; Michel 2015: 48; *contra* Tomei 2011d: 228; Coarelli 2012: 459–62.

. . . and taking other roads they came to the House of Germanicus, the father of Gaius (Caligula), whom they had just killed, which was connected (to the imperial residence). For the imperial residence (*basileon*), although a single entity, was made up in part from buildings belonging to those born into imperial power. These received their names from those who built them or even began some part of the dwellings.

2.11 Nero's Domus Aurea

The great fire of 64, which severely damaged or destroyed ten of Rome's fourteen regions (Tac. *Ann*. 15.33–41), facilitated Nero's expropriation of a vast area of central Rome (c. 50 hectares = 124 acres) for the construction of the Golden House (Domus Aurea). It represented an experimental phase in the development of palace architecture in Rome that involved an attempt to insert a complex inspired by seaside and country villas into the centre of Rome. The Esquiline wing of the villa is partially intact, since it was mostly filled in and formed the foundations of the Baths of Trajan (finished in 109). On the Domus Aurea, see Pflug and Wulf-Rheidt, **Vol. 1, 207–11** (with **fig. 9.2**), George, **Vol. 1, 245–6**, Boëthius 1960, and Ball 2003.

(a) Suetonius, *Life of Nero* 31.1–2

There was nothing in which he was more profligate than in building, for he constructed a house that extended all the way from the Palatine to the Esquiline Hill.[1] He first called it 'the House of Passage',[2] but after it was destroyed by fire and rebuilt, he called it 'the Golden House'. Its size and magnificence can be conveyed by the following description. The vestibule was lofty enough to hold a colossal statue of the emperor 120 feet high[3] and wide enough so that it had a triple colonnade a mile long; there was also a lake like a sea, surrounded by buildings that looked like cities. Furthermore, there were rural landscapes of different kinds – ploughed fields, vineyards, pastures, and woods – with a multitude of both wild and domesticated animals in every variety.[4] The rest of the house was completely overlaid with gold and decorated with gems and mother-of-pearl, and there were dining rooms whose ceilings had ivory panels that pivoted so that flowers could be released, and with pipes so that perfume might be sprinkled on guests.[5] The main dining room was circular, and constantly revolved day and night like the heavens.[6] The baths were supplied with both salt and sulphurous water.[7] Once the house was finished in this style, he dedicated it and gave no more approval other than to say that he could finally begin to live like a human being.

1 The imperial estates on the Esquiline included the Gardens of Maecenas (Horti Maecenatis); see above, **2.9 (b)**, with n. 6.

2 Domus Transitoria (cf. George, **Vol. 1, 245**), a construction that was a 'passage' in that it served as a link between imperial properties on the two hills.

3 The colossal statue was later converted to a statue of the Sun god with the addition of the radiate crown by the emperor Vespasian in order to dissociate it with Nero. The emperor Hadrian had it moved near the Flavian Amphitheatre, which subsequently received the nickname 'ad Colosseum' ('at the Colossus'); hence, 'the Colosseum'.

4 With inclusion of pastures and woodlands to the Domus Aurea, Nero built a miniature estate for himself in the heart of Rome, in imitation of real villas which yielded their own wine and agricultural produce. The opportunity for hunting, an important leisure activity at elite villas, was afforded by the presence of wild animals on this urban property.

5 Cf. Sen. *Ep.* 90.15.

6 The octagonally shaped hall in the east wing of the remaining structure (see **2.11 [c]**) may have been the circular banquet hall referred to in this passage. It perhaps had a revolving ceiling that consisted of a wooden shell inside the concrete dome which was turned by slaves. In the alternative, recent excavations in the Vigna Barberini have revealed archaeological remains that could be the substructures of a dining room with a rotating floor; see Roller, **Vol. 1, 332–3** for literature and discussion.

7 I.e. the water in the baths could replicate both sea-bathing and the medicinal waters of hot sulphur springs common to Roman spas.

(b) Tacitus, *Annals* 15.42.1

Meanwhile, Nero took advantage of his fatherland's disaster (i.e. the fire) and built a house whose gems and gold – both now commonplace and made vulgar by excess – were not as miraculous as its fields and lakes, and its woods on one side and open spaces and vistas on the other, in the manner of solitary places. The architects and engineers were Severus and Celer,[1] who had the talent and audacity to attempt through art what nature had denied and to squander an emperor's riches.

1 PIR^2 C 619, S 638.

(c) The remains of the Domus Aurea

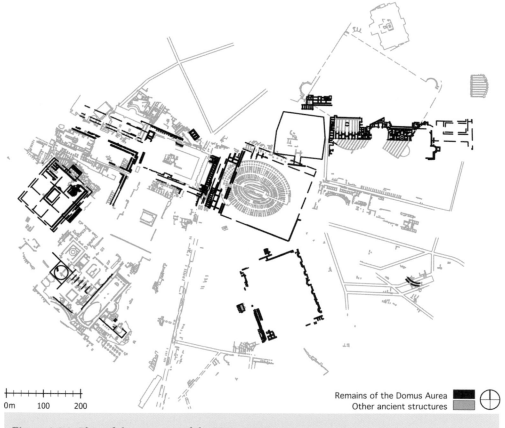

0m   100   200

Remains of the Domus Aurea
Other ancient structures

Figure 2.3.2 Plan of the remains of the Neronian Domus Aurea, Rome.
Courtesy of the Archivio dello scavo dell'area della Meta Sudans e del Palatino nord-orientale - Ex Vetrerie Sciarra - Dipartimento di Scienze dell'Antichità, Sapienza Università di Roma. Plan by Clementina Panella, Marco Fano, and Emanuele Brienza.

2.12 The layout of the Flavian Palace

The first phase of the Flavian Palace was completed by the emperor Domitian in 92. It was used as the residence for emperors when they were in the city of Rome well into Late Antiquity, and, although there were some changes, the major elements of its layout endured over time. The remains were excavated by Alfonso Bartoli in the early twentieth century, and the results partly published: Bartoli 1929, 1938. Beginning in 1998, there was then a major reinvestigation of the remains of the palace buildings; the results of this are summarized by Pflug and Wulf-Rheidt, **Vol. 1, 211–33**; see too Wulf-Rheidt 2011, 2012b, 2015; Sojc 2012a; Pflug 2013. There were also excavations from 1985 to 1999 in the area of

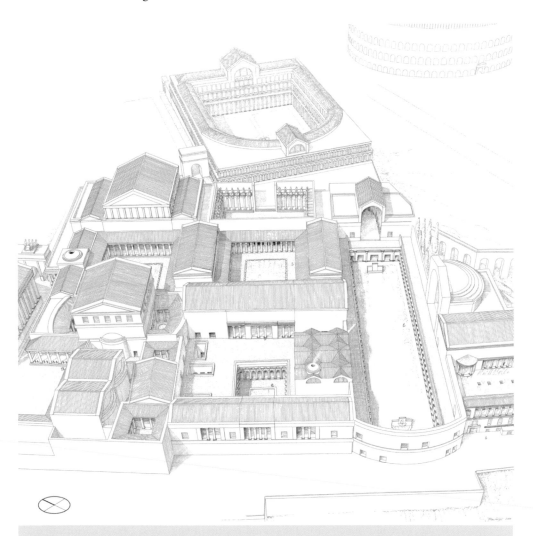

Figure 2.3.3 Hypothetical reconstruction of the Flavian phase of the palace, Palatine Hill, Rome.
Courtesy of the Architekturreferat DAI Zentrale, Berlin. Artwork: Jörg Denkinger.

the Vigna Barberini, on the north-east of the Palatine; these have established the presence there of elaborate gardens that were part of the Flavian Palace complex: André et al. 2004: 114–23; Villedieu 2013.

(a) Reconstruction of the Flavian Phase of the palace (**fig. 2.3.3**)

In the north-west part of the Flavian Palace, which archaeologists conventionally call the Domus Flavia, a peristyle courtyard is surrounded by three very large rooms. The room to the south-west of the peristyle is probably the Cenatio Iovis ('Dining Room of Jove') mentioned in an ancient text: SHA *Pert.* 11.6; cf. **4.27** below. To the north-east were the Aula Regia and the Basilica (names given by modern archaeologists), probably used for audiences and legal hearings, although their functions were likely flexible: Zanker 2002: 112–14. The Cenatio Iovis, Aula Regia, and Basilica all feature apses, which are evocative of temple architecture.

The south-east part of the palace, conventionally called the Domus August(i)ana, has another expansive peristyle courtyard, with a large space to the north-east that was most likely a *vestibulum* (forecourt). To the south are spaces for *otium*, including the Garden Stadium (see below, **2.14**), a place for leisurely strolling and conversation, and the Sunken Peristyle, with its small dining rooms (cf. **4.28**) – an area with a pre-Domitianic construction phase: Pflug 2013: 190–3. The substructures under the main floor of the palace contain many rooms; these were most likely service areas for the palace: Wulf-Rheidt 2012b: 110.

The Domus Flavia and Domus Augustana have been seen as respectively the 'public' and 'private' wings of the palace. However, the Vestibulum and peristyle of the latter would have been used for the *salutatio*, which included visitors who had not been specifically invited. The emperor would also have entertained invited guests in the Garden Stadium and the Sunken Peristyle: Zanker 2002: 111; Wulf-Rheidt 2011: 11–12, 2012b: 106–8, 2015: 6–7. Rather than seeing a separation between 'public' and 'private', it would be better to see different spaces allowing different degrees of intimacy between the emperor and guests. The term 'Domus Flavia' is a modern coinage and does not reflect any Roman perception that different parts of the palace were somehow separate. The so-called Domus Severiana, to the far south of the palace, has been shown by recent investigations to have had a Flavian phase with more spaces for leisurely dining, so it is not aptly named either: Wulf-Rheidt 2011: 8–10, 2015: 11–12.

(b) The remains of the imperial palaces on the Palatine Hill

This plan shows the current state of the structures and remains on the Palatine Hill dating from Antiquity and subsequent eras. It demonstrates the persistence into later periods of the basic plan of the Flavian Palace established at the time of Domitian. At the same time, several post-Flavian modifications to the palace can be seen. These include the Grand Exedra in the south-west, which created a façade symbolically engaging with the Circus Maximus and its crowds; this is now known to have been created in the Trajanic period (as was a bridge linking the palace to the emperor's personal box in the Circus): Wulf-Rheidt 2011: 14, 2015: 8–9, 13. The Sunken Peristyle and associated rooms were also modified in the second century: Pflug 2013: 199; Wulf-Rheidt 2015: 6, 13. Within the Vigna Barberini are the remains of the large temple dedicated by the emperor Elagabalus to his homonymous patron god: André et al. 2004: 123–39;

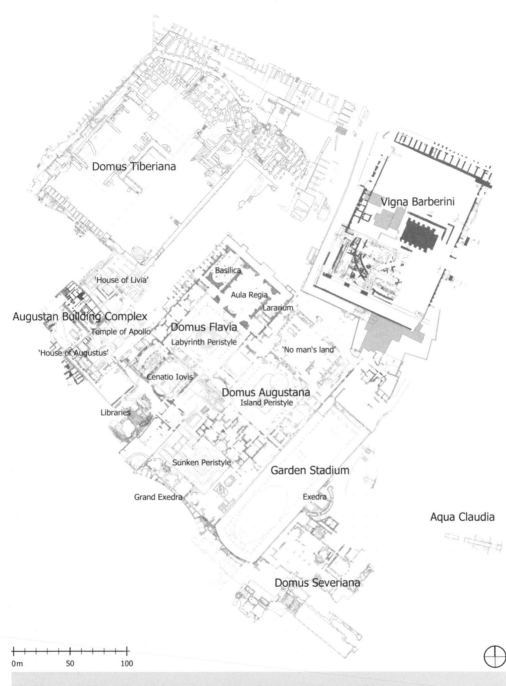

Figure 2.3.4 Plan of the remains of the imperial palaces, Palatine Hill, Rome.
Courtesy of the Architekturreferat DAI Zentrale, Berlin. Plan by Jens Pflug, after Maria Antonietta Tomei and Giovanna Tedone (Augustan complex), Daniel Studer (Domus Tiberiana), École française de Rome (Vigna Barberini), and Architekturreferat DAI Zentrale, Berlin.

Villedieu 2013: 164–75. The structures now visible in the area of the so-called Domus Severiana reflect rebuilding under the Severans and, later, Maxentius: Wulf-Rheidt 2011: 16, 2015: 15.

2.13 Sight-lines in the Flavian Palace

The architecture of the Flavian Palace afforded visitors some very long sight-lines into the depths of the building. A visitor entering the Domus Flavia from the north-west would be afforded a view to the south-east into the Domus Augustana (**2.13 [a]**). If a visitor entered 'No man's land' (the probable Vestibulum) to take part in the emperor's *salutatio*, his or her gaze would pass through the peristyle of the Domus Augustana, to the rooms to the south of the peristyle (in which the emperor might position himself), and then possibly through another opening over the top of the Sunken Peristyle (**2.13 [b]**). This would be evocative of the *atrium–tablinum*–garden view that the *salutator* visiting a traditional *atrium* house would see (see **2.3** above). For discussion, see Pflug and Wulf-Rheidt, **Vol. 1, 220–1**, Wulf-Rheidt 2012b: 105.

(a) The view from the Domus Flavia into the Domus Augustana

Figure 2.3.5 Hypothetical reconstruction of the sight-line from the western portico of the peristyle of the Domus Flavia into the Domus Augustana, Palatine Hill, Rome.
Courtesy of the Architekturreferat DAI Zentrale, Berlin, and Lengyel Toulouse Architekten. Rendering: Lengyel Toulouse Architekten, on the basis of a reconstruction by Ulrike Wulf-Rheidt, Jens Pflug, and Armin Müller.

(b) The central sight-line of the Domus Augustana

Figure 2.3.6 Hypothetical reconstruction of the sight-line from the northern entrance of the Domus Augustana to the central room at the south of the peristyle, Palatine Hill, Rome. Courtesy of the Architekturreferat DAI Zentrale, Berlin, and Lengyel Toulouse Architekten. Rendering: Lengyel Toulouse Architekten, on the basis of a reconstruction by Ulrike Wulf-Rheidt, Jens Pflug, and Armin Müller.

2.14 Spaces for *otium* in the Flavian Palace: the Garden Stadium

The Garden Stadium **(fig. 2.3.7)** provides a striking example of one of the *otium* spaces of the palace. Similar garden spaces are paralleled in villas outside of Rome. This feature is 48 m wide and 161 m long, and is sunk 11 m below the main level of the palace. A portico – probably a cryptoportico – ran around the structure, perhaps providing a shaded area for strolling. On the north and east sides were rooms with views out into the garden area – much like the rooms looking out onto the peristyle gardens of elite houses in earlier eras (cf. **2.3**). The remains visible today reflect the rebuilding after the Garden Stadium was badly damaged in the fire of 191/2. For analysis of this space, see Riedel 2008; Bukowiecki and Wulf-Rheidt 2015: 347–8; Iara 2015.

2.15 Martial on the Flavian Palace

Two poets closely connected with Domitian, Martial and Statius, give contemporary reactions to the Flavian Palace – reactions designed to be congenial to

Figure 2.3.7 Photograph of the Garden Stadium, Flavian Palace, Rome, taken from the north end of the structure.
Photo: Jens Pflug.

the emperor. Statius' poetic account of dining with Domitian (*Silv.* 4.2 = **4.29 [a]** below) stresses the size of the palace and the opulence of its decoration; cf. *Silv.* 1.2.144–57; Klodt 2001: 37–62. It also puts the emperor on the same plane as the gods, and intimates that the palace is a kind of temple or an earthly Olympus: see Newlands 2002: 260–83. These themes are all visible in the epigrams of Martial translated as **2.15 (a–c)** below; see too Mart. 8.39, 13.91. Domitian's Jovian self-presentation and the architecture of the palace, which borrowed features of temple architecture such as apses, perhaps invited some of these literary reactions: Zanker 2002: 117–19.

(a) Martial, *Epigrams* 7.56

You have understood the stars and the heavens with your pious mind, Rabirius[1] – you who build the Parrhasian[2] residence with astonishing skill. If it makes preparations to bestow a worthy temple on Phidias' statue of Jupiter,[3] Pisa will request these hands from our Thunderer.[4]

1 Presumably the architect responsible for the Flavian Palace; on the palace's astrological motifs, see below **2.15 (c)** n. 2.
2 Parrhasia was a region of Acadia in Greece. In legend, the Arcadian Evander and his band of exiles first settled the Palatine: Verg. *Aen.* 8.51–6, 97–368.

3 The sculptor Phidias' cult statue of Zeus, located at Olympia, in the region of Pisa in the Peloponnese.

4 That is, if an architect is needed to upgrade the Temple of Zeus at Olympia, there will be a request that Rabirius be sent by Domitian, whom Martial assimilates with Jupiter Tonans ('Jupiter the Thunderer').

(b) Martial, *Epigrams* 8.36

Laugh at the regal wonders of the pyramids, Caesar! Barbarous Memphis[1] is now silent about oriental achievements; the Mareotic undertaking[2] is equivalent to such a small fraction of the Parrhasian palace (*aula*)! The sun sees nothing more illustrious in the whole world. You would believe that the seven hills rose up together; Ossa was shorter when it bore Thessalian Pelion.[3] It penetrates the heavens in such a way that hidden in shining stars the clear peak resounds with thunder because of the cloud below and it is covered by the hidden light of Phoebus before Circe sees the face of her rising father.[4] Nevertheless, Augustus, this house, which strikes the stars with its top, is equal to heaven, but less than its master.

1 A royal capital of Egypt in pharaonic times with pyramids nearby. There was a Hellenistic palace there too.

2 The building of Alexandria (situated on Lake Mareotis), commenced by Alexander the Great.

3 During their war with the gods, the giants piled Mt. Pelion onto Mt. Ossa to try to reach heaven: Ov. *Met.* 1.151–5.

4 Circe was the daughter of Helios, the sun god. Thus, the height of Domitian's palace allows it to catch the first rays of the sun (= Phoebus) before day breaks on the rest of the earth (including Circe's island).

(c) Martial, *Epigrams* 9.91

If the inviters[1] of both Caesar and Jupiter were to ask me to dinner in different heavens,[2] even if the stars were nearer and the palace (*Palatia*) further away, I should give this reply to be taken back to the gods: 'Look for someone who would prefer to be the Thunderer's dinner guest. My Jupiter[3] keeps me on earth, you see!'

1 The *invitator* was an imperial slave or freedman tasked with issuing invitations to dinners with the emperor; see, for example, *CIL* 6.3975, 8792, 8857–62.

2 Domitian's new palace is therefore another heaven, comparable to that of the gods. The comparison was prompted by architecture: the palace's main dining hall, the Cenatio Iovis, was decorated with astrological imagery: Stat. *Silv.* 4.2.10, 4.2.31 (= **4.29** [a] below); Henriksén 1998–9: 2.135–6.

3 Domitian.

2.16 Reimagining the Flavian Palace after Domitian

The Flavian Palace presented a challenge to authors writing after Domitian: it reflected the luxurious tastes of a now-reviled emperor, but Domitian's successors continued to inhabit the structure for centuries. Plutarch (*Publicola* 15), writing in the relative safety of Greece, felt free to directly attack the palace's cost and luxury. Other authors were more indirect, some reporting anecdotes and aphorisms in which prominent figures attacked the corruption of the palace: Dio Cass. 68.5.5 (Xiph.), 74(73).7.3 (Xiph.); Philostr. *V A* 7.31.2 = **4.4 (b)** below. In one post-Domitianic poem, Martial praised the public splendour of the palace and downplayed the space available for Trajan's private life (12.50 = **2.16 [a]**); in a second, he also criticized not the building but Domitian's luxurious moveables, which had been relocated from the palace to public display in temples by Nerva or Trajan (12.15). (See Lugli 1962: 181–213 docs. 319–521 for a full collection of literary references to the Flavian Palace from Domitian to Late Antiquity.)

In **2.16 (b)** below, Pliny the Younger pursues another strategy. He attacks not the structure, but its use, claiming that Domitian treated it as a tyrant's citadel – a place of isolation, filled with paranoid (and ultimately unsuccessful) security measures. In contrast, the palace is open under Trajan (cf. 47.3–48.5 = **4.7 [b]** below) and the love he provokes provides the best kind of security; for the *topos*, see Roche 2011: 60–5; Kelly, **Vol. 1, 392**. Suetonius' stategy in **2.16 (c)** is not dissimilar. He nowhere mentions in his *Life of Domitian* that Domitian was largely responsible for the massive palace in the heart of Rome. Instead, Suetonius' only description of the palace's physical fabric is an (apocryphal?) anecdote about a paranoid security measure.

(a) Martial, *Epigrams* 12.50

You[1] alone have groves of laurel, plane, and lofty pine trees, as well as baths for more than one person. For you a high portico with a hundred columns stands, and alabaster shines as it is trodden under your foot. The fast hoof beats the dusty hippodrome, and a flood of squandered water[2] resounds on all sides. Long halls (*atria*) stretch out. But there is no place anywhere for diners or for sleep. How well you are housed – not![3]

1 Trajan.
2 From fountains; in the absence of mechanical pumps for recirculation, such water just flowed into drains.
3 Martial's point (which is not literally true) is that the gardens, porticos, and grand representational spaces of the palace are so large as to leave no room for living areas.

(b) Pliny the Younger, *Panegyric* 49.1–3

However, by means of the very walls and battlements that he thought would preserve his life, he shut himself in with treachery, plots, and a god who avenges crime.[1] Punishment pushed aside and broke through the guards, and burst in through the narrow, barricaded entrances, just as if through open doors and inviting thresholds. His divinity was of no use to him then, nor were those secret lairs and cruel places of seclusion,[2] into which he was driven by fear, arrogance, and misanthropy. How much safer, how much more secure is the same house, now that its master is guarded not by cruelty but by love, and not by solitude and locks, but by crowds of citizens. What follows, therefore? We learn from experience that the most faithful guard for an emperor is his own innocence. This is the inaccessible citadel, this is the impregnable stronghold: not needing a stronghold. He who is not surrounded by affection girds himself in vain with terror; for arms are provoked by arms.

1 Domitian was assassinated in his palace in 96; cf. **6.3**.
2 On stereotypical tyrants' proclivity for solitude, see Braund 1996.

(c) Suetonius, *Life of Domitian* 14.4

Moreover, with the time of suspected danger[1] approaching, he became more anxious by the day. He lined with phengite stone the walls of the porticos in which he was accustomed to stroll, so that he could see reflections of whatever was going on behind his back because of the stone's sheen. He used to give a hearing to most prisoners in private and alone, even holding their chains in his hand ...

1 Astrologers had made a prediction about the date of his death: Suet. *Dom.* 14.1 (= **6.3** [a]).

IV | Imperial Villas

What is known in modern Italian as *villeggiatura*, the pleasures of the country retreat that allowed a peaceful refuge from the bustling capital, was an essential part of elite experience in the Republican era and was readily taken up by Rome's emperors. The concept of 'the country in the city' (*rus in urbe*: Mart. 12.57.21), as exemplified by the large urban estates such as the Gardens of Maecenas that appeared in Rome in the first century BC, had a corollary in the luxury villa, which in many ways reproduced the amenities as well as the aesthetics of urban life: Purcell 1987. At these estates, whether in the country or by the sea, the emperor could enjoy different forms of leisure (*otium*) in a sublime setting while still attending to his duties. Imperial villas varied in size and magnificence, but all featured a refined rusticism set amid meadows, groves, and streams, and offering scenic vistas of hills and coastline. Embellished with sculpture and fine mosaic floors, these villas were endowed with porticos, gardens, elaborate fountains, and audience halls on a scale and of a quality that imitated features of the imperial residence at Rome. Small theatres and baths provided diversion for the imperial family and their guests, and dining rooms (*triclinia*) of different dimensions allowed the emperor to host large formal banquets and intimate gatherings, or, as in the unique case of the villa at Anagnia (modern Anagni) (see below, **2.22**), to feast *en famille* in a dining room where treading on grapes from the villa's own vineyards provided an evening's entertainment. Starting with Augustus at the beginning of the Principate, emperors sought moments of isolation from the burdens of court, and villas offered the best opportunity for respite; among the earliest structures built at Tibur was the small island retreat of the emperor (see below, **2.21 [e]**), a space for imperial solitude among the grandeur of vaults and porticos that mark the rest of the villa. Roman engineering prowess enabled architects to alter the natural landscape as desired, leading to the complex terraces that support Tiberius' villa on a rocky cliff on the island of Capreae (modern Capri) and the veritable riot of unusual design features that characterize Hadrian's villa at Tibur. The vast extent of Tibur offered numerous buildings for housing members of the imperial court and administrative staff, as well as the slave workforce, when the emperor was in residence; other villas, such as those frequented by the Antonine emperors (see below, **2.17, 22–3**) were smaller in scale, suggesting that only a limited cohort of secretarial personnel accompanied the imperial family during their visits.

2.17 The pleasures of *villeggiatura*: Marcus Aurelius on the climate at various imperial villas

Fronto, *Letters to Marcus as Caesar* 2.11.3 (ed. vdH 31 = Haines 1.142–4)

On a visit to Naples, the future emperor Marcus Aurelius wrote a letter to his tutor M. Cornelius Fronto in Rome comparing the climate in Naples (ancient Neapolis) to that of other imperial villas, indicating that both he and Fronto were well acquainted with the different locations. This letter dates to either 142 (van den Hout 1999: 80) or 143 (Davenport and Manley 2014: 67–8).

The climate of Naples is thoroughly pleasant, but extremely changeable; from minute to minute it becomes colder or warmer or too hot. At first, midnight is warm, as at Laurentum;[1] but then, as the cock crows, a bit chilly, as at Lanuvium;[2] frosty in the earliest dawn until sunrise, exactly like at Algidum;[3] after that, sunny before noon, as at Tusculum;[4] then at midday as scorching hot as Puteoli;[5] but when the sun goes to bathe in the ocean, finally the temperature becomes milder, the way it is at Tibur.[6] So it goes on like this into the early evening and the first sleep of night, 'until the dead of night hurls itself down', as M. Porcius[7] says.

1 Laurentum was west of Rome not far from the coast, in the area of modern Castelporziano; see George, **Vol. 1, 260**; Lauro 1998.
2 Lanuvium (modern Lanuvio), south of Rome in the Alban hills (see Chatr Aryamontri and Renner 2017) and the site of the imperial villa where the emperors Antoninus Pius and Commodus were born.
3 A town in Latium near Tusculum and Albanus Mons: Strabo 5.3.9.
4 Tusculum, a Roman town in the Alban Hills near modern Frascati, and the location for many elite villas. The imperial villa referred to in this passage has not been found.
5 Modern Pozzuoli on the Bay of Naples. Several imperial villas are known from this area, including Pausylipon (De Caro 2002), the Claudian villa at modern Punta Epitaffia, Baia (Belli 2009), and the large imperial villa and thermal complex at Baiae (modern Baia) (Maniscalco 1997); see also D'Arms 1970.
6 The vast imperial villa built by Hadrian; cf. **2.21**.
7 M. Porcius Cato (234–149 BC; *RE* Porcius 9), more commonly known as Cato the Elder. The quotation is from an unknown work of Cato: Jordan 1860: 86 frag. 17.

2.18 The imperial villas on Capreae

The villa of Tiberius on the island of Capreae, called the Villa Iovis ('Villa of Jove'), was one of twelve estates on the island owned by the imperial family. Construction of the villa was initiated by Augustus, but the majority of the structure dates to the reign of Tiberius, who chose to reside here, rather than in Rome, from AD 27 until his death in 37. Villas thus offered the emperor a place for permanent seclusion as well as temporary retreat.

(a) Tacitus, *Annals* 4.67.1–3 (excerpt)

Meanwhile, after dedicating temples in Campania, Tiberius, who had issued a warning by edict that his tranquillity not be disturbed, restrained the throng of townsmen by posting soldiers in various places. But he so loathed the towns, colonies and everything on the mainland that he hid himself away on the island of Capreae, which is separated by a strait of three miles from the end of the promontory of Surrentum.[1] Its solitude, I assume, pleased him greatly, since it is surrounded by the sea and without a harbour, barely offering even small vessels a refuge, and no one can put ashore unseen by sentries. In winter the weather is mild because the mountains keep away fierce winds; in summer it catches a western breeze and is very pleasant, encircled by open sea. It used to look out over a most beautiful bay, before Mount Vesuvius caught fire[2] and changed the landscape. According to tradition, that area was held by Greeks, while Capreae was inhabited by the Teleboi,[3] but by this time Tiberius had settled there in twelve villas, each massive and with its own name, and as concerned as he had once been for public responsibilities, he now relaxed into secret debauchery and base indolence.

1 Modern Sorrento.
2 The eruption of Mount Vesuvius in 79, which covered numerous villas and towns on the Bay of Naples, including Pompeii and Herculaneum.
3 The Teleboi were a tribe originally from Acarnania on the west coast of Greece.

(b) A Reconstruction of the Villa Iovis of Tiberius, Capreae

This model reconstruction, shown here from the south-west, is an approximation of the original building based on archaeological investigations of the enormous but piecemeal substructures that remain: Krause 2003; for a plan, see **Vol. 1, 243**, fig. 10.1. Built on a rocky promontory on several massive terraces, the villa block is multi-storeyed, with six storeys on the west side but only four on the north, while a vast cistern beneath the peristyle (visible at top of model) not only stored a much-needed supply of fresh water, but also served as the structural core around which ran corridors with perhaps as many as forty rooms placed off them; windows on the outside provided light to the interior. Entered through the small vestibule via a ramp (lower right on model), the villa seems to have been divided into sectors by function: the bath suite with its large, arched, southern-facing windows immediately off the vestibule; the east wing with a wide semi-circular colonnade open to the sea (top right on model) for the reception of guests; and the emperor's apartments on the north side

Figure 2.4.1 Model of the Villa Iovis, Capreae. Model by Niklaus Deschler (Skulpturhalle Basel), based on the archaeological excavations of Clemens Krause. Photo: Clemens Krause.

(top left on model), at furthest remove from the entrance, with a dining room, bedroom, and a long private terrace offering a spectacular view. The service quarter, comprising a kitchen, latrine, residential and storage space, was located in a structure that was attached to the main villa block (lower left on model) and at a lower level than the areas designated for the emperor's own use.

2.19 Caligula's pleasure boat

Suetonius, *Life of Caligula* 37.2

Ships also functioned as court spaces, either as locations for leisure or as more practical means of transport. Suetonius, in full moralizing mode, tells a tale below of lavish leisure vessels used by Caligula. The story is given some plausibility by the fact that brick stamps and a lead pipe identify two ships found at the bottom of Lacus Nemorensis (modern Lago di Nemi) south of Rome with Caligula; one was propelled by oars, while the other, lacking rowing positions, functioned as a floating barge and was probably steered into the middle of the lake by the other ship. Both were equipped with running water and baths, and decorated with mosaics, fresco, copper, bronze, and ivory: Uccelli 1950; Barrett 2015: 230–3. These were perhaps lacustrine equivalents of the seagoing vessels reported by Suetonius. For a Hellenistic royal precedent, see above, **2.1**.

He also built Liburnian 'tens',[1] sterns studded with precious gems and sails in many colours, equipped with large baths, colonnades, and spacious dining rooms, as well as a great variety of vines and fruit trees, so that he could sail throughout the day by the Campanian shore, reclining amid music and dancing. In building palaces (*praetoria*)[2] and villas he gave no thought to expense, striving to do nothing more than what others considered impossible.

1 A galley probably with two banks of oars, each manned by five rowers: Wardle 1994: 281, citing further literature.
2 On the use of *praetorium* ('palace'), see George, **Vol. 1, 242.**

2.20 The villa at Centumcellae

Pliny the Younger, *Letters* 6.31.1–2, 13–17

Pliny describes a sojourn in c. 107 at Trajan's villa at Centumcellae (modern Civitavecchia), 60 km north of Rome on the coast. The villa has not been found. Other emperors used this villa: Marcus Aurelius, with his tutor M. Cornelius Fronto: Fronto, *Ad M. Caes.* 3.21, 5.74 (ed. vdH 51–2, 85 = Haines 1.52–4, 173); Commodus: SHA *Comm.* 1.9.

To Cornelianus,[1]

I took great pleasure in being summoned by our emperor to Centumcellae – for this is its name – to serve on the council,[2] for what could be more gratifying than to observe the justice, dignity, and affability of our ruler at a retreat where these qualities are particularly revealed? There was a variety of different kinds of legal cases which highlighted the virtues of the judge from many different perspectives ... (*Pliny then describes the details of these legal cases at length: 6.31.3–12.*)

You see how conscientiously and how soberly we spent our days, but they were followed by the most delightful recreation. We were invited to dine with the emperor every day, quite a modest repast when you consider that he is the emperor. Sometimes we listened to recitations, sometimes we spent the night in delightful conversation, and on our last day he sent us gifts, for so thoughtful and well-mannered is he. Just as the importance of the cases, the honour of being on the council, and the straightforward amiability of our interactions with him were very agreeable to me, so too was the place itself. The villa is very beautiful, surrounded by the greenest fields and perched above the coast where a harbour is being built at this very moment in the curve of a bay, the left arm strengthened by the sturdiest masonry, while the right arm is under construction. At the harbour's entrance an island is rising as a breakwater against the waves blown in by the wind and to provide safe passage to ships on both sides. But the island rises by means of an ingenuity that must be seen: a wide barge carries huge rocks up to it, which are piled on top of one another so that they stay in place by their own weight, and in this way, little by little, a breakwater is piled up. The ridge of stones already appears projecting up above the sea and, as the waves hit, it breaks them and throws them upwards; from this comes a huge crash and the sea all around is white with foam. Next mortar will be added to the stones so that in time it will look like a natural island. The harbour will bear the name – in fact already bears the name – of its founder, and will be of great benefit, for on this long stretch of coast with no harbour it will be used as a place of refuge. Farewell.

1 *PIR*[2] C 1301. His identity is unknown.
2 On the emperor's council (*consilium principis*) see below, **3.6–8**, and Wei and Kelly, **Vol. 1, 105–7**.

2.21 The villa at Tibur

Hadrian's villa at Tibur, the largest and best-preserved Roman imperial villa, was built between 117 and 130 at times when the emperor was travelling across the empire: De Franceschini 1991; MacDonald and Pinto 1995; Salza Prina Ricotti 2001. A 'landscape villa' with three groups of buildings sited on a high plateau to take greatest advantage of the surrounding vistas, the complex covered 120 hectares.

(a) *Historia Augusta, Life of Hadrian* 26.5

The *Historia Augusta* description of the villa suggests that the unusual variation in its structures inspired fanciful names in Antiquity, and, by convention, these are still used now. However, there is no evidence that Hadrian himself used any of these terms.

The villa he built at Tibur was extraordinary, and to its parts he assigned the most famous names from both provinces and places around the empire, so that he called them names such as the Lyceum,[1] Academy,[2] Prytanium,[3] Canopus,[4] Poecile,[5] and Tempe[6]. And so that no place would be neglected, he even created an Underworld.

1 The school in Athens established by the philosopher Aristotle in the mid-fourth century BC.
2 The school in Athens set up by the philosopher Plato during the first quarter of the fourth century BC.
3 The meeting place of the executive councillors (*prytaneis*) in Greek cities, including Athens.
4 An Egyptian town at the mouth of the most westerly branch of the Nile, linked by canal to Alexandria. A major temple to Serapis was located there.
5 A reference to the *stoa poikile* ('painted stoa'), a monumental portico built in c. 500–450 BC in the agora at Athens and decorated by large panel paintings of mythical and historical battles.
6 The Vale of Tempe, a narrow gorge in Thessaly (northern Greece) near Mount Olympus, was the mythical home of the Muses and sacred to the god Apollo.

(b) The layout of the villa at Tibur

Archaeological investigations of the villa have revealed multiple spaces for entertaining guests, more intimate areas for the emperor's personal use, offices for secretaries and administrative staff, as well as a Greek theatre (**a** on plan), an Odeon (**o** on plan), baths (**t** on plan), and a small amphitheatre. A visitor to the villa entered a monumental

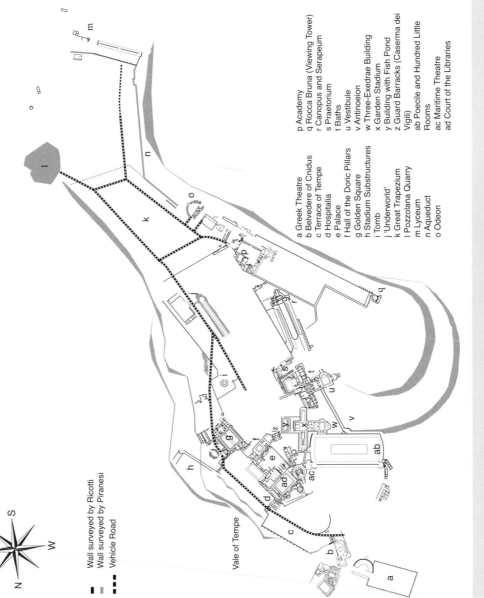

N
S
E
W

Wall surveyed by Ricotti
Wall surveyed by Piranesi
Vehicle Road

Vale of Tempe

a Greek Theatre
b Belvedere of Cnidus
c Terrace of Tempe
d Hospitalia
e Palace
f Hall of the Doric Pillars
g Golden Square
h Stadium Substructures
i Tomb
j 'Underworld'
k Great Trapezium
l Pozzolana Quarry
m Lyceum
n Aqueduct
o Odeon

p Academy
q Rocca Bruna (Viewing Tower)
r Canopus and Serapeum
s Praetorium
t Baths
u Vestibule
v Antinoeion
w Three-Exedrae Building
x Garden Stadium
y Building with Fish Pond
z Guard Barracks (Caserma dei Vigili)
ab Poecile and Hundred Little Rooms
ac Maritime Theatre
ad Court of the Libraries

Figure 2.4.2 Plan of the Villa of Hadrian, Tibur. After Salza Prina Ricotti 2001: 62, fig. 10.

vestibule (**u** on plan) with an apsidal room for audiences with Hadrian, while a similarly-shaped space (the Hall of the Doric Pillars, **f** on plan) retains the masonry dais for the emperor's throne. The so-called Golden Square ('Piazza d'Oro', **g** on plan), a vast columned court equipped with fountains and culminating in a domed, octagonal vestibule, furnished a magnificent setting for reception activities. Substantial resources were also devoted to practical concerns so that the villa's many facilities could function on demand: an aqueduct supplied water for the decorative pools, fountains, baths, and latrines, and a set of subterranean passageways almost 5 km in length extending beneath the villa's main structures provided storage space for goods and discreet accessibility for the many domestic slaves who worked here. Quarters for the slave workforce were scattered throughout the villa, but were concentrated in the so-called 'Hundred Little Rooms' ('Cento Camerelle', **ab** on plan), a four-storied structure with rooms for up to 700 slaves. A colonnaded precinct beside the main entrance road (**v** on plan) was dedicated to Antinous, Hadrian's lover and companion who drowned in the Nile river (Mari and Sgalambro 2007; cf. **5.14**).

(c) The 'Serapaeum'

The so-called 'Serapaeum' was a large outdoor dining area set at the end of a long pool ('Canopus') that was surrounded by columns and statues of gods and other mythological figures: De Franceschini 1991: 297–314, 563–76; MacDonald and Pinto 1995: 112–16; Salza Prina Ricotti 2001: 241–76. The names are taken from two Egyptian reference points: the town Canopus at the mouth of a branch of the Nile delta where there was a

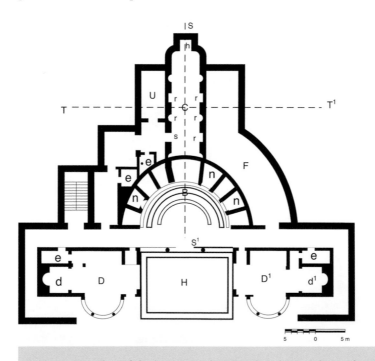

Figure 2.4.3 Plan of the 'Serapaeum', Villa of Hadrian, Tibur. After Salza Prina Ricotti 2001: 244, fig. 82.

temple to the Egyptian god Serapis; whether inspired by Hadrian's enthusiasm for this region or because of his lover Antinous' premature death by drowning in the Nile, there is no ancient support for these labels. The main feature is the curved dining couch or *stibadium* (**B** on plan) on which diners would recline while they ate; over their heads arched a half-dome originally covered with multicoloured mosaic that was meant to create the impression of dining in a vast cave. A square area in front of the diners (**H** on plan) provided space for entertainment during the meal, and water features enhanced the grotto-like effect, with a large central fountain (**h** on plan) and four smaller stepped fountains flowing into a channel behind the dining couch. Latrines built in two small structures to the side of the couches (**e** on plan) were for guests, while a more private toilet was probably reserved for the emperor.

(d) The Imperial Residences and Administrative Block

The core of the villa includes a series of interconnected porticos and structures that probably comprised the imperial residence and the main administrative offices. The

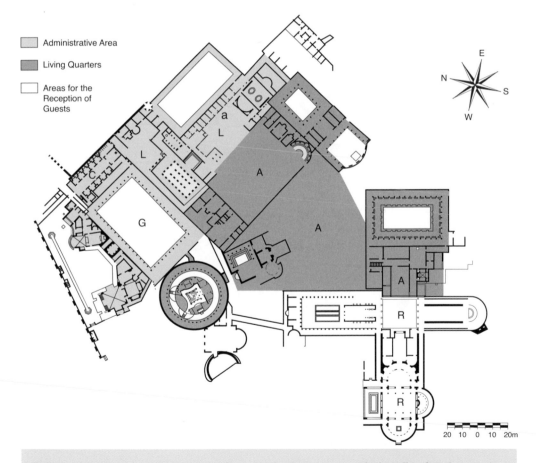

Figure 2.4.4 Plan of the Imperial Residences and Administrative Block, Villa of Hadrian, Tibur. After Salza Prina Ricotti 2001: 204, fig. 70.

living quarters (all labelled **A** on plan) have been seen as having two areas. The main residence was likely located in the northern areas of the living quarters. The part of the living quarters on the south side was more likely used in winter. Both had porticos for strolling, proximity to planted areas and bath suites, *triclinia* (dining rooms), and even heated floors: De Franceschini 1991: 405–16, 541–7; MacDonald and Pinto 1995: 187;

A - Portico
B - Atrium
C - *Tepidarii*
D - Pool
E - *Frigidarium*
F - Guest Bedroom
G - *Tablinum*
M - Hadrian's Bedroom

N - Hadrian's Study
P - Winter *Triclinium*
S - Toilets
T - Niches for Dining Couches

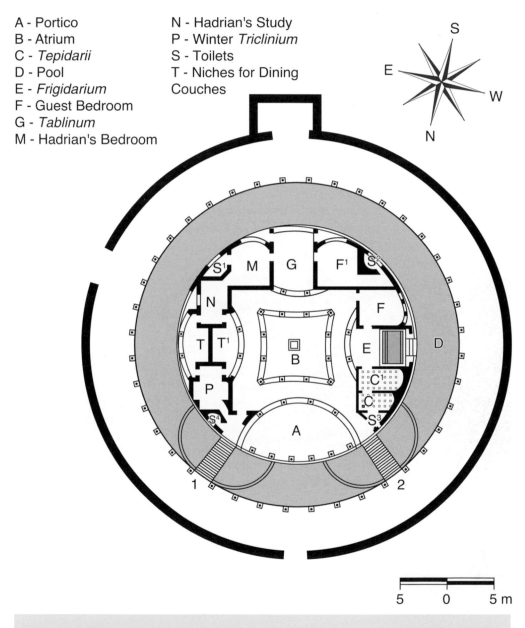

Figure 2.4.5 Plan of the 'Maritime Theatre', Villa of Hadrian, Tibur. After Salza Prina Ricotti 2001: 131, fig. 43.

Salza Prina Ricotti 2001: 199–210, 221–30. Sabina, Hadrian's wife, or other elite guests might have been housed in the so-called 'Academy' (Accademia, **p** on **fig. 2.4.2**), a large peristyle surrounded by many finely decorated rooms that was at a remove from the central block: De Franceschini 1991: 321–56, 581–91; Salza Prina Ricotti 2001: 167–70. One of the villa's underground passages connected the imperial residence to the large peristyle and set of surrounding rooms (**a** on plan) to the north; this was probably the sector where imperial secretaries ate, slept, and conducted their business when the emperor was in residence. The 'Hospitalia' (**C** on plan) is a two-storey structure which might have served as living quarters for administrative staff, who would have been near enough to the emperor to do his bidding, but distant enough to afford him privacy: De Franceschini 1991: 32–54, 358–66; Salza Prina Ricotti 2001: 153–6.

(e) Plan of the 'Maritime Theatre' (**fig. 2.4.5**)

The misnamed 'Maritime Theatre' (Teatro Marittimo) is in fact a small, circular island built in the first phase of the villa's construction to furnish Hadrian with a haven for solitude and contemplation: De Franceschini 1991: 185–98, 428–36, 490; MacDonald and Pinto 1995: 81–9; Salza Prina Ricotti 2001: 127–38. Set off from the rest of the villa and enclosed within its own walls, the 'island' is surrounded by an internal ring of columns that creates a small promenade and serves as an attractive camouflage for the wall behind, while a water channel spanned by two small footbridges surrounds the suite of rooms in the middle. A dining room (**P** on plan), bedroom (**M** on plan), study (**N** on

Figure 2.4.6 Aerial photograph of the 'Maritime Theatre', Villa of Hadrian, Tibur.
Photo: © Raimondo Luciani.

plan), bathing suite with a small pool (**C** and **E** on plan), four latrines (**S** on plan), and two potential guest bedrooms (**F** on plan) are elegantly punctuated by porticos that screen one part from another. This imperial hideaway is connected to the Hall of Philosophers (immediately to the south-west of the 'Maritime Theatre'), a small audience chamber which Hadrian could use to receive guests or conduct business; narrow staircases (**1** and **2** on plan) led to the administrative block and an underground passage to the Garden Stadium, a planted courtyard attached to the winter residence (**x** on **fig. 2.4.2**). With this arrangement, the emperor could isolate himself from the formal residence while also permitting easy access to the island refuge for administrative staff and slaves, who could move quickly from office or imperial quarters as required.

(f) Aerial view of the 'Maritime Theatre' (**fig. 2.4.6**)

In this aerial photo of the 'Maritime Theatre', the small audience hall can be seen on the lower left; the structure on the upper right is part of the administrative block (the so-called 'Greek Library', **ad** on **fig. 2.4.2**).

2.22 The Villa Magna at Anagnia

The Villa Magna, located south of Rome, has been identified as the imperial villa where Marcus Aurelius, then in his early twenties, wrote three letters to his teacher M. Cornelius Fronto detailing the imperial family's sojourn there c. 141–3: Fentress and Maiuro 2011; Fentress, Goodson, and Maiuro 2016. Excavation has revealed the poor remains of an imperial residence, quarters for slaves and other agricultural workers, and a winery, including the wine-press room mentioned in the letters to Fronto.

(a) Fronto, *Letters to Marcus as Caesar* 4.6 (ed. vdH 62–3 = Haines 1.180–2)

Hail, my sweetest teacher,

We are well. I went to bed early because of a slight cold, which now seems to have eased off. I spent from five to nine o'clock in the morning partly reading Cato's 'Agriculture',[1] and partly writing, less wretchedly, by Hercules, than I did yesterday. After attending my father's *salutatio*, I swallowed some honey water and then spat it out, 'comforting my throat', as I prefer to say, rather than 'I gargled', for I think the phrase is found in Novius[2] as well as elsewhere. After soothing my throat I went to my father and attended him as he sacrificed. We then had a bite to eat for lunch; can you guess what I ate? Just a little piece of bread, although I saw others polishing off beans, onions, and sardines full of roe. Then we worked hard at harvesting grapes, sweating and making cheerful shouts, and, as the poet says, 'we left some hanging high, survivors of the vintage'.[3] We returned home shortly after noon. I studied a little bit, but mostly in vain. I then had a long chat with my mum as she sat on my bed.[4] Our conversation went like this: 'What do you think my Fronto is doing now?' Then she said: 'Well, what do you think my Cratia[5] is doing?' Then I said: 'And what do you think little Cratia,[6] our little sparrow, is doing?' While we were chatting and quibbling about which one of us loved the one or other of you more, the gong sounded, a signal that my father had gone to the baths. So we ate dinner after we had bathed in the wine-press room – we did not bathe in the wine-press room, but we ate there after we had bathed – and we happily listened to the peasants ribbing each other.[7] Then I came back, and before I turned over on my side and started to snore, I did my day's work and I set out an account of my day for my sweetest teacher; I would gladly miss him more, if I could, even if it hurts. Farewell, my Fronto, wherever you are, sweetest, my love, my delight. How is it between us? I love you even though you are not here.

1 Cato the Elder (cf. above **2.17**, n. 7) wrote a 'how-to' treatise on farming (*De Agricultura*), suitable reading for the young emperor during his stay at this villa.
2 Q. Novius (*RE* 5), a writer of the first century BC who wrote comic plays in a genre called Atellan farces (*Atellanae Fabulae*) which were often set in the countryside. The fragment here is Frag. 109 (ed. Ribbeck 1898).
3 A quote possibly from Novius' play 'The Grape-gatherers' (*Vindemiatores*): Frag. 110 (ed. Ribbeck 1898); cf. van den Hout 1999: 174.
4 Marcus Aurelius' mother, Domitia Lucilla.
5 Cratia was Fronto's wife.
6 'Little Cratia' refers to Fronto's daughter, also named Cratia.
7 See the reconstruction of the wine-press room (below, **2.22 [b]**); the set of bathing rooms referred to by Marcus Aurelius was found near the dining area.

(b) The Winery at the Villa Magna

In this reconstruction of the winery, based on archaeological investigations of the structure (see **Vol. 1**, **262**, fig. 10.5 for a plan), the baths referred to in Marcus' letter

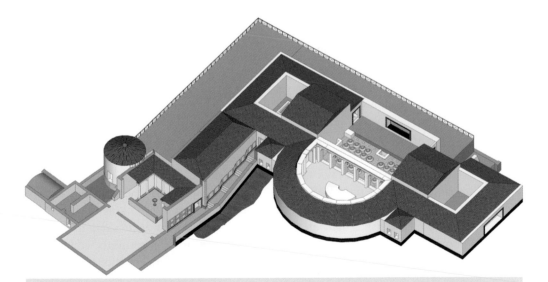

Figure 2.4.7 Reconstruction of the winery at the Villa Magna, Anagnia. From Fentress, E. and Maiuro, M. (2011) 'Villa Magna near Anagni: The Emperor, his Winery and the Wine of Signia', *JRA* 24: 350, colour fig. F. Reconstruction by Dirk Booms.

are visible at the lower left: a colonnaded *atrium* with a pool gave access to the series of rooms with increasing temperature, one a circular room with a domed roof. Although scant decoration survives, the stepped corridor that leads from the baths to the wine-press room had a white mosaic floor and the walls were faced with polychrome marble in an ornamental design that was unusually elegant for such a functional space. At the end of the corridor and at a slightly lower level is the wine-press room (*cella vinaria*), with large circular storage vessels (*dolia*) set in the ground; the grape-treaders stood on a platform (*calcatorium*), and must from the grapes was caught in a vat in its centre to be pressed elsewhere in the complex and then stored in the *dolia*. In front of the wine-press room, and open to it through an arcaded screen, is the semi-circular dining room in which were placed couches for reclining; a small curved table for the deposit of food and dishes is restored here. This room and those approaching it were paved in coloured marbles. As Marcus describes in his letter to Fronto, the winery was designed so that the emperor and his family could see the grapes being trod through the arcade and hear the banter of slaves as they worked.

2.23 The imperial villa at Alsium

Fronto, *On the Holiday at Alsium* 3.1 (ed. vdH 227–8 = Haines 2.4–6)

In this letter, Fronto discusses Marcus Aurelius' visit to the imperial villa at Alsium, on the coast 35 km west of Rome near modern Ladispoli, of which there are currently only a few traces such as mosaics, fishponds, and foundations: Marzano 2007: 389–99; Grüner 2013: 261–3. Although the letter is damaged, the meaning is clear.

To my Lord Antoninus Augustus,[1]

What? Do I not know that you went to Alsium intending to indulge yourself there and focus on entertainment and games and unchecked idleness for four whole days? And I do not doubt that you have gone about enjoying the holidays at your coastal retreat like this: you allow yourself a nap at noon, then call Niger[2] and order him to bring in your books; soon, when the desire to read comes over you, you refine yourself with Plautus[3] or satisfy yourself with Accius[4] or calm yourself with Lucretius[5] or inspire yourself with Ennius[6] until the fifth hour which is appropriate to the Muses; [- - -] and if someone troubles you with some stories, you listen to them, [- - -] then you hurry to the shore [- - -] and loiter around, [- - -] or, if it strikes you as a good idea, you set out to sea on some ship, so that in calm weather you can delight in the sight and sound of the oarsmen and the time-giver's baton; then straightaway you head for the baths to work up a good sweat, then knuckle down to a feast fit for a king of shellfish of every type, a fish caught on the hook à la Plautus – or as he says, 'fish on the rocks',[7] birds fattened for a long time, sausages, fruit, sweetmeats, confections, appropriate wines, and translucent cups without any imperfections.

1 Fronto addresses Marcus using one of his formal titles.
2 Presumably the name of Marcus Aurelius' secretary, librarian, or reader.
3 T. Maccius Plautus (c. 254–184 BC; *RE* 1), Roman comic playwright of the Republican era.
4 L. Accius (170–c. 86 BC; *RE* 1), Roman poet and tragedian, from whom only fragments and titles of works survive.

5 T. Lucretius Carus (99–55 BC; *RE* 17), Latin philosopher and poet whose didactic poem *De rerum natura* ('On the Nature of the Universe') sets out in verse an explanation of Epicurean philosophy, a school of thought developed by the Greek philosopher Epicurus in the third century BC (cf. **3.32** below).

6 Q. Ennius (c. 239–169 BC; *RE* 3), a major Roman writer of the Republican era who wrote in a variety of literary genres.

7 A reference to a line (299) in Plautus' play 'The Rope' (*Rudens*).

V | Imperial Residences of the Tetrarchic Period

The Tetrarchic period saw a new spate of palace building in the Roman world. There were now four emperors, all of whom were forced by political and military necessities to spend most of their time away from the heart of the empire. This led to the building of substantial palace structures in the 'capitals' where particular Tetrarchs spent much of their time. These included Antioch (modern Antakya, Turkey), Mediolanum (modern Milan), Sirmium (modern Sremska Mitrovica, Serbia), Thessalonica (modern Thessaloniki, Greece), and Augusta Treverorum (modern Trier, Germany) (see **2.24**). The period also saw at least two emperors build palatial retirement residences: Galerius built such a complex in Felix Romuliana (modern Gamzigrad, Serbia), although his death in 310 thwarted his retirement plans; Diocletian was more fortunate, retiring in 305 to a substantial residence in Spalatum (modern Split, Croatia) (see **2.25**).

2.24 The palace at Augusta Treverorum (Trier)

The best preserved element of the palace at Augusta Treverorum is the so-called Basilica of Constantine (or Aula Palatina), a massive imperial audience hall (length: c. 70 m; width: c. 27 m; height: c. 32 m). Although its original decoration is almost entirely gone, the basic structure of the building survives – albeit in reconstructed form after American bombing in 1944 – and is used now as a church. The high windows and apse at the end of the long north–south axis ensured that in the audience room, all attention was directed towards the enthroned emperor. A second, smaller hall connected to the south end of the main audience room perhaps was a space to marshal visitors before they were admitted to the imperial presence, and additional entrances to the main hall on the long sides allowed flexibility in the staging of ceremonial: Wulf-Rheidt 2013: 302, 2014: 15–16. The other areas of the palace complex have been heavily built over, but there are hints that it echoed some of the elements of the Flavian Palace complex at Rome. A literary source mentions a hippodrome (*Pan. Lat.* 6[7].22.5); the remains of this have not been securely identified, but it was likely to the east of the Basilica (just off the plan in **fig. 2.5.1**). The remains of a portico have been excavated to the west of that site, and this may have provided a connection between the palace and the hippodrome – a feature of the Flavian Palace shared by many Tetrarchic palaces: Wulf-Rheidt 2013: 288–95, 2014: 17–20. To the west of the portico, remains consistent with the foundations of a temple have been found; this would therefore be another case of a temple being included in a palace complex: Wulf-Rheidt 2014: 21–4. Like other palaces, there were also baths,

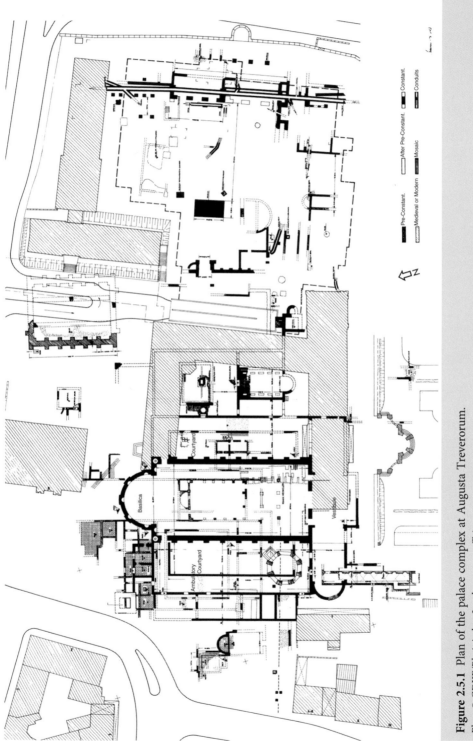

Figure 2.5.1 Plan of the palace complex at Augusta Treverorum.
Plan: © GDKE/Rheinisches Landesmuseum Trier.

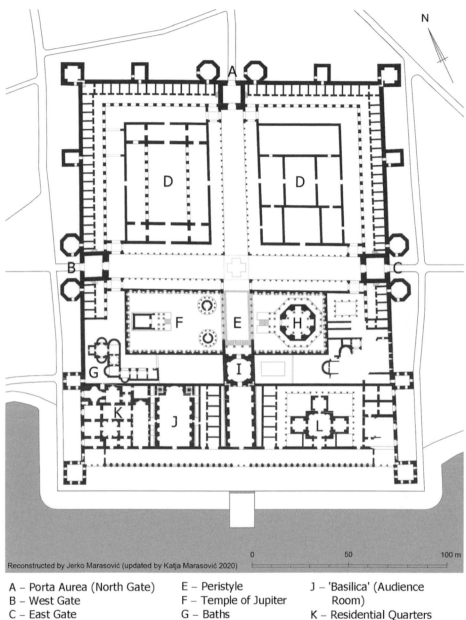

Figure 2.5.2 Reconstructed plan of Diocletian's Palace at Spalatum.
Plan by Jerko Marasović (updated by Katja Marasović, 2020).

the so-called Kaiserthermen (to the south of the Basilica, off the plan in **fig. 2.5.1**). On the palace complex, see most recently Kiessel 2011, 2012–13; Wulf-Rheidt 2014; see too Wightman 1970: 103–10.

2.25 Diocletian's palace at Spalatum (Split)

The palace at Spalatum (modern Split, Croatia), near Salona, became Diocletian's residence upon his retirement in 305 (**fig. 2.5.2**). Oddities and imperfections in its execution have prompted the suggestion that not only was the complex built in haste, but also it was originally meant to be something else (perhaps an installation for manufacturing military clothing) before being converted to a palace: Nikšić 2011. Parts of the palace are very well preserved, including sections of the walls and gates, the mauseoleum, and the temple. The plan of the main floor of the residential part of the palace can be reconstructed from the surviving substructures. The rest of the complex has been absorbed by the town that subsequently grew up inside the walls, but the general plan can be reconstructed. While the structure was unusual, in that it catered for a retired emperor, some elements of earlier palace architecture were repeated. As with the Roman palaces and various of the Tetrarchic residences, the complex had three temples, the largest of which was perhaps of Diocletian's patron god, Jupiter: Wulf-Rheidt 2013: 296–9. There were also baths and an audience room featuring an apse. On the complex, see Wilkes 1993; Nikšić 2011.

3 | Court Relationships

ANGELA HUG, BENJAMIN KELLY, AND NEIL W. BERNSTEIN

Introduction

The Roman imperial court was not a place but a diverse group of people, made up of those who had 'reasonably regular verbal interaction with the emperor and/or who provided him with domestic or security services': Kelly, **Vol. 1, 7.** Like Roman society more generally, court society was heavily stratified. Unlike Roman society, however, these stratifications were based not on traditional markers of status differentiation – gender, citizenship, wealth – but on the strength of individual connections to, and relationships with, the emperor. As a result, the status hierarchy at any court could be both complex and unstable, with courtiers shunted between 'inner' and 'outer' circles, or expelled from the court entirely, as their standing with the emperor changed. Interpreting court dynamics and identifying who enjoyed imperial favour was a challenge for anyone outside court circles but essential if they wished to benefit from those who had the emperor's ear. Specific power groups existed at the court – friends (*amici*), relatives, lovers, domestic servants, bodyguards, and so on – but rarely acted in a unified fashion. Instead, according to the court narratives in our literary sources, alliances were most often made (and broken) between individuals from these disparate groups; for this pattern at monarchical courts in general, see Duindam 2016: 291. This dynamic is most apparent during times of crisis: see below, **6.3–4.**

We face two main challenges when interpreting the relationships we find in the literary sources. Firstly, since the majority of our narratives were written by elite men, they ooze resentment at the influence imperial women, domestic servants, and other low-status but high-ranking individuals could wield at court if they had close relationships with the emperor. Their animosity results in sordid and lurid tales, often so extreme as to be unbelievable. Epigraphic evidence, on the other hand, suggests a more pragmatic acknowledgement of such courtiers' influence, and a willingness by outsiders, including provincial communities and foreign royals, to use it to achieve their goals (**3.27, 29, 32**). Secondly, no behaviour of the emperor was exempt from moralizing judgements, including his relationships. 'Bad' emperors invariably surrounded themselves with the wrong sorts of people, abused and disparaged their aristocratic advisers, and reduced their court to immoral chaos. 'Good' emperors did nothing of the sort. Underpinning such judgement, of course, is anxiety: that the emperor might not respect traditional conventions of aristocratic friendship (**3.10–11**).

All relationships with the emperor were founded on an unequal division of power that had to be carefully negotiated. The delicate balancing act required for any successful courtier is well-documented: the demands on the *amici* (**3.5–6**); the difficulty of refusing an imperial request (**3.16, 25**); the small errors with potentially catastrophic consequences (**3.13, 54 [b–c]**); the fierce competition between courtiers (**3.31, 51, 4.23**). For those in favour, the rewards could be practically boundless (**3.9, 50 [a]**). But elevation came with a price. The higher courtiers rose, the further they had to fall (**3.12, 14**).

I | *Amicitia* at Court

One of the most important kinds of relationship at the imperial court was that of *amicitia* ('friendship'). The conceptualization and performance of friendship between the emperor and aristocrats (and, occasionally, others) drew on a tradition of aristocratic friendship that stretched back to the Republic: see Brunt 1988a; Winterling 2009b. The emperor's position and resources meant that his friendships were in many respects different from those between aristocrats: his friends could accrue extraordinary wealth and power (**3.9**), but the relationship could be time-consuming (**3.5**), and losing imperial favour could entail social and even physical death, either during the emperor's lifetime (**3.12–13, 19**) or after a regime change (**3.14–15**). In spite of its exceptionality, imperial *amicitia* was nevertheless expected to conform to the performative scripts of aristocratic friendship, which included warm displays of affection; there was also an expectation that the emperor should not act coercively towards friends (**3.10–11**). Complexity is added to the topic by the fact that the language of *amicitia* was very flexible, with some people being called *amici* out of politeness (**3.3–4**): Brunt 1988a: 360–1; Millar 1992: 115; Eck 2006: 71; Michel 2015: 137. A variety of other terms (e.g. *intimus, familiaris*) could be used to refer to closer friends (**3.1–2**), but these were never deployed in a systematic fashion. For the Romans – as for us – context mattered greatly in determining the sense in which someone was a 'friend'. For imperial friendships in general, see: Brunt 1988b; Millar 1992: 110–22; Winterling 2009b; and Wei and Kelly, **Vol. 1, 92–109**, citing further literature.

a. Becoming a Friend of the Emperor

3.1 The future emperor Vitellius wins the friendship of three emperors

Suetonius, *Life of Vitellius* 4–5

The emperor's favour could be manifested in political, administrative, and priestly appointments, as Suetonius makes clear in his account of the early life of the future emperor Vitellius. The biographer's claims that shared pastimes and flattery were the basis of Vitellius' close friendships with three emperors may reflect rumour and speculation, but they are important for the underlying assumption that imperial friendships were based on quite subjective criteria; there was nothing automatic about them. To be a close friend of multiple emperors was a well attested phenomenon: Gaudemet 1982: 46–8; cf. **3.5** below. That the biographer counts Vitellius as part of the *aula* also shows that for the Romans, this group of people included the emperor's aristocratic friends (cf. above **1.8**).

In the subsequent part of his life[1] he was also polluted with every vice and held a leading position in the court (*aula*). He was an intimate (*familiaris*) of Caligula because of his zeal for charioteering and of Claudius because of his enthusiasm for dicing. But he was even more well-liked by Nero, not only because of these interests but also because of a particular service. For when he was presiding at the Neronian Games,[2] Nero longed to compete amongst the cithara-players. However, even though the crowd was clamouring for this, Nero did not dare to undertake to do so, and he therefore left the theatre. Vitellius called him back, claiming that he acted as an envoy of the insistent populace, and presented him with the chance to be won over by entreaties.

   Thus, because of the favour of three emperors, he was glorified not only with magistracies but also with the most distinguished priesthoods; he subsequently governed the province of Africa as proconsul and served as Supervisor of Public Works[3] – with varying willingness and reputation.

1 Suetonius has just related Vitellius' boyhood and early youth, which he allegedly spent as one of Tiberius' male prostitutes on Capreae (cf. **2.18** above).
2 An artistic competition along Greek lines instituted by Nero in Rome in 60; it involved musical, poetic, and rhetorical contests. See Tac. *Ann.* 16.4 for another version of the same incident.
3 Vitellius (*PIR*² V 740) was *cos. ord.* in 48 and proconsul in Africa probably in 60/1. Two priestly positions are known: he was *frater arvalis* and a *quindecemvir sacris faciundis*. The date of his appointment as *curator operum publicorum* is unknown.

3.2 Petronius and Nero

Tacitus, *Annals* 16.18.1–2

Even more unreliable is Tacitus' account of the friendship between Nero and Petronius (*PIR*² P 294), who was very likely also the author of the racy Latin novel, the *Satyrica*, which still survives in part. Tacitus perhaps extrapolated Petronius' character and lifestyle from the sordid tone of the novel (Murgatroyd 2013: 245); at the very least, Tacitus' Petronius plays a role in the historian's complex literary strategies (Haynes 2010), so we are not dealing with an artless report on a historical figure. Nevertheless, the account is historically valuable because it shows Tacitus' assumption that the emperor could have close friends who were not givers of sober political, administrative, or legal advice, but rather had other roles in the emperor's court. The moralizing assumption that lurks behind the passage – that extravagant emperors prone to vice will choose friends who share these traits – also illustrates a common theme in ancient discussions of the inner court.

Petronius requires a short retrospect. His days were passed in sleep and his nights with the duties and pleasures of life, and just as hard work had brought fame to some, idleness had brought it to him. Unlike many who burn their way through their fortunes, he was not considered a glutton and a spendthrift, but as learned in the art of luxury. The more his words and actions were unrestrained and displayed a certain carelessness in regards to himself, the more gladly they were accepted as an outward manifestation of his simplicity. However, as proconsul in Bithynia and a little later consul,[1] he showed himself to be energetic and equal to the job. Then, having relapsed to vice – or because of the imitation of vice – he was added amongst the few intimates (*familiares*) of Nero as the arbiter of taste. For Nero thought nothing to be pleasant and agreeable in its abundance[2] except what Petronius had approved for him.

1 Tacitus' 'Petronius' is often taken to be P. Petronius Niger *cos. suff.* 62, but see Völker and Rohmann 2011. The date of his proconsulship is unknown.
2 *Adfluentia*; on varying scholarly interpretations of the meaning of this word in the passage, see Haynes 2010: 85.

3.3 An equestrian friend of Vespasian?

Corpus Inscriptionum Latinarum 10.8038 (= *FIRA* 1^2.72) – northern Corsica; AD 77 (?)

This bronze tablet, found in a village in northern Corsica, contains a letter from the emperor Vespasian to the community of the Vanacini concerning a boundary dispute they had with the Colonia Mariana: for analysis, see Zucca 1993. The inscription also tends to disprove the argument that all aristocrats welcome at the *salutatio* of the emperor were considered his *amici*; see Mommsen 1887–8: 2.2.834–5, followed by Winterling 1999: 161–9, 2009a: 90–1; Schöpe 2014: 86–94. Senior equestrians would have been welcome at the emperor's *salutatio* when in Rome, yet two of the three equestrian governors mentioned in the text are not called *amici*: Eck 2006: 75. Otacilius Sagitta (*PIR*^{2} O 175), the governor who is so called, was not a prominent figure and could be called an *amicus* out of politeness. On the other hand, the fact that he is singled out could indicate a genuine personal connection with Vespasian.

The emperor Caesar Vespasian Augustus greets the magistrates and senators of the Vanacini.[1] I am delighted that my friend and procurator Otacilius Sagitta governed you in such a way as to deserve a positive testimonial from you. On the topic of the boundary dispute that you have with the Mariani relating to the lands which you purchased from my procurator Publilius Memoralis,[2] I have written to my procurator Claudius Clemens[3] to determine the boundaries and I have sent him a surveyor. I confirm the privileges granted to you by the deified Augustus after his seventh consulship, which you continued to have up until the time of Galba.

Lasemo, son of Leucanus, priest of Augustus, and Eunus, son of Tomasus, priest of Augustus, served as envoys. In the consulships of C. Arruntius Catellius Celer and M. Arruntius Aquila, on the fourth day before the Ides of October.[4]

1 For the Vanacini, see Zucca 1993: 191.
2 *PIR*² P 1053.
3 *PIR*² C 835.
4 12 October. The year is probably 77; cf. Zucca 1993: 187–8 n. 10 on the date.

3.4 Pompeius Planta – a 'friend' of Trajan

Oxyrhynchus Papyri 42.3022, verso, ll. 1–16, *BL* 9.199 (= *Greek Constitutions* 46) – Oxyrhynchus, Egypt; October – December, AD 98

In this letter of Trajan, the prefect of Egypt, Pompeius Planta (*PIR*² P 637), is called a friend (*philos*) of the emperor; see too Plin. *Ep.* 10.7. Planta had a distinguished equestrian career under earlier emperors, and Trajan probably appointed him to govern Egypt (cf. Bastianini 1988: 507). But after Planta left the office in 100, no further public roles are known for him, and literary sources contain no hint of his being personally close to Trajan. His designation as a friend of Trajan may not have reflected genuine friendship; it could have been a mere politeness.

[The emperor Caesar Nerva, son of the deified Nerva, Trajan Augustus] Germanicus, *pontifex maximus*, holding [tribunician] power for the second time, consul,[1] [to the city of the] Alex[andrians,[2] greetings].

[Since I approve of your] city's remarkable [goodwill] towards (previous) emperors, and I remember the benefactions that my deified [father] bestowed upon you [- - -] in the early days of his reign, and I myself have a positive disposition towards you [over and above][3] these rights (of yours), I commend you firstly to myself, and then to my friend and prefect, Pompeius Planta, so that taking every care he can provide for your undisturbed peace and your grain-supply and your rights, communal and individual. *(The papyrus becomes fragmentary here.)*

1 Trajan was in his second consulship by the time of the letter, so there may be a copyist's error here: Harker 2008: 51.
2 This letter was likely written in response to an embassy sent by the city to Trajan in Germany upon his accession in 98. For the survival of such letters concerning Alexandria in the Egyptian countryside, see Harker (2008: 49–59, esp. 50–1), who judges this one genuine.
3 Here we translate, *exempli gratia*, Parsons' suggested restoration of [μετ]ά. *Pace* Oliver, a photo of the papyrus confirms Parsons' view that [ἕνεκ]α cannot have stood in the gap: see comm. to *P. Oxy.* 42.3022 l. 9.

b. The Duties of Friends of the Emperor

3.5 An *amicus* of Titus and Vespasian: Pliny the Elder

Pliny the Younger, *Letters* 3.5.7–9, 18–19

Friendship with emperors was often seen as an onerous and time-consuming burden, as Pliny the Younger stresses in this letter about his uncle, Pliny the Elder; cf. Plin. *Ep.* 4.24.3. The passage presents a variation on the standard theme of the literary man exercising independence and refusing to write at the emperor's command; according to his nephew, Pliny the Elder managed to write prolifically in spite of friendship with the emperor: see Bernstein, **Vol. 1, 454**.

Are you amazed that such a busy man completed so many books, many of them highly detailed? You will be even more amazed if you know that for some time he frequently pleaded cases before the courts, that he died in his fifty-sixth year, and that the intervening period was busy and impeded both by very important public duties and by friendship (*amicitia*) with emperors. But he had a sharp intellect, unbelievable concentration, and could get by without much sleep. From the time of the festival of Vulcan[1] he used to begin work by lamplight, not to take the auspices,[2] but to start studying straight away in the depths of night, in winter from the seventh or, at the latest, eighth hour – and often from the sixth. He certainly fell asleep very easily, and sometimes he would nod off and then wake again even while he was studying. Before dawn he used to go to the emperor Vespasian[3] – for he too made use of the nights – and then to the duties assigned to him.[4] ... *(Pliny then describes his uncle's routine when at home, on journeys, and in retirement.)*

When you think about how much he read and wrote, surely you would assume that he had never served in any public positions or maintained a friendship (*amicitia*) with the emperor? On the other hand, when you hear about how much toil he devoted to studies, perhaps you think he did not write or read enough? For his official occupations hindered him in every way, but such mental concentration could achieve anything. Thus I tend to smile when someone calls me studious, since compared with him I am very lazy.

1 On 23 August.
2 Magistrates often took the auspices by night to ensure the gods approved of the public business they planned for the following day: Driediger-Murphy 2019: 149 n. 77.
3 To attend Vespasian's *salutatio* (cf. **4.8** below).
4 On the duties (*officia*) assigned to Pliny the Elder, see Sherwin-White 1966: 222–3.

3.6 The *amici* of Domitian gather to debate a big fish

Juvenal 4.72–118

The premise of Juvenal's fourth *Satire* is that Domitian, when staying at his villa at Lacus Albanus (modern Lago Albano), is presented with a fish too large for any serving plate. He calls a *consilium* to advise him in this crisis. The meeting of the *consilium* then described parodies a scene in Statius' lost *On the German War*, which is known from a fragment: see Stat. *De Bello Germanico* (frag.) ap. Valla *Schol. ad Iuv.* 4.94 = Morel, Büchner, and Blänsdorf 2011: 330. Although writing satire, Juvenal gives a plausible list of men serving on the *consilium*, since it includes a combination of nine senators and two equestrians; see the notes below for specifics, and for extended prosopographical analysis, see Vassileiou 1984; Jones 1992: 51–61; Eck 2000a: 196–8. Juvenal claims that there was *amicitia* between these men and Domitian, but that Domitian hated them and they in turn were terrified of Domitian. This reflects the broader moralizing complaint that friendship had become debased under the Principate: Seager 1977. But Juvenal was perhaps also aware that some men served as advisers because of their senior status and were called *amici* out of politeness, without necessarily having an emotional connection with the emperor.

Therefore the leading men are called into a *consilium* – men whom Domitian hated, on whose faces lay the pallor of that wretched and mighty friendship (*amicitia*). First of all, when the Liburnian slave was shouting 'Hurry up! He is seated already', Pegasus[1] grabbed his cloak and began to hurry there. He had only recently been appointed as the slave-driver of the gobsmacked City – were the prefects at that time anything else? He was the best of prefects and a most upright jurist; he used to think that, although the times were dreadful, everything should be dealt with by bloodless justice.

Crispus,[2] an agreeable old fellow, also came. His disposition was similar to his eloquence; he was a gentle spirit. Who would have been a more beneficial travelling companion (*comes*) to the ruler of seas, lands, and peoples, if, in that time of calamity and pestilence, he had been permitted to denounce savagery and proffer morally upright advice? But what is more savage than the ear of a tyrant? On him depends the fate of the friend who merely intends to talk about the rain or the hot weather or the cloudy spring.[3] Crispus thus never swam against the current; he was not the sort of citizen who was able to speak his mind freely and throw away his life for the truth. In this way he saw many winters and his eightieth summer; with this armour he was safe even in that court (*aula*).

Next to Crispus was hurrying Acilius,[4] who was the same age. With Acilius was his youthful son,[5] who did not deserve the cruel death in store for him – a death so accelerated by the swords of his master. But old age has long been like a marvel in the nobility; hence I prefer to be a complete nobody. It was therefore of no advantage to the wretched youth that as a naked beast-fighter in the Alban arena he speared Numidian bears at close quarters. For who by now does not see through such patrician stratagems? Who marvels at your ancient shrewdness, Brutus? It is easy to trick a bearded king.[6]

Rubrius was coming,[7] who was no more cheerful, although of low birth. He was guilty of an old and unspeakable wrong, but was nevertheless more shameless than a catamite who writes satire. Montanus'[8] paunch is also there; his belly slows him down. So too Crispinus,[9] sweating already at dawn with exotic perfume – two funerals scarcely reek so much – and Pompeius,[10] more savage than him, who slit throats with a faint whisper. Likewise Fuscus,[11] who was reserving his innards for the Dacian vultures, having planned the battles in his marble villa, and wise Veiento,[12] accompanied by death-dealing Catullus,[13] who used to burn with love for a girl he had never seen. Catullus was a large and notable monstrosity even by the standards of our age, a blind flatterer, a dreadful henchman, who deserved to be begging from axles at Aricia and tossing fawning kisses at a carriage that had come down (the hill).[14]

---

1 [L. Plo?]tius Pegasus (*PIR*² P 512), *cos.* under Vespasian and governor of several provinces. Possibly urban prefect already under Vespasian: *Dig.* 1.2.2.53.

2 L. Iunius Q. Vibius Crispus (*PIR*² V 543, cf. I 847) was *cos.* I under Nero, *cos.* II *suff.* 74, *cos.* III under Domitian; curator of the water supply (AD 68–71); and governor of Africa and Spain.

3 That is, a friend who visits a tyrant intending mere small-talk can find the conversation taking a dangerous (possibly lethal) turn.

4 Acilius Glabrio (*PIR*² A 62), *cos.* under Domitian.

5 M'. Acilius Glabrio (*PIR*² A 67) *cos. ord.* in 91. Glabrio successfully fought a lion in the arena at Domitian's Alban villa, supposedly earning the jealousy of the emperor, who later executed him: Dio Cass. 67.14.3–4 (Xiph.); Suet. *Dom.* 10.2.

6 According to legend, L. Iunius Brutus feigned stupidity so as not to seem a threat to his uncle, the wicked King Tarquin: Livy 1.56.7–9. Tarquin, like many early Romans, was imagined as bearded by later generations.

7 Rubrius Gallus (*PIR*² R 127), *cos. suff.* under Nero, governor of Moesia. His 'old and unspeakable wrong' was allegedly the seduction of Domitian's wife in his youth: *Schol. ad Iuv.* 4.105 (ed. Wessner 1931: 63).

8 Probably T. Iunius Montanus (*PIR*² I 781, cf. M 681), *cos. suff.* 81; for other possibilities, see Jones 1992: 54.

9 'Crispinus' (*PIR*² C 1586) was certainly an equestrian (Juv. 4.32); scholars once thought he was a praetorian prefect, but more recently he has been seen as a buffoon at court (Baldwin 1979; Vassileiou 1984) or an equestrian administrator (Absil 1997: 217–18).

10 Probably M. Pompeius Silvanus Staberius Flavianus (*PIR*² P 654), *cos. suff.* I 45, II 74 (?), III *desig.* 83, who also held a string of important priestly, military, and administrative positions; see Eck 1972 for details.

11 Cornelius Fuscus (*PIR*² C 1365), praetorian prefect in the first part of Domitian's reign; he was killed in action in Dacia: Suet. *Dom.* 6.1.

12 A. Didius Gallus Fabricius Veiento (*PIR*² F 91), *cos. suff.* I under Vespasian, II 80, III 83 (?), and holder of four priesthoods; cf. below **4.30**.

13 L. Valerius Catullus Messalinus (*PIR*² V 57), *cos.* I *ord.* 73, *cos.* II *suff.* 85; see below **4.30** for his posthumous reputation.

14 The village of Aricia was on the Appian Way just south of the Alban Villa; a steep dip in the road forced carriages to slow down, making it a perfect place for beggars to solicit travellers: cf. Mart. 2.19.3, 12.32.10.

3.7 The members of the *consilium* of Marcus Aurelius

Année épigraphique 1971.534 ll. 22–3, 29–53

This text is one of three documents contained on the so-called *Tabula Banasitana*, a Latin inscription on bronze discovered at Banasa (modern Sidi Ali bou Jenoun, Morocco) in 1961. The documents concern the grant of Roman citizenship to two leaders of the Zegrenses, a father and son both named Iulianus, and to their wives and children. The third document, translated below, provides an authenticated extract from the records (*commentarii*) of people granted citizenship, proving that the wife and children of the younger Iulianus had been made citizens. The list of the twelve men who authenticated the document provides vital evidence for the emperor's *consilium*. The first five men (and probably also the sixth) are distinguished senators; the other six men are all equestrians, four of whom are known to have been holders of senior equestrian offices. Although these men acted as authenticators of this document, rather than advisers, they were presumably gathered together on the occasion in question for a meeting of the *consilium*, and were asked to act as witnesses as an extra duty: Eck 2000a: 199. On the inscription generally, see Seston and Euzennat 1971; Sherwin-White 1973; Williams 1975.

Transcribed and authenticated from the register of people given Roman citizenship kept by the deified Augustus and Tiberius Caesar Augustus and ... (*there follows a list of the other emperors up to Commodus, excluding Otho and Vitellius*). Asclepiodotus[1] the freedman produced the register. Extract below:

In the consulships of the emperor Caesar L. Aurelius Commodus Augustus and M. Plautius Quintillus, the day before the Nones of July,[2] at Rome.

Faggura, the wife of Iulianus, the chief of the Zegrensian people, aged 22; Iuliana, aged 8; Maxima, aged 4; Iulianus, aged 3; Diogenianus, aged 2, children of the said Iulianus.

At the request of Aurelius Iulianus, the chief of the Zegrensians, made by petition, with Vallius Maximianus[3] lending his support by letter, we have given Roman citizenship to these people, with their tribal rights preserved and with no reduction of the tribute and taxes due to the people and the imperial *fiscus*.

Done on the same day, in the same place, under the same consuls. I, Asclepiodotus the freedman, have authenticated it.

Sealed by:

M. Gavius Squilla Ga[l]licanus,[4] son of Marcus, Poblilia tribe

M'. Acilius Glabrio,[5] son of Manius, Galeria tribe

T. Sextius Lateranus,[6] son of Titus, Voturia tribe

C. Septimius Severus,[7] son of Gaius, Quirina tribe

P. Iulius Scapula Tertullus,[8] son of Gaius, Sergia tribe

T. Varius Clemens,[9] son of Titus, Claudia tribe

M. Bassaeus Rufus,[10] son of Marcus, Stellatina tribe

P. Taruttienus Paternus,[11] son of Publius, Poblilia tribe

Sex. [Tigidius Peren]nis,[12] [son of - - -, - - - tribe]

Q. Cervidius Scaevola,[13] son of Quintus, Arnensis tribe

Q. Larcius Euripianus,[14] son of Quintus, Quirina tribe

T. Flavius Piso,[15] son of Titus, Palatina tribe

1 This is possibly the same man attested in c. 185–9 as *a memoria* and *a rationibus* (*CIL* 6.41118 = *AE* 1961.280), but the identification is not completely certain: see Haensch 2018: 292 n. 27.

2 6 July 177.

3 *PIR*² V 251, the governor of the province (Mauretania Tingitana).

4 *PIR*² G 114, *cos. ord.* 150, proconsul of Asia c. 165.

5 *PIR*² A 73, *cos. ord.* 152. His grandfather and great-grandfather were probably the Acilii Glabriones on Domitian's *consilium* (above **3.6**): see *PIR*² A 62, 67–8.

6 *PIR*² S 666, *cos. ord.* 154.

7 *PIR*² S 485, *cos. suff.* 155 or 160.

8 *PIR*² I 556, *cos.* c. 160–6.

9 *PIR*² V 274, previously an *ab epistulis Latinis* (c. 162–5), and probably adlected to the Senate by the date of this document.

10 *PIR*² B 69, praetorian prefect 168–77.

11 *PIR*² T 35, *ab epistulis* c. 170–2; attested as praetorian prefect by 179, but it is unknown if he held the post in 177.

12 Sex. Tigidius Perennis (*PIR*[2] T 203) had a distinguished equestrian career and rose to being praetorian prefect under Commodus, but was executed in c. 185/6, perhaps on charges of conspiracy: Hdn. 1.9.1–6; Dio Cass. 72.9.3; cf. SHA *Comm.* 6.2. His name has been deliberately erased from the inscription, providing physical evidence of how *damnatio memoriae* could occur when an adviser of the emperor fell from grace.

13 *PIR*[2] C 681; he had been prefect of the watch (*praefectus vigilum*) in 175; whether he held the post still in 177 is unknown. Also a distinguished jurist.

14 *PIR*[2] L 89, an equestrian, perhaps holding a more junior equestrian office.

15 Presumably an equestrian, perhaps holding a more junior equestrian office.

3.8 Septimius Severus and his *consilium* hear Egyptian ambassadors

Oxyrhynchus Papyri 42.3019 ll. 2–19, 9 March 200

During his visit to Egypt in 199–200, Septimius Severus spent a good deal of time carrying out legal duties. This Greek papyrus from Oxyrhynchus minutes the emperor's decision in a matter that he heard while sitting with a *consilium* (Greek: *to symbouleion*). This included friends, who were clearly travelling with him, but also others – perhaps members of the provincial elite who could provide local knowledge. The document therefore assumes that not everyone sitting on a *consilium* was automatically a friend of the emperor.

In the consulship of Severus and Victorinus, on the seventh day before the Ides of March, in Alexandria. The emperor took his seat in the law-court with his friends (*philoi*) and those who had been invited to serve on the advisory council, and he ordered that the representatives of the Egyptian litigants[1] who were advancing communal requests be called in. After other matters:[2] when Dionysius made a request about the swineherds, since the farmers (?) were already involved in the harvest [---].[3]

1 Cf. Turpin 1981: 154 n. 33.

2 This copy of the record of proceedings, likely made for private purposes or because it illustrated a legal point, omits court business earlier in the day unrelated to the case.

3 The papyrus becomes fragmentary here, before the gist of Dionysius' request becomes clear. For a discussion of the possible background, see Parsons, comm. to *P.Oxy.* 42.3019 l. 15 ff.

c. Negotiating Imperial Friendship

3.9 Augustus' relationships with his friends

Suetonius, *Life of Augustus* 66

In this passage, Suetonius reveals his assumptions about how *amicitia* with the emperor would (and should) work. Friendship with the emperor is seen as a reciprocal affair and as having an emotional dimension. In a very few cases, Augustus brought his friendships to an abrupt end, just as aristocrats sometimes did: cf. Rogers 1959; Kierdorf 1987; Millar 1992: 113; Hurlet 2018. The passage also shows that, despite the ideal, an emperor's friendships were not normal: Augustus' attempt to distance himself from a friend was fatal to the latter, and the emperor realized that his friends were likely to communicate their true sentiments only from beyond the grave.

Augustus did not accept friendships (*amicitiae*) readily, but held on to them resolutely, not only rewarding appropriately each friend's virtues and meritorious services, but also putting up with their defects and misdeeds – or at least their moderate ones. Indeed, out of all those who enjoyed his friendship none who were ruined can easily be found. The exceptions were Salvidienus Rufus, whom he advanced as far as the consulship, and Cornelius Gallus, whom he promoted to the governorship of Egypt – and both from the lowest social station. He handed the former over to the Senate to be condemned for plotting revolution.[1] The latter he barred from his house and his provinces because of his ungrateful and spiteful spirit.[2] However, when Gallus was also hounded to his death by the allegations of his accusers and by senatorial decrees, Augustus praised the devotion of those who were so very indignant on his account, but wept and lamented his plight, since he alone was not allowed to get as angry as he liked with his friends.

Augustus' other friends had power and wealth right up to the ends of their lives, each being distinguished as leading members of their respective orders, albeit with resentments sometimes cropping up. I shall not multiply examples, but he sometimes found that M. Agrippa lacked patience and Maecenas discretion. The former left everything behind and took himself off to Mytilene because of an idle suspicion of coolness (on Augustus' part) and because Marcellus was preferred over him.[3] The latter (Maecenas) betrayed the secret of the discovery of Murena's conspiracy to his wife Terentia.[4]

He himself in turn demanded reciprocal goodwill from his friends – as much from the dead ones as from those living. For although he certainly did not hunt inheritances, and could never stomach the idea of taking anything from a stranger's will, he would nevertheless obsess over the final judgements of friends in a pernickety way.[5] He did not conceal his resentment if someone had rewarded him too stingily or with less than honourable words, nor did he conceal his joy if someone did so with gratitude and devotion. . . .

1 Salvidienus Rufus (*RE* 4), *cos. des.* 39 BC, one of Octavian's commanders in the early Triumviral period. In 40 BC, he was condemned by the Senate for plotting to go over to Mark Antony and probably committed suicide: Liv. *Per.* 127; App. *B Civ.* 5.66; Dio Cass. 48.33.1–3.

2 Cornelius Gallus (*PIR*² C 1369), a distinguished writer of love elegy, was appointed to command positions in Octavian's army and as the first governor of the province of Egypt. The sources diverge on whether he alienated Augustus with revolutionary or merely inappropriate behaviour: Ov. *Tr.* 2.446; Suet. *Gram.* 16; Dio Cass. 53.23.5; Amm. Marc. 17.4.5; Serv. *ad* Verg. *Ecl.* 10.1.

3 For this episode see too Vell. Pat. 2.93.2; Suet. *Tib.* 10.1; Tac. *Ann.* 14.53.3, 55.2; Dio Cass. 53.32.1. The claim that tensions with Marcellus prompted Agrippa's voluntary withdrawal may not be historically true: Wardle 2014: 424–5 for discussion and literature.

4 On Murena and his conspiracy, see Cogitore 2002: 123–35. Maecenas' wife Terentia (*PIR*² T 98) was Murena's sister: Dio Cass. 54.3.5.

5 This began the custom, which built on older Republican practices, of *amici* making the emperor a beneficiary in their wills; see Rogers 1947; Millar 1992: 153–8; Winterling 2009b: 50–2.

3.10 Trajan's friendships, according to Pliny

Pliny the Younger, *Panegyric* 86.1–4

Imperial friendships involved significant power imbalances between the emperor and his friends (cf. Winterling 2009b: 48–9). The precarious position of the friend necessarily inclined him to do the emperor's will at the expense of his own liberty. But the ideal, which is well reflected in the passage below from Pliny's panegyric for Trajan, was rather different: the emperor was expected to allow friends to exercise their free will, even if it conflicted with his own inclinations. Moreover, the scene Pliny paints of Trajan's farewell to his departing friend illustrates that imperial friendship was supposed to be accompanied by a warm emotional performance.

It is worth referring to the anguish you inflicted on yourself to avoid denying something to a friend. Even though you were reluctant and unhappy, you allowed the retirement of an excellent man who was most dear to you, just as if you were not able to retain him. Torn apart and cut off from him as you gave way and yielded to his pressure, you found out how much you loved him from your longing. Thus, something happened that was unheard of: when the emperor and a friend (*amicus*) of the emperor wanted different things, the friend's wishes prevailed.

This is something that should be committed to memory and written down! A praetorian prefect[1] was selected not from those who thrust themselves forward but from those who withheld themselves.[2] The same prefect also returned to the leisure (*otium*) that he so persistently loved,[3] and even though you yourself were so busy with the responsibilities of supreme power (*imperium*), you did not begrudge to someone the honour of peace and quiet. We understand, Caesar, how much we owe you for (holding) this toilsome and troublesome post when leisure (*otium*) is sought and given by you on the ground that it is the best thing.

Your consternation was considerable, so I hear, when you escorted him as he was departing! For you escorted him and you did not refrain from giving the departing man hugs and kisses on the shore. Caesar stood on that lookout post – a special place for friendship![4] – and prayed for favourable seas for the departing man and a swift return, if he wanted to return. Nor could Caesar refrain from following his friend more and more with prayers and tears as he receded into the distance.

1 His identity is unknown: Syme 1980b: 65.
2 Thus, the friend showed the imperial virtue of *recusatio*, and avoided the appearance of wishing to use his friendship with the emperor to obtain positions of power.
3 On the ideal of *otium*, see above **2.11, 14, 17–23**.
4 Lat.: *in illa amicitiae specula* – literally: 'in this lookout post of friendship'.

3.11 Marcus Aurelius on Antoninus Pius as a friend

Marcus Aurelius, *Meditations* 1.16.8–12

This passage from Marcus Aurelius' *Meditations* shows an emperor reflecting on the realities of imperial *amicitia*. Again, we are not dealing with an objective record: the

Meditations were not intended for publication, but Marcus did idealize his adoptive father, Antoninus Pius. Pius' friends may well have felt rather more constrained in their decisions. See too SHA *Ant. Pius* 11.

(I also admired my father's) consideration for other people's feelings, the fact he absolved his friends (*philoi*) from the obligation of dining with him and travelling with him by compulsion, and the way that those who were left behind because of some pressing necessity always found him the same when he arrived back.[1] (I admired) his dedication to making pointed enquiries in *consilia* and his persistence.[2] (Likewise I was impressed) with his ability to keep friends[3] and his never being fickle or obsessed with them,[4] and with his self-sufficiency in all matters and his cheerfulness, and with his tendency to look well into the future and make provisions in advance for the smallest matters, without drama.

1　On the expectation that emperors should not resent excusing friends from attending on them when necessity intervened, see **4.7 (b)**; Antoninus Pius ap. Fronto *Ad Ant. Pium* 6 (ed. vdH 165 = Haines 1.228).
2　Here we omit a probable interpolation in one branch of the manuscript tradition; for the textual issue, see Dalfen 1974: 52–3.
3　Suetonius praises the same trait in Augustus: **3.9** above.
4　Infatuation with a friend could create a favourite with an unhealthy degree of influence.

d. Terminating *amicitia*

3.12　Tiberius' advisers – and their fates

Suetonius, *Life of Tiberius* 55

While friends of the emperor enjoyed wealth and power, they also risked a spectacular fall if they lost imperial favour. With some emperors, this entailed not only social death for the friend but also physical extinction. It was a cliché that tyrannical emperors would murder their friends, so Suetonius' discussion below of the fate of Tiberius' friends could be dismissed as overstatement, except that specific cases of Tiberius executing his friends or driving them to suicide are known.

Besides his old friends (*amici*) and intimates (*familiares*), Tiberius had requested twenty leading men of the state to serve as members of his *consilium* – as it were[1] – to advise him on public affairs. Of all of these, he kept scarcely two or three unscathed;[2] he destroyed the others for one reason or another, amongst them Aelius Sejanus, whose fate brought the ruin of many others.[3] Tiberius had promoted Sejanus to the highest position of power not so much out of goodwill but more so that by this man's support and guile he might ensnare the children of Germanicus and secure the imperial succession for his natural grandson, whom his son Drusus had sired.

1　Suetonius' words here (*velut consiliarios*) hint that this group of men was somewhat like a *consilium*, but not quite – perhaps because it still owed something to the Augustan senatorial council: see Crook 1955: 18–19, 36. *Consiliarii* in this sense should not be confused with the salaried equestrian officials who appeared at a later date.

2 Specifically documented cases of friends whom Tiberius had executed or drove to suicide
   include Cn. Cornelius Lentulus Augur (*PIR*[2] C 1379; Suet. *Tib.* 49.1, cf. Tac. *Ann.* 4.29.1),
   Vescularius Flaccus and Iulius Marinus (*PIR*[2] V 431, I 406; Tac. *Ann.* 6.10.2), and Sex.
   Vistilius (*PIR*[2] V 727, Tac. *Ann.* 6.9.2).
3 Cf. **5.5** below.

3.13 The future emperor Vespasian loses the favour of Nero

Some emperors attempted to break off friendships in rather gentler ways, by
barring former friends from their residence as an ordinary aristocrat would do:
Tac. *Ann.* 6.29.2; Plut. *Mor.* 508a–b; **3.9**. Vespasian briefly suffered such a fate,
according to the passages below; for the anecdote see too Tac. *Ann.* 16.5.3; Dio
Cass. 65(66).11.2 (Xiph.); cf. Acton 2011: 111–13. At times, emperors also
attempted to signal the end of a friendship with other prohibitions: Tac. *Ann.*
6.9.2, 13.46.3, 15.23.4. These additional signs of estrangement are diverse and
rarely attested, so emperors do not appear to have developed a special, ritual-
ized way to end friendships.

(a) Suetonius, *Life of Vespasian* 4.4

During the Greek tour, when Vespasian was amongst the travelling companions
(*comites*) of Nero, he caused most serious offence, since, when the emperor was
singing, he either left too often or stayed and fell asleep. He was barred not only
from close association with the emperor (*contubernium*),[1] but also from the
public *salutatio*. He withdrew to a small and remote town until a province with
an army was offered to him while he was still lying low and even fearing death.[2]

1 See Hurlet (2018: 278–9) on the connotations of *contubernium*.
2 If Suetonius is correct that the incident happened during Nero's Greek tour of AD 66/7, then
   Vespasian's disgrace was short-lived, since he was appointed commander in the war in Judaea
   within months: Drinkwater 2019: 96. Tacitus (*Ann.* 16.5.3) dates the affair to the
   Quinquennial Games in Rome in 65, implying a slightly longer period of disgrace.

(b) Suetonius, *Life of Vespasian* 14 (excerpt)

When he was alarmed at being barred from the court (*aula*) under Nero and
asked what he should do and where he should go, somebody from the admissions department[1] had told him to go to hell[2] as he sent him away. Afterward,
when this man begged for mercy, Vespasian's rage was confined to words, and
their number and tenor were about the same.

1 For the admissions staff of the court, see below, **4.5**.
2 Lat.: *abire Morboviam*; literally 'to go to Disease-ville'; cf. *OLD* s.v. *Morbovia*. The term is not
   paralleled elsewhere and was possibly coined in the moment.

3.14 The rise and fall of Galba's *amici*

Although many emperors took over their predecessors' friends and advisers, a
change of regime could sometimes involve a rupture, with key *amici principis*

being marginalized (or worse). The sources claim that three favourites – one a senator, one an equestrian, and one a freedman-turned-equestrian – exercised immense influence over Galba, an alleged example of 'monarch capture': cf. Wei and Kelly, **Vol. 1, 111–12**. The senator, T. Vinius, was killed in January 69 in the same affray as Galba, and the other two soon after.

(a) Suetonius, *Life of Galba* 14.2

Galba was controlled by the wishes of three men, who dwelt together with him in the palace and were attached to him always; people regularly used to call them Galba's nannies.[1] They were: T. Vinius, Galba's legate in Spain,[2] a man of boundless desires; Cornelius Laco, a former legal adviser[3] who was now praetorian prefect and was insufferably conceited and torpid; and the freedman Icelus, who a short time before was honoured with the gold ring[4] and the cognomen of Marcianus, and now was a candidate for the highest equestrian position.

1 Lat.: *paedagogi*; these were low-status people (usually slaves) who supervised children, accompanying them (especially in public) and playing a role in their general socialization.
2 Galba governed Hispania Tarraconensis (AD 60–8); Vinius (*PIR*[2] V 666) was legate (either a legionary legate or *legatus iuridicus*) in the province for some or all of this time.
3 Cornelius Laco (*PIR*[2] C 1374) perhaps acted as Galba's legal adviser in Spain: Syme 1980a: 81.
4 The wearing of the gold ring (*anulus aureus*) was a symbol of equestrian status, and could also be granted to freedmen by the emperor to bestow fictive free birth: Davenport 2019: 216–18. For Icelus, see *PIR*[2] I 16.

(b) Tacitus, *Histories* 1.42

They then fell upon T. Vinius. Regarding him also, it is unclear whether pressing fear took away his voice or whether he shouted that there was no order from Otho for him to be killed. Perhaps he made this up out of terror or perhaps he revealed his complicity in the conspiracy; his lifestyle and notoriety rather dispose one to the view that he was complicit in the crime of which he was the cause. He fell before the Temple of the Deified Julius by an initial blow to the knee; a legionary soldier, Iulius Carus, ran him through soon after.

(c) Tacitus, *Histories* 1.46.5

The prefect Laco, ostensibly banished to an island, was run through by a senior soldier, whom Otho had sent ahead to kill him. Marcianus Icelus was executed in public, as happens to freedmen.

3.15 Maximinus Thrax dismisses Severus Alexander's friends

Herodian 7.1.3–4

Regime change could entail the large-scale replacement of imperial friends and advisers with new ones. Herodian claims something like this happened at the accession of the soldier-emperor Maximinus Thrax in 235; the *Historia Augusta* makes a similar claim

(*Max.* 9.6–8), although it has Maximinus resorting to murder where Herodian speaks of gentler means. Both authors may be guilty of overstatement, and Maximinus certainly still had senatorial supporters (cf. Hdn. 7.9.1–3). It is plausible, however, that a Thracian of low origins who had risen through the army would not want the friends and advisers of the pro-senatorial Severus Alexander.

Maximinus immediately got rid of all the friends (*philoi*) who were attending on Alexander, as well as[1] the members of his *consilium* picked by the Senate.[2] Some were dispatched to Rome; others were ejected from the administration on some pretext. He wanted to be alone with his army and not to have any people around him who were his superiors thanks to their awareness of their own nobility. He would then have the opportunity for tyrannical deeds, just like someone from an acropolis[3] who has nobody around him to whom he needs to pay respect.

1 Here, in spite of the doubts of some modern editors, we retain the Greek τε, which appears in the manuscripts; cf. Crook 1955: 87 n. 1. Again, then, advisers and friends are not entirely overlapping categories; cf. above **3.6**, **3.8**.
2 On the *consilium* of Severus Alexander and its composition, see Hdn. 6.1.2; Zonar. 12.15; SHA *Alex. Sev.* 16.1–3, 68.1, to be read with Crook 1955: 86–91.
3 I.e. a tyrant, who stereotypically lived on an acropolis or citadel.

II | Cultural Patronage

Like many courts through history, the Roman court attracted poets, philosophers, physicians, and other intellectuals. Indeed, some of the most important surviving literary, philosophical, and medical writings of the Principate were produced by men with close court associations, at the encouragement of emperors or members of the imperial family. This category of courtier overlapped to some degree with that of the *amici principis*: some were members of the senatorial or equestrian aristocracies, and were spoken of as *amici* of the emperor (**3.17**, **19**, **23** [a], **26** [c]). Like friends, cultural figures were enmeshed in the web of patronage that centred on the court, receiving considerable material and intangible benefactions from the emperor (**3.18–19**, **21** [a, c], **23** [a]), and also acting as brokers themselves (**3.21** [a]). Writers and intellectuals faced an especially complex challenge in negotiating their relationship with the emperor: offending him was dangerous (cf. **3.19**, **23** [b]), but at the same time there was a need to appear to maintain artistic or intellectual independence (**3.16**, **17**, **25**), and to avoid being criticized as sycophants for appearing too accommodating to the regime (**3.18**).

3.16 Vergil and Augustus

Ti. Claudius Donatus, *Life of Vergil* 31–3

This anecdote describes events of the 20s BC, when Vergil (70–19 BC; *PIR*[2] V 407) was engaged in the composition of the *Aeneid*. Augustus left Rome for the

Cantabrian campaign in 26 BC, and his nephew Marcellus, his sister Octavia the Younger's son, died in 23 BC. Ti. Claudius Donatus wrote in the fourth century, but is thought to have reproduced material from Suetonius' life of Vergil; see most recently McGill 2013. Like the other ancient lives of the poets discussed in this chapter, however, some of its claims must be treated with scepticism, as they may have been either exaggerated or developed from the poet's own works. This anecdote has been the basis of numerous subsequent imaginings of Vergil's performance at Augustus' court, most famously Ingres' painting *Tu Marcellus Eris* (1812); see Bernstein, **Vol. 1, 439**.

Augustus indeed demanded in his letters – because he happened to be away on his Cantabrian campaign – using prayers and even joking threats, that Vergil send him 'something from the *Aeneid*'. In his own words, 'either the first draft of the poem or any section he chose'. But not until much later, when the material was finally complete, did Vergil recite three complete books to him: the first, fourth, and sixth books of the *Aeneid*. The sixth book greatly affected Octavia, who was present at the reading. When Vergil reached the line about her son, 'You will be Marcellus', it is said she fainted and was revived with difficulty. He also recited to many people, but never to a large group. He usually selected passages about which he was in doubt, the better to get his listeners' critique.

3.17 Horace, Vergil, and Augustus

Suetonius, *Life of Horace* (excerpts)

While Vergil mentions very little about his life in his poetry, Horace (65–8 BC; *PIR*[2] H 198) creates a detailed narrative of his rise from a freedman's son to the emperor's favoured poet. Suetonius' life of the poet accordingly interacts with an image carefully constructed by the poet himself. All of Horace's works include an address to Maecenas, as the patron who guaranteed his connection to the emperor. For Horace's negotiations over his creative independence, see Bowditch (2001), McCarter (2015), and Bernstein, **Vol. 1, 452–4**.

Horace first won Maecenas' favour, and Augustus' soon after, and held a prominent place among their circles of friends (*in amborum amicitia*). A well-known epigram shows well enough how much Maecenas loved him: 'If I do not love you, Horace, more than my own vital organs, then you may see your friend skinnier than a rag doll.' But this eulogy to Augustus in Maecenas' last will witnesses their friendship even more: 'Remember Horace as you remember me.' Augustus offered Horace the post of secretary for correspondence, as his letter to Maecenas shows: 'Earlier, I was strong enough to write letters to my friends, but now I am too busy and sick, and I want to take our mutual friend Horace from you. So he will come from your parasitic table to my royal table, and help me write letters.' Augustus showed no resentment at all when Horace refused, nor became angered, and did not stop trying to gain his friendship. *(Suetonius then quotes some extracts of letters from Augustus to Horace.)*

Augustus greatly approved of Horace's writings and believed that they would last forever. He not only commissioned him to write the *Secular Hymn*,[1] but also compelled him to celebrate his stepsons Tiberius and Drusus' victory over the Vindelici.[2] Thanks to this commission, Horace added a fourth to his three books of *Odes* after a long interval. Furthermore, after reading some of his *Satires*, Augustus complained that he found no mention of himself . . .[3]

1 The *Secular Hymn* (*Carmen Saeculare*) was performed in 17 BC as part of the *Ludi Saeculares*, a three-day festival.
2 Tiberius and Drusus the Elder campaigned against the Vindelici, a Celtic people of Switzerland and southern Germany, in 15 BC.
3 In response to Augustus' complaint of not being mentioned in his work, Horace composed the *Epistle to Augustus* (*Epist.* 2.1).

3.18 Seneca the Younger and Nero

Tacitus, *Annals* 14.52

Seneca was a successful writer in many genres, who had court connections stretching back to the time of Claudius and who flourished under Nero's patronage. As will happen to any successful courtier, Seneca attracted the criticism of his competitors as a result. Even his early *Consolatio ad Polybium*, written from exile in the 40s, was later remembered as a work of shameful flattery: Dio Cass. 61.10.2 (*EV*). For the stories surrounding Seneca's career, see Ker 2009, Wilson 2014.

Burrus' death diminished Seneca's influence, as virtuous endeavours no longer had the same strength after one of their two leaders had been removed.[1] Nero was also inclined to listen to worse counsellors. These men attacked Seneca with various accusations, such as: he continued to add to enormous wealth, carried well beyond a private citizen's standard; he turned the citizens' affection to himself; he also seemed to outdo the emperor in his gardens' loveliness and his villas' magnificence. They also charged Seneca with arrogating praise for eloquence to himself alone, and writing verse more frequently, now that Nero had developed a love of poetry. For Seneca was openly hostile to the emperor's amusements: he disparaged the emperor's skill at driving his horses, and he made fun of his voice when he sang. How long, they asked, would there be nothing outstanding in the state, unless Seneca was thought to have discovered it? Nero's childhood was certainly over, and he was now in the full strength of young manhood.[2] He should discharge his teacher, as his own ancestors, who were learned enough, could guide him.

1 In 62. Tacitus' chronology therefore does not entirely match the narrative presented by two late-antique authors of 'Nero's five good years' (*quinquennium Neronis*), ending in 59: Aur. Vict. *Caes.* 5.1–4; *Epit. de Caes.* 5.1–5. On the tradition, see Murray 1965.
2 Nero was 25 in AD 62.

3.19 Lucan and Nero

Suetonius, *Life of Lucan* (excerpts)

Lucan (M. Annaeus Lucanus, AD 39–65; *PIR²* A 611) was Seneca's nephew and author of a ten-book epic on the civil war between Julius Caesar and Pompey. The ancient biography's account of Lucan's quarrel with Nero has greatly affected interpretation of his epic on the civil war. It has been hypothesized, for example, that the poem's criticism of the Caesars derives from the poet's quarrel with Nero described below. Such views should be treated with scepticism, however, as they may derive from a reading of the poem rather than independent evidence for the poet's life. See Fantham 2011 for the most recent review of the evidence and its relevance to reading the *Bellum Civile*.

Lucan of Corduba made the first trial of his poetic skill with a *Eulogy of Nero* at the emperor's Quinquennial Games.[1] He next recited from his poem on the *Civil War* fought between Pompey and Caesar … Nero recalled him from Athens, added him to his circle of intimate friends (*cohors amicorum*), and also honoured him with a quaestorship; but Lucan did not remain in the emperor's favour. He took it badly that while he was reciting, Nero suddenly called a meeting of the Senate and left, for no other reason than to put a chill on his performance. After that, Lucan did not hold back from words and deeds against the emperor, which are still well known … (*Some examples of Lucan's hostile acts and deeds then follow.*) At last, he revealed himself almost as the standard-bearer of the Pisonian conspiracy.[2] He openly spoke a great deal about the glory of tyrannicides,[3] and he was full of threats. He was so unbalanced that he boasted to anyone close to him that he would give him Caesar's head. But he did not show the same constancy of spirit at all when Nero uncovered the conspiracy. For he confessed easily and sunk to the lowest begging. He even named his own innocent mother among his confederates, hoping that his lack of dutifulness would help him with the parricidal emperor.

1 The Neronian Games (the Neronia) of 60.
2 The plot to murder Nero in 65, which had C. Piso as its figurehead. On the breakdown of Lucan's relationship with Nero and his involvement in the conspiracy, see too Tac. *Ann.* 15.49.3, 56.4, 70.1; cf. Dio Cass. 62.29.4 (Xiph.).
3 M. Iunius Brutus (*RE* 53), C. Cassius Longinus (*RE* 59), and the other conspirators who murdered Caesar in 44 BC.

3.20 Statius and Domitian

In the envoy to his epic *Thebaid*, Statius indicates an eager readership that includes the emperor. Suetonius (*Dom.* 2.2, 20) offers a hostile account of the emperor Domitian's interest in poetry. In the proem to his later, briefer epic *Achilleid*, Statius joins the other Flavian poets in representing the emperor as skilled both in poetry and military command, with the latter superseding the former. In these encomiastic passages, Domitian is no passive recipient of compelled praise, but a discriminating consumer of sophisticated poetry. For recent discussion of both passages, see Parkes 2015.

(a) Statius, *Thebaid* 12.810–15

Will you endure longer and will you outlive your master to be read, o my *Thebaid* on which I laboured much for a dozen years? Certainly Rumour here at hand has already made a welcome path for you and begun to show my new work to future generations. Already great-souled Caesar thinks it worthwhile to recognize you, already the Italian youth learn you and recite you with eagerness.

(b) Statius, *Achilleid* 1.14–18

Italian and Greek courage both wonder at you, Domitian, as the first by far. The twin laurels of poets and commanders flourish for you in competition, and one long since regrets that the other won. Give me your favour and permit me to sweat briefly in this dust, anxious as I am. I am working on an epic about you; it has been long in preparation, and I am not yet confident in it. Great Achilles plays a prelude for you here.[1]

1 Statius refers here to a proposed epic on Domitian's career that he promises to complete in the future, following the convention of the *recusatio*.

3.21 Martial and Domitian

Martial refers to the honours and material rewards that he received from his imperial patrons, Domitian, Nerva, and Trajan. (He also complains frequently about his poverty, but this is a convention of the epigrammatic genre rather than a literal description of his circumstances as an equestrian.) Martial boasts of his precedence thanks to imperial favour (**3.21 a**), his access to the emperor through intermediaries such as Domitian's *a cubiculo* (**3.21 b**), and the connection between his patronage and his choice of poetic genre (**3.21 c**).

(a) Martial, *Epigrams* 3.95.5–6, 9–12

Both Caesars have praised and rewarded me, and given me the rights of a father of three children[1] ... There is also something to be said for this: Rome has seen me made a tribune,[2] and I sit where Oceanus[3] dislodges you from your seat. Thanks to Caesar's gift, I have made so many citizens[4] – I suspect, Naevolus, that you do not have as many slaves.

1 The 'right of three children' enabled a father who had not actually engendered three children to enjoy certain tax immunities and office-holding privileges. Martial was probably granted the right by Titus and had it renewed by Domitian; cf. Mart. 2.91–2, 9.97.5–6; Sullivan 1991: 25 with n. 39.
2 Martial was made an honorary military tribune, presumably as a result of imperial favour: Sullivan 1991: 4.
3 'Oceanus' (*PIR*[2] O 8) is generally assumed to be the (possibly generic?) name of a slave serving as a *dissignator*, who assigned seats in the theatre: Friedländer 1886: 1.332; cf. Mart. 5.23, 6.9. Martial's tribuneship gave him equestrian status (cf. *Ep.* 5.13.2) and he thus enjoyed special seating in the theatre – which the addressee of the poem, Naevolus, did not.
4 Martial presumably used his connections with the Flavian emperors to obtain grants of citizenship for provincials with whom he was connected – i.e. he acted as a broker in the process of imperial patronage.

(b) Martial, *Epigrams* 5.6.1–11

If it is not too difficult or burdensome, Muses, please ask your friend Parthenius: 'So may your late and happy old age end one day while Caesar lives, so may you enjoy good fortune and Envy favour you, so may Burrus[1] soon appreciate his father – admit this timid, slender volume within the threshold of the holier part of the palace (*aula*). You know the times when Jupiter[2] is serene, when he shines with his own gentle countenance, the one he customarily wears when he denies nothing to suppliants.'

1 The son of Parthenius (*PIR*[2] B 176). On Martial and Parthenius, cf. **Vol. 1, 444**.
2 The emperor Domitian, who is often called Jupiter by the Flavian poets.

(c) Martial, *Epigrams* 8.55(56).1–6, 21–4

The time of our forefathers yields to our own, and Rome has grown greater along with her emperor. So you wonder that holy Vergil's genius cannot be found today, and no writer uses such a mighty trumpet to make war thunder.[1] Flaccus,[2] there need to be Maecenases, and then Vergils will not be lacking. Even your own backwater will give you a Vergil ... Why should I speak of Varius and Marsus[3] and the other poets whom Maecenas made rich – so many it would be a great effort to run through them all? So would I be a Vergil if you gave me Maecenas' gifts? I would not be a Vergil, I would be a Marsus.[4]

1 Martial plays on a familiar satiric narrative of stingy patrons.
2 The addressee of the poem is nominally Martial's fellow poet Flaccus (*PIR*[2] F 170); it may be suspected, however, that the ultimate audience for this call for generous patronage is the emperor: Sullivan 1991: 19, 41.
3 L. Varius Rufus (*PIR*[2] V 285) and Domitius Marsus (*PIR*[2] D 153), poets of the Augustan age whose works are now lost.
4 Martial here differentiates his chosen genre of epigram from his contemporaries who pursue tragedy and epic by claiming that he would emulate the epigrammatist Marsus rather than Vergil. For the image of a 'Golden Age' of court patronage under Augustus, see Bernstein, **Vol. 1, 438**.

3.22 Martial under the principates of Nerva and Trajan

Martial, *Epigrams* 10.72

Suetonius (*Dom.* 13.2) corroborates the story that Domitian insisted on being addressed as 'Lord and God' (*dominus et deus*). However, see Davenport's commentary on **4.15 (c)** below for the argument that the initiative for this address came from courtiers. Martial claims that encomia no longer have to feature extravagant flatteries more suitable for the Parthian monarchy.

Flatteries, you are coming to me for no reason. You have rubbed away your lips, you wretched things! I'm not going to say 'Lord and God'. You no longer have a place in Rome; go far off to the turbaned Parthians! You wretched, humble suppliants, kiss those gaudy kings' feet. There is no 'Lord' here, but an Emperor, the most just senator of all. He has brought back rustic, dry-haired Truth from the Styx's Underworld home. Under this emperor, Rome, you will take care, if you are smart, not to speak the words of the prior regime.

3.23 Hadrian's interactions with literary men

The emperor Hadrian travelled frequently throughout the empire with numerous literary figures, including Suetonius and Arrian. Several of the anecdotes regarding Hadrian's relationships with sophists feature elements of the remarkable career of the philosopher and rhetorician Favorinus (*PIR*^{2} F 123), a eunuch from Arelate (modern Arles) in Gaul. See Birley 1997 on Hadrian's entourage; for Favorinus, see Eshleman 2012.

(a) *Historia Augusta, Life of Hadrian* 16.8–11

Hadrian was often ready to criticize musicians, tragedians, comedians, grammarians, and rhetoricians. Yet he still honoured all these professionals and made them rich, even as he constantly harassed them with questions. And though he made many of them leave his court upset, he would say he took it badly to see anyone upset. He included the philosophers Epictetus and Heliodorus among his close friends (*in summa familiaritate*), as well as grammarians, rhetoricians, musicians, geometricians, painters, and astrologers – I cannot mention them all by name. Many people say that Favorinus was pre-eminent among them. He gave teachers who appeared unfit for their profession riches and honours, and then fired them.

(b) Philostratus, *Lives of the Sophists* 489–90 (excerpts)

Though Favorinus had an argument with the emperor Hadrian, he suffered no harm. And so he used to riddle like an oracle that there were these three paradoxes in his life:

a)   though he was a Gaul, he led a Hellenic life;
b)   though he was a eunuch, he had been charged with adultery; and
c)   he had argued with an emperor and yet lived.

Hadrian should be praised for this last instance, since, though he was emperor, he argued as if from a position of equality with a man he could have put to death.
   (Hadrian announces his intention to vote against Favorinus' bid for immunity from public service.)
   Now the emperor was doing this as a form of entertainment, for he attended to sophists and philosophers to divert his mind from affairs of state. This matter seemed outrageous to the Athenians, however. They ran together, especially the magistrates, to throw down Favorinus' bronze statue as if the man were the emperor's bitterest enemy.[1]

1 For other cases of the same phenomenon, see **5.5, 9, 19**.

3.24 The cultural activities of Marcus Aurelius – and their consequences

Cassius Dio 72(71).35.1 (Xiph.; *EV*)

Marcus Aurelius was a lifelong student of Stoic philosophy, which resulted in his book *Meditations*. As Dio's passage below and numerous letters of Fronto attest, however, he also received an education in rhetoric from Fronto; see Fleury (2006) and Champlin (1980) for discussion. The historian Cassius Dio, writing in the subsequent century, reported the assumption made by Marcus' contemporaries that appearing to conform to his cultural programme might bring material rewards.

Marcus had studied both rhetoric and philosophical argument, and his education helped him greatly. Cornelius Fronto and Claudius Herodes[1] had been his rhetoric teachers, and Iunius Rusticus and Apollonius of Nicomedia, both of whom professed Zeno's doctrines, taught him philosophy.[2] As a result, many people pretended to study philosophy in hope that he might make them rich.

1 L. Vibullius Hipparchus Ti. Claudius Atticus Herodes (*PIR*² C 802).
2 Q. Iunius Rusticus (*PIR*² I 814) and Apollonius (*PIR*² A 929) were both adherents of Stoicism, which was founded by Zeno of Citium (c. 335–262 BC).

3.25 Galen and Marcus Aurelius

Galen, *On my own Books* 3.4–8 (= ed. Kühn 1821–8: 19.18–20)

Galen of Pergamum (129–216; *PIR*² G 24) wrote dozens of medical and philosophical treatises in Greek, though many survive now only in Arabic translation. His work became the centre of the medieval medical curriculum. This anecdote takes place shortly after the outbreak of plague at Rome in 169, when Galen was recalled to Rome to serve as physician to Marcus' heir Commodus. Galen would continue in the role of court physician during the reigns of Commodus and Septimius Severus. For Galen's multiple roles as court physician, philosopher, and medical researcher, see Mattern 2008. This anecdote shows the author asserting his independence from the emperor, in the familiar tradition of the *recusatio*. It also demonstrates how imperial patronage could provide the financial stability that permitted a writer to embark on literary projects.

Afterwards Marcus Aurelius concerned himself with the expedition against the Germans.[1] He contrived beyond everything to lead me away with him. But he was persuaded to release me, having heard from me that my ancestral god Asclepius[2] was ordering the opposite. I had declared myself Asclepius' servant from the time when I had a deadly abscess and he saved me. Marcus respected the god and ordered me to await his return, for he expected to succeed swiftly in the war. He set out, leaving behind his son Commodus, who was still quite a young boy. He commanded Commodus' caregivers to try to keep him healthy and to call on me to attend him if he were to become ill.

During this time I collected and brought into a stable condition both the matters I had learned from my teachers and those I had discovered myself. Still investigating certain questions which I had concerning their discovery, I wrote much, devoting myself to many medical and philosophical problems. Most of these were destroyed in the great fire in which the Temple of Peace and many other buildings burned down.[3] And as Marcus lingered on his journey against all hope, that whole time provided to me the most worthy study, so that I completed my work *On the Usefulness of Parts* in seventeen books and I added the remaining matters to the work *On the Teachings of Hippocrates and Plato.*

1 Marcus Aurelius spent much of his reign campaigning against the Marcomanni, a Germanic people living north of the Danube.
2 The Greek god of healing.
3 The fire took place in 191.

3.26 Literary patronage at the court of Septimius Severus

As was the case under earlier emperors, the court of Septimius Severus was an environment that stimulated literary production. The following passages demonstrate various ways in which this could occur. The emperor (and also his wife) could encourage writers to produce particular literary works (**3.26 [a, d]**) – the prospect of further imperial favour serving to concentrate such writers' minds. Philostratus (**3.26 [d]**) also hints that Severus' wife, Julia Domna, was the centre of some kind of intellectual circle interested in rhetoric, and according to Cassius Dio she studied philosophy and spent considerable time with sophists: Dio Cass. 76(75).15.7 (Xiph; *EV*; Suid.); see too Bowersock 1969: 101–9; Levick 2007: 107–23. The figure of P. Aelius Antipater (*PIR*[2] A 137) also represents a Severan case of a well-established phenomenon: men of literary and rhetorical talent being appointed as imperial secretaries: see Bowersock 1969: 50–8; Millar 1992: 83–101. In Antipater's case, being given the highly paid position of *ab epistulis Graecis* (and also that of tutor of Severus' sons: Philostr. *V S* 607; *IEphesos* 2026 [= *Greek Constitutions* 244 l. 16]) apparently allowed him enough spare time to also compose orations and write history: **3.26 (b)**. As with literary figures and their patrons in earlier periods of Roman history, the relationship between Antipater and his imperial paymasters was conceptualized as one of *amicitia*: **3.26 (c)**.

(a) Cassius Dio 73(72).23.1–4 (Xiph.)

Afterwards wars and massive revolts occurred,[1] and I wrote an account of them for this reason. I had written and published a certain book about the dreams and portents through which Septimius Severus had hoped to become emperor. After he read the copy I sent him, he replied with much praise for my work. I received his letter towards nightfall, and soon went to sleep. In my dream, the Divine Power commanded me to write history. And so I wrote the work that I am now engaged upon. And since my work pleased others and especially Severus himself, I aspired next to set down everything else that pertained to the Romans.

1 Septimius Severus came to power as the result of a war between numerous claimants to the throne after the death of Pertinax, the short-lived successor to Commodus.

(b) Philostratus, *Lives of the Sophists* 607

Philostratus' anecdote regarding P. Aelius Antipater from Hierapolis (modern Pamukkale, Turkey) is characteristic of his accounts of contemporary sophists, which detail both the performance style and literary qualities of each figure.

Though Antipater of Hierapolis was talented in extemporaneous improvisation, he did not neglect written compositions. Rather, he would recite to us Olympic and Panathenaic orations and wrote a history of Septimius Severus' achievements. Severus had appointed him as imperial secretary for correspondence, a job in which he succeeded brilliantly. For my part, let me make clear that, though many people declaimed and wrote history better than this man Antipater, yet no one wrote letters better than he did. Like a brilliant actor of tragedy who knows the repertoire well, his expressions were worthy of the emperor's character.

(c) [Galen], *On Theriac to Piso*, 2 (= ed. Leigh 2016: 72 = Kühn 1821–8: 14.218)

Some modern scholars have doubted that Galen is the author of this work; however, if the author was not Galen, he was still likely a physician at the Severan court: see Leigh 2016: 19–61 for the question of authorship.

The emperors Septimius Severus and Caracalla greatly honoured Antipater, their secretary for Greek letters,[1] because of his personal dignity and rhetorical expertise. When he fell ill with a kidney disease and endured serious and painful suffering, I observed the emperors'[2] praiseworthy love of saving their friends and admirable munificence concerning the medical art.

1 *Ab epistulis Graecis*, for which see Davenport and Kelly, **Vol. 1, 123**.
2 Septimius Severus and Caracalla: Leigh 2016: 18.

(d) Philostratus, *Life of Apollonius of Tyana* 1.3.1

Some relative of Damis brought previously unknown notebooks containing his memoirs to the empress Julia Domna's attention. I was part of the empress' circle, for she praised and encouraged all forms of rhetoric. She commanded me to transcribe Damis' writings and take concern for their literary style. For the writer from Ninos had a clear style, but not a skilful one.

III | Familial Relationships

Many relatives of the emperor automatically became members of his court upon his accession, and remained so unless he took explicit steps to signal their expulsion; see, for example, the fall of Agrippina the Younger: **6.2**. When in favour, their connection with the emperor – whether by blood or marriage – gave them significant power and influence, allowing them to act as power brokers: Saller 1982: 58–66. Imperial relatives often used their wealth and status to act as patrons in their own right, attracting both courtiers and those outside court circles, including provincial communities (**3.27**) and ethnic groups (**3.30**). Epigraphic evidence treats this influence as normal, even expected: **3.29, 32**. The portraits of the imperial family in the literary sources, on the other hand, emphasize their potential for destabilizing, or even destroying, the court. Male relatives could be given official positions in the administration of the empire, but too many potential heirs were believed to spark tension over the succession: **3.28**. Female relatives, like domestic servants (**3.37–43**), were judged to be interlopers, their behaviour criticized in formulaic ways. They were thought to make the perfect head for conspiracies, and in narratives of the court in times of crisis, they loom large. There are many monographs on individual relatives (e.g. Barrett 2002; Levick 2007, 2014; Nadolny 2016); for the role of the imperial family at the court, see Hug, **Vol. 1, Chapter 4**, citing further literature. For royal relatives in other monarchical societies, see especially Duindam 2016: 97–155.

3.27 Livia attempts to intervene with Augustus on behalf of Samos

Reynolds, *Aphrodisias* 13 (= *Greek Constitutions* 1)

Although this inscription reproduces a letter written by Augustus to the people of Samos, it was not found there but rather at Aphrodisias, a city in Asia Minor. The Aphrodisians undoubtedly put the text on public display because it emphasized that they alone (at the time the letter was written) enjoyed the privilege of free status. Livia's influence with her husband certainly had limits – Augustus did not accede to her concerted efforts to win freedom for the Samians – but it is interesting that the emperor appeared to feel that some explanation for why he rejected her request was needed. The date of the document is uncertain, but it must have been produced before 20–19 BC, when the Samians did succeed in winning their freedom; whether Livia continued to plead their case is not known. For discussion see Reynolds 1982: 104–6; Barrett 2002: 198, 331–2; Kunst 2008: 76–7.

Imperator Caesar Augustus, son of the divine Julius, wrote to the Samians underneath their petition.

You yourselves are able to see that I have awarded the privilege of freedom to no people except the Aphrodisians, who were on my side in the war and were made captives because of their goodwill towards us. Indeed, it is not right that the greatest privilege of all should be granted indiscriminately and without cause. I am sympathetic to you and I wish I could oblige my wife, who is active on your behalf, but not to the extent that I abandon my usual practice. For the money which you pay towards the tribute is of no concern to me, yet I am unwilling to give anyone the most valuable privileges without reasonable cause.

3.28 Factional strife at the court of Tiberius

Tacitus, *Annals* 2.43.4–6

According to Tacitus, by AD 17, Tiberius had grown wary of the influence enjoyed by his adopted son, Germanicus, and now wanted to give precedence to his own son, Drusus the Younger. Multiple heirs were assumed to guarantee conflict at the court: for the alleged tension between Tiberius and Augustus' grandsons/adopted sons Gaius and Lucius Caesar, see Suet. *Tib.* 10–11; Dio Cass. 55.9.4–8 (Xiph.; *EV*; cf. Zonar.), 55.10.18–19 (Zonar.; Xiph.).

Some people believed that he[1] was even given secret instructions from Tiberius, and without a doubt the Augusta,[2] driven by feminine rivalry, advised Plancina[3] to harass Agrippina.[4] For rifts and schisms were present in the court (*aula*), with support quietly attached either to Drusus or to Germanicus. Tiberius favoured Drusus, since he was his own, a son of his own blood. As for Germanicus, his estrangement from his uncle had only increased the good will felt for him by everyone else, as did the advantage he held in terms of the renown of his maternal line: he presented Mark Antony as a grandfather and Augustus as a great-uncle. With Drusus, on the other hand, his great-grandfather, the Roman equestrian Pomponius Atticus,[5] seemed to dishonour the ancestral images of the Claudian house. The wife of Germanicus, Agrippina, surpassed Drusus' wife, Livia,[6] in both her fertility and her reputation. But the brothers were remarkably amicable, undisturbed by the squabbles of their relatives.

1 Cn. Calpurnius Piso; here we translate Goodyear's (1981: 327) conjecture of *ei* instead of *et*.
2 Livia.
3 Munatia Plancina (*PIR*[2] M 737).
4 Tacitus repeatedly asserts that Livia loathed Agrippina the Elder; see also *Ann.* 4.12.
5 *RE* 102, Suppl. 8.
6 Livilla.

3.29 The influence of Livia receives official acknowledgement

Senatorial Decree on Gnaeus Piso the Father ll. 109–20

In the autumn of 19, Germanicus died under mysterious circumstances in the east. The following year, Cn. Piso (see above, **3.28**) was charged and brought to trial at Rome; he committed suicide before the trial had ended. His wife, Plancina (see above, **3.28**), was also charged but her close friendship with Livia led to her acquittal. The passage here comes from the lengthy inscription known as the *senatus consultum de Cn. Pisone patre* which preserves the senatorial decree outlining the official version of the trial. The contrast between the acceptance the Senate shows here of Livia's intervention with Tiberius and the criticism found in Tacitus (*Ann.* 3.17–18; cf. Woodman and Martin 1996: 178–93, esp. 179–80) is stark. Plancina escaped judgement, but only temporarily: after Livia's death in 29 Tiberius reinstated the charges against her. She committed suicide in 33. For discussion of and commentary on this section of the decree, see Caballos Rufino, Eck, and Fernández Gómez 1996: 193–6; Eck, Caballos Rufino, and Fernández Gómez 1996: 228–30; Griffin 1997: 256–61;

Potter 1998: 448–9. The decree is syntactically very complex; the layout below is designed to help the reader follow the translation – it does not reflect the physical layout of the Latin text on the inscription.

Regarding the case of Plancina, against whom a great many very serious charges had been laid:

> since she conceded that she placed all hope in the mercy of our emperor and of the Senate;

> and (since) our emperor often and carefully has asked this order that the Senate be satisfied with the punishment of Cn. Piso the father and spare his wife as well as his son Marcus;[1]

> and (since the emperor) interceded on behalf of Plancina at the request of his mother, and, as to why his mother wished to obtain this result, she gave him most excellent reasons,

the Senate decided that both

> Julia Augusta[2], who was most worthy of the state not only because she gave birth to our emperor but also because of her many and not insignificant favours towards men of each order – although she, by right and by merit, ought to possess the greatest influence in the things which she asked of the Senate, she made very sparing use of it,

> and our emperor's great respect for his mother

should be supported and indulged,
and that it was pleased to forgive Plancina's punishment.

1 *PIR*[2] C 293.
2 Livia.

3.30 Poppaea acts as a broker for Josephus

Josephus, *Life* 16

The historian Josephus claims that in 62 Poppaea Sabina, Nero's second wife, interceded on behalf of the Jews: Joseph. *AJ* 20.189–96. The anecdote below, set in either 63 or 64, alleges she interceded a second time. Josephus' identification of Poppaea as *theosebēs* ('God-fearing' or 'religious') (*AJ* 20.195) has fuelled much scholarly speculation about her relationship to Judaism; for discussion see Williams 1988: esp. 99–101; Baughman 2014; Dolansky, **Vol. 1, 401–2**. Poppaea's alleged actions, however, do not look unusual when compared with the actions of imperial women in other reigns; the Jewish delegations could have been amongst the groups who successfully used the women's access to and influence with the emperors to achieve their goals.

Having come safely to Dicaearchia, which the Italians call Puteoli, I met Aliturus through a friend; he was a mime-actor, very dear to Nero's heart, and of Jewish ancestry. Through him I became acquainted with Poppaea, the wife of Caesar, and then took care of things very quickly, beseeching her to release the priests. Having obtained substantial gifts from Poppaea in addition to this favour, I returned home.

3.31 Pliny's praise for harmony within the imperial family

Pliny the Younger, *Panegyric* 84.2–4

In the following passage, Pliny the Younger heaps praise on Trajan's wife (Pompeia Plotina) and sister (Ulpia Marciana, PIR^2 V 877) for the harmonious nature of their relationship. Pliny's very public portrait of feminine domestic tranquillity contrasts with the assumption found in most literary sources that the female relatives of the emperor were destabilizing factors at the court, prone to bitter rivalries and factional infighting: e.g. Tac. *Ann.* 2.43.4 (= **3.28**), 4.40.3; Dio Cass. 60.8.4–5, 18.4; Hdn. 1.8.3–4, 6.1.9–10; cf. Hug, **Vol. 1, 79–80**.

Nothing is so inclined to foster animosity, particularly between women, as rivalry. Further, it especially springs from close association, it is nourished by equal rank and inflamed by jealousy, until it ends in hatred. Indeed, it has to be judged all the more laudable, the fact that there is no competition, no dispute between two women who are equals living in one house. They look up to each other, they give precedence to each other, and, since each of them loves you most abundantly, they think it makes no difference which of them you love more.

3.32 Plotina intervenes with Hadrian on behalf of the Epicurean school at Athens

Greek Constitutions 73 (= *AE* 1891.20 = *IG* 2^2.1099 = *CIL* 3.12283 = Smallwood 1966: doc. 442, cf. *ILS* 7784 [ll. 1–17 only]; *Syll*^{3} 834 [ll.17–39 only])

This inscription from Athens neatly illustrates the ability of the women of the imperial family to act as intermediaries between the emperor and those outside court circles. The head of the philosophical school of Epicurus at Athens enlisted Plotina's aid in appealing to Hadrian to revise the regulations concerning the selection of his successor. Three parts of the exchange have been preserved: Plotina's original request to Hadrian (written in Latin), Hadrian's reply (an imperial rescript, also in Latin), and Plotina's jubilant response to the school of Epicurus at Athens (written in Greek). For discussion, see Oliver, *Greek Constitutions*, pp. 178–80.

In the consulship of [M. Annius Verus for the second time and Cn. A]rrius Augur.[1]

From Plotina Augusta.
[The extent of my fondness] for the sect of Epicurus[2] you know very well, lord. His school needs help from you. [At the moment, because] a successor may only be chosen from those who are Roman citizens, [the ability] to choose is restricted. Therefore, [I ask] in the name of Popillius Theotimus, who is currently the successor[3] at Athens, that you permit him both to make a

testament in Greek[4] concerning that part of his decisions which pertains to the management of the succession, and to select as his successor someone of peregrine status,[5] if the experience of that person should recommend it. (I ask) also that thereafter the future successors of the sect of Epicurus enjoy the same rights that are granted to Theotimus, all the more so because, whenever a mistake has been made by the testator concerning the election of a successor, it is standard practice that the best candidate is selected by the members of the same sect at a general meeting. This will be made easier if the candidate is chosen from a larger pool.

Imperator Caesar Trajan Hadrian Augustus to Popillius Theotimus: I grant permission to make a testament in Greek about those matters which pertain to the successor of the sect of Epicurus. And since he will more easily choose a successor, if he possesses the ability to name a successor also from those who are not Roman citizens, I grant this as well. And thereafter, all the rest who become successors will be permitted to transfer this right to either a peregrine or a Roman citizen.

Plotina Augusta sends greetings to all the friends.

We now possess what we were eagerly seeking to obtain. For it has been granted to any successor who leads the school of Epicurus at Athens in the future both to make all dispositions connected with the administration of the succession in a Greek testament and to choose whomever he likes, either a Greek or a Roman, as the new head of the school. An excellent permission has been granted, and for its value we owe a debt of gratitude to him who is truly the benefactor and supervisor of all culture and therefore the most venerable emperor, most dear to me in every way, as an exceptional ruler and as an admirable son. It is therefore fitting for each man entrusted with the decision about the leadership (of the school) always to try and appoint the best of his fellow Epicureans as his successor and give more weight to the views of the whole school than to his private intimacy with certain people. *(Plotina then continues in the same vein, giving detailed advice about the process of selecting new heads for the school.)*

1 AD 121.
2 Epicurus was a Greek philosopher who lived during the late fourth and early third century BC; the philosophical school he founded in Athens was known as 'The Garden'.
3 I.e. the head of the school, who was considered Epicurus' successor.
4 Instead of a Roman will written in Latin.
5 Someone who was not a Roman citizen.

3.33 Pertinax tries to keep his family out of the limelight

Cassius Dio 74(73).7 (Xiph.)

On 1 January AD 193, after the assassination of Commodus (cf. **6.4**), the urban prefect P. Helvius Pertinax was acclaimed emperor. The passage below suggests Pertinax knew accepting the proposed honours for his family would put them in danger if his reign was short-lived. In this he appears remarkably prescient, for he was killed only eighty-six days after he first became emperor. His efforts to protect his family, however, appear to have been only partially successful. The *Historia Augusta* reports that his wife did outlive him (SHA *Pert.* 13.7) but that his son was later killed by Caracalla, precisely because he was the son of an emperor (SHA *M. Ant.* 4.8, *Geta* 6.7–8; cf. Hdn. 4.6.3).

Pertinax then appointed as urban prefect his father-in-law, Flavius Sulpicianus,[1] a man certainly worthy of the office. But he would not name his wife[2] Augusta or his son[3] Caesar, even though we (the Senate) voted in favour; instead, he vigorously refused each honour,[4] either because he had not yet firmly established his own rule or because he did not wish for his licentious spouse[5] to besmirch the name of Augusta or for his son, who was still a child, to be corrupted by the pretension and the expectation of such a name before he had completed his education. He would not even raise him in the palace (*palation*), but on the first day of his reign he straightaway put aside everything which had belonged to him previously and divided it between his children – he also had a daughter[6] – and ordered them to live with their grandfather.[7] Occasionally he would come to meet them, but as their father and not as the emperor.

1 T. Flavius Claudius Sulpicianus (*PIR²* F 373).
2 Flavia Titiana (*PIR²* F 444).
3 Also named P. Helvius Pertinax (*PIR²* H 74).
4 One inscription from Divodurum Mediomatricum in Gallia Belgica (modern Metz, France) does name his wife Augusta and his son Caesar, but this could have been an assumption on the part of the community that Pertinax would follow precedent and accept the proffered titles: *CIL* 13.4323 (= *ILS* 410).
5 Accusing the emperor's wife of adultery was a common literary trope (see Hug, **Vol. 1, 71 n. 63**).
6 Her name is not known.
7 Sulpicianus; cf. Hdn. 2.4.9.

3.34 Julia Domna's influence during the reign of Caracalla

Greek Constitutions 265 (= *AE* 1966.430 = *IEphesos* 2.212)

This passage forms part of an inscription from Ephesus which refers to Caracalla's grant to the city of a third title of *neokoros* – meaning 'temple-keeper' or 'temple-warden', an official designation for a Greek city which housed a provincial temple for the cult of the emperor: Burrell 2004: 5. This section illustrates the difficulties in assessing the influence of imperial women. Julia Domna's name appears before that of Caracalla, and she addresses the Ephesians directly. This might suggest that they had originally sent their petition directly to her, that she had handled the correspondence even though it was addressed to her son – Cassius Dio claims that Caracalla put her in charge of petitions and his correspondence in both languages (78[77]18.2 [Xiph.]) – or just that she actively advocated on their behalf (like Livia did for Samos; see above, **3.27**). Ultimately, however, it was the emperor's decision; the degree of Julia Domna's involvement remains obscure. For discussion see Robert 1967: 44–64; Burrell 2004: 70–4; Levick 2007: 96; Bertolazzi 2015: 422.

Julia Augusta to the Ephesians. I join in the prayers of all cities and all peoples to receive [benefactions] from my sweetest son, the emperor, and those of your city above all because of [its stature], its beauty, and its remaining gifts, and because it is a [school] for those who [come] from all over [to its] seat of learning.[1]

(The constitution of Caracalla then follows)

1 For ἐργαστήριον as 'school' or 'seat of learning', see Lifschitz 1970: 57–60.

3.35 The persistent power of Victoria, mother of the Gallic emperor Victorinus

Aurelius Victor, *On the Caesars* 33.14

From AD 260–74 men who called themselves emperors ruled the breakaway Gallic Empire, which at its peak controlled Britannia and Hispania, as well as the Gallic and German provinces; see Drinkwater 1987. Although deemed usurpers at Rome, these emperors behaved much like their central counterparts, naming imperial capitals, minting coins, and adopting imperial trappings, like the praetorian guard. The *Historia Augusta* claims Victoria also received the official titles of *mater castrorum* and *Augusta*, and minted her own coins: SHA *Tyr. Trig.* 6.3, 7.1, 31.1–4.

Meanwhile Victoria,[1] after the loss of her son Victorinus,[2] secured the approval of the legions thanks to a considerable sum of money and made Tetricus[3] emperor.

1 *PIR*[2] V 626. Victoria, unusually, is presented as supporting a man who is not related to her. Compare with Didius Iulianus, who became emperor in 193 by bribing the praetorians (Dio Cass. 74[73].11 [Xiph.; *EV*]; Hdn. 2.6.7; SHA *Did. Iul.* 2.6–7) and Maesa, who allegedly used her own money to convince the legions to support her grandson Elagabalus against Macrinus in 218 (Hdn. 5.3.11, 5.4.1; SHA *Macr.* 9.5).
2 *PIR*[2] P 401. He died in 271.
3 *PIR*[2] E 99.

3.36 Maximinus propositions Valeria, wife of the late emperor Galerius

Lactantius, *On the Deaths of the Persecutors* 39

When Galerius, the Augustus for the eastern half of the empire, died in 311, he was said to have given over his wife, Galeria Valeria (*PLRE* 1.937), to Licinius, the Augustus in the west, for protection: Lact. *De mort. pers.* 35. Valeria, herself the daughter of Diocletian, instead took refuge with Galerius' own Caesar, Maximinus Daza (or Daia), who was married; Licinius was not. Lactantius presents this as the main reason behind Valeria's actions, alluding to her awareness of the prize she offered any new husband – legitimate imperial authority by virtue of her status as the widow of one emperor and the daughter of another; cf. Suet. *Otho* 10.2 on Otho's plan to marry Statilia Messalina (*PIR*[2] S 866), the widow of Nero.

Indeed, once Maximinus had made up a new rule to suit his own wantonness – that whatever he wanted should be considered morally right – he could not even restrain himself from pursuing the Augusta, whom he had just recently addressed as mother.[1] Valeria had come to him after the death of Galerius, believing that she could stay more safely in Maximinus' part of the empire, especially because he had a wife. But that contemptible brute straight away burned with desire. The woman was still wearing black clothes, as the time for mourning was not yet ended. He sent messengers to her demanding marriage; he said he would put away his wife if he succeeded with his proposal. She responded frankly as only she could do:[2] first, she was not able to think upon marriage while she wore mourning clothes and while the ashes of her husband, his father, were still warm; next, he was acting impiously by proposing to divorce a faithful wife; undoubtedly he would do the same to her; finally, it would be immoral, without custom, and without precedent, for a woman of her name and rank to take a second husband.[3] This bold answer was reported to the man. His lust was changed into anger and fury. At once he outlawed the woman, seized her property, removed her attendants, tortured her eunuchs to death, and sent both her and her mother[4] into exile, but not to any fixed location. Rather, he toyed with them, driving them out from this place and that place, and he condemned the women who were her friends (*amicae*) on trumped up charges of adultery.

1 Maximinus was adopted by Galerius in 305.
2 Note the suggestion that only Valeria, with the ingrained authority of her position, could speak to the emperor in this manner.
3 Some scholars (e.g. Creed 1984: 116) have seen this reluctance to remarry as a reflection of a Christian viewpoint. The emphasis on her 'name and rank' (*nomen ac locus*) suggests there is more to it than this.
4 Prisca (*PLRE* 1.726), the wife of Diocletian. She must have accompanied her daughter when Valeria sought refuge at Maximinus' court.

IV | Other Relationships of Influence and Power

a. Domestic Workers

From the beginning of the Principate slaves and freedmen surrounded the emperor, both as domestic servants and as office holders in the emerging imperial bureaucracy. The emperor's household differed from those of wealthy aristocrats both in terms of scale – there are numerous job descriptions not attested anywhere else – and in the potential for social mobility; for job titles, see Edmondson, **Vol. 1, 170–87**; Treggiari 1975; Winterling 1999: 93–107. Although a very few positions in the imperial bureaucracy could reasonably be identified as 'court offices', for the vast majority, membership in the *familia Caesaris* did not automatically mean access to the court; see Davenport and Kelly, **Vol. 1, Chapter 6**. For imperial slaves and freedmen who did become courtiers, however, influence with, and control over access to, the emperor made them into power brokers, and the opportunities for self-enrichment were numerous. The influence these low-status individuals could wield did not sit well with the senatorial authors of the literary sources; the resulting narratives are universally critical. With a few exceptions, the servants who are imagined as possessing the greatest influence with the emperor are domestics, particularly the emperor's chief bedroom attendant (*a cubiculo*), whose duties guaranteed frequent, close contact with the monarch: see below, **3.41**, **51**; cf. Michiels 1902; Boulvert 1970: 241–7. For the *familia Caesaris*, Weaver 1972 remains indispensable. For the political and administrative roles of imperial slaves and freedmen, see Boulvert 1970: esp. 23–35, 1974; Millar 1992: 69–83.

3.37 Caligula and Helicon

Philo, *Embassy to Gaius* 168, 171–3, 175, 178 (excerpts)

Early in the reign of Caligula, the Greek-speaking Jewish philosopher Philo was appointed the leader of an embassy to Rome after extensive conflict between the Greek and Jewish communities in his native city of Alexandria (for his account of the conflict, see *In Flacc.* 41–96; cf. Joseph. *AJ* 18.257–60). At court, Philo's diplomatic efforts reportedly made little headway: he emphasizes their repeated failure to get and hold Caligula's attention: Philo *Leg.* 181, 185–94, 349–73 (= **4.19**). Philo's efforts to achieve his goals using less official channels were equally frustrated: many of Caligula's household slaves, he claims, were 'Egyptians', by which Philo means Alexandrian Greeks, who he feels were predisposed to hate the Jews: *Leg.* 165–6. But the largest thorn in his side, by far, was their leader, Helicon (*PIR*[2] H 49), whose outsized influence with Caligula meant Philo's mission could not succeed without his support. According to Philo, Helicon was a bit player at Tiberius' court, since the dour emperor did not approve of his comportment: *Leg.* 167. But after the death of Tiberius, everything changed.

When Tiberius died and Gaius (Caligula) succeeded him as emperor, Helicon, attending a new master who was sliding into indulgence and licentiousness in all his senses, said to himself, 'Now's your moment, Helicon! Wake up! You have the best possible audience for your show!' … *(Philo then imagines Helicon's self-congratulatory checklist of his own talents.)*

Stirred up by these absurd and accursed arguments and pulling himself together, he stuck close to Gaius and treated him with honour, never leaving his side whether day or night, but shadowing him everywhere so that he might use his periods of solitude and of rest to make accusations against our people[1] …

It is said that the Alexandrian ambassadors[2] knew this[3] well and had secretly bribed him at considerable expense, not just with money but also with the expectation of honours which, they implied, they would procure for him in the near-future, when Gaius came to Alexandria. Helicon promised them everything, dreaming of that time when he would be honoured by the greatest and most esteemed city,[4] in the presence of his lord and practically the whole world with him. For there was no doubt that, in order to pay homage to Gaius, the most eminent people – the leading lights of their cities – would come together, setting out from all corners of the world. . . .

For he played ball with him, exercised with him, bathed with him, breakfasted and lunched with him, and, when Gaius went to go to bed, he was there, for he had been appointed to the posts of bedroom attendant (*katakoimistēs*) and chief of the bodyguards (*archisōmatophylax*) belonging to his household – a rank which had never been granted to anyone else – with the result that he alone had the emperor's ear when he was relaxing or resting, free of external distractions and able to listen to what he most wanted. . . .

So we were helpless and at a loss when, although we had left no stone unturned in order to conciliate Helicon, we found no way to achieve this. No one dared to speak to or approach him, because of the arrogance and rudeness which he inflicted on everyone and, at the same time, because we did not know whether there was some personal animosity towards the Jewish people which led to him forever inciting his lord and schooling him in hatred against our race.

1 The Jews.
2 The Greek delegation, Philo's rivals. Note too the suggestion that Helicon's relationship with Caligula was so familiar that he had access to the emperor even at times when most courtiers would not.
3 That Helicon was pouring poison into Caligula's ear about Philo and the Jews.
4 Note the assumption that Helicon would accompany Caligula on any journey to Egypt.

3.38 The career of C. Stertinius Xenophon

A native of the Greek island of Cos, the freeborn C. Stertinius Xenophon belonged to a prominent family which claimed descent from the god Aesculapius. After gaining Roman citizenship in 23, he entered court circles as Claudius' personal physician: *CIL* 6.8905 (= *ILS* 1841); *Syll.*[3] 806. He (along with Ti. Claudius Balbillus: below, **3.45**) accompanied Claudius to Britain in 43 as military tribune and chief of the engineers (*praefectus fabrum*); both men were honoured in Claudius' triumph the following year with the *hasta pura* (a spear made without iron) and a gold crown. Xenophon later became Claudius' *ad responsa Graeca*, literally his secretary 'for replies written in Greek'; on the meaning of this title, see Millar 1992: 226; cf. Buraselis 2000: 74 n. 43 with further bibliography. Xenophon's influence in court circles, according to Tacitus, led directly to Claudius' decision in 53 to grant Cos immunity: **3.38 (a)**. Many surviving inscriptions from Cos attest to his patronage, prestige, and influence; his personal connections with the emperor are emphasized repeatedly: **3.38 (c)**. Xenophon's influence, however, came at a price: when Claudius died under mysterious circumstances in 54, Xenophon did not escape suspicion: **3.38 (b)**. He likely returned to Cos early in the reign of Nero. For Xenophon's career in Rome and patronage on Cos, see Herzog

1922: 216–47; Sherwin-White 1978: 149–52 and 283–5; Wolters 1999: 51–60; Buraselis 2000: 66–110.

(a) Tacitus, *Annals* 12.61

Next, Claudius proposed to grant immunity to the people of Cos, and he spoke at length on their antiquity. The earliest inhabitants of the island, he said, were either the Argives or Coeus, the father of Latona.[1] Soon after, with the arrival of Aesculapius, the art of healing was introduced, which achieved the greatest fame among his descendants. Here Claudius recounted the names of some individuals and the period in which each one had flourished. And furthermore, he continued, Xenophon, whose expert knowledge he himself made use of, descended from that same family; they should acquiesce to his entreaties by granting that in the future the Coans be free from every kind of tribute and inhabit a sacred island devoted to the service of the god alone. There is no doubt that the many services of those same islanders to the Roman people, as well as the victories in which they had shared, could have been cited. But Claudius did not cover up with any extraneous arguments a favour which he, with his typical indulgence, had granted to one individual.

1 Coeus was a Titan, one of the children of Uranus and Gaia in Greek mythology. His daughter, Latona, known to the Greeks as Leto, was the mother of Artemis and Apollo.

(b) Tacitus, *Annals* 12.67

The whole affair soon became so notorious that contemporary writers have recorded that the poison was drizzled on a particularly choice mushroom, although the potency of the drug was not noticed immediately, either from carelessness or because Claudius was drunk. At the same time, a bowel movement appeared to have remedied the issue. Then Agrippina was terrified and, seeing that the most extreme penalties were to be feared, she defied the ill-will attached to immediate actions and called upon the complicity of the doctor Xenophon, which she had already secured. While appearing to assist the emperor's efforts to vomit, Xenophon, it is believed, pushed a feather, smeared with a swift-acting poison, down his throat. He was not at all unaware that the greatest crimes are begun with danger but are finished with profit.

(c) *Sylloge Inscriptionum Graecarum*[3] 804 (= *ICos* 345 = *IGR* 4.1086): Greek inscription from Cos; Reign of Nero

[. . . C. Stertinius] Xenophon, son of Heracleitus, (of the tribe) Cornelia, Chief Physician of the gods Augusti and secretary for responses written in Greek,[1] former military tribune,[2] former Chief of Engineers[3] and decorated in the triumph [over] the Britons with a gold crown and a spear, [son] of the People, [devoted to Nero,][4] devoted to the emperor, devoted to Augustus, devoted to Rome, devoted to his country, benefactor of the fatherland, high priest of the gods and priest for [life] of the Augusti, Asclepius, Hygia, and

Epione.[5] When M. Septicius Rufus, [son] of Marcus, and Ariston, son of Philocles, both devoted to the emperor, were temple-treasurers.

1 Cf. Maiuri 1925: no. 475 l. 4–5.
2 I.e. *tribunus militum* (Gr. χιλιάρχης).
3 I.e. *praefectus fabrum* (Gr. ἔπαρχος τῶν ἀρχιτεκτόνων). The duties involved were not necessarily related to engineering by this era.
4 The identification of Xenophon as 'devoted to Nero' has been erased (also in *AE* 1934.93), likely a reaction to the *damnatio memoriae*. Inscriptions dating from before the reign of Nero name Xenophon *philoklaudios* ('devoted to Claudius'). Identifying Xenophon as 'devoted to the emperor', 'devoted to Claudius', 'devoted to Augustus' forms part of the standard text of the dedications to the 'paternal gods' (*patroioi theoi*) for Xenophon's health found on Cos (fifty-eight are collected in Buraselis 2000: 158–9, with discussion at 101–7).
5 A further eleven priesthoods held by Xenophon in Cos are attested in Maiuri 1925, no. 475, l. 6ff.; cf. Sherwin-White 1978: 150 n. 365; Buraselis 2000: 98–9.

3.39 Epaphroditus in a brokerage role

Arrian, *The Discourses of Epictetus* 1.26.11–12

This anecdote is generally taken to refer to the Epaphroditus (*PIR*[2] E 69) who served as Nero's secretary for petitions (*a libellis*): Millar 1992: 78, 298; Weaver 1994: 476–7. It shows how a powerful freedman of the imperial court was in a position to intercede with the emperor on behalf of a senator whose fortune was dwindling: cf. Millar 1965: 144.

I know a certain man who howled as he clasped the knees of Epaphroditus and swore that he was in distress, for he had nothing left but a million and a half.[1] What, therefore, did Epaphroditus do? Did he laugh at him just as you are laughing? No, but he said in amazement, 'Poor man, how, then, did you keep silence? How did you bear it?'

1 The man was in danger of losing his senatorial status (which required a minimum of 1 million sesterces), and he hoped that Nero could be prevailed upon to provide a subvention. The literary sources do record such actions by Nero: Suet. *Ner.* 10; Tac. *Ann.* 13.34.

3.40 The story of Felicio, the emperor's cobbler

Arrian, *The Discourses of Epictetus* 1.19.16–22

In this anecdote, Epictetus, in spite of his own freedman status, reflects the aristocratic distaste for imperial slaves and freedmen whose proximity to the emperor gave them outsized power; for the status dissonance of imperial freedmen, see Roller 2001: 264–72. He highlights the particular authority enjoyed by the bedroom attendant (*koitōnitēs* = *cubicularius*) and even by lowly servants like shoemakers who had somehow gained the emperor's ear. On the question of the identity of 'Epaphroditus' and 'Felicio' in this passage, see Weaver 1994: 472–3.

Whenever people hold bizarre opinions about things that they cannot control, considering them good or evil, it necessarily follows that they will pay court to tyrants. Would that it were only tyrants, and not their bedroom attendants (*koitōnitēs*) too! How does a man instantaneously develop wisdom once

Caesar puts him in charge of his piss-pot? Why do we immediately say, 'Felicio has spoken to me wisely'? I wish he were thrown down from his shit-heap, that you may once more think him foolish. Epaphroditus owned a certain shoemaker, whom he sold because he was useless. Then, as luck would have it, he was bought by someone from Caesar's household, and became Caesar's shoemaker. You should have seen how Epaphroditus lauded him! 'How goes it with the worthy Felicio, pray?' Then, if one of us inquired,[1] 'What is he up to?', he was told, 'He is deliberating with Felicio about something.' Yes, but had he not sold him because he was useless? Who, then, had suddenly made him wise? This is what it is to honour something outside that which is under our control.

1 I.e. another member of the household of Epaphroditus.

3.41 An imperial servant's successful career

Année épigraphique 1972.574 (= *IEphesos* 3.852 = *SEG* 30.1308 = *IK* 59.122), Ephesus, early second century AD

This bilingual inscription from Ephesus in Asia Minor describes the career path of Ti. Claudius Classicus, an imperial freedman whose service spanned the reigns of four emperors. The absence of any formal employment under Domitian is notable and suggests either that he fell out of favour, able to return to court circles only after the accession of Nerva, or that it was judged prudent to pass over his positions during that reign. Some scholars (e.g. Weaver 1980: 151–6; Boulvert 1981) believed he achieved equestrian status under Trajan, but others have suggested he remained an imperial freedman (Bruun 1990, with further bibliography). We translate the Latin portion of the inscription below; the account of Classicus' career given in the Greek portion of the inscription is substantially identical.

For Ti. Claudius Classicus, freedman of the Augustus, chief bedroom attendant[1] and procurator of the household[2] of the deified Titus, procurator of entertainments[3] of the deified Nerva, procurator of entertainments and the morning school[4] and procurator of Alexandria[5] of the emperor Nerva Trajan Caesar Augustus Germanicus Dacicus. C. Iulius Photinus Celer, assistant in the procuratorship of Alexandria, (set this up) because he deserved it.

1 *A cubiculo.*
2 *Procurator castrensis*; see Edmondson, **Vol. 1, 172**.
3 *Procurator a voluptatibus* (or *voluptatum*); see Edmondson, **Vol. 1, 179**.
4 The Ludus Matutinus was one of four gladiatorial schools built by Domitian. It was responsible for training the *venatores* (wild-beast hunters) for the arena. The wild-beast hunts took place early in the daily programme, hence the school's name (*matutinus* = morning): Dunkle 2014: 389.
5 *Alexandriae* is frequently used in inscriptions as a synonym for *in Aegypto* ('in Egypt'), and does not necessarily mean the position's responsibility was confined to the city of Alexandria: Bruun 1990: 276.

3.42 Castor: the fall of a favourite

Regime changes could be dangerous for courtiers, as this tale of the imperial freedman Castor (*PIR*² C 537) illustrates (for other examples, see above, **3.14**, and Edmondson, **Vol. 1, 198–200**). It is perhaps an indictment of Caracalla that Castor's influence with Septimius Severus is judged to be exemplary. Had Caracalla not been a 'bad' emperor – and thus required to be the villain – Dio's assessment of Castor, and his holding of two influential positions, might not have been so positive. The context of the first passage suggests Caracalla resented Castor's influence, but, unlike with the praetorian prefect Plautianus, could not expel Castor from the court while his father still reigned; for Caracalla's alleged role in the fall of Plautianus see Dio. Cass. 77.2–4; Hdn. 3.12.

(a) Cassius Dio 77(76).14.1–2 (Xiph.)

Caracalla astonished Septimius Severus and kept him in a state of never-ending anxiety because his lifestyle was profligate, because he obviously intended to murder his brother, if he could, and, finally, because he plotted against Severus himself. In fact, once he suddenly bolted out of his military quarters shouting and bellowing that he was being wronged by Castor. He was the best man in Severus' household and he had been entrusted with the positions of *a memoria* and bedroom attendant.[1] Then certain soldiers, who had been prepared by Caracalla beforehand, banded together and shouted along with him, but they were subdued shortly thereafter when Severus himself appeared among them and chastised the more disorderly ones.

1 For the secretary *a memoria*, see Davenport and Kelly, **Vol. 1, 130–1**. Castor presumably held the post of *a cubiculo*; on his posts, see Peachin 1989: 172.

(b) Cassius Dio 78(77).1.1 (Xiph.)

After this Caracalla seized total power. According to the law, he ruled with his brother, but in fact, he ruled alone right from the start. He came to terms with the enemy, retreated from their lands, and abandoned the forts.[1] He dismissed some of his own retinue, like Papinianus, who was praetorian prefect;[2] others he put to death, including his tutor Euodus,[3] Castor, and his wife Plautilla and her brother Plautius.[4]

1 In Britain, where Septimius Severus died on 4 February 211. He had been campaigning there with his sons since 208.
2 Aemilius Papinianus (*PIR*² A 388), a jurist who became praetorian prefect after the fall of Plautianus in 205. His dismissal took place in 211; the *Historia Augusta* reports that Caracalla had him executed the following year: SHA *M. Ant.* 8, *Sev.* 21.8.
3 *PIR*² E 117. An imperial freedman. Dio states as a first-hand witness that the Senate intended to honour Euodus for his role in the fall of Plautianus, but Septimius Severus overruled their decision, considering an imperial freedman to be too low-ranking to deserve such accolades: Dio Cass. 77.6.1.
4 *PIR*² F 555, 564. The children of Plautianus, originally only exiled after their father's execution: Dio Cass. 77.6.3.

3.43 Eunuchs at the court of Diocletian

Lactantius, *On the Deaths of the Persecutors* 15.1–3

One of the key distinctions between the later Roman imperial court and the court during the period covered by this volume is the presence of eunuchs, who became an established power group at the court by the early fourth century; see Tougher (1999) and Sidéris (2000) on eunuchs in the court narratives of Ammianus Marcellinus. Exactly at which point this transition occurred, and why eunuchs became so closely associated with the court, is still a matter of scholarly debate: if a sudden change occurred under Diocletian, as argued by Hopkins (1978: 184, 192–3), it is hard to see how eunuchs could already hold power at his court, as Lactantius here claims. Yet the evidence for powerful eunuchs at court in the mid-third century is mostly found in the *Historia Augusta* (SHA *Alex. Sev.* 23.4–7, 34.3, 45.4–5, 66.3–4; *Gordiani* 23.7, 24.2–5), and could well reflect the late-antique court of the author's own day, rather than the reigns it purports to describe. For eunuchs at the later Roman and Byzantine imperial courts, see Hopkins 1963, slightly revised as 1978: 172–96; Guyot 1980: 130–76; Patterson 1982: 299–333; Stevenson 1995; Tougher 2008: esp. 36–53.

And now Diocletian raged, not only against his household staff, but against everyone. In the first instance, he compelled his daughter Valeria and his wife Prisca to be polluted through a sacrifice.[1] The eunuchs who had once been the most influential, and on whom the palace (*palatium*) and Diocletian himself had previously depended, were killed. Church elders and ministers (*presbyteri ac ministri*) were arrested and, convicted without any trial or confession, were led away along with their entire families. People of every sex and age were seized and carried off to be burned, not individually, because their numbers were so great, but they were encircled with fire in a group. His domestic servants, after millstones had been tied around their necks, were thrown into the sea.

1 Lactantius believed that both women were Christians. For both, see **3.36**.

b. Astrologers

Using the positions of the stars and other heavenly bodies to predict the outcome of human affairs was an accepted part of life at the Roman court. Emperors from Augustus onwards are recorded as consulting astrologers, although astrology's prominence at court waxed and waned depending on each individual ruler's interests. A few emperors, like Hadrian and Septimius Severus, were said to have been proficient practitioners themselves (Hadrian: SHA *Hadr.* 16.7, *Ael.* 3.9; Septimius Severus: SHA *Sev.* 2.8–9, 3.9, *Geta* 2.6; Dio Cass. 77(76).11.1–2 [Xiph.]), although they needed to exercise some caution: emperors who were thought to rely too heavily on astrology and other forms of divination could face criticism. Most men who practised astrology and who came to court remain anonymous figures in our literary sources, but a small number became prominent enough to rightly be considered courtiers. For astrology during the Principate in general see Barton 1994a: esp. 41–9, 1994b, and 1994c; and Potter 1994: 17–20; for astrologers at the court see Dolansky, **Vol. 1, 412–15**. Ripat (2011: 122–3) cautions against the casual use of the term 'court astrologers'.

3.44 Tiberius and Thrasyllus

Cassius Dio 58.27.1–58.28.4

Thrasyllus (*PIR*[2] T 190), a Greek perhaps from Alexandria, first appears in court circles late in the reign of Augustus; Suetonius identifies him as a companion (*comes*) of Tiberius: Suet. *Aug.* 98.4. Thrasyllus likely first encountered Tiberius during the latter's self-imposed exile at Rhodes (6 BC–AD 2). The power imbalance in their relationship is marked by the anecdote, which both Suetonius and Tacitus record, that while at Rhodes Thrasyllus convinced Tiberius of the accuracy of his predictions at the very moment when Tiberius determined to throw Thrasyllus – believing him to be a charlatan – from a high, rocky path into the sea below: Suet. *Tib.* 14.4; Tac. *Ann.* 6.20.2–22. Thrasyllus' close association with Tiberius possibly paid dividends: he was perhaps awarded Roman citizenship (*ISmyrna* 2.1.619, but cf. *PIR*[2] T 190); and on one view, his descendants gained an enduring foothold at court (below, **3.45** and Dolansky, **Vol. 1, 413–14**). Thrasyllus, as the passage shows, remained a close confidant of Tiberius until his death. He enjoyed a prominent position at court, but he was unlikely to have been the only astrologer who had access to the emperor; Juvenal claims that while Tiberius was on Capreae he had a 'swarm' (*grex*) of astrologers around him: Juv. 10.93–4.

Thrasyllus, in fact, died at that time, and Tiberius himself died early in the following spring, when Cn. Proculus and Pontius Nigrinus were consuls.[1] It happened that Macro had been plotting against Domitius and many others, and had fabricated against them charges and evidence collected through torture; but not everyone who had been accused was put to death, thanks to Thrasyllus, who dealt with Tiberius in a very clever way. Indeed, although he named with great precision both the day and the hour at which he himself would die, Thrasyllus falsely asserted that the emperor would live for ten more years, so that Tiberius, since he was thinking he would live for longer, would not be so eager to kill them. And this is what happened, since Tiberius, believing that he would be able to do everything that he wanted to do at his leisure, did not hurry at all; and even when the Senate delayed passing judgement because of the accounts given by the accused which contradicted the testimony collected under torture, he did not become angry. . . .

(A few details about the trials then follow.)

Tiberius died at Misenum[2] before he learned anything about the situation. He had been sick for quite a long time, but since he expected to live thanks to Thrasyllus' prediction, he did not consult his doctors or make changes to his lifestyle. Given he was elderly and his illness was not that grievous, he was fading away little by little, and often he would almost stop breathing, only to rally again. And these fluctuations caused both great pleasure for Caligula and the others, when they believed he was going to die, and great terror, when they believed he was going to live. Finally, Caligula, since he was alarmed at the prospect that Tiberius might actually recover, did not comply with his requests for something to eat, on the grounds that it could harm him, and piled on him many heavy clothes, on the grounds that he needed warmth, and in this way asphyxiated him; Macro was his accomplice in this matter in some way, for he, already while Tiberius was seriously ill, was cultivating the young man, especially since he had led him on into desire for his own wife, Ennia Thrasylla.[3] Tiberius, suspecting this, had said to him once, 'Well done! You have deserted the setting and hurry to the rising sun.'[4]

1 In 36.
2 Modern Miseno.
3 Ennia Thrasylla (*PIR*[2] E 65) was possibly Thrasyllus' granddaughter (but cf. *PIR*[2] T 190).
4 This acknowledgement of the shift in the balance of power at court as courtiers turned their attention from the ruler to his chosen successor is found in Tacitus as well: *Ann.* 6.46.4. Cassius Dio (72[71].34.1 [Xiph.]) also has the dying Marcus Aurelius repeat the quip to a military tribune.

3.45 Nero and Balbillus

Suetonius, *Life of Nero* 36.1

The astrologer Balbillus (*PIR*[2] B 38) has often been taken to be the son of the astrologer Thrasyllus (above, **3.44**). Thrasyllus' son predicted the accession of Nero (Tac. *Ann.* 6.22.4), and it seems probable Balbillus was a valued member of Vespasian's court: Dio Cass. 65(66).9.2 (*EV*). The astrologer Balbillus has often been assumed to have been Ti. Claudius Balbillus (*PIR*[2] C 813), an equestrian who held a series of offices in the imperial civil service (*AE* 1924.78; cf. Faoro 2016), and eventually rose so high as to become the prefect of Egypt from 55 to 59: Bastianini 1975: 273. For the debates regarding the astrologer Balbillus and his family connections, see Dolansky, **Vol. 1, 413–14**, citing further literature; for the parallels between the careers of Ti. Claudius Balbillus and C. Stertinius Xenophon (above, **3.38**), see Buraselis 2000: 68, 70, 73.

A comet had become visible for several nights in a row, something which is believed by the lower orders to foretell destruction for those with the greatest power.[1] Distressed by this matter, since he learned from the astrologer (*astrologus*) Balbillus that kings were accustomed to forestall such omens through the murder of some illustrious subject, and thus divert the omens from themselves onto the heads of the leading men of the state, Nero resolved on the deaths of the noblest men, every one of them. Indeed, this resolution was strengthened and emerged for a more or less just reason after two conspiracies were discovered. The earlier and more serious of the two was that of Piso[2] at Rome; the other was hatched by Vinicius at Beneventum[3] and was exposed there.

1 For comets in the ancient world, see Ramsey 2006: esp. 3–28.
2 C. Calpurnius Piso.
3 This conspiracy is not mentioned in any other literary work. For discussion, see Bradley 1978: 220–1.

3.46 Vespasian and Seleucus

Tacitus, *Histories* 2.78.1

This passage follows a speech by C. Licinius Mucianus (*PIR*² L 216), the governor of Syria, encouraging Vespasian to challenge Vitellius in the civil war which erupted after the death of Nero in 68. On Vespasian's astrologer Seleucus, see *PIR*² S 335, cf. P 1027; Cramer 1954: 132–5.

After Mucianus' speech, the others, emboldened, gathered around Vespasian, urged him on, and recited the predictions of seers (*vates*) and the movements of heavenly bodies. And he was not free from such superstition,[1] for he was the sort of man who, not long after, when he was emperor, openly retained a certain Seleucus, an astrologer (*mathematicus*), as his guide and seer (*praescius*).

1 Vespasian's credulity made him vulnerable to manipulation: Ash 2007: 301–2, with bibliography.

3.47 Caracalla seeks guidance on the future

Herodian 4.12.3–5

Given the very real challenges concerning security at court (on this see Kelly, **Vol. 1, 378–83**), it is not surprising that several emperors are recorded as using astrology to uncover their enemies: Tiberius: Dio Cass. 57.19.3–4 (Xiph.; Zonar.); Nero: Suet. *Ner.* 36.1; Domitian: Dio Cass. 67.15.6 (Xiph.; Zonar.); Septimius Severus: SHA *Sev.* 15.5–6. Sometimes the horoscopes of prominent men identified them as potential challengers; others became targets of imperial wrath by showing too much interest in the horoscope – and the predicted date of death – of the emperor himself. Here, the emperor Caracalla's need to uncover potential plots is depicted as bordering on paranoia.

The following thing now happened, for it was inevitable that the life of Antoninus (Caracalla) had to end. Since he was exceedingly inquisitive, he not only wanted to know everything about other people, but he was also curious about the affairs of gods and spirits. Given he always suspected that everyone was conspiring against him, he made much use of every kind of oracle and summoned from all over seers (*magoi*) and astrologers (*astronomoi*) and diviners (*thytai*).[1] And no one who proffered such chicanery escaped his notice. Suspecting, however, that they were not prophesying the truth to him but were motivated by flattery, he sent a message to a certain Maternianus,[2] whom he had entrusted with all the administration of affairs at Rome and whom he considered to be the most trustworthy of his friends (*philoi*) and the only one privy to his secrets. He ordered him to track down the finest seers and, through a summoning of the dead, to find out about his death and whether anyone had designs on the empire. Maternianus straight away carried out the emperor's orders, and then, either because the spirits really prophesied these things to him or otherwise he was hatching some scheme, he replied to Antoninus that Macrinus was plotting against the empire and it was necessary to get rid of him.

1 Marcus Aurelius includes *thytai* in his list of members of the court of Augustus (above, **1.8** [**g**]); cf. North 1990 for diviners at Rome.
2 Flavius Maternianus (*PIR*[2] F 317).

c. Sexual Partners

Roman emperors, like most Roman men, did not have to confine their sexual experiences to their wives. Although in one sense these 'unofficial' sexual partners could not replace wives – only wives had the ability to produce legitimate children who could become heirs – in almost all other respects they could occupy a similar role at the court. Relationships with servile or low-status individuals did not disrupt Roman cultural *mores*. Some emperors, however, are also depicted engaging in sexual relationships with freeborn (and sometimes married) women and/or boys: e.g. Caligula: Suet. *Calig.* 36; Nero: Suet. *Nero* 28; Commodus: SHA *Comm.* 2.8, 5.4. In these cases, the emperors' behaviour threatened the status of the freeborn Romans. Sex became a way for the emperor to assert his power over his subjects; see Chrol and Blake, **Vol.1, 366–70.**

3.48 Augustus' affairs and Livia's tolerance of them

Suetonius, *Life of Augustus* 69.1, 71.1

It may come as a surprise to see adulterous behaviour assigned to Augustus, who became the 'model' emperor against whom all future monarchs were judged and who famously sponsored legislation targeting adultery (the *lex Iulia de adulteriis* of 18 BC). The passage reminds us that 'good' and 'bad' emperors were often said to have done the same things. Whether their actions met with criticism or approval in the literary sources largely depended on their reputation after their death.

That he indeed engaged in adultery not even his friends deny, although they make excuses that this was committed not out of lust but out of calculation, so that he might more easily discover the plans of his adversaries through their women.[1] Besides his hasty marriage with Livia,[2] Mark Antony[3] reproached him for having led away the wife of a former consul from her husband's dining room – before his very eyes! – into a bedroom, and for bringing her back to the dinner party with her ears pink and her hair dishevelled[4] ... He held on to his lusty character and – so they say – even later in life he was eager to deflower virgins, who were procured for him from all quarters, even by his wife.[5]

1 Cassius Dio implicitly condemned the same behaviour in Sejanus: Dio Cass. 58.3.8 (*EV*).
2 Augustus took Livia away from her husband, Ti. Claudius Nero (*RE* 254), when she was pregnant with Nero's second child: Suet. *Aug.* 62.2.
3 M. Antonius (*RE* 30), Augustus' one-time ally and brother-in-law, later rival for control of the Roman empire. Augustus' defeat of Antony at the Battle of Actium in 30 BC left him as sole ruler.
4 For a similar story about Caligula's sexual predations against aristocratic women during dinner parties, see Suet. *Calig.* 36.2.
5 Dio Cassius (58.2.5 [Xiph.]) has Livia claim that she maintained her influence over Augustus by preserving her own sexual virtue and by turning a blind eye to his various love affairs.

3.49 Acte and Nero

Tacitus, *Annals* 13.13.1

Early in his reign, Nero entered into a relationship with the freedwoman Acte, a relationship which was perceived as threatening the position at court of both his mother, Agrippina the Younger, and his wife, Octavia: [Sen.] *Oct.* 104–5; Dio Cass. 61.7.1 (Xiph.). According to Suetonius (*Ner.* 28.1), Nero bribed ex-consuls to claim Acte was of royal birth in order to make their relationship more palatable. After Nero's death, it was allegedly Acte, along with two of Nero's nurses, who deposited his ashes in his family tomb: Suet. *Ner.* 50. For Acte and her role at the court, see Mastino and Ruggeri 1995; Holztrattner 1995: 133–45; Strong 2016: 80–4; Wellebrouck 2017; Edmondson, **Vol. 1, 196–7**; Chrol and Blake, **Vol. 1, 361–2**.

But Agrippina, like a typical woman, complained loudly about 'her rival the freedwoman', 'her daughter-in-law the slave girl', and so on, and she refused to wait for her son's regret or for his lust to be sated. The viler her rebukes of Acte, the more she incited Nero's passion, until he, spurred by the force of his love, threw off his obedience to his mother and put himself in the hands of Seneca. One of Seneca's friends, Annaeus Serenus,[1] had screened the first passions of the young man by feigning a desire for the same freedwoman, and had made his name available to Nero, so that the gifts which the emperor bestowed on the girl in secret were ostensibly lavished upon her by Serenus.

1 *PIR*² A 618.

3.50 Vespasian's concubine, Caenis

Vespasian's relationship with Caenis was said to have started in the 30s AD. Since she was a freedwoman of Antonia the Younger, this suggests that Vespasian moved in court circles during the reign of Tiberius. Vespasian resumed their relationship after the death of his wife; as emperor he was said to treat Caenis almost like she was in the position of a legal wife: Suet. *Vesp.* 3; cf. Herodian (1.16.3) on Marcia, the concubine of Commodus. Suetonius suggests that Vespasian's son, Domitian, resented Caenis' influence, relaying an anecdote where Domitian refused to accept her kiss of greeting: Suet. *Dom.*

12.3. After Caenis' death, Vespasian took up with other women, but they did not rise to prominence at his court: Suet. *Vesp.* 21; cf. Chrol and Blake, **Vol. 1, 363**. Charles and Anagnostou-Laoutides (2012) examine the portrayal of Vespasian and Caenis' relationship in Suetonius. For a possible identification of a house and baths owned by Caenis, see Frighetto 1977–8. For other imperial concubines, including Marcia, see Strong 2016: 85–93.

(a) Cassius Dio 65(66).14.1–4 (Xiph.)

At this time too, Caenis, the concubine of Vespasian, passed away.[1] I mention her because she was extremely trustworthy and because she had an exceptional memory. Her mistress, Antonia, the mother of Claudius, once secretly dictated to her a letter to Tiberius about Sejanus[2] and then immediately ordered her message to be erased so that no evidence might be left behind. In reply, Caenis said, 'In vain, mistress, do you command this. Not only this message but also everything else which you dictate to me, I forevermore carry in my mind, never able to be forgotten.' And I marvel at her for this thing and, over and above this, because Vespasian exulted so immoderately in her. For this reason she became enormously influential and built up uncountable riches, so that it was even believed that he made money through Caenis herself. For she took large sums of money from many people, selling to some magistracies, to others procuratorships, military commands, and priesthoods, and also to some the decisions of the emperor.[3] For Vespasian never put anyone to death on account of money, but he did preserve the lives of many people who gave it. It was Caenis who received the money, but Vespasian was suspected to have willingly permitted her to do this.

1 Sometime between 71 and 75: Murison 1999: 166.
2 For Sejanus, see below, **5.5**. On Antonia's role in uncovering Sejanus' treachery, see also Joseph. *AJ* 18.180–2.
3 See Dio Cass. 60.17.8 for a nearly identical description of the privileges allegedly for sale by Messalina.

(b) *Corpus Inscriptionum Latinarum* 6.12037: Funerary altar for Caenis (from Rome; c. AD 71–5)

This elegant funerary altar has decorated columns on the edges of all four sides, and elaborate motifs depicting cupids, geese, vegetation, and garlands on the three sides not pictured; for images and discussion, see Saladino 2008 and Nonnis 2009. Funerary inscriptions for court personnel often boast of their official positions (see **4.5**, **5.11**), but Caenis' makes no mention of her relationship with Vespasian or her role at his court.

To the spirits of the dead. For Antonia Caenis, freedwoman of the Augusta,[1] the best patroness, Aglaus, (her) freedman, with his children Aglaus, Glene, and Aglais (set this up).

1 Antonia the Younger was given the title of *Augusta* under Caligula.

Figure 3.3.1 Funerary altar for Antonia Caenis (*CIL* 6.12037), from Rome. Museo Storico della Caccia e del Territorio, inv. A 231.
Photo: Gallerie degli Uffizi, Gabinetto Fotografico.

3.51 Competition for attention from (and influence with) Elagabalus

Cassius Dio 80(79).15.1–2, 15.4–16.3, 16.6 (Xiph.; *EV*)

The narratives of the reign of Elagabalus are sensationalist in the extreme. Despite the hyperbole, underneath the scandals and the accusations lie recognizable elements of a functioning court. Here, Dio relates the fierce competition for the emperor's favour between two sexual favourites, both men, an inversion of the norm which serves to mark out Elagabalus as a deviant. Dio's criticism of their undue influence with the emperor, however, is identical to that levied against other, female, sexual favourites in earlier reigns; see above, **3.49–50 (a)**. The account in the *Historia Augusta* goes even further, claiming that Zoticus wielded so much influence at court that he appeared to some to be almost like the emperor's 'consort' (*maritus*); SHA *Heliogab.* 10.2; cf. Hdn. 1.16.3 on Marcia, the concubine of Commodus.

Her[1] husband was Hierocles, a slave from Caria who once was the darling of Gordius,[2] from whom he learned to drive a chariot. And it was because of this that he became pleasing to Elagabalus in a most irregular way. For in a certain race Hierocles fell out of his chariot opposite the very seat of Sardanapalus (sc. Elagabalus), his helmet knocked aside in the fall. When he was so revealed to the emperor – for he was still beardless and adorned with golden hair – he was immediately carried off to the palace (*palation*); and he increased his grip on the emperor even more by his nightly labours, and became extremely influential, with the result that he was more powerful than even the emperor himself. It was even considered a trivial thing that his mother, when she was still a slave, should be escorted to Rome by soldiers and be counted among the wives of ex-consuls[3] . . . (*Dio then gives an account of Elagabalus' sexual exploits with other men.*) Elagabalus actually wanted to proclaim Hierocles Caesar; when his grandmother[4] became an impediment in this matter, he threatened her, and he quarrelled with the soldiers above all on account of this man. . . .

Aurelius Zoticus, a man from Smyrna, whom they nicknamed 'cook' because of his father's trade, was both intensely loved and then intensely hated by Elagabalus, and because of this (hatred) his life was saved. For not only was his entire body beautiful, since he was an athlete,[5] but he also vastly eclipsed everyone else in the sheer magnitude of his genitalia. This was reported to the emperor by those who scrutinized such things, and all of a sudden he was snatched away from the games and led to Rome under an immense escort, more than Abgarus had had during the reign of Severus, or Tiridates under Nero.[6] He was made bedroom attendant[7] even before he was seen by Elagabalus and honoured with the name of the emperor's grandfather, Avitus[8]. . . . (*Dio then gives an account of Elagabalus' enthusiastic reception of Zoticus.*)

But Hierocles, since he was afraid that Zoticus would enslave Elagabalus more than he, and that he might suffer something terrible thanks to him, as typically occurs between rivals in love, made him impotent with a certain drug, thanks to the cupbearers who were somewhat sympathetic towards him.[9] And in this way, Zoticus, hamstrung by his impotence, which lasted the entire night, was stripped of everything which he had gained, and was banished from the palace (*palation*), from Rome, and later from the rest of Italy, and this saved his life.[10]

1 Dio uses the feminine pronoun αὐτή to refer to Elagabalus. Nero was also said to have 'married' a man: Suet. *Ner.* 28–9; Dio Cass. 62(63).13.1–3 (Xiph.).

2 *PIR*[2] C 1289.

3 The inversion of status here – Hierocles' mother, as a slave, has no business being ranked alongside the wives of former consuls – illustrates the subversive nature of the court. Compare this with Nero's alleged efforts to procure elevated status for Acte: Suet. *Ner.* 28.1.

4 Julia Maesa.

5 Zoticus is identified by name and depicted alongside two other athletes on a mosaic from Puteoli: Caldelli 2008.

6 L. Aelius (Aurelius) Septimius Abgar VIII, the client king of Osrhoëne; see Ross 2001: 46–57; *PIR*[2] A 8. Tiridates, the king of Armenia, was received at Rome by Nero in 66; see below, **4.20** and Strootman, **Vol. 1, 17**. The comparison to the entourages of foreign kings emphasizes the absurdity of the situation.

7 πρόκοιτος = *cubicularius* or *a cubiculo*. For the position see above, **3.21 (b)**, **40** and Edmondson, **Vol. 1, 180–1**.

8 His maternal grandfather, (C.) Iulius Avitus Alexianus (*PIR*[2] I 190, 192), husband of Julia Maesa.

9 Note the suggestion that other domestic servants could be expected to take sides in such conflicts.

10 Dio records that Hierocles, among others, was killed with Elagabalus: Dio Cass. 80(79).21.1 (Xiph.). In the account in the *Historia Augusta*, Zoticus becomes a key figure at the court, using his influence with Elagabalus to manipulate others and amass great personal wealth (SHA *Heliogab.* 10.3), but his fate and the fate of Hierocles are not specified. For analysis of the fall of Elagabalus, see Kemezis 2016.

d. Foreign Royalty

Two categories of foreign royals are most often attested at the Roman imperial court: the children of monarchs, who were raised at the court and later returned there as adults, and royal family members from semi-autonomous states, who sought refuge at the court during dynastic conflicts. Their presence made the court into an important 'contact zone', a term drawn from postcolonial theory for 'social spaces where cultures meet, clash, and grapple with each other, often in contexts of highly asymmetrical relations of power': Pratt 1991: 34 (quotation), 1992: 6. The court became a meeting place where foreign royals from disparate kingdoms were integrated into international social networks, and where they, like all other courtiers, competed to gain the emperor's favour. On this, see Jussen, **Vol. 1, Chapter 7**.

3.52 The children of King Phraates IV of Parthia

Strabo 16.1.28 (excerpt)

Phraates IV ruled Parthia from 37 to 2 BC. In 20 BC he made a treaty with Augustus that led to him sending four of his sons to Rome a decade later. Augustus also benefitted from the arrangement: Suetonius (*Aug.* 43.4) says that the Parthians accompanied Augustus to at least one public spectacle and were seated only one row behind the emperor, a very public reminder of Augustus' diplomatic successes.

The next king, Phraates, was so eager for friendship (*philia*) with Caesar Augustus that he both sent to him the trophies marking their victory over the Romans[1] which the Parthians had set up and also summoned Titius,[2] who was in charge of Syria at that time, to a meeting and put into his hands as pledges[3] four of his legitimate sons – Seraspadanes, Rhodaspes, Phraates, and Vonones[4] – and two of their wives and four of their sons, because he was afraid of insurrections and attacks against his own life.[5] He knew that no one could prevail against him unless they won over someone from the family of Arsaces,[6] because the Parthians were exceedingly loyal to that house. He therefore got his children out of the way, seeking to deprive troublemakers of that hope. In fact, his surviving children are maintained in a kingly fashion at public expense in Rome, and the subsequent kings have continued to send ambassadors and come to meetings.

1 The lost standards from the battle of Carrhae in 53 BC, where the Parthians routed the Roman army led by M. Licinius Crassus.
2 M. Titius (*PIR*[2] T 261).
3 Ὅμηρα. Translating *homēra* (and other similar terms like *obsides*) as 'hostages' can be misleading: Jussen, **Vol. 1, 148**; Allen 2006: 17–22.
4 Seraspadanes and Rhodaspes likely died in Rome: *CIL* 6.1799 (= *ILS* 842). Vonones and Phraates eventually returned to Parthia: Tac. *Ann.* 2.2.1, 6.31.1.
5 The idea that factional strife motivated the king to send his sons to Rome is also found in Josephus (*AJ* 18.42) and Tacitus (*Ann.* 2.1.2). Augustus himself claims that Phraates did this 'because he was seeking his friendship (*amicitia*)': *Mon. Anc.* 32; cf. Vell. Pat. 2.94.4; Suet. *Aug.* 21.3.
6 Arsaces I (r. 247–217 BC) was the first king of Parthia.

3.53 Roman influence at the court of Herod the Great

Josephus, *Jewish Antiquities* 17.10

The most detailed accounts we have of foreign royals and the Roman imperial court come from Josephus, whose works reflect his close connections with the Herodian dynasty of his native Judaea; on this, see Jussen, **Vol. 1, 148–9**. Other foreign royals may have been equally enmeshed in the court, but they lacked a historian to record their exploits: Braund 1984: 11; Hekster 2010: 53. This passage shows the contact moved in both directions: Livia's relationship with Salome I (*PIR*[2] S 108), the sister of Herod the Great (*PIR*[2] H 153), is depicted as strong enough to influence court politics in the independent kingdom of Judaea. For Salome, see Roller 2018: 59–78; her relationship with Livia is discussed at 69.

Herod forced Salome to marry Alexas, although she desired marriage with Syllaeus the Arab and longed for him out of amorous passion; in this Julia (i.e. Livia) helped him, persuading Salome not to renounce the marriage lest hatred be established between them[1] . . . And so she listened to Julia both because she was the wife of Caesar and because she always advised her in advantageous ways.

1 At *BJ* 1.566, Josephus suggests that Livia tried to intercede with Herod on Salome's behalf.

3.54 Herod Agrippa I at the Roman court

Here, Josephus embarks on a lengthy description of the trials and tribulations of Herod Agrippa I; for Josephus' portrait of Agrippa, see Kushnir-Stein 2003. Agrippa first entered court circles in 7 BC, when he came to Rome with his mother, Berenice (*PIR*^{2} B 108), after the death of his father, Aristobulus IV (*PIR*^{2} A 1050). Agrippa was only five at the time. In his youth, Agrippa formed friendships with both Drusus the Younger and Claudius, the latter made possible by his mother's own friendship with Antonia the Younger. For Agrippa at the court in Rome, see Jussen, **Vol. 1, 157–60**.

(a) Josephus, *Jewish Antiquities* 18.143–6

Shortly before the death of Herod the king,[1] (Herod) Agrippa was living at Rome; he was brought up and was on very close terms with Drusus (the Younger), the son of the emperor Tiberius. He also formed a friendship (*philia*) with Antonia (the Younger), the wife of Drusus the Elder, for his mother Berenice was highly esteemed by her and had asked for her son's advancement.[2] Agrippa was noble in his character and extravagant in the gifts which he made, but while his mother was still living he did not reveal this tendency of his spirit, thinking it best to avoid her anger concerning such matters. When Berenice died, however, and Agrippa came to be guided by his own character, he spent part of his money on the extravagance of his daily life, part on the generous presents which he gave away freely, but most of it he paid to the emperor's freedmen[3] in the hope of some support from them. Within a short time, he was reduced to poverty and this was an impediment for his life in Rome. In addition, Tiberius refused to allow the friends of his deceased son to come before his eyes, because seeing them stirred up his grief by calling to mind his son.

1 In 4 BC.
2 Cf. Joseph. *AJ* 18.156.
3 Note how Herod Agrippa considers Tiberius' freedmen to be the best people with whom he should cultivate a relationship.

(b) Josephus, *Jewish Antiquities* 18.161–7

By AD 35 or 36, Herod Agrippa found himself once again in financial trouble: he owed the imperial treasury 300,000 drachmas; see Smallwood 1976: 189; Kushnir-Stein 2003: 155–6. In this passage, Herod Agrippa needs to use his old court connections to restore his favour with Tiberius.

When (Herod) Agrippa had come to Puteoli, he wrote a letter to the emperor Tiberius, who at that time was living on Capreae, explaining to him that he wanted to visit and pay homage to him and requesting permission to cross over to Capreae. Tiberius did not hesitate but replied to him in a kindly manner, indicating his delight that he had returned in safety to Capreae. After Agrippa arrived, Tiberius welcomed him kindly, no less than he had said he would do in his letter, and received him as a guest. But on the next day, a letter reached Caesar from Herennius Capito[1] informing him that Agrippa had borrowed 300,000 drachmas, had failed to make the payments at the appointed time, and, when the sum was demanded back from him, had fled out of the places under his control, leaving him without any authority to exact the money. When he had read this letter, the emperor was greatly pained by it, and he gave orders that Agrippa should be forbidden from his presence until he had settled the debt. Not at all bothered by the emperor's anger, Agrippa appealed to Antonia, the mother of Germanicus and of Claudius, who later became emperor, to give him a loan of 300,000 drachmas so that he might not lose the friendship (*philia*) of Tiberius. She, because of the memory of Berenice his mother – for the two women had been very close to each other – and because he had been brought up together with Claudius and his associates, gave him the money; once he had paid the debt in full, there was no barrier to Tiberius' friendship (*philia*). Afterwards the emperor Tiberius introduced to him his grandson[2] and requested that Agrippa always accompany him on his expeditions. But when Agrippa received friendship (*philia*) from Antonia, he turned to cultivating her grandson Gaius (Caligula), who enjoyed the greatest esteem because of the goodwill felt towards his father. Now there was besides a certain imperial freedman from Samaria; Agrippa procured a loan of a million drachmas from this man and repaid the debt which he owed to Antonia. What remained went on the costs of paying court to Gaius, with whom his status increased.[3]

1 C. Herennius Capito (*PIR*[2] H 103) was the procurator of Iamnia in Judaea. He had failed to prevent Agrippa from sailing to Italy before the debt had been repaid (Joseph. *AJ* 18.158–9).
2 Ti. Gemellus.
3 Cf. Joseph. *BJ* 2.178–80. At *AJ* 18.188, Josephus claims that Agrippa's focus on Caligula, rather than Ti. Gemellus, became a long-standing grievance with Tiberius.

(c) Josephus, *Jewish Antiquities* 18.202–4

Herod Agrippa's close friendship with Caligula eventually led to him making yet another mistake with Tiberius: Josephus claims he expressed the hope to Caligula that he would soon become emperor, either because Tiberius would step down (Joseph. *AJ* 18.168) or because he would die (Joseph. *BJ* 2.179). The remark found its way back to Tiberius, who had Agrippa arrested and imprisoned, despite Antonia's intercessions on Agrippa's behalf: Joseph. *AJ* 168–9, 183–91. Josephus emphasizes how much respect Tiberius had for Antonia (Joseph. *AJ* 18.180–2), but, as this passage shows, there were limits to her influence.

Antonia (the Younger), although grieved at the tribulations of (Herod) Agrippa, perceived that to argue with Tiberius on his behalf would be too difficult and besides would achieve nothing. But she did obtain from Macro for

Agrippa the following: that the soldiers who were to watch over him should be moderate and likewise the centurion who had authority over them and who would be bound to Agrippa, that he should be allowed to bathe every day, that his freedmen and his friends should be permitted to visit, and that other things which comforted his body be permitted.[1]

1 In *BJ* 2.180, Josephus maintains that Agrippa was treated very strictly while in jail.

3.55 Berenice and Titus

Cassius Dio 65(66).15.3–4 (Xiph.)

Tacitus states that the relationship between Berenice, the daughter of Herod Agrippa I, and Titus began in Judaea, after Vespasian was declared emperor in 69: *Hist.* 2.2.1, 81.2. When Titus returned to Rome, Berenice came with him, but their relationship proved controversial: Jussen, **Vol. 1, 160–1**; Anagnostou-Laoutides and Charles 2015. The relationship between the third-century emperor Gallienus and the German princess Pipa, daughter of King Attalus of the Marcomanni, also evoked a hostile response from the literary sources: SHA *Gall.* 21.3; *Epit. de Caes.* 33.1; Aur. Vict. *Caes.* 33.6.

Berenice was at the height of her power and consequently even came to Rome, with her brother Agrippa.[1] He was thought worthy of the civic honours of a praetor; she took up residence in the palace (*palation*), and was living with Titus. She was expecting to marry him[2] and already in every way was acting as if she were his wife, but after he became aware that the Romans were unable to endure this arrangement, he sent her away.[3]

1 Herod Agrippa II (*PIR*² I 132).
2 Suetonius records it was rumoured (*ferebatur*) that Titus had promised to marry her: Suet. *Tit.* 7.1.
3 Dio here places Berenice's banishment during the reign of Vespasian, and adds that she returned to Rome once Titus became emperor, but he did not resume the affair: Dio Cass. 66.18.1 (Xiph.). Suetonius has Titus send Berenice away unwillingly once he becomes emperor: *Tit.* 7.2; cf. Juv. 6.156–8; *Epit. de Caes.* 10.7; Anagnostou-Laoutides and Charles 2015: 36.

4 | Rituals and Ceremonial

CAILLAN DAVENPORT, MATTHEW B. ROLLER, AND FANNY DOLANSKY

Introduction

All monarchical societies are regulated by rituals and ceremonies, acts and observances that through their formal nature, repetition, and adherence to a set of rules and expectations articulate the majesty, permanence, and cosmic significance of kings and queens: Bell 1997: 138–69; Geertz 1999: 15; Duindam 2016: 255–7. When grouped together, these individual observances form part of a larger system of performative acts which we collectively call ceremonial or ritual: *OED* s.v. ceremonial B (2), ritual B (3); on these terms as synonyms, see Duindam 2016: 255. Monarchical ceremonial can be divided into different categories: state ceremonial, such as accessions and funerals, which mark the performance of a monarch's office, and the change from one ruler to the next; domestic ceremonial, the regulation of daily life at court, from greeting ceremonies to dinners; diplomatic ceremonial, the reception of foreign ambassadors; and religious or liturgical ceremonial: Giesey 1987: 42–7; Duindam 1995: 103–4, 2003: 181–3. There is, of course, often slippage and overlap between these categories, since in most cultures state ceremonial also has a religious dimension. Nor can we apply the distinctions wholesale to the Roman Principate, in which there was no separate diplomatic protocol, for example. But these categories assist us in conceptualizing the range of rituals which involved the court.

The texts and images in this chapter feature events at the Roman imperial court which can be regarded as rituals by their adherence to the criteria set out above. These included regular occurrences that took place on a daily or near-daily basis, such as the *salutatio*, dinners, and religious sacrifices. They also included special occasions like diplomatic receptions, lavish banquets, and the acclamation of a new emperor, which were still performed often enough to develop the characteristic rules and routines that defined them as rituals; on definitions and categories, see Davenport, **Vol. 1, 291–2**. Many of these ceremonies would have been familiar from late Republican aristocratic households, whose heads (*patres familiarum*) greeted their clients in order of precedence, entertained them at dinner to display their wealth and generosity, and celebrated their sons' coming of age in *toga virilis* ceremonies: see Neel, **Vol. 1, 44–6** on Republican precedents. Their retention under Augustus and his successors was the natural consequence of a monarchy that slowly evolved from Republican government and society. But these rituals soon gained monarchical implications, as expressed by all the members of the Senate coming to pay their respects to Augustus each morning, and the celebration of the attainment of manhood by imperial sons and grandsons becoming intertwined with the future of the Roman state itself; on the latter, see Dolansky, **Vol. 1, 405–8**. Hence, these ceremonies became 'traditionalized', to use the terminology of Catherine Bell (1992: 124): their continued existence provided the impression of stability and continuity from the Republic, even though their form and meaning now served new monarchical purposes. Even ceremonies which were specifically monarchical in nature, such as the accession of an emperor, drew upon Republican forms and precedents, and only gradually developed into a defined 'rite of enactment': see Muir 1997: 247–8 for such royal rituals.

The rituals presented in this chapter involved the court in different ways. The reception of foreign embassies, imperial accessions, and religious processions, such as that depicted on the Ara Pacis, did not consistently take place in court spaces, but merit inclusion here because they involved key members of the court community, such as the imperial family, prominent senators, and praetorian prefects. In contrast, events such as the *salutatio*, banquets, and the celebration of festivals and anniversaries involved a wide cross-section of the court community, from members of the imperial family and the senatorial and equestrian orders to the guards and officials who regulated admissions, the slaves who served food and drink, and the actors and musicians who provided entertainment; on dining and banqueting, see Roller, **Vol. 1, 319–36**. These ceremonies functioned as displays of consensus among members of the court community, as their actions demonstrated shared values and expectations. When an emperor greeted fellow senators with a kiss or shared his evening meal with them, this performance showed that he regarded them as his peers, rather than as his inferiors: Wallace-Hadrill 1982. The rules and expectations of these rituals were subject to modification both by emperors and courtiers, who experimented with new types of address, greeting, and physical contact, either to demonstrate their superiority (the emperor) or to flatter and curry favour (courtiers). Such innovations would usually only lead to long-term changes in ceremonial – such as the transformation of the ritual of greeting the emperor to one of adoration – if they were accepted by the court community at large; on this negotiation of ritual, see Bell 1992: 123–4.

See Bell 1992 and 1997 for theories and definitions of ritual; Giesey 1987 and Geertz 1999 on rituals and kingship; and Duindam 1995: 97–136 on types of ceremonies involving monarchical courts. For Roman ritual and ceremonial during the first three centuries AD, see Alföldi 1970; Wallace-Hadrill 1996: 285–95; and Winterling 1999: 117–94; and on the change to Late Antiquity, MacCormack 1981.

I | The *salutatio*

The *salutatio*, or morning greeting, was a fundamental ritual of Roman social relations. Clients would assemble daily at the house of their patron to pay their respects; the greater the throng, the greater the patron's power and influence: Cic. *De Off.* 1.139. By the end of the late Republic, morning callers were divided into groups according to their intimacy with the patron. Seneca attributed this innovation to C. Sempronius Gracchus and M. Livius Drusus; see **4.6 (a)**.

Augustus retained this ceremony at his house on the Palatine, but it took on an exponentially larger scale, as all senators and high-ranking *equites* were expected to attend. The *salutatio* became the most important ritual interaction between emperor and courtiers, as the public nature of the ceremony dramatized power relationships and networks of favour: Wallace-Hadrill 2011. As the following sources make clear, emperors could modify parts of the *salutatio* ceremony, such as location, security measures, and hierarchies, according to the public image they wished to project. For full discussion, see Alföldi 1970: 25–8; Wallace-Hadrill 1996: 290–1; Winterling 1999: 117–44; Paterson 2007: 146–8; Goldbeck 2010 (covering both the Republic and the empire).

4.1 The beginnings of the imperial *salutatio*

Suetonius, *Life of Augustus* 53.2–3

This passage comes from a section of Suetonius illustrating the emperor's *civilitas*: Wardle 2014: 371. Senators were expected to attend Augustus' house every day, except if the Senate was in session (Dio Cass. 54.30.1), when Augustus came to the Senate instead. From AD 12 onwards, when Augustus was ill, he did not come to the Senate house, nor were senators required to attend a *salutatio* at the emperor's house: Dio Cass. 56.26.2. See too Winterling 1999: 125–7.

He even admitted ordinary people to his public *salutationes*, receiving the petitions of those visiting him with such great affability that when a fellow hesitated as he held out his petition, Augustus chided him, joking that he looked 'like he was offering a coin to an elephant'.[1] On senatorial sitting days, he would only ever greet the senators in the Senate house itself, and he did so one by one as they were seated, never needing a reminder of their names.[2] He would leave in exactly the same way, saying farewell to the senators as they were in the seats.

1 For versions of the same anecdote, see Quint. *Inst.* 6.3.59; Macrob. *Sat.* 2.4.3.
2 Many Romans used a *nomenclator* to remind them of names; see Vogt 1978; Goldbeck 2010: 101–3. It was a mark of Augustus' *civilitas* not to rely on one.

4.2 The *salutationes* of Julio-Claudian women

Cassius Dio 57.12.1–2

In this passage, Dio describes the significant public role of Livia in the reign of Tiberius; see further Barrett 2002: 146–73. Prominent women had received friends and associates at home during the Republic, especially in the absence of their male relatives. But Livia was the first woman to be formally granted the right to hold an audience, as indicated by the recording of this privilege in the public registers. This same honour was later granted to Agrippina the Younger: Tac. *Ann.* 13.18.2–19.1 = **6.2 (c)**. For discussion, see Goldbeck 2010: 67–73; Foubert 2016: 138–45.

Tiberius also ordered his mother to behave in much the same way (i.e. with humility), to the extent that it was fitting for her to do this, both for the sake of emulating him and to put a check on any haughtiness.[1] For Livia had been raised to great and lofty heights, far beyond that of any woman who had gone before her, as she regularly received the Senate and the members of the populace who wished to greet her at her house.[2] This was formally recorded in the public registers.[3] There was a time when the letters of Tiberius were also written in Livia's name, and people wrote to them both alike.

1 The idea that members of the imperial family should emulate Tiberius can also be found in the *SCPP* ll. 132–6.
2 It is uncertain whether this house refers to the so-called 'Casa di Livia' on the Palatine, or to another structure: Foubert 2010: 66–7.
3 The 'public registers', known either as the *acta publica* or *acta diurna*, were instituted by Julius Caesar: Suet. *Iul.* 20.1.

4.3 The expectation to attend the *salutatio*

(a) Cassius Dio 69.7.2 (Xiph.)

All senators were required to attend the *salutatio* at the imperial *domus* when the emperor was in residence in Rome. It was regarded as the mark of a *civilis princeps* not to enforce this condition too strictly: see **4.3 (b)**. Cassius Dio thus includes Hadrian's desire not to hold the *salutatio* every day among the emperor's good qualities.

When Hadrian returned home he was carried in a litter, so as to spare people the burden of accompanying him. He stayed home on those days on which no religious or administrative business was scheduled, and allowed no one to enter, not even to pay their respects, unless it were absolutely necessary, in order that no one would be troubled at all.

(b) Fronto, *Letters to Verus as Emperor* 1.12 (ed. vdH 115–16 = Haines 1.296–300)

When Fronto, previously tutor in Latin rhetoric to Marcus Aurelius and Lucius Verus, visited the palace for the first time after their accession in 161, he only called upon Marcus. Verus then wrote to Fronto to complain, asking why he did not inform him as well that he was coming to the palace: *Ad Verum Imp.* 1.11 (ed. vdH 114–15 = Haines 1.294–6). The letter below is Fronto's reply.

I shall demonstrate a little later that it was not my fault that yesterday, when I had come to the palace to see both of you, I did not see you – sad to say! But if I had willingly and with conscious and sober mind <not> discharged this duty

<to the best of my ability>,[1] I should not regret it at all. For this very thing was the <reason why you>[2] remonstrated with me in such a friendly letter. Nor, if I had come to you and had been greeted with great honour, would I rejoice as much as I do now, since to judge from such a scolding, I am longed for. Certainly, in keeping with your most remarkable kindness, you address respectfully all the men of our order[3] when they present themselves to you. Yet you do not earnestly ask after all of them when they are absent. This is indeed the nub of the matter: I should rather you be severely angry with me than gladly pardon me. For we get angry when in fact we long for someone keenly. But we are unfavourably disposed towards people and do not get angry with or long for them if we have stopped loving them.

Indeed, you and your brother have been assigned such great power. You are surrounded by such a great throng of people of all kinds and all social levels, on whom you shower your love. You share no small part of your love with me. What, then, should I do, since all my hopes and fortunes rest on you alone. [---] ...[4]

But I should not postpone my defence any longer. It was not my fault that I did not visit you. For I returned to Rome from my gardens on the fifth day before the Kalends of April[5] at daybreak, so that if possible I might embrace you both on that very day, after such a long time. Your letter to me, however [---][6] So as to do what? To enquire whether all is well? Or to embrace you or kiss you or converse with you? Or should I have come to look at your tears and show mine after four months?[7] What, then, did I do the following day? I did not dare to write to your brother[8] or to you that I was going to come to you; instead I wrote to your freedman, Charilas,[9] with these words, if memory serves: 'Do you know whether today is convenient for me to come before them? Tell me as a kindly man and a friend of mine. Send me word if there is any news.'[10] [---]

---

1 Several words are missing from the manuscript in this clause, and some words are possibly corrupt. Here we translate van den Hout's suggestion of <*non quantum*> *persolvissem* (1999: 283).

2 The manuscript is again illegible here; we translate (*exempli gratia*) Mai's conjecture of <*causa, cur tu tam*>.

3 The senatorial order.

4 Damage to the manuscript has made some parts of the next lines illegible; without full context, Fronto's train of thought is unclear from the remaining words.

5 28 March 161.

6 The sense is again lost due to damage to the manuscript.

7 The grief is for the deceased Antoninus Pius, as argued by Davenport and Manley (2014: 130). Cf. van den Hout (1999: 282), who prefers to identify the dead relative as L. Ceionius Commodus, the grandfather of Verus.

8 Marcus Aurelius.

9 Charilas (*PIR*[2] C 713) may have been one of the admissions staff, perhaps the *ab admissione* himself (see **4.5 [a]**).

10 Fronto wrote to Charilas in Greek. The manuscript becomes illegible after the note to Charilas, so the rest of the letter is lost.

4.4 Waiting for admittance at the *salutatio*

(a) Suetonius, *Life of Claudius* 35.1–2

This passage comes from the section dealing with Claudius' cowardly and distrustful nature: Hurley 2001: 211–12. Claudius made an initial show of *civilitas*, Suetonius says, but this was belied by his paranoia and tough security; see also Dio Cass. 60.3.3. It was not unusual for visitors to be searched before entering the emperor's presence (e.g. Suet. *Aug.* 35.2); what made Claudius' measures so exceptional was the harsh manner in which they were enforced. On security at the palace, see Kelly, **Vol. 1, 385–93**.

From this point on, Claudius always assigned staff to search those who came to greet him, and they roughed up all visitors terribly. For it was not until later that he relaxed this slightly, so that women, boys who had not yet reached the age of manhood,[1] and girls would not be manhandled, and so that pen cases and stylus boxes would not be confiscated from accompanying attendants and secretaries.[2]

1 Literally: 'boys clad in the *toga praetexta*', the garb they would exchange for the *toga virilis* once they reached puberty; cf. Dolansky, **Vol. 1, 406**.
2 Writing implements could be used as weapons: Suet. *Iul.* 82.2, *Calig.* 28, *Claud.* 15.4.

(b) Philostratus, *Life of Apollonius of Tyana* 7.31.2

In Book 7 of Philostratus' biographical novel, Apollonius is arrested on Domitian's orders for seditious speeches against the emperor. The passage below describes the scene in which Apollonius and his disciple, Damis, are escorted from the prison to meet with Domitian in the gardens of Adonis (Diaeta Adonaea) on the Palatine (now the area known as the Vigna Barberini, on which see Coarelli 2012: 515–30).

As Apollonius came near to the palace, he could see some people being flattered and others flattering, and the bustle of people coming and going.[1] He said, 'It seems to me, Damis, that this scene could be compared to a public bath, for I see many who are outside hastening to get in, and vice-versa, and there are equal numbers of clean and unclean men.'[2] I would urge this line to be kept unaltered, and not attributed to any random person, because it belongs entirely to Apollonius, who has placed it on record in a letter. When he saw a man of advanced years who had set his heart upon a governorship, and so was subordinating himself and paying court to the emperor, he said: 'Sophocles[3] has not yet convinced this fellow to escape from his mad and cruel overlord, Damis.' And Damis replied: 'We have adopted the same overlord ourselves, Apollonius: it is for this reason that we are now stopped at these very gates.'

1 Likely the Area Palatina (on which see **4.4 [c]** below).
2 Apollonius' point was that those who have not yet entered the palace are still morally clean, and those already inside are sullied by the experience – and also want to escape.
3 In Plato's *Republic* (329 C), the Greek playwright Sophocles says that he had escaped the desire for sex, as though he had run away from a savage and cruel master.

(c) Aulus Gellius 20.1.1–3, 55

In this passage, Gellius reports a learned discussion of the Twelve Tables that took place on the Area Palatina, where the men are waiting to be admitted to the *salutatio*.

In the practice of law and in the study and interpretation of the laws of the Roman people, Sex. Caecilius[1] was renowned for his erudition, practical experience, and authority. In this story, the philosopher Favorinus[2] approached him in the Area Palatina,[3] where we were waiting for the emperor's[4] *salutatio*, and he engaged Caecilius in conversation in front of me and many others who were present.

(Gellius then gives a lengthy account of a conversation concerning the laws of the Twelve Tables.)

When Sex. Caecilius had discussed these things, and others of similar character, all those who were present, including Favorinus himself, endorsed and praised him. It was announced that the emperor's *salutatio* had begun, and we were separated.[5]

1 Sex. Caecilius Africanus (*PIR*² C 18).
2 For Favorinus, see above, **3.23**. For his representation in Gellius, see Holford-Strevens 2003: 98–130.
3 The Area Palatina in the Antonine age was probably the plaza directly at the top of the Clivus Palatinus before the main north-east façade of the palace. See Pflug and Wulf-Rheidt, **Vol. 1, 222**.
4 Antoninus Pius.
5 The Latin perfect passive form *separati sumus* ('we were separated') suggests that the waiting crowd was organized into groups.

(d) Fronto, *Letters to Marcus as Caesar* 5.45 (ed. vdH 77 = Haines 1.228–30)

This letter was sent by Fronto to Marcus Aurelius, then Caesar under Antoninus Pius, to apologize for his absence from the New Year's Day celebrations of 148 or 149: van den Hout 1999: 206–7. The New Year's Day celebrations would have started with a crowded *salutatio* that Fronto was at pains to avoid for health reasons.

To my lord,

I pray that your New Year will be happy and fortunate in everything that you wish for, and I also pray for our lord your father,[1] your mother,[2] your wife,[3] your daughter,[4] and everyone else who deserves your love. I was worried about giving myself up to the close quarters of the crowd, since my body is still not recovered.[5] If the gods will it, I will see you on the day after tomorrow when you pronounce your vows.[6] Farewell, my dearest lord. Pay my respects to your lady.[7]

1 Antoninus Pius.
2 Domitia Lucilla.
3 Faustina the Younger.
4 Domitia Faustina, b. 30 November 147.
5 Fronto's health issues were legendary: many of the letters in *Ad M. Caes.* Book 5 are concerned with his complaints.

6 The vow for the health and safety of the emperors (*nuncupatio votorum*) was offered annually empire-wide on 3 January: Reynolds 1962; Rüpke 2007: 163.

7 This is usually taken to be Domitia Lucilla, but may be Faustina the Younger.

(e) Cassius Dio 78(77).17.3–4 (Xiph.)

The emperor Caracalla wintered in the city of Nicomedia in Bithynia (modern İzmit, Turkey), probably in 213/14; cf. Scott 2018: 1 n. 3. In this passage, Dio recounts his experience waiting to be received by Caracalla, a passage which is designed to contrast with his much more positive experiences under that emperor's father, Septimius Severus: Dio Cass. 77(76).17.1–3 (Xiph.). There are different scholarly views on the extent to which Dio's account of Caracalla can be assumed to be representative of senatorial sentiments in general: see Meckler 1999; Davenport 2012; and Scott 2015.

Caracalla, on the other hand, used to announce that straight after dawn he would begin hearing legal cases or managing state affairs,[1] but then he left us waiting until midday, and often as late as the evening. He did not let us into the entrance vestibule, but we were made to stand somewhere outside. It was his practice to decide, sometime later, that he was not going to receive us after all. During this time, he occupied himself in other ways, just as I have said, as he used to drive chariots, massacre wild animals, engage in single combat, drink, and revel to excess.[2] And for the soldiers who served as his protective detail, to add to all their other bounty, he mixed craters of wine, and sent cups of it around, as those of us who were present looked on. After this, he would sometimes hear cases.

1 Emperors continued to engage in the business of government while travelling through the provinces: see Halfmann, **Vol. 1, 271–5**.

2 Cassius Dio frequently complained about Caracalla's preference for such pastimes and his fondness for the soldiers: 78(77).6.2 (Xiph.), 9.1–10.4 (*EV*; Xiph.), 11.2–4 (*EV*; Xiph.), 13.1–2 (Xiph.).

4.5 The admissions staff

(a) *Corpus Inscriptionum Latinarum* 6.8698, cf. 33748

This is an epitaph for the freedman M. Aurelius Hermes, who was the *ab admissione*. He was aided by other officials, such as his deputy, the *proximus* (*CIL* 6.8701) and assistants, *adiutores* (*CIL* 6.8700), and announcers of names, *nomenclatores* (*CIL* 6.8931). See Weaver 1972: 252–4; Winterling 1999: 102–4; and Edmondson, **Vol. 1, 174–5**.

Sacred to the spirits of the dead. To M. Aurelius Hermes, freedman of the emperor, the official in charge of admissions, Aponia (?) Graphis (?) Claudia Philotis, his wife, made this for a man who well deserved it, and for herself, and their descendants.

(b) *Corpus Inscriptionum Latinarum* 6.604

This inscription indicates that the emperor's staff played a role in organizing the emperor's *amici* during receptions. For the *amici*, see Eck 2006; Wei and Kelly, **Vol. 1, 92–103**.

Fortunatus, freedman of the emperor, official in charge of the *amici*, son of Fortunatus, a most devoted father, gave this offering to (the god) Silvanus.

(c) *Corpus Inscriptionum Latinarum* 6.8649

Curtain attendants (*velarii*) such as the one commemorated here regulated access between rooms in the palace: Winterling 1999: 98.

To the spirits of the dead. Ti. Claudius Thallus, head of the curtain attendants in the Augustan palace, made this for himself and his children, and for his freedmen and freedwomen, and for their descendants.

4.6 Hierarchy at the *salutatio*

(a) Seneca the Younger, *On Benefits* 6.33.3–34.2

In his philosophical treatise *On Benefits*, Seneca attributes to two tribunes of the late Republic, C. Sempronius Gracchus (*tr. pleb.* 123, 122 BC; *RE* 47) and M. Livius Drusus (*tr. pleb.* 91 BC; *RE* 18), the practice of dividing callers at the *salutatio* into ranked groups. The practice was then adopted at the imperial *salutatio* (below, **4.6 [b–c]**). For Gracchus' *salutatio*, see Goldbeck 2010: 217–24.

You are ignorant of the true value of friendship if you do not appreciate that the gift of a friend is worth a great deal indeed. This is rarely recognized, not only in the great houses, but also in the contemporary world generally,[1] meaning that there is no greater lack of such appreciation than in the places where one would most expect to find it. You might object to this, but do you think that those registers, which a *nomenclator* can barely keep hold of in his mind or in his hands, are composed of friends' names? People who queue in a long line to knock at the door, and who are categorized into groups according to whether they enter first or second,[2] are not really friends.

It has long been the custom of monarchs, and those who pretend to be monarchs, to classify their large number of friends in groups. But it takes a special type of arrogance to consider that passing over – or even simply touching – the threshold is some kind of honour. In the same way, they might seat someone slightly closer to the door, or place him higher in the order of entering the house, only for that individual to discover later that inside there are in fact many other doors, designed to exclude even those who have already been welcomed.

At Rome, it was Gracchus[3] and soon after him, Livius Drusus,[4] who instituted the practice of dividing up the morning crowd, so that they received some men in private, others in groups, and the rest altogether. So it was the case that these men had friends of the first rank and friends of the second rank, but they never had true friends.

---

1 *On Benefits* was written during the reign of Nero.

2 Seneca (*Clem.* 1.10.1) uses similar language to describe Augustus' friends who made up 'the whole group entitled to be admitted first'.

3 For C. Gracchus' following, see Plut. *C. Gracch.* 6.4, 12.1–2.

4 Livius Drusus is known to have had a crowd around him in the forum (Vell. Pat. 2.14.1) and at his house (App. *B Civ.* 1.36).

(b) *Corpus Inscriptionum Latinarum* 6.2169 (= *ILS* 1320)

This epitaph for C. Caesius Niger (*PIR*[2] C 202) dates to the reign of Augustus or Tiberius. The inscription is controversial, as it contains the Latin phrase *ex prima admissione*, which most scholars of the nineteenth and twentieth centuries took to mean 'from the first admissions group' (for example, Mommsen 1887–8: 2.2.834 n. 2; Crook 1955: 23). Similar language can be found in Seneca to indicate this (**4.6 [a]** above; and Seneca, *Clem.* 1.10.1). Winterling (1999: 131–3) has disagreed, arguing that Niger must have been an official on the admissions staff, which means that *ex prima admissione* should be translated as 'a former admissions official of the first-rank'. However, there are several facts which count against this. A member of the admissions staff would have been an imperial slave or freedman, and Niger's full name, including tribe and filiation, indicates he was a freeborn citizen. Moreover, Niger's priesthood (*curio minor*) was held by *equites* and occasionally by senators: Mommsen 1887–8: 3.1.101 n. 4; *CIL* 2.1262, 8.1174. Crook (1955: 23) suggests that the high favour shown to Niger could mean he was an associate of one of the princes of the imperial house, such as Germanicus or Drusus. The inscription could in fact be referring to a position in the first admissions group at the *salutatio* of the imperial prince in question, and not at that of the emperor.

Sacred to the spirits of the dead. To C. Caesius Niger, son of Quintus, of the Teretina tribe, from the first admissions group, a member of the four judicial panels,[1] and a *curio minor*. Caesia Theoris, freedwoman of Gaius, (dedicated this tomb) for her patron and herself.

1 This expression helps to date the inscription, as Augustus introduced the fourth judicial panel and Caligula later increased the number of panels to five: Davenport 2019: 197.

(c) *Corpus Inscriptionum Latinarum* 6.41111 (= 31746 = *ILS* 1078)

This is the epitaph of the senator L. Plotius Sabinus (*PIR*[2] P 517). The inscription records that he had the right of *salutatio secunda* of Antoninus Pius, which must mean the privilege of entering the *salutatio* in the second group. For the separation of *salutatores* into such groups in the Antonine period, see **4.4 (c)**, above.

Sacred to the parental spirits. L. Plotius Sabinus, son of Gaius, of the Pollia tribe, praetor, member of the college of priests for the emperors (Vespasian and) Titus,[1] curule aedile, one of the six men (heading divisions) of Roman equestrians, urban quaestor, senatorial tribune of the First Minervan Legion Pius and Faithful,[2] a member of the board of ten men for judging lawsuits, also possessing the right of admission in the second group at the *salutatio* of the Emperor Antoninus Augustus Pius. The praetor Sabinus, a great man, died at Formiae.[3]

1 The title of *sodalis Titialis* indicates that Sabinus was a member of the college of priests for the worship of both Vespasian and Titus, the *sodales Flaviales Titiales* (as correctly recorded on *CIL* 6.41112 = *AE* 1998.285). See Rüpke 2008: 843 no. 2736.

2 The legionary title was *Legio I Minerva Pia Fidelis*; the legion, formed by Domitian in 83, was given the last two elements in its title for its loyalty to the emperor during the revolt of L. Antonius Saturninus (*PIR*[2] A 874) in 89.

3 The final phrase of the inscription – *praetor magna res Formis* (or *formis*) *peri(i)t* – is not altogether clear, and various interpretations have been suggested. Here we follow the interpretation of Lambertz, *RE* Plotius 13; see too Winterling 1999: 130 n. 62.

(d) Cassius Dio 69.19.1–2 (Xiph.; *EV*)

Ser. Sulpicius Similis (*PIR*[2] S 1021) was praetorian prefect in the last years of Trajan's reign and also served the emperor Hadrian until he retired in 119. This anecdote refers to an incident earlier in Similis' career when he was still a centurion. It shows the importance of the praetorian prefects in the hierarchy of the imperial court.

Similis was Turbo's[1] superior in both age and status, and, I would say, ranked second to none in his character. This can be ascertained from even the most minor events. For once, when he was a centurion, Trajan summoned him inside before the praetorian prefects, and Similis said: 'It is shameful, Caesar, for you to be talking with a centurion while the prefects are being made to stand outside.'

1 Q. Marcius Turbo Fronto Publicius Severus (*PIR*[2] M 249) was Hadrian's praetorian prefect from c. 117–18 to 136/7.

(e) *Historia Augusta, Life of Marcus Aurelius* 3.3–5

This passage describes the relationship between the emperor Marcus Aurelius and the senator (and philosopher) Q. Iunius Rusticus (*PIR*[2] I 814), whom Marcus appointed *cos.* II *ord.* in 162 and urban prefect. The anecdote demonstrates the high standing of praetorian prefects at the Antonine court.

Marcus also received instruction from Claudius Severus,[1] who was a disciple of the Peripatetics, and especially from Iunius Rusticus, whom he revered and imitated. Rusticus was esteemed at home and abroad and was the most learned of the Stoic philosophers. Marcus consulted him on all state and family matters, and he even made it a habit to kiss him before the praetorian prefects. He designated Rusticus consul for the second time, and requested that the Senate erect statues of him after his death.

1 Cn. Claudius Severus Arabianus (*PIR*[2] C 1027), *cos. ord.* 146; cf. M. Aur. *Med.* 1.14.1–2.

(f) *The Code of Justinian* 9.51.1 (Caracalla)

This entry from the sixth-century *Code of Justinian* preserves an original constitution of the emperor Caracalla. It records a hearing which took place before the emperor in Antioch (modern Antakya, Turkey), probably in June/July of 216: Peachin 1990: 105. It shows the order of precedence of officials at the court of Caracalla on that occasion: the praetorian prefects entered first, followed by the emperor's friends (*amici*), the heads of the imperial bureaux (*principales officiorum*), then all other senators and equestrians. This is very similar to the order at a hearing before Caracalla on 27 May 216 in Syria: *AE* 1947.182 (= *SEG* 17.759). For the evolution of such imperial councils, see Millar 1992: 119–22.

The emperor Antoninus Augustus (i.e. Caracalla). When the emperor had been greeted (*salutatus*) by Oclatinius Adventus and Opellius Macrinus, praetorian prefects, most distinguished men,[1] and in addition by his friends[2] and the heads of the imperial bureaux[3] and the men of both orders,[4] and had proceeded forward, Iulianus Licinianus, who had been deported to an island by Aelius Ulpianus, then a provincial governor, was presented to him.[5] Antoninus Augustus said: 'I restore you to your province with your full rights.' And he added: 'And so that you might know what "full rights" means: (I restore you) to your political offices and your order and to everything else.'

1 Caracalla's praetorian prefects, M. Oclatinius Adventus (*PIR*[2] O 9) and M. Opellius Macrinus (the future emperor; *PIR*[2] O 108) are recorded with the senatorial title of 'most distinguished men' (*viri clarissimi*). In the previous hearing at Antioch in May they were styled 'most eminent men' (*viri eminentissimi*), the most senior equestrian status. This indicates that they had been awarded consular decorations (*ornamenta consularia*) in the intervening period. See Salway 2006: 121–6; Schöpe 2014: 278–9.
2 The friends (*amici*) would be senators and equestrians who were part of Caracalla's retinue (*comitatus*). For their identities, see Davenport 2012: 806–7.
3 Officials such as the secretary of letters (*ab epistulis*) and secretary of petitions (*a libellis*), but not the financial secretary (*a rationibus*), who usually stayed in Rome: see Davenport and Kelly, **Vol. 1,** 136–7.
4 The 'men of both orders' (*utriusque ordinis viri*) were senators and equestrians who did not fit into the preceding categories, perhaps members of the local elite in Antioch: Schöpe 2014: 47.
5 Aelius Ulpianus (*PIR*[2] A 279) was probably the consular governor of Syria Coele: Peachin 1990: 105–6.

4.7 Interactions at the *salutatio*

(a) Suetonius, *Life of Claudius* 37.1

As with **4.4 (a)** above, this excerpt deals with Claudius' fears and anxieties. It shows that on some occasions individuals could have private conversations with the emperor during the *salutatio*.

Moreover, no rumour was too small and no source too unreliable to cause the emperor to be on his guard and plot revenge whenever he was seized by a slight anxiety. On one occasion, one of the two men involved in a lawsuit took Claudius to the side during the *salutatio*, and swore that he had seen the emperor killed by a certain individual in one of his dreams.[1] Then, not long afterwards, when his opponent in the lawsuit was handing over his petition,[2] the man gestured towards him, as though he had just recognized him as the emperor's murderer. The man's opponent was immediately carried off for punishment, just as if he had really been apprehended committing a crime.

1 For another case of a man being condemned under Claudius because someone else dreamt he was going to harm the emperor, see Dio Cass. 60.14.1–4.
2 For petitions being presented at the *salutatio*, see **4.1** above and Mart. 8.82.

(b) Pliny the Younger, *Panegyric* 47.3–48.5

In this passage, Pliny describes the relaxed atmosphere of the imperial palace under the *civilis* Trajan compared with Domitian, who had treated the building like his fortress. For an extended analysis of this theme, see Roche 2011: 60–6.

For surely there is no one educated in the liberal arts who does not support everything you do and, most especially, your accommodation at public receptions? Indeed, it was your father[1] who, with greatness of spirit, had inscribed the title of 'Public House'[2] on what had been a fortress prior to your new generation of emperors. But such action would have been in vain, if he had not adopted a man who could spend his life under public scrutiny. How well that inscription matches your own character, and your every deed makes it seem like no one else could have inscribed it! What forum, what temples are made so accessible? Not the Capitoline Temple, that very place at which you were adopted, is more public, more available to all. There are no barriers, no hierarchies of humiliation, and on top of that, no innumerable gateways which forever lead to yet more doors standing severe and obstinate.[3] Now there lies true tranquillity before you, behind you, and all around you: so mighty is the peace, and so noble the sense of propriety, that radiate out as paradigms of modesty and serenity from the prince's home to humble households and ordinary dwellings.[4]

Then there is you – how you welcome everyone, how you wait for them! How it is that you spend much of each day occupied with the many burdens of state but adopt the manner of a man of leisure! And so we now assemble, no longer pallid and paralysed with fear, nor dragging our heels as though in fear of our lives, but free of anxiety and light of heart, at our own convenience. Sometimes when the emperor is receiving people, there is perhaps a more pressing issue that keeps us at home, but you always excuse us without requiring us to plead excuses.[5] For you know that each of us competes with each other to see you and visit you, and so you offer more free and extensive occasions for this pleasure. So your audiences are not followed by our escape and your desolation: we remain behind, we linger, as if this house belongs to all of us. Until recently it was a place where that most brutal beast[6] barricaded himself in,[7] protected by his countless acts of terror. For example, sometimes, in his secret grotto[8] he would lick up the blood of his relatives,[9] while at other times he showed himself in order to destroy and slaughter citizens of senatorial rank.[10] Dread and menace guarded his gates, as did the twin fears of admission and rejection. Then there he was, equally frightening to see and to meet. His countenance was marked by arrogance, his eyes by anger, his body by a womanly pallor, and his face by the tell-tale blush of shamelessness.[11] No one dared to approach or address him, while he always sought shadows and seclusion, never emerging from his place of desolation except to make new miseries elsewhere.

1 The emperor Nerva, who adopted Trajan in October 97.

2 Nerva lived on the Palatine in the same palace as Domitian. This inscription indicated that this did not mean his approach to imperial rule would be the same: Roche 2011: 60.

3 Domitian's use of gateways and barriers – if accurate – suggests that security procedures could be modified depending on imperial preferences.

4 In the same way that the emperor serves as an *exemplum* for people to imitate, so his residence is a model for other houses.

5 For the senatorial obligation to attend the *salutatio*, and to offer explanations if absent, see **4.3**.

6 The image of Domitian as a monstrous emperor echoes the depiction of Claudius in Seneca's *Apocolocyntosis* (5), in which he is portrayed as an inhuman beast.

7 Emperors who shut themselves off from their fellow senators were objects of suspicion (such as Tiberius on Capreae). Domitian's desire for privacy was notorious (e.g. Suet. *Dom.* 3.1).

8 Domitian is supposed to have enjoyed interrogating prisoners alone: Suet. *Dom.* 14.4.

9 He executed his cousins T. Flavius Sabinus, T. Flavius Clemens, and M. Arrecinus Clemens: Suet. *Dom.* 10.4, 11.1, 15.1, with Jones 1992: 42–8.

10 For Domitian's senatorial victims, see Jones 1992: 180–8.

11 Physiognomy was an important way in which Romans assessed their emperors, as appearance was supposed to reflect character. Blushing was normally a sign of *pudor*, or shame, but in Domitian's case, the natural red complexion on his face gave the impression that he was shameful, although he was really shameless; see also Suet. *Dom.* 18.1; Tac. *Agr.* 45.2. On this and other aspects of the blush, see Barton 2002.

4.8 Informal receptions of friends

Cassius Dio 65(66).10.4–5 (Xiph.)

Receptions in the emperor's bedroom are first attested under Vespasian; see also Suet. *Vesp.* 21; *Epit. de Caes.* 9.15; cf. Plin. *Ep.* 3.5.9. This was regarded as a mark of imperial simplicity and *civilitas*, though it was still a regulated court ritual. See Davenport, **Vol. 1, 295–6**.

Vespasian settled upon the following routine for his day-to-day life. He rarely resided on the Palatine,[1] instead passing most of his time in the gardens called 'Sallustian',[2] where he would receive anyone – senators and everyone else besides – who wished to see him. Before dawn, still lying in his bed, his closest friends would join him there in discussions, while other friends would pay their respects to him as he walked the streets. The gates of the imperial residence lay open throughout each day and there were never any guards placed there as a garrison.[3]

1 The imperial residence on the Palatine underwent substantial modifications from Vespasian's reign onwards, which may explain why the emperor resided in another location: Krause 1995. See Pflug and Wulf-Rheidt, **Vol. 1, Chapter 9** for the Flavian building programme.

2 The 'Sallustian Gardens' (Horti Sallustiani) was an estate owned by the Roman historian C. Sallustius Crispus (better known as Sallust; *RE* 10). It passed into imperial hands in the Julio-Claudian period. Vespasian's residence there signalled the difference between his court and that of Nero on the Palatine: Acton 2011: 107–10.

3 Vespasian was regarded as an accessible emperor in contrast with rulers such as Claudius (**4.4 [a]**) and Domitian (**4.7 [b]**).

II | Special Occasions

Throughout the year, courtiers participated in a variety of commemorative events, such as New Year's Day, anniversaries, birthdays, and festivals; Herz 1978 offers a full account. Members of the court, such as the praetorian prefects, played an increasingly important role in the development of Roman imperial accession ritual. The Palatine itself became a location at which imperial acclamations could take place, but this never solidified into a firm ritual procedure.

4.9 Accession ceremonial

(a) Josephus, *Jewish Antiquities* 19.223, 226, 247

Caligula was murdered on the Palatine on 24 January 41 by members of the praetorian guard, including the tribune Cassius Chaerea (*PIR*[2] C 488). In the panic which followed, Claudius hid behind a curtain, but was discovered by a guardsman called Gratus, who proposed that they acclaim him emperor: Joseph. *AJ* 19.216–20. The story continues in the passage below from Josephus, who provides the most detailed narrative of the murder of Caligula and accession of Claudius. The actions of the guardsmen were only part of the accession ritual, however, since Claudius still needed to be acclaimed by the Senate and people, which happened on the following day. For Josephus' account, see Wiseman 2013a, and for accession ceremonial, Davenport, **Vol. 1, 309–11**.

They (sc. Claudius and the soldiers) then came out into the open space on the Palatine:[1] the story handed down about this area is that it is the place where the city of Rome was first settled.[2] And by the time they reached the public building,[3] there was an even greater gathering of soldiers, who greeted the appearance of Claudius with delight, and they intended to establish this fellow as emperor because of their goodwill towards Germanicus, his brother, who had left an excellent impression on all those with whom he had come into contact.

(Josephus reports that the soldiers considered the benefits of proclaiming Claudius emperor.)

Learning of the enthusiasm (sc. for Claudius), they took up the challenge, encircling him and turning about-face, they carried him off to the camp, lifting him up in a litter, so that nothing would stop their onward motion.

(After a confused period, in which the Senate showed some unwillingness to have a new emperor, and Herod Agrippa played a double game by conciliating the Senate and steeling Claudius' resolve, Claudius decided to seize the purple.)

Claudius addressed the assembled army, and after administering the oath as a pledge of their loyalty to him,[4] he distributed five hundred *denarii* a head to the members of the praetorian guard,[5] an amount for the officers in proportion to their standing, and undertook to give equivalent amounts to the armies stationed elsewhere.

1 This Area Palatina was probably directly outside the Augustan Vestibulum on the north-western façade of the imperial *domus*. See the discussion and plans in Wiseman 2013a: 101–8.

2 For the location of Romulus' hut on the south-western Palatine, see Plut. *Rom.* 20.5; Ov. *Fast.* 3.183–4; Coarelli 2012: 119–20, 130–2.
3 The identity of this building is unknown; it may simply refer to the imperial residence as a whole. See Wiseman 2013a: 87.
4 The oath of loyalty to the *princeps* became a regular part of imperial accessions in the Julio-Claudian period: Campbell 1984: 25–32.
5 Suetonius (*Claud.* 10.4) gives a figure of 15,000 sesterces per head, on which see Hurley 2001: 100.

(b) Suetonius, *Life of Nero* 8

Suetonius' account of the accession of Nero reveals the importance of the steps to the palace as a location at which one key accession ritual could take place: the imperatorial acclamation. This was followed by a visit to the praetorian camp and then the Senate. See too Tac. *Ann.* 12.69 for the same episode.

Nero was seventeen years old when news of Claudius' death became public. Between the sixth and seventh hour,[1] he presented himself to the watchmen;[2] because there had been terrible portents throughout the whole day, no other time could be regarded as promising for inaugurating his reign. After he was hailed *imperator* before the steps of the Palatine,[3] he was taken to the praetorian camp by litter, gave a hasty speech to the troops, and then was brought to the Senate house, only leaving there in the evening.[4] Out of all the immense honours heaped upon him, only the name of 'Father of the Fatherland'[5] was rejected, because he was still a youth.

1 I.e. in the hour after midday.
2 These are the *excubitores*, the soldiers on guard duty. Tacitus regarded these guards as part of the 'trappings of a court' (above **1.8 [c]**).
3 The steps to the palace (*gradus Palatii*) are mentioned in different accounts: see e.g. Suet. *Vit.* 15.2; Dio Cass. 68.5.5 (Xiph.). They are not necessarily the same steps on each occasion, since the imperial residence evolved significantly over time. For example, Augustus' Vestibulum did not have steps up to it, whereas the Flavian Vestibulum did: Wiseman 2013b: 262; cf. Tamm 1963: 82–4; Coarelli 2012: 398–9. The *gradus* referred to in pre-Flavian accounts must be in other locations; see Perrin 2003 for the possibilities.
4 Cassius Dio gives the same order of events in much less detail: 61.3.1 (Xiph.).
5 Nero would become *pater patriae* in late 55/early 56.

4.10 Celebrating accession anniversaries at court

Fronto, *Letters to Antoninus Pius* 5 (ed. vdH 164 = Haines 1.226–8).

Emperors' accession days were celebrated each year with sacrifices and vows for the continuation of their reigns: Mommsen 1887–8: 2.797; Herz 1978: 1140. In this letter to Pius, Fronto writes to apologize for his absence from Antoninus Pius' accession day (10 July 138) on grounds of ill-health.

Fronto to Antoninus Pius Augustus,
   I long to offer part of my soul, emperor, so that I may embrace you on this most fortunate and long-desired anniversary of your accession, which I regard

as the birthday of my welfare, public standing, and security.[1] But serious shoulder pain, which grows much more painful up my neck, has struck me so badly that I can barely bend, raise myself upright, or turn around. Therefore, I must keep my neck completely still.[2] Nevertheless, I have made and given an undertaking to fulfil my vows before my Lares, Penates, and household gods. I have prayed that next year I will embrace you twice on the day itself, and that I will fondly kiss your breast and hands twice over,[3] so that I will complete this year's and next year's vow at the same time.

1 Like many senators, Fronto had an ambivalent relationship with Pius' predecessor and adoptive father Hadrian. See *Ad M. Caes.* 2.4.1 (ed. vdH 25 = Haines 1.110); Champlin 1980: 94–7.
2 Fronto's health problems often kept him away from court; cf. **4.4 (d)** n. 5.
3 The *civilis princeps* would normally be expected to kiss senators on the cheeks as his peers. However, here Fronto flatters the emperor by greeting him in a more subservient fashion. See **Section III** below and Davenport, **Vol. 1, 304–6**.

III | Greeting the Emperor: the Imperial Kiss and *adoratio*

Roman aristocratic men usually embraced and kissed each other on the lips in greeting, and the continuance of this tradition by the emperor marked him out as a *civilis princeps*, who treated courtiers as his peers. There were many dynamics to imperial kisses, which were closely observed by contemporaries. They noted if an emperor kissed a courtier only briefly, regarding it as a sign of disfavour; see Tac. *Agr.* 40.3. At the other spectrum, too much intimacy with an emperor could arouse jealousy; see **4.14**. Emperors who offered other parts of their body to kiss, such as their hands or feet, were regarded as breaking with tradition by emphasizing the power differential between themselves and the aristocracy. Yet very often it was courtiers themselves who made the first move, introducing new sycophantic ways of kissing the emperor's body and clothes: **4.12**. See Paterson 2007: 136–7, 147–8, 155–6.

Indeed, from a relatively early stage, aristocrats experimented with ceremonial procedure by prostrating themselves before the ruler. When a courtier such as L. Vitellius veiled his head and abased himself before Caligula, there was no doubt that he intended it to be regarded as the act of *proskynēsis*, the rite of prostration before a god: **4.15 (b)**. The introduction of such behaviour to the Roman imperial court was regarded as more befitting the tyranny of Persian monarchy, and indeed many Roman writers thought it had been imported from there: Alföldi 1970: 9–15; Matthews 1989: 244–6. That said, by the mid-third century, it had become much more common for courtiers to prostrate themselves before the emperor. This led to the emperor Diocletian introducing the new ceremonial of *adoratio*, which required people to lower themselves before the emperor's figure and kiss his purple robe: **4.16**. For discussion of the change from *salutatio* to *adoratio*, see Alföldi 1970: 38–79; Smith 2007: 175–8, 215–20.

4.11 The custom of aristocratic kissing – and its hazards

Pliny the Elder, *Natural History* 26.2–3

Pliny's description of the spread of an unsightly skin disease highlights the prevalence of kissing as a form of greeting between male members of the nobility. The disease appears to be why the emperor promulgated an edict which forbade kissing: Suet. *Tib.* 34.2.

The most serious of these (sc. diseases of the face) is known as *lichen*,[1] which comes from the Greek. Our Latin term for it started as a naughty joke – since many people are shameless enough to mock the sufferings of others – but was soon taken up into common usage. It is thus called *mentagra*,[2] because it usually starts on the chin. In most cases, the disease completely takes over the entire face, with only the eyes spared, and then its unsightly scales descend over the skin on the neck, chest, and hands.

This contagion did not exist when our parents or ancestors were alive, but only first crept into Italy in the middle of the reign of Ti. Claudius Caesar,[3] when a certain Roman equestrian from Perusia brought the disease with him on his return from the province of Asia, where he had been serving as secretary for the quaestor. Neither women, nor slaves, nor people of humble or middling background are affected by this malady, but it especially afflicts leading men who pass it during their fleeting kisses.

1 *OLD* s.v. *lichen* 2.
2 *OLD* s.v. *mentagra*, literally 'chin gout', derived from *podagra* ('foot disease, gout').
3 The emperor Tiberius.

4.12 Kissing the tyrant: Caligula

(a) Seneca the Younger, *On Benefits* 2.12.1–2

Seneca the Younger criticizes Caligula for demanding that Pompeius Pennus (*PIR*[2] P 636), a man of consular rank, kiss his slippered feet in gratitude for being spared execution. Seneca does not say what the senator did to earn Caligula's wrath. Pompeius may be identical with the Pomponius in Cassius Dio (59.26.4 [*EV*]) who was accused of conspiring against the emperor, or the Pompedius in Josephus (*AJ* 19.32–6) who apparently uttered treasonous sayings.

C. Caesar (Caligula) gave Pompeius Pennus his life, if by 'gave', one means not depriving him of it. After Pennus had been spared and was offering thanks, the emperor stretched out his left foot so he would kiss it. There are some who offer excuses and deny that it was supposed to be an insulting gesture.[1] They say that the emperor wanted to show off his gold-covered slipper[2] – or more accurately, his slipper made of gold – which was covered with pearls. And so, how could it be insulting, if a man of consular rank kissed gold and pearls, since he could not find another part of the emperor's body which would be purer to kiss? This being, who was created to transform the ways of a free state into a Persian-style servitude, thought that it would not have been enough for an elderly senator, who had been exalted with honours, to lower himself as a suppliant in full view of the leading aristocrats, in the same way that defeated foreigners offer themselves to their enemies. Instead, he discovered how to force freedom down lower even than the knees. Does this not represent our state being trampled underfoot? And indeed, one might say, for it does matter in this case, with the left foot? For, it is surely the case that a slipper-clad judge, hearing the capital case of a man of consular rank, would not have displayed enough insulting and infuriating arrogance unless he had acted like a general (*imperator*) and thrust his hobnails[3] into the senator's face.

1 This remark suggests that there were some courtiers who supported innovations in court ceremonial. See further **4.12 (b)** below.
2 The Latin word *soccus* (the diminutive *socculus* appears here) specifically refers to a slipper traditionally worn by Greeks and actors: *OLD* s.v. *soccus* a, b. Caligula is also criticized for wearing this same style of Greek shoe in Suetonius: *Calig.* 52; cf. Olson, **Vol. 1, 465**.
3 *OLD* s.v. *epigrus*. Griffin (2013: 193) suggests that the pearls acted like a soldier's hobnails, and that this may be an ironic reference to Caligula's own nickname 'little boots'.

(b) Cassius Dio 59.29.5–6 (Xiph.; Zonar.)

This anecdote about Caligula demonstrates that not all innovations in ceremonial emerged from the emperor himself. Often it was the courtiers themselves who tried to find new ways to flatter the ruler, as in the case of the consul who kissed Caligula's feet.

In the palace, Gaius (Caligula) was taking part in a festival and putting on a show,[1] and as part of this he was eating and drinking along with others he had received into his hall. It was then that Pomponius Secundus,[2] that year's consul, thoroughly gorged himself, and while sitting next to the emperor's feet, he frequently bent over to kiss them. Chaerea[3] and Sabinus,[4] although they found these shameful acts revolting, patiently waited another five days.[5]

1 The *ludi Palatini* were held in honour of Augustus each year, beginning in January AD 17.
2 Q. Pomponius Secundus (*cos. suff.* 41; *PIR*[2] P 757).
3 Cassius Chaerea (*PIR*[2] C 488), praetorian tribune and a leader in the conspiracy to kill Caligula.
4 Cornelius Sabinus was another praetorian tribune who joined in the conspiracy: Joseph. *AJ* 19.46–8; Suet. *Calig.* 58.2.
5 I.e. before murdering Caligula.

4.13 Trajan's courteous kisses

Pliny the Younger, *Panegyric* 24.2

Unlike Caligula, described above (**4.12**), Trajan kisses his senatorial peers as fellow citizens, demonstrating that he has retained his *humanitas*. See Kühn 1987.

You (i.e. Trajan) do not force citizens to embrace you at the level of your feet, nor do you repay their kiss by holding out your hand;[1] your kiss remains that of a fellow man, even though you are now an emperor, and your right hand remains respectful.

1 As Caligula reportedly did to Cassius Chaerea: Suet. *Calig.* 56.2.

4.14 The politics of kissing at the Antonine court

(a) Fronto, *Letters to Marcus as Caesar* 3.14.3 (ed. vdH 46 = Haines 1.220–1)

In this excerpt from a letter to Marcus Aurelius from the late 140s, Fronto explains why he did not kiss Marcus farewell on a recent occasion, seemingly because he feared causing jealousy on the part of other courtiers, which would rebound negatively on Marcus. Kissing was a normal part of court life, but Fronto evidently thought that his kiss from Marcus would be misinterpreted, and the Caesar needed to be seen to distribute his affections more equally in public. The letter is infused with amatory language indicating Fronto's desire to be close to Marcus, and he explicitly compares himself to a lover: Richlin 2006a: 123–6; 2006b: 150. Kissing often features in the correspondence as an indication of Fronto's desire to be esteemed and honoured by Marcus, as well as his anxiety at their separation: *Ad M. Caes.* 2.13, 4.12 (ed. vdH 32, 65–7 = Haines 1.144–6, 202–8). However, this discourse is not evidence of a sexual relationship: Laes 2009; Davenport and Manley 2014: 9–11.

What is more delightful to me than your kiss? For me, that delightful scent, that reward which flows from it, can be found on your neck and on your mouth. But most recently – when you were embarking on a journey and your father[1] had already climbed into the carriage – there was a crowd of people who were wishing you farewell and kissing you and so delayed you all the longer. Then, it was for your benefit that I alone, out of all those gathered, neither embraced you nor kissed you. Likewise, in all other further matters, I will never put my personal considerations before your own needs; for, if it were necessary, I would go to great trouble and effort to ensure that you would be entirely free and untroubled.

1 Antoninus Pius.

(b) Fronto, *Letters to Verus as Emperor* 1.7 (ed. vdH 111–12 = Haines 2.238–40)

This letter from Fronto to Lucius Verus probably dates to 161–2, the year after Verus became joint Augustus with Marcus Aurelius: van den Hout 1999: 275. The beginning of the letter is lost, but it seems that the affection Verus showed for Fronto had aroused misgivings at court (similar to the situation described in **4.14 [a]** above with Marcus). We must remember that in both letters we view the jealousy of courtiers through the lens of Fronto's own experience; he was a somewhat anxious courtier who took every opportunity in his correspondence to signal his yearning to be close to both Marcus and Verus.

<To my lord Verus Augustus>
   [- - -] the honour would be desired, and someone seeks that which he hopes for just as much, if the honour seems to have been shared with others. You

approved and praised my advice, but nevertheless, for more than three or four days you could not bring yourself even to reply to me with a word. But you then devised the following: first, you would order me to be sent into your bedroom,[1] so you could give me a kiss without anyone's resentment. I believe that you had come to the conclusion in your mind, that I, the one to whom you had entrusted the custody of and care for your speech and style,[2] also had a right to your kisses, since all teachers of public speaking, by the rights of their own labour, receive the enjoyments of their cultivation, as derived from the voice's own vessel.

1 Emperors often held audiences for their *amici* in the imperial bedchamber (see **4.8**, above), but Fronto was especially privileged to be received alone.
2 Fronto was Verus' tutor in Latin rhetoric, as he had been for Marcus: SHA *Ver.* 2.5.

4.15 Early experiments with *adoratio*

(a) Tacitus, *Annals* 1.13.6

Q. Haterius (*cos. suff.* 5 BC; *PIR*[2] H 24) had aroused Tiberius' ire because he asked how long he would put off taking up his imperial duties. Suetonius (*Tib.* 27) gives a version of the same story. For grasping people by the knees as a traditional gesture of supplication, see Alföldi 1970: 48–9.

It is reported that Haterius, when he had come to the Palatine to seek a pardon, grovelled before Tiberius by taking hold of the emperor's knees as he was walking. He was almost killed by the soldiers, because Tiberius had fallen face-forward, either accidentally or because he had become entangled with Haterius' hands. However, even the threat to the life of such a great man did not mollify Tiberius, until Haterius pleaded with the Augusta,[1] and he was shielded by her solicitous prayers.

1 Tiberius' mother, Livia. See **3.29** for another example of her influence.

(b) Suetonius, *Life of Vitellius* 2.5

This anecdote concerns the distinguished consular and ex-censor, L. Vitellius, who faced execution, allegedly after his successful governorship of Syria provoked Caligula's jealousy and fear; cf. Dio Cass. 59.27.2–6 (Xiph.; *EV*). The gestures with which he ingratiated himself with Caligula have the appearance of *proskynēsis*, and Dio gives them this label.

L. Vitellius had a remarkable natural talent for flattery, being the first man who decided to adore C. Caesar (Caligula) as a god. After his return from Syria, he would not dare to approach Gaius except with his head covered, then turning himself around and lying prostrate before him.[1] He used every trick to win the approval of the emperor Claudius, who was controlled by his wives and freedmen. As if it were some great privilege, he asked Messalina to offer up her feet so he could remove her shoes. After he had taken off her dainty right slipper, he constantly carried it about between his toga and tunic, sometimes giving it a kiss.[2]

1 Dio Cass. 59.27.5 (Xiph.; *EV*) uses the Greek verb προσκυνέω to describe L. Vitellius' action.
2 For Vitellius' adherence to Messalina, see Tac. *Ann.* 11.2.2–4.2.

(c) Cassius Dio 67.13.3–4 (Xiph.)

Iuventius Celsus (*PIR*[2] I 880) was a senator implicated in a conspiracy against Domitian, probably in 93: Murison 1999: 256–7. Again, a courtier resorts to *proskynēsis* and flattery in a desperate attempt at self-preservation.

However, a certain Iuventius Celsus escaped with his life in an extraordinary way. He was one of several men who had taken a leading role in fomenting a conspiracy against Domitian, and he had been arraigned on this very charge. When he was about to be convicted, he pleaded for the opportunity to speak to the emperor in private, and performed *proskynēsis* before him then and there, hailing him again and again as 'lord' and 'god', honorifics which some men were already using to refer to the emperor.[1] Celsus said: 'I am not guilty of the sort of crime of which I am accused, but if I receive a reprieve, I will investigate anyone and anything, and I will charge and convict many individuals on your behalf.' After he had been freed on this condition, he did not denounce any individuals, but instead, by constantly offering a range of different excuses, he managed to prolong the matter until Domitian had himself died.

1 According to Suetonius (*Dom.* 13.2) and Zonaras (11.19 = Dio Cass. 67.4.7), Domitian used these titles to refer to himself in his letters, though this has been rightly doubted by Jones (1992: 108–9), who points out the lack of corroborating evidence. It seems better to regard this combination of titles as adulation by courtiers. *Dominus* had become a conventional honorific for addressing emperors by this period (indeed, Pliny uses it to refer to Trajan in his *Letters*). The addition of *deus* was a new way to flatter Domitian (e.g. Mart. *Ep.* 5.8.1, 9.66.3), to which he was no doubt receptive. For discussion, see Jones 1992: 108–9; Dominik 1994: 158–60; Murison 1999: 228–9.

(d) Philostratus, *Lives of the Sophists* 589–90

Hadrian of Tyre (*PIR*[2] H 4) was a famous sophist from a part of the province of Syria that is now in modern Lebanon. He served as professor of rhetoric at Athens and Rome: Philostr. *V S* 585–9. During the second century, it had become common practice for the emperors to appoint such distinguished Greek intellectuals as their secretary of Greek letters (*ab epistulis Graecis*); see Millar 1992: 91–3; Davenport 2019: 363–5. In Hadrian's case, this honour only came at the end of his life.

When Hadrian of Tyre had fallen ill at Rome, and indeed had reached his end, Commodus awarded him the office of *ab epistulis*, with an apology for not appointing him earlier. Hadrian called upon the Muses, as he usually did, and performed *proskynēsis* before the imperial letter.[1] As he exhaled his final breath over the words before him, the grant became a funereal honour.

1 For individuals performing gestures of obeisance before an emperor's images, edicts, and letters, see Alföldi 1970: 65–70; Ando 2000: 106–8, 232–9.

(e) [Aelius Aristides], *To the King* 19 (ed. Keil 1898: 257–8)

The oration *To the King*, although once ascribed to the second-century orator Aelius Aristides, is generally dated now to the third century, with the emperor Philippus Arabs as the likely honorand: Swift 1966; de Blois 1986; for other views cf. Jones 1972, 1981; Körner 2002. By the time the speech was composed, *proskynēsis* had evidently become routine before the emperor, at least when he was acting as a judge.

For there is no one who leaves the emperor's presence without justice having been done or finds fault in what he has decided, neither the accuser who has been defeated nor the accused who has been convicted, for both men are satisfied, and having performed *proskynēsis*, they take their leave, the decision in the case being borne equally by the defeated and the victorious.

4.16 *Adoratio* under Diocletian

(a) Aurelius Victor, *On the Caesars* 39.2–4

Victor and other Roman historians of the fourth century believed that a dramatic change in court ceremonial had occurred during the reign of Diocletian, marking a caesura between their world and that of the early empire: Matthews 1989: 244–6. These accounts (see also **4.16 [b–c]**, below) all rely to some extent on a lost series of mid-fourth century imperial biographies, which modern scholars have termed the *Kaisergeschichte*: Alföldi 1970: 6–9. Victor identified two specific innovations of Diocletian: the emperor's decadent and foreign dress, and the introduction of the ceremony of *adoratio*, on which see Avery 1940; Stern 1954.

Indeed, Diocletian was the first emperor who desired, together with clothes made out of gold, a quantity of silk and purple, and gems for his feet.[1] Although these were not the characteristics of a Roman citizen,[2] but of a mind inclined to pride and extravagance, they were inconsequential when compared to his other actions. For he was the first of all the emperors, after Caligula and Domitian, to allow himself to be publicly hailed as 'lord', and to be adored and addressed as if he were a god.[3]

1 Caligula is also said to have worn studded slippers: see **4.12 (a)**. This criticism is applied to Elagabalus and Carinus: SHA *Heliogab.* 23.3–4; *Alex. Sev.* 4.2; *Carinus* 17.1.
2 Diocletian's ceremonial marked a break with the imperial virtue of *civilitas*, or citizen-like behaviour. In Late Antiquity, emperors could be criticized for showing too much *civilitas*; e.g. Amm. Marc. 22.7.3–4 on Julian.
3 Cf. **4.15 (b–c)**.

(b) Eutropius, *Short History* 9.26

Eutropius wrote the *Short History*, offering an abbreviated account of Roman history from 753 BC to AD 364, for the emperor Valens, drawing on the lost *Kaisergeschichte*. His work offers an account of Diocletian's ceremonial innovations that is similar to

Aurelius Victor's (**4.16** [**a**]). Eutropius specifically identifies the new 'monarchical customs' which contrasted with Roman practice – the monarchy being Rome's largest neighbour, Persia. This belief that the *adoratio* ritual came from Persia was widespread, but inaccurate: Canepa 2009: 64–6, 149–52.

Diocletian was an artful character, a man who was perceptive and naturally quick-witted; indeed, he was the sort of man who was prepared to satiate his own cruel desires even if others bore the blame. Nevertheless, he was a most industrious and intelligent emperor, and it was he who first introduced into the Roman empire a ritual that owed more to monarchical customs[1] than to the liberty familiar to Romans. He commanded that he should be adored, although all his predecessors had been greeted.[2] He studded his robes and shoes with decorative gemstones.[3] Prior to this point, the emperor had been marked out only by his purple cloak (*chlamys*), with his other clothes being no different from his peers'.

1 For the *adoratio* as a Persian custom, see also SHA *Alex. Sev.* 18.3.
2 Eutropius explicitly draws a contrast between *salutatio* and *adoratio*.
3 See above, **4.16** (**a**) with n. 1.

(c) Ammianus Marcellinus 15.5.18

Ammianus Marcellinus was a fourth-century military officer, who wrote a history of the Roman empire from Nerva to Valens in thirty-one books. In this passage, Ammianus describes the events of 355, when the master of the soldiers (*magister peditum*) Silvanus (*PLRE* 1.840–1) staged a coup against the emperor Constantius II. In response, the emperor and his advisers resolved to call on Ursicinus (*PLRE* 1.985–6), the master of the cavalry (*magister equitum*) whose popularity had led to him being accused of treason, though his life had been spared. Ammianus goes on to describe Ursicinus' reception by Constantius II at court in Mediolanum (modern Milan) and the ceremony of *adoratio*.

After Constantius (II) had been hit by this unexpected and weighty blow like a heavenly thunderbolt,[1] he summoned a council at the second watch, and all his foremost advisers came quickly to the palace. Since no one's mind or tongue had sufficient power to choose an appropriate course of action, Ursicinus' name cropped up in hushed conversations, as he was far and away the most outstanding expert in military matters and had been unjustly wronged by a grave miscarriage of justice.[2] He was summoned by the *magister admissionum*[3] – as the proper protocol dictates – and was admitted by that same official into the consistory.[4] Ursicinus was presented with the purple[5] in a manner that was much more gracious than his previous experiences. It was <Diocletian Augustus>[6] who had been the first of all the emperors to institute the foreign and monarchical ritual of adoration, since we have read that before his time the emperors were always greeted as if they were like all other magistrates.

1 The usurpation of Silvanus at Cologne.
2 Ammianus describes the intrigues against Ursicinus earlier in the book (15.2.1–6).
3 The master of admissions (*magister admissionum*) was the late Roman equivalent of the *ab admissione*; see Jones 1964: 1.103, 368–9.

4 The late-antique emperor's council of state, descended from the *consilia* of the Principate.
5 The act of kissing the purple was a high honour. Flavius Abinnaeus, for example, used this as evidence that he had been rightfully appointed to a military post when other men claimed the same position: *P.Abinn.* 1. The emperor could withhold the privilege from courtiers as a mark of his displeasure: Amm. Marc. 22.9.16.
6 There is a gap in the Latin text of Ammianus at this point, into which modern editors have plausibly inserted the name of Diocletian.

4.17 *Adoratio* for Diocletian and Maximian

Latin Panegyrics 11(3).11.1–3

This is an excerpt from a speech delivered by an anonymous orator at Augusta Treverorum (modern Trier, Germany) in 291 as part of the birthday celebrations for the emperor Maximian, who ruled as co-Augustus with Diocletian: Nixon and Rodgers 1994: 76–80. The panegyrist gives an extended account of the formal *adventus* of the emperors to the city of Mediolanum in the winter of 290/1. In this passage, he provides the first contemporary account of the ceremony of *adoratio* under Diocletian.

What a sight, good gods! What a show your piety staged, when the crowd who came to adore your sacred visage[1] entered the palace at Mediolanum (*in Mediolanensi palatio*) and gazed upon you both together, and you unexpectedly upset the custom of venerating a single emperor with your twofold godhood![2] The established rules for the order of deities could not be followed: everyone remained still, prolonging the act of adoration, unyielding in their duty to offer their devotion twice over. However, just as if this act of exclusive veneration had taken place in the inner chambers of a sanctuary, it stunned only the minds of those who were sufficiently high ranking to merit admittance to your presence.[3] Still, after you crossed over the palace threshold, and journeyed together through the midst of the city, I am told that the buildings themselves almost started to shake, as everyone, men and women, little children and old people, either rushed outside into the streets or leant out from the upper stories of their houses.

1 In the late Roman empire, the *adventus* ceremony was envisioned as the arrival of a living god: MacCormack 1981: 22–33.
2 The ceremony of *adoratio* was already established by 290/1; what caused confusion was the fact that there were two emperors who both required veneration: Nixon and Rodgers 1994: 96 n. 65.
3 The panegyrist's language assimilates the entrance into the emperor's presence with entering a temple: Alföldi 1970: 33–6; MacCormack 1981: 25–6.

4.18 *Adoratio* for Constantine

Latin Panegyrics 5(8).1.3–4

This passage comes from a speech praising the emperor Constantine, delivered at Augusta Treverorum in 311 by an orator from the Gallic city of Augustodunum (modern Autun, France). The speaker had come to Augusta Treverorum as part of an embassy: Nixon and Rodgers 1994: 254–63. The speech is valuable because the orator provides a first-hand account of *adoratio*, particularly the way in which participation in the ceremony was seen as a mark of favour bestowed by the emperor.

Most sacred emperor, I was intent on rendering thanks to your godhood, when, in the entrance of your palace, you raised up the line of men lying before your feet with the divine voice of your beneficence and by extending this, your unconquered right hand. Although I was caught off guard, I did not lose the ability to speak. For who could have been prepared for favours so unexpected or who could have restrained himself from offering great thanksgiving?

IV | The Reception of Embassies and Foreign Dignitaries

In the Republican period, the reception of embassies traditionally lay within the purview of the Senate: Polyb. 6.13.7–8. From the Augustan period onwards, foreign embassies increasingly approached the emperor directly: Talbert 1984: 411–25. The emperor also often received delegations from provinces or cities within the Roman empire, as he was regarded as the ultimate arbiter in disputes: Millar 1992: 375–85.

4.19 Caligula's reception of the Alexandrian embassies

Philo, *Embassy to Gaius* 351–3, 358, 364–6

The city of Alexandria in Egypt was racked by serious conflicts between the Jewish and Greek communities in the 30s AD. In 39, separate delegations of Jews and Greeks travelled to Italy to ask the emperor Caligula to settle their differences: see Barrett 2015: 207–14. In his account of the delegation he led, Philo describes the proper actions of a judge who is charged with settling disputes, and then continues:

For Caligula behaved in the opposite way to the procedure I have described. He summoned the procurators of the two gardens, named after Maecenas and Lamia, which lay close to each other in Rome.[1] Caligula had whiled away three or four days in these gardens. And it was there, with those of us on hand serving as representatives of our entire people, that a dramatic scenario was going to be staged. Caligula gave orders for the residences to be left totally open for him, for he wanted to examine each of them closely. After we were brought before him, we beheld him with all due reverence and respect, and then we paid our respects, with heads bowed low towards the ground, calling him 'Emperor Augustus'. He addressed us in turn in such a mild and friendly manner, that we not only despaired of our petition but even for our lives. For sneering and bearing his teeth, he said: 'Are you the sacrilegious individuals who do not consider me to be a divinity,[2] as already agreed by all others, but still nameless to you?' He lifted up his hands towards the heavens and delivered a supplication, which was sacrilegious to listen to, let alone to set down word for word.

(Philo then reports how the Alexandrian Greek ambassadors and Caligula engaged in hostile dialogue with the Alexandrian Jewish ambassadors, and then continues.)

All the time he was speaking he was moving through the residences, considering the men's apartments, then the women's, the lower floor, and the upper ones, each and every one, alleging that some had construction problems, while observing others he made additional arrangements for them to be embellished.

(Philo reports how the Alexandrian Greeks and Caligula continued to ask mocking questions of the Alexandrian Jews regarding their customs, and then continues.)

We began to speak and explain, but after he had a taste of our complaints and realizing that they were hardly negligible, he cut us short when we were making our preliminary arguments, before we presented our stronger evidence. He sprang up, rushing into the great chamber, and while touring it he gave instructions that the windows around it should be brightened up with translucent stones, which are much like clear glass in that they do not prevent light entering but do shut out the wind and the harshness of the sun. And then he approached us again, now without any haste, and asked us more reasonably, 'What are you saying?' We began to string together our next points, but he rushed off again into another room, where he commanded that original paintings should be displayed.

1 The Gardens of Maecenas (Horti Maecenatis) and Lamian Gardens (Horti Lamiani) were imperial estates on the Esquiline hill.
2 For Caligula's divine pretensions, see Barrett 2015: 190–205.

4.20 Nero receives Tiridates of Armenia

Suetonius, *Life of Nero* 13.1–2

Ceremonial which involved members of the imperial court not only took place within the palace, but also in full view of the public, as shown by this passage in which Nero crowns Tiridates as king of Armenia. For much of Nero's reign, Rome and Parthia had been engaged in conflict over Armenia, an important buffer state between the two empires. The tension was resolved when Tiridates was installed on the throne in 63, and three years later he travelled to Rome to receive the crown from the emperor. For these events, see also Dio Cass. 62(63).1.2–6.7 (Xiph.). Modern scholarly accounts can be found in Griffin 1984: 223, 226–7, 232–3; Champlin 2003: 221–9.

It would not be unwarranted for me to describe, among the spectacles staged by Nero, the entrance of Tiridates into Rome. This man was the king of Armenia, whom Nero had enticed there with grand promises. Although the day which had been publicly announced for the presentation of Tiridates to the people had to be postponed on account of inclement weather, Nero exhibited him as soon as there was a convenient opportunity.[1] After stationing armed cohorts around the temples of the forum, the emperor, clad in triumphal dress, seated himself on a curule chair on the rostra, flanked on all sides by military emblems and standards. Tiridates ascended up a sloping platform, kneeled down, and Nero received him;

then, the emperor raised him up with his right hand and kissed him warmly. After removing the headdress from Tiridates as he made his entreaties, Nero placed a diadem on his head. The words of the suppliant king were translated and announced to the crowd by an ex-praetor. From the forum, Tiridates was taken into the theatre,[2] and after again supplicating himself, Nero indicated he should sit next to him, on his right. On account of these events, Nero was proclaimed *imperator*,[3] and after placing laurels in the Capitoline temple, he closed the twofold doors of Janus,[4] on the ground that no other wars were being waged.

1 In May 66.
2 The Theatre of Pompey on the Campus Martius.
3 Nero received his eleventh imperatorial acclamation: Griffin 1984: 232.
4 The closing of the doors of the Temple of Janus Geminus in Rome symbolized that there was peace throughout the Roman empire. This act was commemorated on Nero's coinage, e.g. *RIC* 1^2 Nero 50–1, 58, 263–71.

4.21 Agrippina the Younger and the reception of embassies

Tacitus, *Annals* 13.5.2

As wife to the emperor Claudius, Agrippina had received the submission of the British king Caratacus when sitting on a separate tribunal: Tac. *Ann.* 12.37.4; Dio Cass. 61(60).33.7 (Xiph.). When her son Nero became emperor in 54, Agrippina went further by attempting to receive an Armenian embassy alongside him on the same tribunal, as Tacitus recounts below. The same story can be found in Dio Cass. 61.3.3–4 (Xiph.).

Indeed, when the Armenian ambassadors were entreating Nero with their people's cause, Agrippina started to climb up to the emperor's tribunal and to take her seat beside him; most people stood crippled by fear, but Seneca[1] urged Nero to go to meet his mother as she approached. Thus this show of dutifulness averted what could have been a shameful incident.

1 Seneca was Nero's tutor. In Dio's version of the story, Seneca takes this action with Burrus, the praetorian prefect.

V | Dining

4.22 Augustus dines with Vedius Pollio

Seneca the Younger, *On Anger* 3.40.2–5

In this portion of the third book of his dialogue *On Anger*, Seneca the Younger discusses ways in which anger can be controlled: whether internally by the person experiencing it, or via external forces acting on the angry person. In the passage quoted here, the emperor Augustus (here called Caesar) attends a dinner party hosted by a friend, P. Vedius Pollio (*PIR*^{2} V 323). Here we see an instance of the latter form of anger control – a powerful external force (the emperor) constraining the angry person (his friend, the host, even in that person's own residence). It is unclear whether Vedius, a wealthy equestrian of low birth, interacted frequently enough with Augustus to count as a courtier: however, this seems at least possible, since Augustus accepted his invitation – albeit at Vedius' villa on the bay of Naples, no doubt when Augustus was travelling. See Roller 2001: 168–71 and **Vol. 1, 334–5** for further discussion.

To censure someone who is angry and become angry yourself inflames things. You should approach him in varied ways and in an agreeable manner, unless your position is so great that you can crush his anger, as the deified Augustus did when he dined at Vedius Pollio's house. One of Vedius' slaves had broken a crystal goblet.[1] Vedius ordered him seized, to die in no ordinary manner: he ordered him to be thrown to the lampreys, the giant ones he kept in his fishpond. Who would not think he did this just for display? It was savagery.[2] The boy escaped his captors and took refuge at Caesar's feet, intending to seek nothing but to die in some other way, and not be fish bait. Disturbed by this innovation in cruelty Caesar ordered that the boy be released, and that all the crystal goblets be smashed before his eyes and the fishpond be filled in.[3] It befitted Caesar that his friend be censured in this way; well did he employ his power. 'You order that people be snatched away from *convivia* and be torn to pieces with novel sorts of punishments? If your cup has been broken, someone's guts will be torn apart? Are you so full of yourself that you order someone to be led off to execution in a place where Caesar is?'[4] This is how someone may give anger rough treatment, if he has enough power to attack it from an advantageous position.

1 Beautiful, sexually attractive young male slaves were (stereo)typically employed in the role of wine servers at Roman *convivia* – at least by hosts who could afford to purchase or rear such slaves, for they were very expensive (for these 'Ganymede' figures, see also Chrol and Blake, **Vol. 1, 358** and **4.29** below). As Vedius was very wealthy, it is probably such a slave who is portrayed here as handling, and fumbling, an expensive and luxurious drinking vessel as he serves his master's guests. Vedius' extravagance, then, is manifested not only in having such cups and slaves, but in being willing to kill so costly a slave for so trivial a reason.

2 Lamprey eels were a Roman culinary delicacy. That Vedius had large, live ones close at hand in his no doubt lavish fishpond suggests they were on the menu for this dinner party – as well as being conveniently located to discharge the punishment Pollio intended for the slave. One wonders, however, how appetizing it would be to dine upon an eel that has just consumed a slave (the lurid scenario Seneca conjures at *Clem.* 1.18.2, followed by Tert. *De pallio* 5.6). On the archaeological evidence for fishponds at the maritime villa commonly identified as Vedius Pollio's 'Pausilypon', see Higginbotham 1997: 191–4.

3 By breaking the rest of the crystal, Augustus makes it difficult for Vedius to justify punishing the slave for a lesser version of the same offence (so Dio Cass. 54.23.4).

4 The emperor (among other people) was empowered to issue judgements on legal cases and potentially consign defendants to execution. Hence Seneca can present it as inappropriate for someone else to usurp this role in the emperor's presence.

4.23 Tiberius dines with Agrippina the Elder

Tacitus, *Annals* 4.54

In this passage, the ambitious courtier Sejanus, who is unrelated to the imperial family, seeks to clear a path for his own advancement and breach the emperor Tiberius' innermost circle of courtiers. To this end he aims to eliminate other courtiers who might stand in his way, including Tiberius' closest relatives. Here he devises and executes a strategy to alienate Tiberius from Agrippina the Elder, Tiberius' recently widowed and still grieving daughter-in-law. The social dynamics and protocols of the *convivium* are revealed as a brutal arena for competition among courtiers.

But Sejanus wounded her deeply as she grieved and was off her guard, unleashing people to warn her, under the pretext of friendship, that poison had been prepared for her, and that she must avoid meals hosted by her father-in-law.[1] And she, oblivious of the deception, as she reclined near him was unmoved by anyone's look or conversation and touched no food, until Tiberius noticed – whether by chance, or because he had heard.[2] To make a more incisive trial of this, he praised some fruit just as it had been set before them, and gave it to his daughter-in-law with his own hand.[3] Agrippina's suspicion was increased by this, and she passed it, untouched by her lips, to her slaves.[4] No remark directly to her from Tiberius followed, but turning to his mother he declared that it would be no surprise if he decided on stern measures against a woman by whom he was being accused of poisoning.[5] Hence the rumour that her destruction was being readied, but that the emperor did not dare to do it openly, and an isolated place was being sought for its commission.[6]

1 Tiberius.
2 I.e. had heard of her suspicions.
3 That Tiberius can offer Agrippina fruit from his own hand, without mediation, implies that she is reclining very near to him – proximity that normally indicated favour and intimacy.
4 Aristocratic guests commonly brought their own, trusted slaves to help attend them at *convivia*; these slaves would normally stand behind their master's couch and be prepared to assist as needed (as here, to take the fruit): see **4.29 (b)** below for the alarm courtiers felt when their own slaves were removed from their service in a *convivium* hosted by the emperor.
5 That she rejects food given directly from Tiberius' own hand, with no intermediary who might introduce poison (as happens at **4.26** below), is to suggest that Tiberius is knowingly administering poison to her directly. Tiberius recognizes the implication and bristles at it; a shorter version of this story at Suet. *Tib.* 53.1 says he never invited her again. His mother Livia is also present and reclining sufficiently nearby that he can speak to her readily, without his words being loud enough that they might seem addressed to Agrippina.
6 Agrippina's behaviour after receiving from Sejanus the false information that Tiberius was planning to poison her leads, ironically enough, to Tiberius hatching an actual plan to punish or kill her (or so Tacitus says). Her fall from Tiberius' good graces is another step forward for Sejanus.

4.24 Caligula dines with his sisters and humiliates other courtiers

Suetonius, *Life of Caligula* 24.1, 26.2 (excerpts)

In these passages Suetonius shows Caligula to be a master manipulator of the symbolism of posture, position, and dress in the *convivium*, which he uses to create and articulate hierarchies and connections among the participants. By these manipulations he puts every participant in her or his place, both literally and figuratively.

He made a habit of committing incest with all his sisters, and in well-attended
convivia he used to position them by turns in the place below him, while his
wife reclined in the place above him.[1] ... In no way more respectful or gentler
toward the Senate, he allowed certain men who had discharged the highest
offices to run alongside his chariot over a distance of several miles while
wearing their togas, and also to stand in girt tunics now at the head and now
at the foot (sc. of his couch) as he dined.[2]

1 When two reclining diners were juxtaposed on a couch such that person A had his or her
   back toward the front side of person B, then person B was said to recline directly 'above'
   person A, and A was said to recline directly 'below' B. This juxtaposition was commonly used
   by couples who were married or sexually involved, with the man reclining 'above' and the
   woman 'below.' Thus the fact that Caligula places his sisters, one after another, in the 'below'
   position in *convivia* (with his actual wife displaced to the other side of him) is taken as
   announcing that he is having sexual relations with them. See Roller 2006: 120–1.
2 Far from hosting high-ranking senators (some of whom are liable to be courtiers) as reclining
   diners at a *convivium*, he instead dresses and positions them as slaves in service to himself,
   standing by his couch to manage the flow of food, drink, and so on (for attending slaves, see
   4.23 above). The girt tunic was the stereotypical dress of the slave standing in attendance on a
   diner. See Roller 2006: 85–6.

4.25 Claudius' big dinner parties

Suetonius, *Life of Claudius* 32 (excerpts)

This passage briefly describes the dining practices of the emperor Claudius, remarking
upon very large-scale events (which are likely to have included courtiers, though were
certainly not limited to them: cf. **4.29 [a]** below) and also upon what appear to be
smaller events that included 'noble children' – whose parents are more likely to have
been among Claudius' aristocratic courtiers. The large-scale events must have been
considerably less 'personal', given the numbers and social range, than the smaller ones,
and hence achieved different social and political ends: see Winterling 1999: 150–1.

He put on *convivia* that were both ample and very frequent, and usually in
locations with the largest capacity, so that often six hundred guests reclined at
once.[1] ... To every dinner he also invited his own children along with noble boys
and girls, who in the ancient manner ate sitting at the ends of the couches.[2]

1 In Latin 'six hundred' can mean this precise number or, more colloquially, a generically large
   number, i.e., 'a lot' (*OLD* s.v. *sescenta* 2), which might be the sense here. Six hundred
   simultaneous guests is probably not out of the question in the Flavian Palace (see **4.27** below).
   But for the Julio-Claudian emperors (prior to Nero, at least) we know very little about the
   enclosed spaces available on the Palatine, so cannot judge whether a banquet for this actual
   number might have been possible indoors for Claudius. For Winterling (1999: 150 n. 36),
   Suetonius' wording implies enclosed space(s) in the then-extant imperial residential complex.
   But it may, alternatively, point to public places in open air.
2 Children, when their presence at *convivia* is noted at all, are usually portrayed as sitting
   while the adults to whom they are connected recline: Roller 2006: 159–69. We can infer
   that their parents, likely courtiers, were present as well. The 'noble' children presumably
   constituted a proto-court for Claudius' own children, on the assumption of familial
   succession (see **4.26** below).

4.26 Nero murders Britannicus at dinner

Tacitus, *Annals* 13.16

In the first year of his reign, the emperor Nero came to view Claudius' son Britannicus –
the direct male descendant of the previous emperor – as a dire threat to his position, and
determined to do away with him. This passage narrates the fatal poisoning of
Britannicus at a dinner party, along with the dynamics of the aristocratic, courtly
gathering taken off guard by this harrowing event. Suetonius (*Ner.* 33.3) relates this
event much more briefly.

The custom was maintained that the children of the imperial family, seated with
other nobles of the same age, should dine under the eyes of their relatives at their
own, more frugal, table.[1] As Britannicus banqueted there, because his food and
drink was taste-tested by a select slave, the following trick was devised in order not
to violate the custom or reveal the crime by the death of both. A drink was handed
to Britannicus, harmless so far but very hot, and already sampled by the taster.
Then, after he rejected it due to heat, the poison was administered in the cold
water, which raced through all his limbs so fast that his voice and breathing were
snatched away at the same time. Alarm ran through those sitting around him;
those who lacked foresight fled. But those whose understanding was deeper
remained pinned in their seats, gazes fixed on Nero.[2] Without changing his
reclining posture, and pretending ignorance, he declared this was normal due to
the epilepsy by which Britannicus had been troubled from his earliest infancy, and
that his sight and senses would slowly return. But such fear and mental disturb-
ance flashed forth from Agrippina, however much it was suppressed in her
expression, that it was established that she was just as unaware as Octavia the
sister of Britannicus: for Agrippina grasped that her last support had been taken
away and that there was a precedent for familial murder.[3] Octavia too, although of
tender years, had learned to conceal her pain, her affection, and all her emotions.
And so, after a brief silence, the pleasures of the *convivium* were resumed.[4]

1 The imperial children and their noble age-mates dine sitting while their parents recline. Here,
   however, the children are portrayed as having a separate table and simpler fare than the adults
   (hence not sitting on the couches on which the adults recline, as in **4.25**). Again, the point
   may be to groom future courtiers to the imperial children by having them follow the example
   of their parents.
2 These are the children's reactions, who are said to be *sitting* around Britannicus (the adults
   recline, like Nero in the next sentence). The distinction between those with lesser and greater
   understanding may point to a diversity of ages among the children, and/or of their familiarity
   with the ways of Nero's court.
3 The focus has now turned to the reaction of one of the reclining adults, Nero's mother (and
   Claudius' last wife) Agrippina the Younger, who seeks unsuccessfully to conceal her surprise
   and alarm at what Nero has done.
4 Nero imposes his fiction as truth upon the guests (so Bartsch 1994: 13–16). In Tacitus'
   portrayal they must accept the pretence, which (it is implied) they know to be only a pretence,
   that Britannicus has merely suffered a seizure. Here, then, is a group of courtiers cowed by the
   brutality of the emperor, desperately calculating the consequences of this murder for power
   relations within the court, and each trying to determine what this event augurs for them.

4.27 Dining Spaces in the Domus Flavia

The Domus Flavia is the north-western part of the Flavian Palace complex on the Palatine (cf. **2.12**). In this plan (**fig. 4.5.1**) a space commonly identified as a large dining room (the 'Cenatio Iovis') is at bottom left, with two large flanking garden installations. It opens onto a large peristyle to its north-east, on the far side of which is a very large reception hall ('Aula Regia'), itself flanked to the

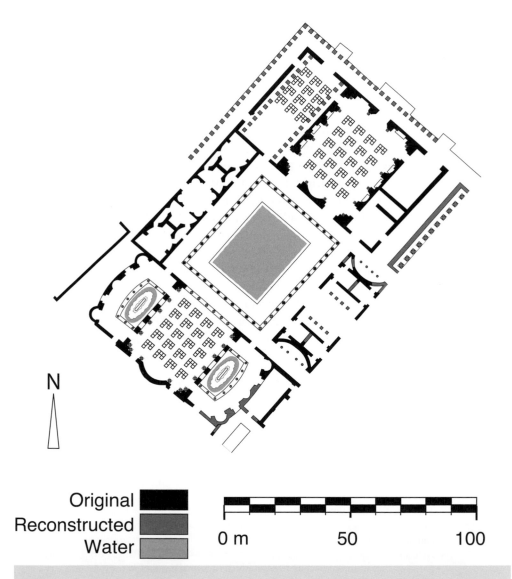

Original
Reconstructed
Water

0 m   50   100

Fig. 4.5.1 Plan of the possible dining spaces in the Domus Flavia, Palatine Hill, Rome. After plans by Jens Pflug and Ulrike Wulf-Rheidt, and F. Rakob and P. Zanker.

north-west by a somewhat smaller reception room ('Basilica'). In this plan, *triclinia* (arrangements of three couches accommodating nine diners at a time) are shown set up in all three of the large rooms, with a notional capacity of a bit under 500 diners (though only c. 180, as estimated here, in the dining room itself). One might imagine couches set up in the flanking gardens and peristyle as well, for even greater capacity. Dinners at this scale could include courtiers, but also other guests at greater social distance from the emperor. On this dining room and its capacity see, for example, Mar 2009; Zanker 2002.

4.28 Dining spaces in the Domus Augustana

The Domus Augustana is the central portion of the Flavian Palace complex, located south-east of the Domus Flavia. The complex of rooms shown in **fig. 4.5.2**, located at the south-west end of the Domus Augustana and on a lower level, is called the Sunken Peristyle. It is plausibly interpreted as a suite of dining rooms of various sizes and configurations, and with various lines of sight into the large central water installation or into smaller light-wells (on which see Sojc and Winterling 2009; Sojc 2012b: 29–37; Pflug and Wulf-Rheidt, **Vol. 1, 214–16, 225–6**). These rooms could flexibly accommodate smaller, more intimate parties than the great dining room in the Domus Flavia allowed: **4.27, 29 (a)**. One might imagine that *convivia* involving small numbers of the emperor's close associates and family members (relatively 'courtly' company) could be hosted in one or more of these spaces: see **4.29 (b)** and **4.30** below. These rooms seem to have remained in use, when emperors were resident in Rome, for at least two centuries after the palace's completion.

4.29 Dining with Domitian in the palace

The next two passages invite comparison thanks to the strikingly divergent images they provide of the emperor Domitian as a host to his courtiers (and others). Statius writes in a panegyrical mode about his own experiences, while Cassius Dio, 130 years later, presents the emperor as a kind of virtuoso in terrorizing but also in rewarding his courtiers. In general, literary texts tended to panegyrize Domitian richly while he lived, and pilloried him after his death; this pairing is no exception.

(a) Statius, *Silvae* 4.2.1–45

The poet presents himself as having attended a vast banquet hosted by Domitian in the new Flavian Palace on the Palatine Hill. A banquet of this scale would have involved guests from beyond the ambit of the court, and indeed Statius himself was unlikely to have been a courtier. For while he certainly interacted with the emperor from time to time, there is no reason to think that interaction was regular, or that he received much special attention or favour from Domitian – for instance, the invitation described in this poem is presented as the *first* such invitation the poet has received. Yet this panegyrical poem, offering thanks for the honour of attending the dinner, quite possibly seeks to

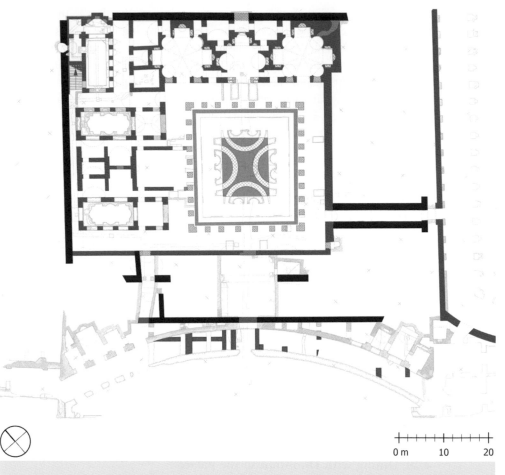

Fig. 4.5.2 Reconstructed ground plan of the Flavian phase of the Sunken Peristyle, Palatine Hill, Rome.
Courtesy of the Architekturreferat DAI Zentrale, Berlin. Plan: Jens Pflug.

elicit a further invitation or other honour from the emperor in its turn, hence to open the door to more regular interaction and a closer relationship between poet and emperor. It is the gesture of an *aspiring* courtier, not an established one. On Statius and Domitian, cf. Bernstein, **Vol. 1, 448**.

The man who brought great Aeneas into Laurentian lands praises the royal dinner-parties of Sidonian Dido; the man who wore Ulysses out with a long sea-voyage as he returned home tells of the feast of Alcinous, in a poem that will be immortal: as for me, to whom Caesar has now, for the first time, granted the novel joy of his sacred meal and whom he has allowed to stay reclining at his lordly table, with what song am I to praise the fulfilment of my prayers, and what thanks do I avail to repay? Not even if Smyrna and Mantua together wove sweet-smelling laurel for my joyous head, could I produce a worthy utterance.[1] I seem to be reclining amidst the stars with Jupiter, and to take up deathless drink offered by the Trojan prince's right hand.[2] Barren are the years I have already passed: this is the first day of my allotted time, this is the threshold of my life. Is it you, ruler of the lands, great parent of the subjected world, you the hope of mankind, you the gods' ward, that I look upon as I recline? Is it granted – is it really granted – to gaze upon this visage from close at hand, among the wine and dinner courses, and is it permissible not to rise to my feet?[3]

The building is venerable and immense, distinguished not by one hundred columns, but by as many as could support the gods on high and the heavens if Atlas were dismissed.[4] The neighbouring palace of the Thunderer is astounded at it, and the divinities rejoice that you are installed in a residence equal to theirs.[5] But do not hurry to go up to great heaven! The mass of the building extends so much, and the push of the far-spreading hall, freer than an open field, enclosing much land and covered sky, lesser only than its master; he fills the household and delights it with his huge spirit. There gleam the African and Trojan mountains in rivalry; also there is much granite from Syene and Chian marble, and stone rivalling the green sea. Luna marble is placed only underneath, to carry the columns. The view above extends far: you would scarcely discern the ceiling with your exhausted vision, and you would think it the coffers of gilded heaven.[6] Here, when Caesar has bid the leading descendants of Romulus and the trabea-wearing throngs to recline together at a thousand tables,[7] Ceres herself, her garment girded up, and Bacchus toil to meet the demand. Thus flowed the fruitful path of Triptolemus through the air; thus Lyaeus shaded the barren hills and sober countryside with his grape-bearing vines.[8]

But it is not the food, and the tables of Moorish wood resting on Indian supports, and the regiments of slaves one after another,[9] but rather himself, himself alone, that I in my eagerness have had time to behold: placid in his expression, but softening his radiance with serene dignity, and temperately lowering the banner of his lofty station; yet the worth he dissembled shone out in his face. Such an appearance even a barbarian enemy and peoples unknown could apprehend.

1 The poet modestly declares that his own efforts cannot compare to earlier poetic descriptions of mythological royal banquets. He mentions the banquets of the Carthaginian queen (= 'Sidonian Dido') found in the *Aeneid* of Vergil (from Mantua), which tells of Aeneas' journey to Latium (= the 'Laurentian lands', modern Lazio). Statius also alludes to the *Odyssey* of Homer (sometimes said to have come from Smyrna, modern İzmir, Turkey), which concerns Odysseus' (Lat.: Ulysses') trip home to Ithaca after the Trojan war, during which he enjoyed the hospitality of Alcinous, king of the Phaeacians. However, the effect of this declaration is precisely to present Domitian's banquet as being on or above the level of these epic feasts, and to present the poet as capable of transmitting a positive image of the ruler and his banquets far and wide and also into the future, just as Vergil and Homer did.

2 Here and subsequently Domitian appears as Jupiter, with a radiant divine presence, and the dining room itself is presented as having a cosmic or Olympian aspect (e.g. the 'Trojan prince' is Ganymede, the cupbearer to Jupiter on Olympus, who Statius says seems to be serving him: Domitian of course has the choicest slaves; cf. **4.22**, above).

3 The wonder and awe that the poet experiences, in his proximity to Domitian's divine presence and in the context of the cosmic palace, places the emperor at an inaccessible social distance; cf. **4.33 (c)** below. There is no suggestion that the poet is on familiar terms or interacts regularly with the emperor – notwithstanding the emperor's supposed graciousness in not requiring his guests to rise to greet him (a gesture that would indicate their acknowledgement of his higher rank).

4 This section of the poem is usually thought to describe the great dining room or Cenatio Iovis in the 'new' Flavian Palace on the Palatine Hill (see above, **4.27**).

5 The 'palace of the Thunderer' refers to the temple of Jupiter on the Capitoline Hill, just across the valley of the Velabrum from the Palatine Hill. Jupiter, along with his temple-mates Juno and Minerva, is thus presented as residing in his temple, looking on with amazement and pleasure at the new Flavian Palace just across the way, and deeming it a fitting abode for Domitian as the Jupiter-on-earth.

6 The emphasis on the large number of columns in the dining hall, and on the luxurious, imported, coloured marble from which they were made, suggests the resources and reach of the emperor; the same theme recurs in Statius' description of Domitian's Saturnalia: below, **4.33 (c)**. The size of the room and the decoration of the ceiling continue the 'cosmic' theme noted earlier.

7 'The leading descendants of Romulus and the *trabea*-wearing throngs' refer to the leading senators and equestrians; the *trabea* was a brightly coloured and striped garment worn by equestrians on special occasions. At least some of the banqueters were likely courtiers, though the size of the event described here suggests that many non-courtiers (like Statius, in fact) were present as well. 'A thousand tables' is hyperbolic, though some hundreds of guests reclining on couches set up in the great dining room and in adjacent spaces would be plausible (see above, **4.27**).

8 Triptolemus was a mythical prince of Eleusis who learnt agriculture from the goddess Demeter (identifed with the Latin goddess Ceres), and travelled in a winged chariot. Lyaeus is a cult name of Bacchus/Dionysus, the god who taught humans viticulture.

9 Tabletops made from Moorish citrus wood, set on the tusks of Indian elephants, and the large numbers of slaves serving the guests, all continue to develop the image of luxury, imperial reach, and abundant resources, over which the quasi-divine ruler presides.

(b) Cassius Dio 67.9.1–6 (Xiph.)

This passage is an excerpt from or condensation of Dio's original text, made by the Byzantine epitomator Xiphilinus. The broader context appears to be a discussion of the various celebrations Domitian held in Rome following his successes (real or alleged) in his Dacian wars. The dinner described here is presented as one of these events. In contrast to the vast, socially diverse banquet portrayed by Statius, here the circle of invitees seems to have been smaller and highly elite, hence would likely have consisted substantially or entirely of courtiers. This narrative is assuredly the product of a hostile tradition that seeks to present Domitian as a cruel and uncivil host, one who inverts in every way the normal expectation that a host should create a welcoming and comfortable environment for his guests (hence, one could say, 'the dinner is the emperor'). If any dinner like this actually took place, its staging could perhaps have been intended as some kind of sober commemoration of those who died during the Dacian wars. Alternatively, it could perhaps be thought of as an overdone application of the *memento mori* theme – the idea that, even on the most festive occasions, one should recall the fact of one's own mortality. This theme is otherwise attested as playing a role in Roman dining (see notes).

At that time Domitian entertained the people at dinner as I have described, and he entertained the leading men of the Senate and of the equestrians in the following way. He prepared a dining room that was entirely black on all sides: the ceiling, the walls, and the floor. Then, having made ready dining couches that were bare and also black standing directly upon the floor, he summoned the guests by night, alone without attendants.[1] First he set up a slab in the form of a grave marker for each of them, bearing their name and a small lampholder such as is hung up in tombs.[2] Then good-looking naked slave boys, themselves painted black, entered as if they were phantoms, and after going around the guests in a terrifying dance they seated themselves at their feet. And after this everything that is normally dedicated among offerings to the dead was brought out for the guests too – all black and served on similarly-coloured tableware, so that every single one of them was terrified and shook, always expecting that they would be slaughtered at any moment, and especially because there was already profound silence, as if among the dead, from everyone else, while everything Domitian talked about referred to death and slaughter. Finally he dismissed them, having previously removed their slaves who had stood waiting in the vestibule. By (entrusting them to) other slaves they did not know, having provided some with carriages and others with litters, he thrust much greater fear into them. Presently each of them had arrived home and began, so to speak, to catch their breath, when it was announced that someone from the emperor had arrived. As they expected from this that they were then at all events going to perish,[3] someone brought in the grave marker, which turned out to be silver, and then one person after another brought in item after item of the tableware that had been laid on at the dinner, each made of the most costly type of material. And finally, the particular boy who was the spirit for each guest, washed and adorned, <came in> (sc. as a further gift). And thus, having passed the whole night in terror, they received gifts.[4]

Such were the victory celebrations that Domitian performed – or such were the funeral offerings, as the people called them, for those who died in Dacia and for those who died in Rome.

1 This dinner might be imagined to have taken place (if anything like this took place at all) in one or more of the dining rooms on the Sunken Peristyle at the south-west end of the Domus Augustana (see above, **4.28**) in the newly-completed Flavian Palace. These spaces, being subterranean and considerably smaller than the great dining room upstairs, could be imagined to allow for the kind of decoration and treatment described here.

2 Roman religious practice included meals at or in tombs on certain occasions. One such meal was the *silicernium*, held by the family directly following the inhumation of a deceased family member; another, called the *cena novendialis*, was held nine days later. Such meals may also have been held subsequently during certain festivals or on anniversaries. Perhaps the dinner described in this passage could be understood as a kind of funerary meal for those who had died in the Dacian wars, or in the subsequent games held in Rome (see last sentence of the passage). Alternatively, the *memento mori* idea was often associated with dining in Roman culture: some reminder of mortality was present to those participating in perhaps the quintessential experience of living; see, e.g., Petr. *Sat.* 34.8–10, Dunbabin 1986. The guests, however, are presented as imagining that this is a funeral meal for themselves, in advance,

hence their terror. On all these matters and their relationship to the dinner described here, see Edwards 2007: 161–78, esp. 161–71, with further bibliography; also Levi 2012 for the long post-antique tradition of such dinners.

3 Messengers from the emperor were sometimes known to arrive bearing instructions that the recipient should commit suicide; see Edwards 2007: 116–18.

4 The large quantity of silver (in the slab) and the sexually desirable, expensive slave boys (Ganymede figures; see above, **4.22** and **4.29 [a]**) were gifts of great value, suggesting that the guests were elite courtiers in our sense – closely enough associated with the emperor that it was worth his time and effort both to terrorize them and to display the scale of the rewards he could confer. Both were strategies for keeping them docile and cooperative. This text itself represents the elite courtiers' counterstroke – a lurid portrayal that brands Domitian for posterity as an uncivil, brutal host (again, 'the dinner is the emperor'), and that puts future emperors on notice regarding the long-term costs of mistreating such courtiers.

4.30 Speaking truth to power at Nerva's table

Pliny the Younger, *Letters* 4.22.4–6

Here Pliny the Younger speaks of Iunius Mauricus (PIR^2 I 771), a man he admires for having endured exile under Domitian; Domitian also executed Mauricus' brother, Q. Iunius Arulenus Rusticus (PIR^2 I 730). Recalled from exile when Nerva succeeded Domitian, Mauricus is portrayed here as dining with a small group of leading men, hosted by Nerva himself. The story is also told at *Epit. de Caes.* 12.5.

You would say (sc. Mauricus spoke) with integrity and bravery, would you not?[1] But this is nothing new from Mauricus. He also spoke no less bravely before Nerva as emperor. Nerva was dining with a few guests;[2] reclining next to him and even on his breast was Veiento: when I named the man, I said it all.[3] The conversation turned to Catullus Messalinus who, deprived as he was of vision, had augmented the evils of blindness with his savage disposition. He displayed no respect, no shame, no pity; wherefore he was regularly hurled by Domitian like a javelin, which themselves fly blindly and without foresight, against all the best men.[4] Over the meal, everyone was speaking openly about Messalinus' wickedness and bloodthirsty decisions, when the emperor himself asked, 'What do we reckon would be his lot if he were still living?' Mauricus replied, 'He would be dining with us.'[5]

1 Pliny has just recounted another occasion on which Mauricus spoke frankly while serving on Trajan's *consilium*.

2 This intimate gathering could be imagined to have taken place in one of the rooms on the Sunken Peristyle of the Domus Augustana in the Flavian Palace, which was still quite new during Nerva's reign (see above, **4.28**).

3 A. Didius Gallus Fabricius Veiento (PIR^2 F 91). Pliny evidently does not think highly of Veiento. The Latin expression for 'on his breast', *in sinu*, suggests that Veiento occupied the position on the couch directly 'below' the emperor – that is, reclining directly next to Nerva, his back to Nerva's front (see above, **4.24**). However, *in sinu* also connotes 'under the care or protection of'.

4 L. Valerius Catullus Messalinus (PIR^2 V 57) is portrayed here and elsewhere as the kind of adviser who always urged Domitian to impose harsher punishments (Juv. *Sat.* 4.113 = **3.6** above calls him *mortifer*, 'death-dealing') – and while Pliny does not say that Messalinus

himself was responsible for Mauricus' exile or his brother Rusticus' execution, he implies that Messalinus was central to the system that produced such outcomes under Domitian.

5 The implication is that Veiento and Catullus Messalinus were similar characters (they are also paired as monstrous, ludicrous advisers to Domitian in Juv. *Sat.* 4.113–29, cf. **3.6**). Hence, notwithstanding the criticism of Catullus Messalinus apparently circulating at this dinner, Veiento's own presence, and the favour Nerva is said to have shown him, implies that Catullus Messalinus, too, would have been present and shown favour at this dinner were he still living. Thus the anecdote depicts tensions within Nerva's court between surviving pillars of the previous regime (like Veiento) and rehabilitated victims of that regime (like Mauricus), and shows the latter landing a blow against the former.

4.31 Trajan dines with Sura

Cassius Dio 68.15.4–6 (Xiph.; *EV*; JA)

As in **4.22**, the following passage depicts an emperor dining out, hosted by a friend – in this case Trajan and his close associate and confidant L. Licinius Sura (*PIR*[2] L 253). Sura was thought to have intervened decisively in establishing Trajan as Nerva's successor (*Epit. de Caes.* 13.6; cf. Aur. Vict. *Caes.* 13.8); he accompanied Trajan on his Dacian campaigns and is portrayed repeatedly on Trajan's Column; and he also was said to have played some kind of role in establishing Hadrian as Trajan's successor (SHA *Hadr.* 3.10). Migliorati (2003: 115–17) provides further discussion.

So great was the friendship and trust that Sura enjoyed from Trajan, and Trajan from Sura, that – as seems naturally to happen regarding all who have any influence with emperors – despite Sura often being slandered, Trajan neither suspected nor hated him.[1] Indeed, when those who envied Sura became very insistent at Trajan, he went uninvited to Sura's house for dinner, and dismissing his entire bodyguard he first summoned Sura's doctor, and had him put a salve on his eyes; then he summoned his barber, and had him shave his chin.[2] For everyone including emperors used to follow this long-standing practice; Hadrian was the first to introduce the beard. Having done these things, and thereafter bathing and dining, on the next day he said to his friends whose habit was always to say petty things about Sura that 'if Sura wanted to kill me, he would have killed me yesterday'. He did a great thing in putting himself at risk at the hands of a person who had been slandered, but a far greater one in trusting that he would suffer no harm from him. Thus he augmented his confidence in an opinion deriving from what he knew about Sura's deeds rather than from others' suppositions.[3]

1 This passage presents rivalry among courtiers as the background to and occasion for Trajan inviting himself to dinner at Sura's house. Sura's pre-eminence among Trajan's courtiers is presented here as prompting others to try to undermine him and reduce his standing with Trajan – presumably to establish more equal power relations within the court and to enhance their own standing at Sura's expense.

2 Dismissing his bodyguard, having Sura's doctor treat his eyes, and letting Sura's barber shave him puts him at risk of being poisoned or having his throat cut. Thus the passage shows Trajan confidently entrusting all aspects of his personal well-being to his host for the duration of the dining event, precisely what one would 'normally' expect a guest to do at his host's

house. The ostentatious display of normal friendship and ideal guest–host relations is the implement Trajan employs to tamp down a dimension of competition among his courtiers that has become excessive ('when they became *very* insistent', evidently in alleging that Sura wished to kill Trajan and usurp imperial power for himself).

3 With these approving statements at the end, Dio's anecdote not only presents Trajan as exemplary and praiseworthy in his ability to maintain a 'normal friendship' despite being emperor, but also shows Trajan managing rivalries within the court in a way that a high-status courtier like Dio can approve of: ostentatiously honouring and valuing an aristocratic courtier (and not some other segment of the court), and modifying the competitive dynamics within his court without resorting to violence (in contrast to Nero's approach: see above, **4.26**).

VI | Household Religion and the Court

4.32 The *toga virilis* ceremony

Coming of age for freeborn boys was celebrated by a series of rituals which revolved around exchanging the purple-bordered *toga praetexta* boys wore (mainly on formal occasions) for the plain white *toga virilis* worn by adult male citizens. The ceremony typically began in the family home where the boy dedicated the emblems of his free birth – his *toga praetexta* and *bulla*, a golden locket believed to have apotropaic properties – to the Lares. Next he donned the white toga which symbolized his achievement of adulthood. Typically the newly togate boy, accompanied by family and friends, progressed then to the Forum followed by the Capitol, where he sacrificed, likely to Jupiter and Juventas, in the temple of Jupiter Optimus Maximus. He probably then registered his name at a *tabularium* which held records of citizenship. For further details see Dolansky 2008 and **Vol. 1, 405–8**.

Toga virilis ceremonies within the imperial family and among members of the court differed from other aristocratic celebrations largely in scale. Aristocratic families typically distributed *sportulae* (gifts of food or money) and members of the imperial family dispensed largesse (*congiaria*), which was usually more lavish: see **4.32 (b)** and **(d)**, cf. Tac. *Ann.* 3.29.3; Ehrenberg, Jones, and Stockton 1976: 41. We are told that when Caligula provided retroactive compensation to the people in AD 37 because largesse had not been dispensed when he came of age, individuals received the significant sum of HS 240 apiece plus interest (**4.32 [d]**). On occasion, the internal politics of the imperial court could also result in deviations from standard aristocratic practices when it came to the *toga virilis* ceremonies of individual members of the imperial family.

(a) Nicolaus of Damascus 4.8–10

Nicolaus of Damascus (born c. 64 BC) was a historian and philosopher, as well as a close associate of King Herod the Great of Judaea. He wrote a biography of the early life of Augustus that survives only in fragments. Nicolaus of Damascus' account of Octavian's *toga virilis* ceremony illustrates the components of the ritual celebrated in civic spaces once the domestic rites were complete, although Octavian's exchange of togas in the forum itself is unique. The visual dimension of the ritual transition and attendant atmosphere are highlighted by Nicolaus' language, including labelling Octavian's toga *kathara* ('pure'), which corresponds to the Latin *pura*. Both designations emphasize the whiteness of the toga in contrast to dark or bordered togas, but also convey moral and ethical connotations related to sexual and moral purity and free birth (*ingenuitas*). The passage establishes how the ceremony could be used for public display by elite families during the Republic; the imperial family then built on this custom.

At about the age of fourteen,[1] he went down into the Forum to lay aside the purple-bordered toga and take up the pure white one, which is a symbol of enrolment among men. While he was gazed upon by the whole people because of his striking appearance and the brilliance of his noble birth, he was enrolled in a priesthood in place of L. Domitius,[2] who had died, and the people elected him with great enthusiasm. And at the same time as he changed his toga and was adorned with this very illustrious honour, he sacrificed <to the gods>.

1 While the day of the ceremony is certain as 18 October, the year is not and arguments have been made for both 48 and 47 BC; see Wardle 2014: 110 for discussion with references.
2 Octavian was enrolled in the college of pontiffs in place of L. Domitius Ahenobarbus (*cos.* 54 BC; *RE* 27), who died fighting Julius Caesar at Pharsalia in August 48 BC.

(b) Suetonius, *Life of Tiberius* 54.1

Soon after receiving the toga, many embarked on a preparatory period called *tirocinium fori* ('training for the forum'), which Suetonius refers to in connection with Germanicus' sons (**4.32 [b–c]**). In this period, young men acquired practical training for politics through apprenticeships with established politicians, orators, or advocates, as well as training for military service.

Since Tiberius had three grandsons by Germanicus – Nero, Drusus, and Gaius – and one by Drusus named Tiberius, and was childless due to the deaths of his own children, he recommended Germanicus' older sons, Nero and Drusus, to the Senate and celebrated the day when each began his *tirocinium* by distributing largesse to the plebs.

(c) Suetonius, *Life of Caligula* 10.1

Certainly not all boys in the imperial family received equal treatment upon coming of age and there were notable irregularities in both Caligula's and Claudius' rites. As Suetonius and Dio detail in **4.32 (c–d)**, Caligula received the toga considerably later than his peers at nineteen (in AD 31), and without distributions of *congiaria*. His ceremony was also followed immediately by his *depositio barbae* ('dedication of the first beard'), but often there was a significant gap between the two rituals; for instance, Octavian received the toga in 48 or 47 BC, then dedicated his first beard in 39 BC: Dio Cass. 48.34.3; cf. Marquardt 1886: 2.599–600. The ceremony persisted: almost two centuries after Caligula, the young emperor Elagabalus celebrated the *depositio barbae*: Dio Cass. 80(79).14.4 (Xiph.; *EV*).

Caligula also accompanied his father on his Syrian expedition. When he returned from there, he lived first with his mother, then, after she was banished, with his great-grandmother Livia Augusta; when she died, though he was still a boy at the time, he delivered her eulogy from the rostra. He moved to the house of his grandmother Antonia, and in his nineteenth year, he was summoned to Capreae by Tiberius and on the same day he assumed the *toga virilis* and dedicated his first beard without any honours of the kind that had marked his brothers' entry into adulthood (*tirocinium*).

(d) Cassius Dio 59.2.2

To the people Caligula paid out the forty-five million,[1] for so much was left to them, and over and above this amount two hundred and forty sesterces a person which they had not received when he received his *toga virilis*, along with sixty sesterces in interest.

1 This occurred following Tiberius' death when Caligula became emperor and was able to use
   funds left to him in Tiberius' will.

(e) Suetonius, *Life of Claudius* 2.2

Claudius' *toga virilis* ceremony was unusual due to his perceived physical and mental disabilities, which caused embarrassment and drew criticism within the imperial family; see Suet. *Claud.* 3–4.

On the day of his *toga virilis* ceremony, Claudius was carried in a litter to the Capitol around midnight without the customary entourage.[1]

1 See *OLD* 2b for *officium* as 'a gathering of people paying respects'.

4.33 Saturnalia celebrations and the court

Lauded for its role reversal between masters and slaves and extension of greater licence (*licentia*) to all and particularly to slaves, the Saturnalia in late December was a highly anticipated celebration. Standard modes of dress and deportment were temporarily set aside and freedom of speech was afforded to all members in both ordinary households and the imperial household. A private feast was the central component, with various dining configurations attested involving role reversal or status inversion as masters feasted alongside their slaves or let slaves dine first. A revel followed the feast, at least for men. Participants exchanged gifts for the occasion, though it is not clear when this occurred. See Dolansky 2011 and **Vol. 1, 408–10** for further details on the festival.

(a) Suetonius, *Life of Augustus* 75

Saturnalia gifts ranged from modest items such as books of poetry and dinner napkins, to more costly ones including slaves and exotic animals. Such diversity is reflected in this passage concerning Augustus' gift-giving habits, which seem to have included a penchant for offering unusual gifts, some of which may have been intended as jokes or 'gag gifts': Leary 1996: 77–8 on Mart. 14.25; see also Gowers 1993: 37 on Stat. *Silv.* 4.9. Other emperors are likewise known to have provided Saturnalia gifts for relatives and friends: Suet. *Claud.* 5; Suet. *Vesp.* 19.1; SHA *Hadr.* 17.3.

Festivals and holidays he used to celebrate lavishly, but sometimes only lightheartedly. On the Saturnalia, and whenever he had the inclination, he would distribute gifts of clothing, gold, or silver, and at other times coins of every denomination, even old issues from kings and foreign currencies; occasionally, he would give nothing except cloth made from goat hair, sponges, pokers and tongs, and other things of that sort bearing mysterious and enigmatic labels.

(b) Tacitus, *Annals* 13.15.1–3

One feature of the revel was a game in which participants took turns being 'king' of the festivities and ordering others around, as Tacitus recounts in this passage regarding the future emperor Nero and his rival Britannicus. Embarrassing and even humiliating others were objectives, as Epictetus (Arr. *Epict. diss.* 1.25.8) and Lucian (*Saturnalia* 4) indicate, since participants were ordered to perform menial tasks or say and do things that would otherwise be considered disgraceful. The free speech and inversion characteristic of the festival are apparent in Nero and Britannicus' interactions, and the occasion exposed some tensions within the inner court to attendees, who presumably included courtiers and invited guests of both the emperor and members of the imperial family.

Upset by Agrippina's threats and the day approaching when Britannicus would complete his fourteenth year, Nero ruminated now about his mother's impetuousness, now about Britannicus' character which recently had become evident through a test, <trivial> indeed, yet by which he had widely gained support. On the Saturnalia, during the various amusements when his age-mates were casting lots in the game 'King of the Saturnalia', the lot had fallen to Nero. A range of commands were issued to the other boys, though not to make them blush. When he ordered Britannicus to stand up, come into the centre of the room and begin to sing a song, he was hoping that the boy would be a laughingstock as a result since he was unaccustomed to sober banquets, let alone drunken ones. Britannicus began resolutely to sing a song in which it was foreshadowed that he would be cast from his father's home and important affairs. A more obvious pity arose from this because night and revelry had taken away pretence. Once this indignation towards him was perceived, Nero increased his hatred. With Agrippina's threats pressing upon him, because there was no criminal charge and he did not dare to openly order his brother's murder, he contrived secret plans and ordered poison to be prepared. Julius Pollio assisted, a tribune of a praetorian cohort, through whose attention Locusta, a condemned poisoner notorious for her crimes, was detained.[1]

1 See **4.26** for Tacitus' narrative of the poisoning.

(c) Statius, *Silvae* 1.6: 'The Kalends of December'

While there is at least one other instance on record of a public banquet held on the Saturnalia (Livy 22.1.19–20), Domitian's Saturnalia feast, as described in lavish detail by Statius, was truly unique. Extant calendars preserve 17 December as the date the festival began, yet according to Statius, Domitian's celebration began on 1 December instead (the year is unknown). As Newlands (2002: 236) proposes, Domitian 'appropriated the Saturnalia for his own political use, placing its celebration in the most prominent position of the month, the Kalends'. His banquet was spectacular, unprecedented in scale and novelty, and staged in an amphitheatre where those in attendance – courtiers and ordinary citizens alike – were literally overwhelmed by a continuous bounty of foods and entertainment hailing from all parts of the empire; see Newlands 2002: 238–52. The emperor himself joined the banquet, but Statius' depiction suggests he sat apart, regarded and behaving more like a god than a man; cf. above **4.29 (a)**. In contrast, the emperor Lucius Verus is said to have invited his home-born slaves (*vernae*) to dine with him during the festival: SHA *Verus* 7.5. Nevertheless, Domitian's feast afforded an opportunity for contact between the emperor and his subjects, as well as interaction between the court and the public.

Father Phoebus and stern Pallas, and festive Muses, go far away: we will call you back on Janus' kalends! Let Saturn, freed from his fetters, be present for me, and December heavy with much wine, and cheerful Mirth and wanton Wit, while I tell of joyful Caesar's blessed day and drunken <feast>.[1]

   Dawn was scarcely raising a new day and already delicacies were raining down from a cord: upon arrival, the East Wind pours forth this dew. Whatever fine produce falls from fertile Pontic nut-groves or Idume's peaks,[2] what pious Damascus grows on her branches[3] and <steamy> Caunus ripens,[4] unbidden and free of charge descends in rich plunder. Soft cookies shaped like little men and fritters made of cheese and honey, Ameria's bounty not scorched by the sun,[5] must-cakes and plump dates from a hidden palm – all kept dropping down. Not with such great showers does tempestuous Hyas or the constellation of the Pleiades releasing its rain overwhelm the earth as such a storm pounded the people with fair-weather hail throughout the rows in the Latian theatre.[6] Let Jupiter draw the clouds over the world and threaten wide fields with downpours, so long as rains like these of our Jove are produced.

   But look: another mass of people moves through the whole theatre, distinguished in appearance and handsome in their attire, a crowd no smaller than the one seated. Some carry bread baskets and white napkins and rather sumptuous fare; others generously serve wine that makes one weak: you would think they were so many cupbearers from Mount Ida.[7] At one time you nourish the Circle where there is a better and more serious class of men together with those dressed in togas,[8] and since you, blessed leader, feed so many people, haughty Annona does not know this day.[9] Go on now, Antiquity, compare the ages of ancient Jove[10] and the golden age: at that time wine was not flowing so freely and the harvest was not getting a head start on the slow year. At one table, every order eats – children, women, common folk, equestrians, senators:

freedom has relaxed reverence. Nay rather, *you*, in fact, entered upon shared feasts with us. Which of the gods could be summoned thus, which could accept an invitation in this way? Now whoever he is, poor or rich, boasts that he is the leader's dinner guest.

Amid these murmurings and novel luxuries, the flitting pleasure of watching flies by. The inexperienced sex,[11] ignorant of the sword, stands ready and shamelessly takes on manly battles! You would think they were troops of Amazons fighting heated battles by the Tanais river and the wild Phasis.[12] Here comes a daring line of dwarves, short in stature as Nature completed them right after their start, whom she has tied up into a knotty mass. They deal out wounds and engage in hand-to-hand combat and threaten one another with death – by what hands! Father Mars laughs, and bloody Valour, as cranes, about to fall upon their wandering prey, marvel at these rather fierce little fighters.[13]

Now, under the approaching shadows of night, what a commotion the rich scattering of largesse[14] stirs up! Here come girls easily bought, here every kind of entertainment is recognized, what pleases the theatre because of its beauty or is approved of for its skill. A company of Lydian ladies brimming with excitement clap, and there are cymbals and jingling girls from Gades. There columns of Syrians make noise, here are actors and those who exchange common sulphur[15] for broken glass.

Among these things, tremendous clouds of birds fall through the stars in sudden flight, birds which the holy Nile and wild Phasis collect, and the Numidians beneath the moist south wind.[16] People to snatch them all up are lacking, and full folds of garments rejoice while novel gains are acquired. They raise countless voices to the stars, sounding the Saturnalia of the leader, and they proclaim him 'master' with kindly approbation: this licence alone did Caesar forbid.[17]

Hardly was dark night yet covering the world when, glittering amid the dense shadows, a fiery orb drops down in the middle of the arena, surpassing the light of the Cretan Crown.[18] The sky is completely illuminated by the flames and does not grant licence to the obscure night. Seeing these things, languid Rest and lethargic Sleep flee and go off into other cities. Who should sing of the shows, the unrestrained jokes, who of the banquets and foods unbought, who of the rivers of lavish Lyaeus? But now I am losing strength because of Bacchus [- - -] and inebriated I am dragged into tardy sleep.

(Memory of) this day will travel through so many years into a distant time! Sacred, it will not fade in any age, as long as the hills of Latium and father Tiber, as long as your Rome will stand and the Capitol, which you restore to the lands,[19] will remain!

1 Here we follow Phillimore's (1918) suggestion of *aparchen* ('festival', 'feast') for the obviously corrupt *parcen* of the manuscript.
2 Dates.
3 Plums.

4 Figs. Here we translate Imhof's (1867) suggestion of *aestuosa* ('steamy', 'sultry') for the corrupt *aebosia* of the manuscript. An alternative suggestion is to read *Ebosea Caunos* ('Ebosean Caunos'): see Shackleton Bailey 2015: 373.

5 Apples and pears.

6 The festivities occur in an amphitheatre that is not specified (Newlands 2002: 228) though some translators take it to mean the Colosseum or Flavian Amphitheatre (e.g. Nagle 2004: 62).

7 This refers to Ganymede, cupbearer of Zeus/Jupiter, who was abducted from Mount Ida.

8 Following the interpretation of Shackleton Bailey (2015: 373–4), the Circle included all of the spectators except the senators, who sat in the orchestra. Within the Circle were the fourteen rows of seating reserved for *equites*, who constituted 'a better and more serious class of men', distinct from 'those dressed in togas', who comprised the general public.

9 There is so much plenty on the occasion of Domitian's Saturnalia feast that the price of grain is irrelevant.

10 Saturn.

11 Women.

12 On the Black Sea.

13 Cranes were mythological enemies of pygmies, and fought battles with them; see, for instance, Hom. *Il.* 3.2–7.

14 The largesse (*sparsio*) can be regarded here as vouchers or coupons (*tesserae*) which Shackleton Bailey (2015: 73 n. 14) proposes would be used to purchase the girls who are 'easily bought'.

15 Matches (cf. Mart. 1.41.4–5). The meaning of this passage as well as similar references that pair sulphur and broken glass have been debated without convincing resolution; see Harrison 1987.

16 Flamingos, pheasants, and guinea fowl respectively.

17 The contrast is between *princeps* (emperor) and *dominus* (master, lord). On Domitian as *dominus*, see above, **4.15 (c)**.

18 The constellation *Corona Borealis*, known also as Ariadne's Crown; Ariadne was from Crete.

19 Statius refers here to Domitian's restoration of the Temple of Jupiter Optimus Maximus Capitolinus, on which see Jones 1992: 92.

VII | Public Cult and the Court

4.34 Religious processions: the Ara Pacis Augustae

The Ara Pacis Augustae (Altar of Augustan Peace) was decreed by the Senate on 4 July 13 BC to celebrate Augustus' safe return after a three-year absence campaigning in Spain and Gaul; it was dedicated on 30 January 9 BC. The monument consists of an altar mounted on a stepped podium and enclosed within a precinct. Both the altar proper and the enclosure are made of white Italian (Luna) marble. A small sculptural frieze decorates the altar table and depicts a sacrifice scene and six Vestal Virgins (priestesses of Vesta) processing.

There are friezes on the eastern and western exterior walls of the precinct depicting deities and mythological scenes respectively. The north and south exterior walls of the precinct feature friezes of sacrificial processions that involve key members of the imperial family and the leading priests of Rome – i.e. members of the court of Augustus. Each frieze measures 1.55 m in height and 9.70 m in width, and the human figures are approximately three-quarters life-size. The left end of the south frieze (**fig. 4.7.1**), now fragmentary, contains the front third of the procession: a lictor (attendant) is identifiable (Pollini 2012: 225), suggesting the presence of magistrates and priests, perhaps *pontifices* (pontiffs). *Augures* (augurs) appear in the middle third, with the first figure of this group being Augustus, who was an augur and also had the right to take the auspices as *princeps* and *imperator*. The *rex sacrorum* (a high priest) stands close behind Augustus, after which follow the *flamines* (priests) of the four state cults: Mars, Quirinius, the deified Julius Caesar, and Jupiter. They are represented wearing leather helmets with spikes on top, and are followed by their lictor who holds an axe over his shoulder (on the order of the priests and their lictor, see Billows 1993: 84–7). It is perhaps possible to identify some specific historical individuals on the frieze, although it should be emphasized that such identifications are necessarily tentative – and sometimes debated. The priest of the deified Julius Caesar bears a clear portrait whose distinctive physiognomic traits identify him as Sex. Appuleius (*PIR*² A 960), husband of Octavia the Elder (*PIR*² O 65) and father of Sex. Appuleius (*cos.* 29 BC; *PIR*² A 961): Torelli 1982: 47. The last third of the procession and the right-hand portion of the frieze is comprised of members of the *domus Augusta* in their ceremonial finery. Agrippa, his head veiled with his toga, is at the head of this section, followed immediately by Livia and her son Tiberius. Antonia the Younger follows her husband Drusus the Elder, who is distinguished by his general's garb; the young child standing between them is likely their son Germanicus. A second couple, Antonia the Elder and her husband L. Domitius Ahenobarbus (*PIR*² D 128), appear towards the end of the procession with the children in front of them presumably being their son Gnaeus and daughter Domitia: Torelli 1982: 50. In contrast, the identity of the young boy who grabs Agrippa's toga has been debated considerably, though it has been convincingly suggested he is a foreign prince, and likewise the barefoot boy wearing non-Roman attire on the north frieze; see Rose 1990; Kleiner and Buxton 2008; Jussen, **Vol. 1, 154–5**.

The north frieze procession (**fig. 4.7.2**) likewise includes members of the imperial family, who occupy the fragmentary left third of the scene, the reverse of the south frieze. Members of the official priestly colleges along with their attendants constitute the remainder of the procession: the *quindecemviri sacris faciundis* (fifteen priests mainly responsible for the prophetic Sibylline Books) are pictured as the middle third followed by the small group of *augures* then the *septemviri epulones* (seven priests in charge of feasts for the gods) in the right third with a lictor at the head. It is significant that all four major priesthoods are represented, as Augustus was a member of each. Zanker (1988: 121) also notes that all of the major priesthoods, including the

Figure 4.7.1 The Ara Pacis: South Frieze.

Photo: © Charles Rhyne Estate; courtesy Visual Resources Center, Eric V. Hauser Memorial Library, Reed College, Portland, Oregon. Reproduction: © Roma, Sovrintendenza Capitolina ai Beni Culturali.

Figure 4.7.2 The Ara Pacis: North Frieze.

Photo: © Charles Rhyne Estate; courtesy Visual Resources Center, Eric V. Hauser Memorial Library, Reed College, Portland, Oregon. Reproduction: © Roma, Sovrintendenza Capitolina ai Beni Culturali.

Vestal Virgins, were instructed by the Senate to make annual sacrifice at the altar (*Mon. Anc.* 12.2); thus their inclusion in the friezes reflects their actual participation in rites performed there. What kind of religious occasion the two processional friezes represent has been the subject of debate. Recently, Pollini (2012: 225–7) has argued that rather than a public sacrifice, the reliefs commemorate one of two augural events: either a ceremony known as *maximum augurium salutis rei publicae* ('supreme augury for the safety of the Roman state'), or a ritual in which Augustus marked out the *templum terrestre* ('terrestrial precinct') where the Ara Pacis would be erected and dedicated. Whatever the case, the friezes are a prime example of how members of the court were depicted engaging in rites in the public spaces of the city. Furthermore, since many of the individuals would have been identifiable to contemporaries, the monument also served to showcase who mattered in Augustus' court.

4.35 Vestals at the House of Augustus

The Sorrento Base, named for its nineteenth-century discovery in Sorrento (ancient Surrentum), provides valuable archaeological evidence for Augustus' installation of the cult of Vesta in his house on the Palatine in 12 BC. This was an important step in creating an imperial residence with special religious associations that made it distinct from an ordinary aristocratic house. The location of the shrine of Vesta in the House of Augustus suggests the emperor would have had regular, personal interactions with the Vestals, an important group of state priestesses, just as he did with members of the major male priestly colleges. Augustus' role as *pontifex maximus* involved oversight of the Vestals, but the establishment of the shrine in his house would perhaps have made his interactions with the Vestals even more frequent. Figurative reliefs decorate the four sides of the base with gods and mythological figures associated with the Palatine and thus Augustus. In the left portion of the scene on side A pictured here, five Vestal Virgins stand facing right towards the centre of the scene, which is badly damaged. On the right end of the monument, Vesta is portrayed seated on a throne and flanked by a sixth Vestal, who stands to her left, and a veiled female figure on her right who is thought to be Livia. The inclusion of Livia is significant as she is the only member of Augustus' court portrayed in this scene. Her presence may reflect in part her long-standing association with the Vestals which dated to the triumviral period, when she, as well as Augustus' sister Octavia, were honoured with some of the same privileges the priestesses enjoyed including immunity from *tutela* (guardianship) and the right of *sacrosanctitas* or personal inviolability: Dio Cass. 49.38.1; DiLuzio 2016: 142. The Vestal beside the goddess, who may be the *virgo maxima* (chief priestess), holds a small figurine that might be the Palladium or a replica of it that she will place in the new Palatine shrine to Vesta. Curtains draped between two Ionic columns suggest an interior setting for the scene that may be the

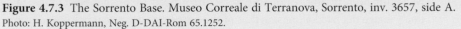

Figure 4.7.3 The Sorrento Base. Museo Correale di Terranova, Sorrento, inv. 3657, side A.
Photo: H. Koppermann, Neg. D-DAI-Rom 65.1252.

House of Augustus. Behind Vesta and Livia, a small circular building in the Ionic order, which is probably Vesta's new shrine, can be seen as the drapery falls away. The Palermo Relief, dated to the late first century BC, may be helpful in reconstructing the central part of side A of the Sorrento Base as it depicts a similar scene: DiLuzio 2016: 219.

5 | Picturing the Court

OLIVIER HEKSTER, KELLY OLSON, ANGELA HUG, AND ROBYN GILLAM

Introduction

Much of our evidence for the Roman imperial court comes from written texts. For the majority of the inhabitants of the Empire, however, their understanding of the court – who was in it and, crucially, who was excluded – depended on images. Images of the emperor were omnipresent, but when should images of the emperor also be considered images of the court? We might answer here that an image of the emperor is also an image of the court when he is depicted in the presence of the sort of people with whom he would be habitually surrounded. Consequently, for Roman viewers to see *aula* rather than just *princeps* in an image, they would have needed a certain amount of knowledge about what the court was and who made it up to serve as an interpretative framework. But that framework, in turn, was influenced by images of emperors surrounded by their inner circle. Having one's image depicted alongside that of the emperor was a clear acknowledgement of imperial favour. For those outside court circles, repeated representations of a particular individual alongside the emperor implied a close relationship with the *princeps*. Without compelling evidence to suggest otherwise, viewers would assume that these favoured individuals also enjoyed a high rank at court. Images reflected the court, but they also helped to create it.

Different media produced different images of the court, even when the same individuals were represented. Images in the possession of individuals, which could be personally handled or displayed to friends – like Ovid's statues (**5.2**) – would create a sense of intimacy impossible for a large statue group or elaborate reliefs. This suggestion of a relationship would be heightened when the image in question was a gift from the emperor himself, like the medallion of Gallienus (**5.23**). The imposing grandeur of monuments or state reliefs (**5.10, 15**), on the other hand, suggests that the men and women depicted alongside the emperor were far above the viewer, a very different impression but an equally valid one. Central coinage (by which we mean coins struck at imperial mints, as opposed to those minted by autonomous towns in the provinces) was perhaps the most effective way to disseminate images of the court; coinage could circulate freely and reach a wide cross-section of the emperor's subjects; for the advantages of central coinage in transmitting imperial ideology see Hekster 2015: 30–1; Elkins 2017: 4–5. There could be clear efforts to establish consistent messaging from the centre, but there was also room for local interpretation. The community of

Amisus (Pontus), for example, set up a statue group in AD 63–5 which included Nero, Poppaea, and, despite his death years earlier and his lack of posthumous status at the court, Britannicus: *SEG* 16.748; Rose 1997: 48, 161, cat. 98.

Publicly displayed physical representations of courtiers could both establish and advertise court hierarchy. Proposing honorific statues for members of the imperial family or other high-ranking individuals was one avenue for power groups outside of the court – the Senate, the soldiers, provincial communities – to attempt to win the emperor's goodwill. The close association between the physical representations of members of the emperor's court and the individuals themselves, however, is best demonstrated by the treatment of these images after a courtier fell from grace. The term *damnatio memoriae* ('condemnation of memory') is a modern scholarly invention, but its effects are well documented in Antiquity; on this see especially Varner (2004) and Flower (2006). We have both the written accounts, in which mobs are depicted as tearing down statues of fallen courtiers in an animal-like frenzy of both rage and joy (**5.5, 9**), and the physical remains: new heads on statues, defaced coins (**5.21**), and blank spaces on reliefs where figures once appeared (**5.20**). The rush to destroy all evidence of the disgraced individual(s) emphasizes both the complex, unstable hierarchy at the court and the need to preserve the emperor's goodwill (**5.19 [a]**). Acting too hastily was likely a less serious error than not acting hastily enough.

I | The Julio-Claudians

5.1 A representation of the mobile court of Augustus

This cup (**fig. 5.1.1**) is part of a hoard found in a villa at Boscoreale (just north of ancient Pompeii) which consists of 109 pieces of silverware, as well as jewellery and gold coins. Items from the hoard vary in date from the fourth century BC to the first century AD; many are considered masterpieces of Roman art. On this silver *skyphos* (a two-handled drinking cup), Augustus sits enthroned on a tribunal, surrounded by seven lictors. At the far right stand two soldiers, one in dress armour and one in plain tunic and helmet; opinions vary on whether these figures represent praetorian guardsmen: Héron de Villefosse 1899–1902: 138; Durry 1938: 218; Kuttner 1995: 94. The left side of the image is taken up with a party of foreigners whom Augustus is greeting, a group of adult males with three children. All are clad in Gallic costume, and are being presented to the emperor by Drusus the Elder, the stepson of Augustus (see Kuttner 1995: 99), clad in dress armour, who steadies a child being ushered forward. This image is not a scene of anguished, newly conquered tribesmen handing over their children as hostages to Rome. It depicts a friendly people, loyal to Rome, and the children are likely being transferred to Augustus to be brought up in the capital, possibly at the court, with the expectation they will

Figure 5.1.1 Boscoreale Cup (1:2). Musée du Louvre, Paris, BJ 2366.
Photo: P. Dujardin; composite from Héron de Villefosse 1899–1902: Plates 31, 33.

become tribal leaders sympathetic to Rome – much like the barbarian children on the Ara Pacis: Kuttner 1995: 99–100; cf. above, **4.34** and Jussen, **Vol. 1, 154–5**. Zanker (1988: 227–8) suggests that this scene was taken from a public relief sculpture (now lost), and referred to a specific historical event or occasion. This has been taken one step further by Kuttner, who suggests that it represents the leading men of Gallia Comata in 13 BC (or possibly 10 BC) petitioning Augustus to take their children with him to be raised at the Roman imperial court, when Augustus was in Gaul with Drusus, responding to an invasion by the German tribes: Kuttner 1995: 122–3.

5.2 Bringing the court home in exile: Ovid receives statuettes of Augustus, Tiberius, and Livia

Ovid, *Letters from Pontus* 2.8.1–22, 57–62.

Private individuals often owned images of the imperial family, allowing people to create some sort of private court by surrounding themselves with miniature members of the court. In a famous lament from AD 13, the poet Ovid, who was sent into exile by the emperor Augustus in AD 8, reflects on the difference between the real persons at the real court on the Palatine in Rome, and the small silver statues that are sent to him in exile at Tomi (modern Constanța, Romania).

A Caesar with a Caesar was returned to me recently; you have sent me these gods, Cotta Maximus;[1] and so that your gift might be a complete set – as it should be – there is Livia, joined with her Caesars. Lucky silver, more blessed than any gold! When it was unwrought it had value; now it is divine.[2] Had you given me riches, it would not have been a greater present than the three deities sent before my sight. It is something to look upon gods and consider them present, to be able to converse with them just as if with a real divinity.[3] As much as you could manage it, I have returned; no distant land holds me, but I linger safe and sound, just like in the old days, in the midst of the City.[4] I see the faces of the Caesars, just as I used to see them before; I have had scarcely any hope of this prayer being answered. I hail, just as I used to hail, the divine majesty. Even if you managed to secure my return, you could bestow nothing, I think, greater. What do my eyes lack except for the Palatine?[5] That place would be worthless, should Caesar be removed. As I gaze on him, I seem myself to be looking at Rome, for he embodies his own fatherland. Am I mistaken,[6] or is the face in his portrait angry at me? Is his appearance somehow grim and threatening? . . .

Happy are they who see not imitations but the reality, the true forms of the gods before their very eyes. Since harmful fate has refused me this, I revere the features and likenesses which art has brought forth. In this way men come to know the gods, whom the lofty heavens hide; they worship Jupiter through Jupiter's image.

---

1 M. Aurelius Cotta Maximus Messalinus (*cos.* AD 20; *PIR*[2] A 1488) was a Roman senator and friend to Augustus and Tiberius and also patron of Ovid.

2 Ovid had presumably sent Cotta a poem, in return for which he sent Ovid silver statues or busts (or a silver relief) of Augustus, Tiberius, and Livia. This gift was perhaps placed in Ovid's *lararium*: Lahusen 1999: 262.

3 This phrase highlights the tension between real people and artistic illusion, by instilling the real presence of the imperial family in their 'miniature cult images': Hardie 2002: 318.

4 This is a clear reference to Rome, linking the imperial family with the capital city (*urbs*).

5 Note how the location of the Palatine (*Palatia*) and the emerging concept of a recognizable court are linked.

6 This 'mimetic' use of language aims to involve the reader in his illusionistic games. Ovid (*Met.* 10.287) uses *fallo* in the passive voice (*fallor*: 'am I mistaken') elsewhere to describe Pygmalion's reaction when his statue comes to life: Hardie 2002: 322.

5.3 Formal honours for the dead Germanicus

Année épigraphique 1984.508 ll. 9–21 + 2012.467 ll. 16–21

It is rare to have insights into the process through which public images of the court were created in the Roman world. One prominent source is the so-called *Tabula Siarensis*, in which the Senate decreed honours for Germanicus, who had just died in the East (AD 19; cf. **3.29**). The reaction in Rome was an outpouring of grief. Consequently, Germanicus received a range of honours, including a marble arch with his whole family on top of it, which is described in the extract from the decree translated below. The formal decree for this has survived in fragments of bronze tablets. These were found in the territory of Siarum (hence the name) in Baetica (near modern Seville, Spain). A fragment of a further bronze plaque with the same decree was also found in Umbria (Cipollone 2011), which shows that the decree must have been disseminated widely throughout the empire. In that way, readers of the inscription would have obtained mental images of members of the imperial family, who formed an important part of the inner circle of the imperial court. People at Rome, of course, would see this inner circle represented on the monumental arch, which the decree discusses.

It pleased the Senate that a marble arch be erected in the Circus Flaminius at public expense, along with an entrance to the place in which statues for the deified Augustus and the *domus Augusta*[1] had been dedicated at public expense by C. Norbanus Flaccus,[2] with images of the defeated peoples.

(It also pleased the Senate that) the following be inscribed on the front of this arch: that the Senate and the People of Rome had dedicated this monument to the memory of Germanicus Caesar, because he died for the sake of the state, saving himself no effort and before entering the city while celebrating an *ovatio*[3] by decree of the Senate; for he had defeated the Germans in war and expelled them from Gaul; he had recovered our military standards,[4] avenged the vile deception of an army of the Roman people, and settled the affairs of the Gauls; he had been sent as proconsul to the overseas provinces [of Asia?] to organize these and the kingdoms of the same area in accordance with the orders of Tiberius Caesar Augustus, and he had installed a king in Armenia.[5]

(It also pleased the Senate that) on top of this arch should be placed a statue of Germanicus Caesar in a triumphal chariot, and around him statues of Drusus Germanicus,[6] his natural father, brother to Tiberius Caesar Augustus, and of Antonia (the Younger), his mother, and of Agrippina (the Elder), his wife, and of Livia,[7] his sister, and of Ti. Germanicus,[8] his brother, and of his sons and daughters.[9]

1 Cf. above, **1.3**.
2 *PIR*[2] N 168, *cos. ord.* 15 with Germanicus' adoptive brother, Drusus the Younger.
3 A form of minor triumph at Rome.
4 The military standards that had been lost during Varus' defeat in 9.
5 Artaxias III, who reigned 18–34.
6 Drusus the Elder.
7 Livilla.
8 The future emperor Claudius.
9 Germanicus had six children, including Gaius (the future emperor Caligula) and Agrippina the Younger.

5.4 A Representation of Living and Dead Members of the Imperial Family

The *Grand Camée de France* (**fig. 5.1.2**) is a five-layered sardonyx cameo dating to either c. AD 23–9 or 50–4: Bartman 1999: 112; Wood 2001: 308. Its dimensions are 31 cm by 26.5 cm. While Wood (2001: 308) believes this was 'a lavish gift to the imperial family', the assumption of other scholars is that such gems come from a courtly context, and were displayed in the imperial treasury: Simon 1967–8: 16; Megow 1987: 1–3; Flory 1995: 48. The identification of the family group pictured here changes depending on the date assigned to the gem, but whatever the date, it is a representation of living and dead members of the Julio-Claudian family; for the identification of individuals see Jucker 1976: 232–3, 241–2; Megow 1987: 202–7; Jeppesen 1993; Wood 2001: 308–13; Varner 2004: 75–6; Smith 2021: 90, 114–15.

In the upper level are (from left): Drusus the Younger, the deified Augustus (crowned and veiled), and, mounted on a Pegasus, either Drusus the Elder or Germanicus. The middle level is more complicated. The seated emperor Tiberius (centre) holds a sceptre, flanked by his mother Livia (also seated), their appearance 'unabashedly divine': Bartman 1999: 112. Standing in front of them is perhaps Nero Caesar (or his father, Germanicus, or Sejanus), as well as a woman who could be Nero Caesar's wife, Julia (or Agrippina the Elder or Antonia the Younger). Behind them are Caligula (or the future emperor Nero or Ti. Gemellus) and a female figure. Behind Livia and Tiberius to the right are Drusus Caesar or Claudius (emperor if the cameo was made in c. 50–4) and Agrippina the Elder or Younger. 'Agrippina the Younger's' hairstyle could confirm a date for the cameo between her marriage to Claudius in 49 and the accession of her son Nero in 54: Wood 2001: 296–7, 309. In the lowest level are captive barbarians. A symbol of the unity of the imperial family and its dynastic stability, this contrasts with the tension and factional conflict found in the accounts of Tiberius' reign: e.g. Tac. *Ann.* 1.33.3. This cameo presents a portrait of a strong, united family with generational depth, and if the jewel is coming

Figure 5.1.2 The Great Cameo of France. Bibliothèque nationale de France, camée 264.
Photo: Bibliothèque nationale de France.

from a court context, it may signal that 'officially' all is well. In addition, if such cameos were on display, it was one way that those outside the court understood who mattered within.

5.5 Public images for Sejanus – and his fall

The praetorian prefect Sejanus is depicted by our literary sources as a master of court politics, rising higher and higher under Tiberius until his abrupt fall from grace in AD 31; for details, see Seager 2005: 151–88; Birley 2007; Champlin 2012. The following three passages track his rise and fall through the treatment of his statues and show the myriad roles public images could play in court dynamics. Such images could be important indicators of an individual's place in the status hierarchy at court, particularly to those outside the inner circle. When other power groups, like the Senate or the military, proposed setting up images of courtiers, especially alongside images of the emperor himself, this confirmed the courtiers' high rank at court, unless the emperor took steps to curtail the honours. And, finally, the destruction of these images echoed the political (and often actual) death of the courtier who had fallen into disgrace.

(a) Tacitus, *Annals* 3.72.2–3

But the rebuilding of the Theatre of Pompey,[1] destroyed by an incidental fire,[2] was guaranteed by the emperor, because no one from the family had the means to pay for restoration; the name of Pompey, however, was retained. At the same time, Tiberius praised Sejanus highly, on the ground that it was through his toils and watchfulness that such a blaze had stopped at one loss. And the senators proposed a statue for Sejanus, to be placed at the Theatre of Pompey.[3]

1 Located in Regio IX, near the Circus Flaminius, the theatre, the first such permanent structure in Rome, was dedicated at the end of September 55 BC, during Pompey's second consulship: Beacham 2007: 218–23.
2 In AD 22. See too Vell. Pat. 2.130.1 for the incident.
3 Dio adds that the statue was made of bronze and that Tiberius set it up. Such an overt sign of imperial approval then led many people to erect their own images of Sejanus: Dio Cass. 57.21.3; cf. Sen. *Ad Marciam de consolatione* 22.4–7. Hennig (1975: 122–38) discusses Sejanus' honours; see also Champlin 2012: 371–3.

(b) Cassius Dio 58.4.3–4

By AD 30, according to Cassius Dio, Sejanus was emperor in all but name; Tiberius, aware of the danger at last, resolved to orchestrate his prefect's fall but did not yet feel secure enough to act openly: Dio Cass. 58.4.1–2. This passage shows the challenges those outside the emperor's inner circle could face when trying to assess the complex and unstable hierarchy of the court: Sejanus was a marked man, but no one other than the emperor knew this yet.

Tiberius then began to attack Sejanus in another way: he appointed him consul, proclaimed him sharer of his cares, and repeatedly called him 'My Sejanus', a title which he used to make public in letters addressed to the Senate and to the people. Men were deceived by these words, taking them to be sincere, and so they erected bronze statues[1] of them everywhere on equal terms, portrayed them together in paintings, and placed gilded chairs in the theatre for both of them. It was finally decreed that they should be appointed consuls together every five years and that when they entered Rome a body of citizens should go out to meet them both. Finally, they sacrificed to the images of Sejanus just as they did to those of Tiberius.[2]

1 As Tiberius' net tightened around Sejanus and his treachery, these statues then became the sites of portents heralding Sejanus' downfall: Dio Cass. 58.7.1–3.
2 Champlin (2012: 373) observes: 'The step from sacrificing for Sejanus to sacrificing to him is of course enormous.'

(c) Juvenal 10.56–67

Sejanus was arrested and executed in October 31. Cassius Dio (58.11.3) records that the people tore down his statues as though they were attacking the man himself. What happened to those statues is here imagined by Juvenal as part of his satire on the dangers of power.

Influence[1] subjected to intense jealousy ruins some people; a lengthy and conspicuous list of offices[2] sinks them. Down come the statues, pulled away by the rope, and then the stroke of the axe smashes the very wheels of chariots and the legs of undeserving nags are shattered.[3] Now the fires are hissing, now that head worshipped by the people blazes in the bellows and the furnaces and mighty Sejanus crackles. Next, out of the face that was number two in the whole world[4] are made little jugs, shallow bowls, a frying-pan, piss-pots. Festoon your house with laurel, drag a great bull, whitened with chalk,[5] up to the Capitol: Sejanus[6] is being dragged by a hook – now that is worth seeing – everyone cheers.

1 *Potentia*, not *potestas* (official power) or *auctoritas* (informal authority).
2 *Honorum pagina*. Here, *pagina* refers to a bronze tablet attached to the base of a statue: Ferguson 1979: 259; Courtney 1980: 460.
3 The statue imagined here is that of a chariot drawn by two horses, the 'characteristic triumphal type': Courtney 1980: 460; cf. Plin. *HN* 34.19.
4 At lines 74–7, Juvenal observes that, had things gone a little differently, the crowd who are now gloating over Sejanus' fall would have been calling him Augustus.
5 The chalk was used to cover any imperfections in the sacrificial animal: Ferguson 1979: 259; Murgatroyd 2017: 48.
6 From discussing the fate of his statue, Juvenal jumps now to the fate of Sejanus himself, connecting the chalk-whitened bull with his white corpse. The bodies of executed criminals were dragged by a hook to the Gemonian Steps: Ferguson 1979: 259; Murgatroyd 2017: 49; cf. Tac. *Ann.* 3.14.4, where the mob drags the statues of Cn. Piso to the Gemonian Steps.

5.6 Caligula and his Praetorian Guards

Fig. 5.1.3 shows a bronze sestertius minted at Rome, dated to 37/8. The obverse shows a bust of Caligula, facing left, laureate, with the legend C. CAESAR

Figure 5.1.3 Sestertius of Caligula, Roman Mint, AD 37–8 (*RIC* 1² Caligula 32; 30.44 g; 34.1 mm). Kunsthistorisches Museum, Vienna, RÖ 5257.
Photo: KHM-Museumsverband.

AVG(ustus) GERMANICVS PON(tifex) M(aximus) TR(ibunicia) POT(estate). The reverse shows the emperor, bare headed and dressed in a toga, standing on a low platform to the right, with his right arm extended towards five soldiers, who wear helmets and carry shields and short blades. Four standards are visible in the background; the standards closely resemble one held by a praetorian standard bearer on the reverse of a coin of Claudius, who is depicted clasping hands with the emperor: *RIC* 1² Claudius 11–12, 23–4, 29. The legend reads ADLOCVT(io) COH(ortium) ('address to the cohorts'). The middle shield depicts a multi-legged creature, which has been identified as a scorpion – the symbol of the praetorian guard: von Domaszewski 1909: 11, 14; Töpfer 2011: 21, 43. The coin provides the earliest physical representation of a key power group at the court – the emperor's bodyguards. Such representations were rare and were only politically palatable during reigns where the praetorians occupied positions of influence: Kelly 2020. In Caligula's case, the praetorian prefect Macro (*PIR*² N 12) was said to have played a key role in his accession: Philo *Leg.* 32–8, 58–9; Tac. *Ann.* 6.50.3–5; Dio Cass. 58.28.3–4, 59.1.2.

5.7 The Image of the Julio-Claudian Family: The Statue Group from the Basilica at Veleia

The Julio-Claudian forum of Veleia (near modern Piacenza) represented the centre of social, commercial, and political activities of the city, surrounded on three sides by porticos with shops (*tabernae*) and public buildings. The southern side is marked by a raised terrace which hosted the basilica, a building with

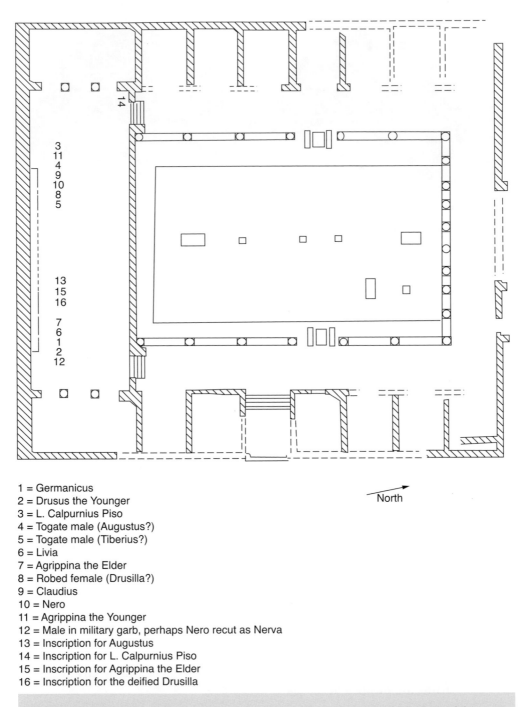

1 = Germanicus
2 = Drusus the Younger
3 = L. Calpurnius Piso
4 = Togate male (Augustus?)
5 = Togate male (Tiberius?)
6 = Livia
7 = Agrippina the Elder
8 = Robed female (Drusilla?)
9 = Claudius
10 = Nero
11 = Agrippina the Younger
12 = Male in military garb, perhaps Nero recut as Nerva
13 = Inscription for Augustus
14 = Inscription for L. Calpurnius Piso
15 = Inscription for Agrippina the Elder
16 = Inscription for the deified Drusilla

North

Figure 5.1.4 Plan of the Forum at Veleia, showing locations of statues of members of the Julio-Claudian family. After Boschung 2002: 30, fig. 2.
Original plan: A. Smadi.

a nave and a rectangular *exedra* intended for the worship of the emperors. Statues were displayed in the basilica and surrounding forum: Boschung 2002: 28–32. There seem to have been three phases of development: Caligulan, Claudian (AD 50–4), and Flavian. Throughout these phases, the statue group was augmented and/or changed as a result of *damnatio memoriae*: several statues are extensively recut from portraits of older family members: Rose 1997: 121–6. The twelve marble statues portraying members of the Julio-Claudian family were on view in the basilica and can be identified with some certainty; among them are images of Livia, Germanicus, Agrippina the Elder, Claudius, Agrippina the Younger, and Nero. Most intriguing is the inclusion in the basilica of a statue of L. Calpurnius Piso (*cos.* 15 BC; *PIR*^{2} C 289), who was only a distant relative of the imperial family but was a confidant of Augustus and Tiberius and a long-serving urban prefect: Boschung 2002: 25, 32–3; *contra* Rose 1997: 124. His presence makes the ensemble more than a family group: it is a court group. All the togas contain traces of red paint, 'usually an under-coating for gilding or for purple', thus indicating the togas were painted a rich colour or gilded to indicate imperial rank: Rose 1997: 125.

5.8 The Reception of Court Fashion in the Provinces: Agrippina the Younger

(a) Bust of Agrippina the Younger

This portrait of Agrippina the Younger (**fig. 5.1.5**) is the so-called Milan type, dated to sometime between the reign of Caligula and early in the reign of Claudius: Gasparri, Capaldi, and Spina 2009: 72, cat. 47. In this type, the hair is parted down the middle, rows of curls partially cover the ears, and there are two shoulder-locks, one on each side of the neck. This type, along with the 'Ancona' type, were the most commonly replicated of Agrippina's portrait types (and the two may have existed simultaneously): Wood 2001: 296, cf. 1995: 465. The curls on either side of the part make her resemble her mother, Agrippina the Elder: Wood 2001: 297. This hairstyle was complicated and almost certainly required time and effort on the part of at least one *ornatrix*; it probably also utilized a hairpiece to augment Agrippina's natural hair.

(b) Tempera Portrait of a Woman on a Linen Shroud

The woman in this portrait (**fig. 5.1.6**) painted on a linen shroud has a hairstyle reminiscent of Neronian Rome (AD 50–70): Walker 2000: 38–9, with references. The hair is parted in the centre and slightly waved with banks of curls at the sides of the head, and long locks at the side of the neck, very like the hairstyle in the portrait of Agrippina the Younger discussed above (**5.8 [a]**). The hair on the proper left side is worn in a knot bound with gold. The woman's jewellery has been added in gold leaf: ball earrings (typical of the first century AD), a gold necklace with central shell pendant, gold snake bracelets, and a gold ring. It used to be thought such portraits were Ptolemaic; only with the realization that the hair and jewellery were Roman styles were the portraits redated to that period: Borg 1995, 1996: 19–84. They are often taken as evidence of the influence of court circles on fashion in the provinces: e.g. Walker 1997: 2. Such fashions may have

Figure 5.1.5 Bust of Agrippina the Younger. Museo Archeologico Nazionale di Napoli, inv. 6190.
Photo: Su concessione del Ministero per i Beni e le Attività Culturali – Museo Archeologico Nazionale di
Napoli – foto di Luigi Spina.

Figure 5.1.6 Tempera portrait of a woman on a linen shroud, Hawara, Egypt, AD 50–70. British Museum, EA 74709.

been circulated through Alexandrian coinage and official statue types (cf. Borg 2012: 614–15), but perhaps also through personal contacts between members of the provincial elite and the court. Such contacts could occur when Egyptian embassies went to Rome and when prominent equestrian administrators were posted to the province.

5.9 The statues of Octavia and Poppaea as targets of loyalty and dissidence

In 62, the emperor Nero made the controversial decision to set aside his wife, Octavia (the daughter of Claudius), to marry his mistress, Poppaea Sabina, a decision which sparked popular unrest. The following passages show how those outside the court looked to physical representations of individuals in order to understand who made up the inner circle around the emperor. For many people in Rome, the statues *were* the court. For a recent comparison of the treatment of the statues in these two passages, see Courrier 2016.

(a) [Seneca], *Octavia* 682–9, 794–803

Here, destroying Poppaea's statues is presented as a conscious effort on the part of the people to effect a change in court hierarchy. Their efforts are ultimately futile, for their will is powerless against the strength of the emperor's favour. They can tear down Poppaea's statues, but they cannot tear down Poppaea herself. For these passages see Ferri 2003: 319–20, 353–5; Boyle 2008: 237–8, 258–9; Kragelund 2016: 255–7, 276–7; Ginsberg 2017: 152–3.

(Chorus) See! Everywhere now Poppaea's likeness, oppressive to our eyes, gleams next to Nero's.[1] Let violent hands hurl to the ground the face – too lifelike – of his Lady,[2] drag the very woman from her lofty couches,[3] then, with savage spears and flames, attack the callous emperor's palace (*aula*). . . .

(Messenger) Any statue – bright marble or gleaming bronze – that stood wearing the face of Poppaea lies struck down by the hands of the mob, toppled by brutal blades. The dismembered limbs they drag away with ropes in all directions, trampled and smothered at length with foul mud.[4] Words converge with these wild deeds, words which my fear keeps unspoken. They intend to ring with flames the emperor's residence unless he, defeated, hands his new wife over to the people's rage and restores to Claudia[5] her proper home.

1 Like with Sejanus (above, **5.5**), the placement of Poppaea's statues next to those of Nero emphasizes her close relationship with the emperor (and implies a high position at the court). For the archaeological evidence for such statue groups, see Ferri 2003: 319, with further bibliography.

2 The Latin *domina* often refers to the female head of the household but can also refer to a female ruler. To translate it as 'empress' is misleading (see Hug, **Vol. 1, 73**).

3 Here the crowd has conflated Poppaea's statues with Poppaea herself; compare with Tacitus on Cn. Piso (*Ann.* 3.14.4) and Cassius Dio on Sejanus (58.11.3). For the blurry boundaries between statue and individual, see Kragelund 2016: 256.

4 Compare with Pliny's description of the visceral pleasure he (and others) took in the destruction of the statues of Domitian: Plin. *Pan.* 52.3–4; cf. Suet. *Dom.* 23.

5 Octavia.

(b) Tacitus, *Annals* 14.60.4–61.1

In Tacitus' version, the riot stems not from rage but from joy, and occurs after the common people (*vulgus*) mistakenly believe that Nero has put Poppaea aside and recalled Octavia. The people are, therefore, reacting to what they think is a change in the court hierarchy, not attempting to force the change themselves. Like in Dio's account of the statues of Sejanus (5.5 [b], above), those not in court circles struggle to successfully interpret court dynamics. It is interesting to note that the statues of Octavia appear to be able to be restored; this suggests that they were taken down after her banishment, but not destroyed.

Soon afterwards, Octavia was banished to Campania and placed under military surveillance. From that arose repeated, open protests by the common people, who are less prudent and who, as a result of their humble fortunes, face fewer dangers. <There followed a rumour>[1] that Nero had regretted his outrageous conduct and recalled Octavia as his wife. Thereupon the people, rejoicing, climbed the Capitol and at last paid homage to the gods. They toppled the statues of Poppaea; the images of Octavia they carried on their shoulders, sprinkled with flowers, and set them up in the forum and the temples. There was even praise for the emperor, and their rivalry in paying homage to him recommenced. They were already filling the Palatine with their numbers and their cries of approval, when bands of soldiers were dispatched who broke up the crowd, thrown into disarray by blows and drawn swords. The changes which they had made in the riot were reversed, and Poppaea's honours were restored.[2]

1 The text as transmitted states that Nero did recall Octavia; this is clearly an error as Tac. *Ann.* 14.61.3 establishes that Octavia is still in Campania. The generally accepted emendation is that the people's protests led to a rumour of Octavia's return; see Furneaux 1891: 464; Miller 1987: 52.

2 Poppaea's statues were pulled down yet again after Nero's death but were reinstated by Otho upon his accession: Tac. *Hist.* 1.78.2.

II | From the Flavians to the Antonines

5.10 The Flavian court in public relief sculpture

The fairly well-preserved Cancelleria reliefs (**fig. 5.2.1**) are now in the Vatican and consist of two friezes, each constructed from several marble panels. The left frieze (known as A; top in **fig. 5.2.1**), shows the emperor Nerva (fourth figure from the left), surrounded by humans and gods. On the far left is a lictor, recognizable through his *fasces*, and on the right and in the background are soldiers. But the viewer also sees the gods Mars, Minerva, and Roma (and a wing of Victory), and the Genii of the Senate and the people who are respectively bearded and bare-chested. The right frieze (B; bottom in **fig. 5.2.1**) shows a similar mixture of human and divine. The emperor Vespasian is greeted by a young man, the goddess Roma or Virtus (seated at the left and accompanied by Vestal Virgins), and the Genii of the Senate and of the people (in the

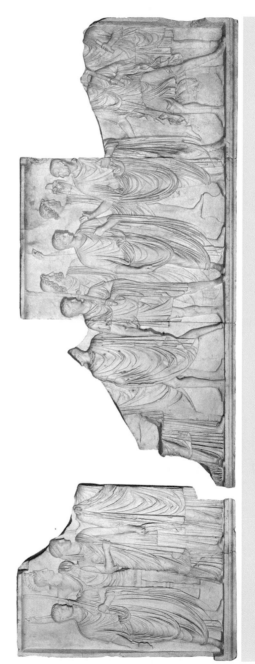

Figure 5.2.1 The Cancelleria reliefs, Rome, c. AD 93–8. Musei Vaticani, Rome, inv. 13389–95. Photo: © Vatican Museums.

background). It is generally agreed that the emperor on Frieze A was originally Domitian, and that after his *damnatio memoriae*, his face was recut to resemble Nerva's. On one view, the face of Vespasian on Frieze B is likewise a re-carving of that of Domitian (Bergmann 1982: 22–5; Baumer 2007: 94–5, 99), although others have argued that the emperor of Frieze B was always Vespasian, and that the young man greeting him depicts the youthful Domitian (Darwall-Smith 1996: 172–7; Varner 2004: 119–20). To Roman viewers the Vestal Virgins would have been directly recognizable. One of them, the third figure from the left on B, is still fully preserved, and feet of more Vestals are visible surrounding the split in the relief. Roman viewers would also have been able to identify the central figure and the two headless figures on the right as lictors from their bundles of rods (*fasces*). The reliefs probably decorated one of Domitian's many arches and showed how the mundane and the divine were focused on the ruler.

5.11 Courtiers in the public eye

Corpus Inscriptionum Latinarum 11.3612 (= *ILS* 1567): Caere (modern Cerveteri)

The ongoing institutionalization of the court meant an increasing number of formalized positions for freedmen functioning as courtiers; see Edmondson, **Vol. 1, Chapter 8**. These courtiers were also visible to the public eye, especially through the many career inscriptions in Rome and the surrounding cities. Those who could read but had no direct experience of the court would still be able to at least obtain a mental image of the domestic and administrative arms of the court from career inscriptions. The substantial staff at court included food tasters, and overseers of various areas of court life, as illustrated in the inscription for Ti. Claudius Bucolas (*PIR²* C 819). Interestingly, the role of overseer of the water supply meant involvement in the water supply of the city in general. This makes Bucolas a relatively rare example of a freedman moving between the domestic and administrative arms of imperial service. The inscription perhaps commemorated how Bucolas built a basilica together with his mother and son: Hemelrijk 2015: 132 n. 71; cf. *CIL* 11.3614 (= *ILS* 5918a).

Ti. Claudius Bucolas, freedman of the Augustus, imperial food taster, head of dining room staff, overseer of the games,[1] overseer of the water supply, overseer of the imperial household,[2] with Q. Claudius Flavianus, his son, and Sulpicia Cantabra, his mother, by decree [of the town councillors].

1 Weaver 1972: 274. See too *CIL* 6.8498 (= *ILS* 1738), the inscription for M. Aurelius Prosenes (AD 217), who was overseer of the games under Commodus, having been overseer of vineyards, and eventually became *a cubiculo* under Caracalla (*PIR²* A 1588; cf. Dolansky, **Vol. 1, 402–3**).
2 On the *procurator aquarum* and the *procurator castrensis*, see Weaver 1972: 6–7; Eck 2000b: 239.

5.12 The women of Trajan's court: Trajan's niece and grand-nieces

One important perception of the court was that of a place where the emperor could be influenced. Members of the court, therefore, came to be prominent figures in their own right. A notable case is that of Trajan's niece and Hadrian's mother-in-law Matidia the Elder and her daughter Matidia the Younger (*PIR*[2] M 367–8). The former appeared on centrally minted coins, which was a type of imagery that allowed people throughout the empire to understand who made up the court: *RIC* 2 Trajan 751–61. On the coin depicted here (**fig. 5.2.2**), the obverse shows a diademed bust of the elder Matidia, surrounded by the legend MATIDIA AVG(usta) DIVAE MARCIANAE F(ilia) ('Matidia Augusta, daughter of the deified Marciana'). On the reverse, Matidia is depicted standing with her hands on the heads of her children Matidia the Younger and Sabina. The legend reads PIETAS AVGUST(ae) ('Piety of the Augusta'). The importance of Matidia the Elder also becomes clear from a statue consecrated to her at Tibur, at the occasion of which the emperor held a laudatory speech. Interestingly, in this speech the emperor stressed that Matidia did not use her position to ask him for favours: *CIL* 14.3579, cf. Jones 2004. Whether this is true or not, Hadrian's denial suggests that people expected Matidia to use her position at court to influence the emperor. Hadrian also allowed for the construction of a temple to his mother-in-law on the Campus Martius – the first temple at Rome to be dedicated to a deified woman: Woodhull 2012: 236–41. Her daughter, likewise, was an important figure at court. Her personal wealth was sufficient to sponsor infrastructure projects, and her prestige was such that she could restore the theatre of Sessa Aurunca in Campania in her own name: Chausson 2008; Bruun 2010; cf. *CIL* 10.4745. It is little surprise that these women were deemed to play an important role at the court – which they probably did. Their prominent role on coins minted in the provinces probably shows local attempts to flatter these important figures.

Figure: 5.2.2 Aureus of Trajan, Roman mint, AD 98–117 (*RIC* 2 Trajan 759 [aureus]; 7.24 g). ANS 1967.153.180.
Photo: Courtesy of the American Numismatic Society.

5.13 Hadrian's inner court at the hunt

Though dedicated to Constantine in 315, the decorative programme on the Arch of Constantine incorporates earlier works of art from the time of the emperors Trajan, Hadrian, and Marcus Aurelius. The eight tondi on the arch are of Hadrianic date and depict a series of hunting scenes paired with depictions of sacrifices to the gods: Aymard 1951: 527–37; Boatwright 1987: 190–202; Martini and Schernig 2000. This pair of tondi (**fig. 5.2.3**) is on the north-west side of the arch. The left-hand tondo in this pair shows (left to right) an attendant, Hadrian (recut to depict the young Constantine), L. Aelius Verus, T. Caesernius Statius Quinctius Macedo Quinctianus (*PIR*^{2} C 182), and an attendant: Martini and Schernig 2000: 148–9; Roller, **Vol. 1, 341–2**. Hunting was a pursuit taken up by some Roman rulers, but does not seem to have been characteristically the sport of emperors. Unlike many courtly hunts throughout history (e.g. those in Early Modern Europe), Roman imperial hunts do not seem to have been large-scale affairs with a significant number of courtiers participating, but smaller events with just a few members of the court's 'inner circle': see Roller, **Vol. 1, 336–46**. Hadrian is one emperor who was a keen huntsman, and the depiction of a lion hunt is appropriate for him, since he was involved in a famous lion hunt in Egypt (*P. Oxy.* 8.1085; Ath. 15.677d–e), and extant medallions of him hunting a lion perhaps refer to this occasion: cf. Boatwright 1987: 198; Toynbee 1944: 219. On Hadrian as a hunter generally, see Dio Cass. 69.10.2 (Xiph.); SHA *Hadr.* 2.1, 26.3; Roller, **Vol. 1, 341–3**; Aymard 1951: 173–82, 523–37; Gutsfeld 2000; Kasulke 2000; Martini and Schernig 2000; Le Roux 2009: 23–5.

Figure 5.2.3 Hadrianic tondi, Arch of Constantine, Rome.
Photo: Alinari / Bridgeman Images.

The lion-hunt tondo is paired on the Arch of Constantine with a relief depicting a sacrifice to Hercules: Holloway 2004: 24. In the centre of the sacrifice scene, Hadrian stands before a small altar in the standard pose of a man preparing to sacrifice as the top of his head is covered by his toga (*capite velato*). Antoninus Pius stands behind Hadrian, and to his left is an attendant; to the right of the altar, a figure identified as T. Caesernius Statius Quintius Statianus Memmius Macrinus (*PIR*² C 183) is shown watching the emperor perform the rites. Statianus and his brother T. Caesernius Statius Quinctius Macedo Quinctianus (*PIR*² C 182) appear in six of the reliefs. The brothers were *amici principis* and accompanied Hadrian during his travels through the East, which earned them the distinction of *comites*: *CIL* 5.865 (= *ILS* 1069), 8.7036 (= *ILS* 1068).

5.14 Egyptianizing depictions of Hadrian and Antinous: The Pinciano obelisk

Few people had closer access to emperors than their lovers, or were better placed to influence them. They are therefore often referred to in our literary sources, but their unofficial position meant that they were hardly ever depicted. The main exception is Antinous, Hadrian's favourite who drowned in the Nile in mystifying circumstances in late 130. There were some rumours that he had sacrificed himself to save Hadrian: Dio Cass. 69.11.2–3; SHA *Hadr.* 14.5–6; cf. Galimberti 2017: 104–5. Antinous was subsequently deified, which gave him official status. The enormous number of images that then appeared indicates how prominent he must have been.

Most commemorations of Antinous were done in a Graeco-Roman artistic style, but one prominent commemoration in the Egyptian style is formed by the 9.25 m high pink granite obelisk that now stands on the Pincian Hill in Rome. This monument was discovered in the early sixteenth century, lying in three pieces in the ruins of the Circus Varianus, near Porta Maggiore, and erected on the present site in 1822 by Pius VII: Boatwright 1987: 242.

Each straight side of the obelisk is surmounted by a relief showing a person (r.) with a god (l.). On the east side, Hadrian as king (partly destroyed) prays before Re-Horakhty, the creator god; on the west Antinous, in a crown that identifies him with Osiris (Grenier 2008: 6 n. a), receives life from Thoth, the god of wisdom and of the Hermopolite Nome (in which Antinoopolis was located); on the north side, he receives wholeness and eternal life from Amun, the oracular god; on the south side, he receives heart/intelligence, stability and eternal rulership from Osiris, god of the dead and resurrection (image destroyed): Kessler in Meyer, Grimm, and Kessler 1994: 133–40. The order given here, which provides the sequence for each part of the inscription, is that of Erman (for discussion see Grenier 2008: 3–5; Panov 2020: 131). The obelisk's original orientation is unknown.

The hieroglyphic text on the four sides of the obelisk is written in Middle Egyptian, a literary and liturgical language whose use continued to the end of the fourth century: Loprieno 1995: 5–6, 23–6. It presents many challenges, both in orthography and basic meaning. It has been suggested that these difficulties stem from it being a translation from Greek, but the text displays the characteristics of a number of well attested Middle Egyptian literary genres, albeit combined in unexpected ways. The study by Adolf Erman (1917) remains the basis of all subsequent translations; for important recent contributions see too Derchain 1991; Meyer, Grimm, and Kessler 1994; Grenier 2008; Panov 2020.

The purpose and location of this monument are disputed. It can be read as an imperial decree that sets up the cult of Antinous and especially his oracle (see SHA *Hadr.* 14.7); it can also be seen as a traditional Egyptian foundation document for a mortuary cult. There is no doubt that it describes the foundation of Antinoopolis. The references to the 'sacred place' of Antinous evidently refer to his tomb. Various localities in Rome as well as the Villa of Hadrian at Tibur have been suggested for the obelisk and tomb: Kessler in Meyer, Grimm, and Kessler 1994: 103; Grenier 2008: 37–45; Renberg 2010: 181–90. However, as the main topic of the text is the foundation of Antinoopolis, the tomb and the obelisk could well have been sited there: Kessler in Meyer, Grimm, and Kessler 1994: 104–9; Panov 2020: 127–9. In this case, like many other such monuments, it would have been moved to Rome at a later date: Boatwright 1987: 258–9.

(a) The West (l.) and East (r.) Side Reliefs

Figure 5.2.4 Reliefs from the Pinciano obelisk, Rome.
Photo: G. Singer, Neg. D-DAI-ROM 71.73, 71.79.

(b) Inscriptions

(i) East – Re-Horakhty

Prayer offered for well-being by Antinous the justified,[1] whose heart is in very great rejoicing since he knows his own form[2] after returning to life and having seen the sun disk [- - -] his heart, saying: 'O Re-Horakhty, overlord of the gods who listens to the appeals of gods, humans, the transfigured and (unjustified) dead, listen to the prayer of one who is near you. Give in return for what your beloved son did for me, The King of Upper and Lower Egypt, who established the instructions[3] (for setting up my cult) in the temples, delighting the hearts of the gods who are there for all the people, ((Whom [Re, Hapy and] all the gods love))[4] Lord of Appearances ((([Hadrian Caesar]))), life, prosperity and health, given life forever, [- - -] (and) a fresh prosperous old age, (as) he is the Lord of Might, ruler of all lands, August(us).[5] The great ones of Egypt are bowed down and the Nine Bows[6] united under his two sandals, as with the (former) rulers of the Two Lands. [They are under all his commands?] every day, his might reaches to every limit of the borders of this land at its four directions. The bulls and their cows mingle with delight and make numerous offspring for him, to make his heart rejoice, and that of the Great Royal Wife, whom he loves, Mistress of the Two Lands and cities, ((Sabina)), Life, Prosperity and Health! ((Sebastē, may she live eternally)).[7] [Hapy], father of the gods, make the fields fertile! Make for them the inundation in its time, flooding the Two Lands.'[8]

1 Reading based on restoration by Panov (2020: 141 n. 77). The epithet 'justified' refers to the judgement of the dead, where the heart is weighed; those who pass the test enter into the entourage of Osiris, the ruler of the dead: Quirke 2001.

2 He becomes conscious of having a divine, imperishable body: Grimm in Meyer, Grimm, and Kessler 1994: 69 n. 6. For the following restorations introducing Antinous' speech, see Panov 2020: 141 n. 79.

3 *Sebayt*: either instructions for setting up Antinous' cult in Egypt (Grimm in Meyer, Grimm, and Kessler 1994: 71 n. 27) or teachings Antinous conveyed to Hadrian (Derchain 1991: 111–12, 114, 117 n. 8).

4 Double brackets (( )) indicate the presence of the cartouche or name ring in the royal titulature. For the restoration, see Panov 2020: 142 n. 81. Hapy is the god of the Nile flood: Hart 2005: 61.

5 These epithets are all part of Hadrian's Egyptian royal titulature: cf. Leprohon 2013. The title *neb was* ('Lord of Might') was a translation of *princeps*: Derchain 1991: 110; Grimm in Meyer, Grimm, and Kessler 1994: 71. *Shepses* means the same thing ('august') in Egyptian as Latin *augustus* or Greek *sebastos*: Derchain 1991: 117.

6 The Nine Bows are the traditional enemies of Egypt, located on its borders: Shaw 2000: 309–11.

7 Following Ptolemaic practice, queens have their own titulary, but not as standardized as that of the king: Leprohon 2013: 180–1, 183, 186–8. *Sebastē* is the Greek version of *Augusta*. This is one of only two hieroglyphic citations for the Roman period: Grenier 2008: 33 with n. b.

8 Upper and Lower Egypt.

(ii) West – Thoth

(As for) the god, the Osiris Antinous,[1] justified, he became a young man, fair of face, who makes festive the eyes. He is great of strength, his heart rejoicing like one with (strong) arms. He accepted the commands of the gods at the time of his death.[2] There was repeated for him every ritual of the Hours of Osiris, together with all his secret ceremonies.[3] His instructions[4] have been circulated throughout the whole land through helpful direction and sharp argument.[5] Never had the like been done by those (who had come) before, up to today. His altars, temples, and so on, are assigned his name, so he breathes the breath of life and it happens that his awe exists in the hearts of the people. Lord of Wenu,[6] Lord of divine speech, Thoth, make (eternally) young his soul like all things in their time, in night and day, at every time, in every second! His love is in the hearts of his followers and his respect [--- of all]. His praise is with the people and they give him adoration. He takes his seat in the hall of the justified, transfigured and excellent, who are in the following of Osiris in the sacred land,[7] while the Lord of Eternity gives him justification. They establish his word on earth because their hearts are delighted by him. He goes to every place that he wants. (As for) the doorkeepers of the underworld, they say to him, 'praise to you,' they loosen the bolts, they open their doors before him for millions and millions of years, every day.[8] His lifetime is forever, without perishing.

1 Everyone who dies and is justified becomes an Osiris, a spirit in the entourage of the god, but not Osiris himself: Grenier 2008: 7 n. b.

2 The opening passage on the west side describes the life and death of Antinous. The phrase 'making festive the eyes' could refer to a divine image of Antinous or his appearance during life: Kessler in Meyer, Grimm, and Kessler 1994: 141; Derchain 1991: 118 n. 1. The latter is more likely, as it is followed by a description of his death and burial. It may be linked to Late Period and Graeco-Roman Period laments for those who die young: Lichtheim 1980: 5–6, 52–4, 58–65; Smith 2009: 9–10, 249, 254. What sets Antinous apart from them is his acceptance of the gods' will. Derchain (1991: 115, 118 n. 3) explains the phrase 'with strong arms' as a translation of 'hero' and therefore a hint that Antinous was 'heroic' in his acceptance of death. For the reading 'great of strength' see Panov 2020: 138 n. 55–6.

3 The Hours of Osiris was a vigil over the model mummies of Osiris, adapted for use in funerary rituals; in myth, Osiris' body was guarded against further dismemberment by Seth: Meeks and Favard-Meeks 1997: 169–72; Riggs 2010. The secret ceremonies or 'works' are the rituals and acts of mummification: Riggs 2010.

4 The word is generally translated as 'instructions', but could be translated as 'regulations' for setting up and running the cult of Antinous: Derchain 1991: 119 n. 8; Grimm in Meyer, Grimm, and Kessler 1994: 75 n. 86.

5 The meaning of this statement is unclear; the interpretation followed is that of Grimm in Meyer, Grimm, and Kessler 1994: 75 n. 81–3. For other views, see Derchain 1991: 118 n. 26; Grenier 2008: 16.

6 An old Egyptian name for Hermopolis, capital of the 15th Upper Egyptian Nome, where Antinoopolis was founded. Thoth was the main god of the city and district; see Montet 1961: 146–9; Grimm, in Meyer, Grimm, and Kessler 1994: 47 n. 90.

7 The underworld or land of the dead.

8 Antinous joins the eternal solar cycle, moving without hindrance through the gates of the underworld and the twelve hours of the night, before rising with the sun every morning: Müller 2001.

(iii) North – Amun

The god, Osiris Antinous, the justified, who is there. They prepared a space for competition in his precinct which [--- is in (Egypt?)], its name being his name, for the strong ones who are in this land, along with the rowers and runners of the whole land[1] as well as for all people who belong to the place where the holy writings of Thoth are.[2] There is bestowed on them praise, wreaths upon their heads. They are rewarded with every good thing and offerings are made on his altars, while, every day, divine offerings are placed before him . . . praise is given to him by the craftsmen of Thoth, in accordance with the extent of his power.[3] He goes out from his sacred place to the many temples of the whole land because he listens to the prayers of those who cry out to him. He heals the sickness of the needy, sending dreams, as he accomplishes his work among the living.[4] He takes every form he desires because the seed of a god is truly in his body [and in?] the healthy body of his mother. He was elevated on the birth stool by [- - -] [5]

1 The 'strong ones' and 'runners' could be understood as 'athletes' or 'sprinters', but there is little agreement on how to translate this passage: see Grenier 2008: 20–3. However, what follows strongly suggests a description of the *Antinoeia*, the games set up in honour of Antinous: Meyer in Meyer, Grimm, and Kessler 1994: 126–9.
2 Perhaps the ritual specialists and scholars in charge of setting up and maintaining Antinous' Egyptian cult (Grimm and Kessler in Meyer, Grimm, and Kessler 1994: 79 n. 138–9, 111–12), or possibly the artists, poets, and athletes who took part in the *Antinoeia* (Derchain 1991: 120 n. 7).
3 Egyptian: *baw*, his power, in the sense of divine manifestation, which Derchain (1991: 120–1 n. 8) suggests is the equivalent of the *virtus* or *aretē* of a hero.
4 Antinous was therefore an oracular and healing god. He goes forth from his temple as a processional oracle in festive procession, where his devotees may appeal to him, as well as communicating through dreams. On healing gods and oracles in this period, see Frankfurter 1998: 46–52, 145–84.
5 Antinous is also reborn as the young, royal god familiar from earlier myths about the divine birth of kings and, at this period, presented as the offspring of divine couples in major religious centres: Meeks and Favard-Meeks 1997: 183–6; Grenier 2008: 59–64. Egyptian *wedjat*, referring to the body of his mother, generally means 'whole' or 'restored': Wilkinson 1992: 43. The idea of physical or sexual virginity is largely absent from Egyptian culture: Grenier 2008: 26 n. d. This fragmentary passage had been restored; Panov (2020: 137 n. 52) has questioned the reference to the mother's body. The name of the god who elevates the child at birth has been lost.

(iv) South – Osiris

(As for) the god[1] who is there, who rests in this sacred place which is the boundary field of the Lord of Might of Rome,[2] he is known as a god in the holy places of Egypt. Temples are built for him and he is worshipped as a god by the prophets and priests of Upper and Lower Egypt, and, likewise, by the (other) inhabitants of Egypt. A town was given his name and (to him) those who belong to the host of Greeks and Egyptians of the Two Lands, who are in the temples of Egypt. They come from their towns [- - -] and there is given to them arable fields to make their lives better (?).[3] There is a temple of this god there, which is called Osiris Antinous, justified. (It is) built of fine, white limestone, sphinxes surround it and statues (and) numerous columns, like those made by the former (kings), and those made by the Greeks.[4] All the gods and goddesses gave to him the breath of life, and he breathes as one rejuvenated.

1 See Grimm in Meyer, Grimm, and Kessler 1994: 81 n. 71. This word is written logographically and has also been read as his name (Erman 1917: 17), Osiris (Derchain 1991: 116) or as *hesy* ('praised one'), someone who died accidentally or by divine intervention, including the drowned (Grenier 2008: 8 n. a); *contra* Renberg 2010: 174 n. 56–7, there is no solid evidence that Antinous is described as *hesy* in the inscription.

2 A literal translation: this passage has been rendered and understood in many ways; the reference to the 'boundary field' is the main clue to the original location of the obelisk; for literature, see above, 205.

3 A reference to the founding of Antinoopolis, with its mixed Greek and Egyptian population: Calament 2005: 1.51–65. Panov (2020: 134 n. 32) reads 'oases' after 'towns'.

4 This could refer to the Canopus complex of the Villa of Hadrian (Boatwright 1987: 143–9; cf. above **2.21** [**a, c**]), to the temple of Isis Campensis in Rome (Lembke 1994), or to an Egyptian equivalent, like the Ptolemaic-period installation at the entrance of the Memphite Serapeum (Kessler in Meyer, Grimm, and Kessler 1994: 116–17).

5.15 The adoption of Marcus Aurelius and Lucius Verus: Relief from the Great Antonine Altar of AD 138–61 (?)

The court itself was not spatially confined to Rome, and images depicting the court were even more widespread. Monumental court scenes can be found in the provinces, often the result of links between a locality and the ruling emperor. An extraordinary series of such reliefs from the so-called 'Parthian Monument' or 'Great Antonine Altar' at Ephesus would have formed approximately 70 metres of narrative, of which c. 45 metres survives in good condition. Centrally depicted within this relief are Antoninus Pius and Hadrian on either side of the imperial sceptre, with Marcus Aurelius standing left of Antoninus, and Hadrian putting his hand on the shoulder of a young Lucius Verus. This part of the frieze is depicted in **fig. 5.2.5**. On another part of the frieze (not reproduced here), Hadrian's wife Sabina and Antoninus' wife Faustina the Elder are both depicted as deities on the right end of the frieze, with Faustina the Younger (Antoninus' daughter and Marcus' future wife) shown as a little girl between them: Liverani 1999; Faust 2012: 149–60. It seems likely that the Ephesians constructed this image of the imperial court to honour Antoninus Pius, who had been proconsul of Asia in 135/6, and apparently promoted several members of the local elite into the Senate: Halfmann 2001: 75.

5.16 Members of the court in civic rituals

After Marcus Aurelius returned to Rome in 176, a triumphal arch was erected to commemorate the victory against the Germans and Sarmatians; *CIL* 6.1014 (= *ILS* 374) records the now-lost dedicatory inscription. Although the arch itself no longer survives, eleven reliefs are preserved today, three in the Musei Capitolini, and eight on the Arch of Constantine, in which Marcus' own head has been replaced with Constantine's. The reliefs depict Marcus' departure

Figure 5.2.5 Adoption scene, Great Antonine Altar, from Ephesus, AD 138–61 (?). Ephesos Museum, Vienna, ANSA I 864.

Photo: KHM-Museumsverband.

Figure 5.2.6 The *liberalitas* panel of Marcus Aurelius, Arch of Constantine, Rome.
Photo: Alinari / Bridgeman Images.

from Rome, his conduct during the war, and then his triumphal return: Ryberg 1967; Boschung 2012: 308–13. The *liberalitas* ('generosity') panel, shown in **fig. 5.2.6**, depicts Marcus Aurelius engaging in a *congiarium*, distributing money to Roman citizens after the end of the campaign. On this particular occasion, we know that each citizen received 800 sesterces: Dio Cass. 72(71).32.1 (Xiph.). The relief presents an idealized illustration of the emperor and members of the court as they would have appeared on the occasion. Marcus Aurelius, seated on the curule chair (*sella curulis*), is flanked by three togate men, the closest of whom is his son-in-law, Ti. Claudius Pompeianus (*PIR*[2] C 973). The two other men also have distinct individual portrait types, which means they are historical figures; see Ryberg (1967: 74–5), who suggests several eminent courtiers as possibilities, including the future emperor Pertinax. The original relief also featured Marcus sitting beside his son Commodus, but the latter was removed after his death and disgrace: Boschung 2012: 312.

III | The Severans

5.17 Septimius Severus and courtiers sacrifice

Sometimes the line between a centrally distributed image of court life and local interpretation is rather blurred. Reliefs on a large four-faced arch (**fig. 5.3.1**) from Lepcis Magna are a case in point. This was the emperor Septimius Severus' hometown, and during his reign the town saw substantial urban renewal, probably sponsored by the imperial family. A large number of imperial statues were locally erected for the extended imperial family, showing how interwoven Lepcis Magna was with the court: Reynolds and Ward Perkins 1952: 120–1, nos. 414, 416–17; Deppmeyer 2008: 2.388–91, no. 202; Bertolazzi 2013. That makes it notable that the attic reliefs (**figs. 5.3.2–3**) of the arch show not only the emperor Septimius Severus with his sons Caracalla and Geta, but also Severus' wife, Julia Domna. She is accompanied by Virtus or Roma. Other deities, such as Fortuna holding the cornucopia and Hercules/Melquart are also present. Melquart was a Phoenician deity who was frequently assimilated with Hercules. Together with Liber Pater, who was often equated to Dionysus, Melquart was tutelary deity of Lepcis Magna. The two men to the right of the emperor may well be the emperor's brother, P. Septimius Geta, and the praetorian prefect Plautianus, who suffered *damnatio memoriae* and had his head removed on the relief (see below, **5.19**). The presence of Plautianus, who at the time was Caracalla's father-in-law, is notable, as is the presence of Julia Domna. Women were not traditionally depicted on arches. In the relief at the north-eastern side of the arch, Domna even seems to be involved in a sacrifice, highlighting her important position at the Severan court: Strocka 1972: 155; Kampen 2009: 90–1.

(a) The Arch of Septimius Severus, Lepcis Magna

Figure 5.3.1 The Arch of Septimius Severus, Lepcis Magna.
Photo: Daviegunn / Wikimedia Commons.

(b) The attic sacrifice panel

Figure 5.3.2 Attic sacrifice panel, Arch of Septimius Severus, Lepcis Magna, AD 203–9.
Archaeological Museum, Tripoli (cast, Museo della Civiltà Romana).
Photo: © Vanni Archive / Art Resource, NY.

(c) The attic *concordia Augustorum* panel

Figure 5.3.3 Attic *concordia Augustorum* panel, Arch of Septimius Severus, Lepcis Magna, AD 203–9. Archaeological Museum, Tripoli.
Photo: © Gilles Mermet / Art Resource, NY.

5.18 Severus, his heirs, and the Senate: The Palazzo Sacchetti Relief

There was inherent tension between the existence of an imperial court and the notion of senators as a group who held power in the empire. Individual leading senators had easy access to the emperor, and could become part of the court, even of its inner circle (cf. Hurlet 2000). But this did not reflect on the Senate as an institution. A dominant court implied less senatorial importance. The hierarchy in Severan times is made clear through the Palazzo Sacchetti Relief (**fig. 5.3.4**), in which the emperor Septimius Severus sits throned in an elevated position, and presents his two sons to assembled senators: Hannestad 1986: 268–9. The emperor's head has been removed, as has that of the smallest figure on the platform, probably Geta (see below, **5.20**). The senators arrive at this scene through an arch showing winged Victories. The image suggests that they come to a public space, to be introduced to their new rulers, with little say in the matter. The position of the emperor and those surrounding him on a platform means that the senators have to look up to their ruler.

Figure 5.3.4 Palazzo Sacchetti Relief, Palazzo Sacchetti, Rome, Severan period.
Photo: Alinari / Art Resource, NY.

5.19 The statues of Plautianus

Pictures of the court were often images of the imperial family. Conversely, setting up images of oneself in connection to the imperial family implied a claim to power. This was a risky mode of self-presentation, since it could cause the emperor to see one as a threat – with fatal results. Sometimes, however, the emperor allowed statues for members of the court to be linked to imperial statues. That clearly showed favour. The destruction of such statues indicated that they had fallen from favour. This was a very visible way to show their loss of influence. The influential praetorian prefect C. Fulvius Plautianus rose high in the court, becoming Caracalla's father-in-law in 202, but overstretched and fell from grace in 205: Levick 2007: 74–86; Bingham and Imrie 2015.

(a) Cassius Dio 76(75).16.2–4 (Xiph.)

At one time, when a great number of statues of Plautianus had been set up – this incident deserves to be reported – Severus, displeased with their number, had some of them melted down; consequently a rumour spread in the cities that the prefect was disgraced and had been overthrown.[1] Some demolished his images, for which they were later punished. Among these was Racius Constans, governor of Sardinia, a distinguished man.[2] My specific reason, however, for reporting the matter is that the speaker who accused Constans declared among other things that the sky would fall before Plautianus would ever suffer harm from Severus, and that with reason one might rather believe even such a report (about the sky), if any account of the sort were to be circulated. Though the speaker made this statement, and though, moreover, Severus himself boldly confirmed it to us who were helping him in bestowing justice, declaring, 'It is impossible that I should do harm to Plautianus', this same Plautianus did not live the year out; he was slain and all his statues destroyed.[3]

1 This took place in 203.
2 *PIR*[2] R 8. The gens *Ra(e)cia* was a plebeian family, prominent in Republican times. It gained importance again in the second century, with C. Raecius Rufus (*PIR*[2] R 10) attested as senator in 173: *CIL* 3.3116 (= *ILS* 3869).
3 Dedicatory inscriptions from which Plautianus' name has been removed, and a range of monuments from which his likeness has been eradicated testify to Dio's text: Varner 2004: 161–4.

(b) *Historia Augusta, Septimius Severus* 14.4–5

Severus had statues erected at his own expense for his father, mother, grandfather, and first wife. Plautianus had been one of his closest friends, but after learning of his lifestyle, Severus came to detest him so much as to declare him a public enemy, throw down his statues, and make him famous throughout the world for the heaviness of his punishment. Severus was especially angry with him because he had erected his own statue amongst those of Severus' kinsmen and relations by marriage.

5.20 The changing image of the Severan court: The Arch of the Argentarii

The well-preserved Arch of the Argentarii served as an entrance into the Forum Boarium and celebrated the military success and dynastic ambitions of the Severan family. It was erected by bankers (*argentarii*) and cattle merchants in AD 203–4 in honour of Septimius Severus; his two sons, Geta and Caracalla; his wife, Julia Domna; Plautianus (praetorian prefect and first cousin of Severus); and Plautilla (daughter of Plautianus and wife of Caracalla). The honorific inscription (*CIL* 6.1035 [= *ILS* 426]) was changed three times as events made it necessary to erase names of family members: when Plautianus was executed for allegedly plotting to overthrow Severus (AD 205; Dio Cass. 77[76].2.4–4.5 [Xiph.], Hdn. 3.11–12); when Caracalla ordered the death of his wife, who had been exiled at the time of her father's execution (AD 211; Dio Cass. 77[76].6.3 [Xiph.]); and when Caracalla had his younger brother Geta put to death (AD 212: Dio Cass. 78[77].2 [Xiph.]; Hdn. 4.4.1–3; SHA *M. Ant.* 2.4–11). Accordingly, in the central panel from the inside of the west pier (**5.20 [a]**, **fig. 5.3.5**), Plautianus and Plautilla have been removed, and only Caracalla remains: Varner 2004: 167–8. In the central panel from the inside of the east pier of the Arch (**5.20 [b]**, **fig. 5.3.6**), Caracalla's brother Geta has been removed, and Septimius Severus and Julia Domna remain: Varner 2004: 176–8.

Before they were the target of *damnatio memoriae*, the reliefs presented a particular image of the inner circle of the court; it is an interesting but insoluble question whether this image was officially endorsed or whether it more reflected the perceptions of the *argentarii*. The reliefs also provide another example of how members of the inner court were routinely pictured as engaging in cultic activities together: see Dolansky, **Vol. 1, 410–11**. The act of *damnatio memoriae* was not the erasure of memory: the erasures are crude, and it is likely that even subsequent generations of Romans would have been able to guess who had been removed. Rather, the *damnatio* was the assignment to certain courtiers of a strong negative value in public memory. Such cases illustrate the way in which changes in court politics could suddenly make certain images of the emperor and particular courtiers impossible (see Kelly 2020), providing tangible reminders of the court's fluid membership: cf. Wei and Kelly, **Vol. 1, 86–92**.

(a) West pier, east side (inside)

Figure 5.3.5 West pier, east side, central panel depicting Caracalla, Arch of the Argentarii, Forum Boarium, Rome.
Photo: G. Singer, Neg. D-DAI-Rom 70.1000.

(b) East pier, west side (inside)

Figure 5.3.6 East pier, west side, central panel depicting Septimius Severus and Julia Domna, Arch of the Argentarii, Forum Boarium, Rome.
Photo: G. Singer, Neg. D-DAI-Rom 70.993.

5.21 The fall of Geta

In his roles as Caesar and Augustus, Geta minted in his own name and also appeared on coin issues celebrating the imperial family, such as this one (**fig. 5.3.7**): Varner 2004: 169. Dio claimed that his brother Caracalla melted down Geta's coinage at the same time as he had his sculpted portraits destroyed (Dio Cass. 78[77].12.6 [*EV*]), but Geta's coin issues 'survive in sufficient quantities to suggest that such numismatic destruction was limited in scope'; the high number of coins featuring Geta with disfiguration or countermarks suggest that these actions served as alternatives to melting down the coins: Varner 2004: 171–2. This coin from Smyrna (modern İzmir, Turkey) is a case where such disfiguration has occurred. For those not in the court context, handling such coins after *damnatio* had taken place would be a reminder of the unstable and changeable nature of the court. On other coins of this type (Head 1892: 283, Smyrna nos. 367–70), the obverse shows Septimius Severus, laurate and holding a globe and roll, flanked on his right by Geta (bareheaded) and on his left by a laureate Caracalla, holding a scroll, each on a curule chair. On this specimen, the figure of Geta has been erased.

The obverse legend originally read ΑΥ(τοκράτωρ) Κ(αῖcαρ) Λ(ούκιος) CE(πτιμίος) CEOYHPOC Λ(ούκος) CE(πτιμίος) ΓΕΤΑC Κ(αῖcαρ) ΑΥ(τοκράτωρ) Κ(αῖcαρ) Μ(άρκος) Α(ὐρήλιος) ΑΝΤΩΝΙΝ(ος) ('Imperator Caesar L. Septimius Severus, L. Septimius Geta, Imperator Caesar M. Aurelius Antoninus'). The obverse legend therefore represented the name and titles of Septimius Severus, Geta, and Caracalla in that order. On this specimen, the

Figure 5.3.7 Bronze coin, Smyrna mint, AD 198–209. British Museum, HPB, p110.24.A.
Photo: © The Trustees of the British Museum. All rights reserved.

name of Geta has been deleted, just as Geta's name and figure have been deleted on several other specimens of the same issue: Head 1892: 283 no. 371; Mowat 1901: 453–4. The reverse legend reads: ΕΠΙ ϹΤΡΑ(τηγοῦ) ΚΛ(αυδίου) ΡΟΥΦΙΝΟΥ ϹΟΦΙ(τοῦ) and (enclosed by a wreath) ΠΡΩΤΑ ΚΟΙΝΑ ΑϹΙΑϹ ϹΜΥΡΝΑΙΩΝ ('Under the *stratēgos* Claudius Rufinus Sophistes. First (games of the) league of Asia. Of the Smyrniotes.'). On the *stratēgos* (magistrate) Claudius Rufinus Sophistes, see Dmitriev 2005: 264–5; on the *prōta koina* as the games of the *koinon* of Asia, see Remijsen 2015: 312.

5.22 Severus Alexander and Julia Mamaea

This coin (**fig. 5.3.8**; an *as*) was minted at Rome. The obverse shows busts of the emperor and his mother, Julia Mamaea, facing each other. Like a coin from 54 which depicts Nero and Agrippina (**6.2 [b]**, below), the two busts show no discernible hierarchy. Severus Alexander wears a laurel crown, his mother a diadem. The obverse legend reads IMP(erator) SEV(erus) ALEXAND(er) AVG(ustus) IVLIA MAMAEA AVG(usta) MATER AVG(usti) ('mother of Augustus'). The reverse legend reads FELICITAS TEMPORVM ('the good-fortune of the times') and shows the emperor seated on a curule chair with the figures of Victory and Felicitas standing nearby. The motif of the bust of the emperor facing that of his mother also appears on gold and silver medallions (*RIC* 4 Severus Alexander 316–17) and on coins with different images and legends on the reverse (*RIC* 4 Severus Alexander 659–67, all *asses*, except 662,

Figure 5.3.8 Bronze *as* of Severus Alexander, Roman mint, AD 222–35 (*RIC* 4 Severus Alexander 661). Münzkabinett, Staatliche Museen zu Berlin, inv. 18205433.
Photo: © bpk-Bildagentur / Münzkabinett, Staatliche Museen zu Berlin / Reinhard Saczewski.

which occurs as an *as* and a *dupondius*). For those outside court circles, such images suggested Julia Mamaea enjoyed high status at court and significant influence with the emperor, perceptions which are echoed in inscriptions and in the literary accounts of Severus Alexander's reign: *AE* 1912.155 ll. 9–11; Hdn. 5.8.10, 6.1.1–2, 6.1.9–10; SHA *Alex. Sev.* 3.1, *Aurel.* 42.4; cf. Kosmetatou 2002; Nadolny 2016: esp. 156–8, 173–8, 194–200.

IV | The Later Third Century

5.23 Gifts from Gallienus' court

In some senses, Roman coins functioned as 'monuments in miniature'. This is especially the case for medallions, larger issues that were not meant to circulate as currency, but were rather meant as gifts from the emperor, especially (but not only) at the New Year. This meant that there was a precise idea as to who would look at the images on medallions. The medallion from Gallienus in **fig. 5.4.1** shows the emperor, with laurel wreath and wearing a cuirass, facing his wife Salonina, who is depicted as being taller than he is. The legend CONCORDIA AUGVSTORVM ('harmony of the Augusti') suggests harmonious cooperation at the court, between husband and wife, and possibly also with Gallienus' father Valerian, with whom Gallienus shared power. But the medallion certainly does not stress the role of Valerian, who was senior emperor at the time, focusing on husband and wife instead. On the reverse is the legend MONETAE AVGG and a depiction of the three *monetae*, the goddesses of the

Figure 5.4.1 Billon 35 mm medallion, Rome, AD 255–6. Museum of Fine Arts, Boston 34.1387. Photo: © 2022 Museum of Fine Arts, Boston.

mint (cf. *LIMC* s.v. *moneta*), who hold cornucopiae and scales, and have piles of coins at their feet. They indicate, not entirely factually, the wealth and plenty which this imperial unity will bring.

5.24 Picturing the Tetrarchic Court

This fragment of a fresco (**fig. 5.4.2**) is preserved on the east side of the south wall of the Imperial Cult Chamber at the Temple of Amun at Luxor (ancient Thebes) in Egypt. The temple was built in pharaonic times, and the chamber

Figure 5.4.2 Fresco fragment, Temple of Amun at Luxor, Egypt, c. AD 293–305.

Photo: Yarko Kobylecky. Reproduced by permission of the American Research Center in Egypt. This project was funded by the United States Agency for International Development (USAID).

and its fresco added in the Tetrarchic period, probably during the First Tetrarchy of Diocletian (293–305). On the east and north walls – and possibly on the west – the friezes, which are now largely lost, depicted processions of soldiers, perhaps in an imperial *adventus:* McFadden 2015: 108–18. At the east end of the south wall a group of richly dressed dignitaries stand below an enthroned emperor, whose purple shoe sitting on a bejewelled footstool is all that remains: Deckers and Meyer-Graft 1979; McFadden 2015: 118–26. The scene anticipates the dress and ceremonial of the late-antique court. The emperor came to use jewellery and costume to elevate himself; costume was also used by the courtiers to mark themselves as members of the court: Parani 2007: 499, 506. In the Luxor Fresco, the courtiers are wearing *chlamydes*, the military cloaks that in Late Antiquity also came to be worn by civilian officials (Morgan 2018: 29; cf. Harlow 2004: 59–62; Parani 2007: 500–4); bejewelled belts, which grew increasingly important in Late Antiquity (Parani 2007: 499, 504, 517; Morgan 2018: 29 n. 12); and embroidered patches (*segmenta*). *Segmenta* could be intricate and colourful, with many varieties of figured designs, decorative or apotropaic; they were worn by people of all social levels, with the status of the wearer reflected in the number, size, quality, and materials of their *segmenta*: Parani 2007: 512–15; cf. Harlow 2004: 55–9. The courtiers also perform the *manus velatae* ('covered hands') gesture; covering one's hands in the presence of the sacred person of the emperor was an act of humility that became a feature of court ceremonial: McFadden 2015: 122, 187 n. 65. Two things may be noted. Firstly, there are more courtiers in this scene (as in the Constantinian *locutio*, below, **fig. 5.4.3**) than in court scenes from the early Empire, a reflection of the increasing scale of the Roman court beginning in the Tetrarchic period: cf. Smith 2011: 135–6. Secondly, the composition of the scene at Luxor Temple is more radically hierarchical than most earlier scenes: the emperor is seated well above the courtiers rather than being depicted on the same level as them.

5.25 The *oratio* of Constantine

The horizontal frieze running around the Arch of Constantine below the Hadrianic tondi (cf. **5.13**) is from the early fourth century (**fig. 5.4.3**). This *oratio* scene, in which the emperor addresses the populace, takes place on the rostrum in the Roman forum; the five columns of the Decennalia monument can be seen clearly behind, with a statue of Jupiter holding a sceptre and globe on top of the centre column, and statues of the four tetrarchs on the other columns: McFadden 2015: 130. On either side of Constantine stand statues of Hadrian and Marcus Aurelius, aligning him with these 'good' emperors. Several things may be noted here: firstly, the increased size of the court depicted; secondly, the fact that, as at Luxor (see above, **5.24**), the emperor is not just in the centre of the composition, but most eyes look towards him (although some courtiers converse amongst themselves, and gesture with their hands);

Figure 5.4.3 The *oratio* frieze, Arch of Constantine, Rome.
Photo: © Vanni Archive / Art Resource, NY.

and lastly, the emperor's semi-divine status, suggested by the 'idol-like position in which he dominates the scenes': Peirce 1989: 415–16. The identities of those who surround the emperor are difficult to determine. The crowd on either side of the rostrum consists of men clad in tunics: these, with the addition of three boys, represent the Roman populace. An attempt has been made to differentiate these figures to some extent: some are bearded and others not; both wavy and curly hair is depicted, and some figures are bald: Kleiner 1992: 450. Those standing on the rostrum with the emperor are wearing togas, and may be senators and/or members of the court. Constantine himself is draped in a *paludamentum*, the cloak of the Roman general (on which see Olson 2017: 77, 79). This panel is matched on the east end of the monument with a scene of *liberalitas* ('generosity'), scenes which can only necessarily occur after the other scenes on the frieze, which depict Constantine's battle with Maxentius and his victorious entry into Rome.

6 | Narratives of Court Crises

ANGELA HUG AND BENJAMIN KELLY

Introduction

Most of the textual sources concerning the imperial court presented in earlier chapters of this sourcebook are relatively short. When drawn from literary histories and biographies, these texts tend to recount anecdotes illuminating a single moment or a specific practice. Thus, with the court, as with so many other aspects of Roman history, we are generally forced to work with fragments to build a (necessarily incomplete) picture of the whole. The surviving works of history and biography do, however, contain a few longer narratives of connected sequences of events at court – narratives that allow our historical imaginations to indulge in a short film, as it were, rather than merely conjuring a static snapshot. We would suggest that such narratives most commonly occur when historians and biographers describe crises, when events at court had wider implications for the political history of the Principate. Prompted by this observation, in this chapter we present a selection of the richest crisis narratives.

It should be stressed that the narratives presented below are not to be taken as accurate accounts of historical events. The events in question took place in the 'inner court', and it is mostly unclear where our sources obtained their information about what happened in this partially secluded social space. Information certainly did sometimes leak out of the inner recesses of the palace – one thinks of the slave boy who witnessed the murder of Domitian (**6.3 [a]**) and apparently gave an account of what he saw to Suetonius or one of his sources. But there is no guarantee that sources of similar quality stand behind all the narratives below; many could be the products of speculation and misinformed rumour – or even malicious fabrication.

Instead of mining crisis narratives for hard facts, we would advocate reading them as reflections of what our authors believed about the workings of the imperial court. In this connection, a number of themes recur in the texts translated below. Firstly, our authors assume that groupings and alliances within the court were somewhat fluid and did not necessarily depend on shared legal and social status. In Tacitus' narrative of the fall of Messalina (**6.1**), there is an assumption that a clique of powerful imperial freedmen were acting together, and were suspicious of Claudius' senatorial *amici* and his equestrian prefects. But in the assassination narratives (**6.3, 4**), freedmen, aristocratic courtiers, and even emperors' consorts are portrayed as acting in concert when necessary. Secondly, all the narratives below assume that, at times, the court could be an arena of competition where key players struggled for control. Nobody – not even the emperor – had an unassailable position, and everyone risked losing control, which could have fatal consequences. Thirdly, our sources assume there was an emotional dimension to court life: they are very interested in recounting how emperors and courtiers felt about events in the social world of which they were a part. With crisis narratives, fear is the dominant emotion ascribed to courtiers, but other emotions occur. (And in Tacitus' account [**6.1**], Claudius' lack of emotion following the death of Messalina hints at his abnormality.) Historians of emotion have observed how other historical courts were seen as having characteristic forms of emotional expression: Rosenwein 2006: 100–62; Holloway and Worsley 2017; cf. Elias 1983: 110–16. The narratives below demonstrate that the same perception existed in the Roman case; cf. Kelly Forthcoming.

I | Narratives

6.1 The fall of Messalina

Tacitus, *Annals* 11.28.1–31.1, 32.2–33, 34.2–35.3, 37.1–38.4

In 48, the court of Claudius was thrown into crisis by his wife's affair with the senator and consul-designate C. Silius; for discussion, see Fagan 2002; Michel 2015: 218–20, with further bibliography. Accusations of adultery against imperial women are a common stereotype in the literary sources (on this, see Hug, **Vol. 1, 71**), but Messalina's relationship with Silius is presented as different: she did not just have an affair, she actually married him. In his account, Tacitus meticulously describes how their actions matched those of a traditional Roman wedding, beginning with his statement that they came together 'for the purpose of having children', an assertion which establishes beyond all doubt that this was meant to be seen as a legitimate marriage: Tac. *Ann.* 11.27; for other accounts, see [Sen.] *Oct.* 257–69; Suet. *Claud.* 26.2; Juv. 10.329–45; and Dio Cass. 61(60).31.1–5 (Xiph.; *EV*; Zonar. 11.10). Messalina had no blood connection to the ruling Julio-Claudian dynasty and her authority at court derived solely from her position as the wife of the emperor. Her position is presented as having acquired its own legitimacy by 48, independent of her relationship with Claudius, to the point that she could be imagined as capable of overthrowing her husband if she married someone else; for similar claims about other imperial women see Tac. *Ann.* 13.19.3 (Agrippina the Younger), 15.53.3–4 (Claudia Antonia); Dio Cass. 72(71).22.3–23.1 (Xiph.; cf. JA) and SHA *Mar.* 24.6, *Avid.* 7.1, 9.6–11.8 (Faustina the Younger). Tacitus' portrait of the ensuing chaos gives us one of our best examples of how the court was believed to operate. We pick up the narrative immediately following his description of the wedding.

A shudder had swept through the emperor's household, and those who held influence (*potentia*), and had much to fear if the established order was overturned, especially aired their grievances, no longer in whispered conversations

but openly. When an actor[1] sullied the emperor's bedroom, they said, shame
had certainly been inflicted, but destruction had been a long way off. Now a
young aristocrat blessed with a distinguished appearance, a keen intellect, and a
forthcoming consulship was preparing himself for a greater prospect. For it was
no mystery what came after such a marriage. Undoubtedly fear washed over
them when they thought about the dull-witted nature of Claudius, his deference
to his wife, and the many killings executed on Messalina's orders. On the other
hand, the very obligingness of the emperor gave some assurance that if they got
the upper hand thanks to the enormity of the charge, she could be crushed,
condemned even before her trial. But the situation hinged on this: whether her
defence would be given a hearing and whether they could close his ears even if
she confessed.

At first Callistus, whom I have already mentioned in connection with the
assassination of Gaius Caesar,[2] along with Narcissus, who was behind the
murder of Appius,[3] and Pallas, whose favour (with Claudius) was then at its
peak, considered whether to divert Messalina from her affair with Silius using
covert threats while pretending ignorance of everything else. Then Pallas and
Callistus, afraid that they in addition might be dragged down and ruined,
developed cold feet – Pallas out of sheer cowardice and Callistus because he
had experience with the previous court (*regia*) as well and understood that
influence was more securely retained by cautious than by energetic schemes.
Narcissus pressed on, making only one change: he would not through any
conversation make Messalina aware of the charge or the informer.

Narcissus, ever alert for opportunities, when the emperor loitered for a long
time at Ostia,[4] prevailed upon two of Claudius' mistresses (*paelices*), whose
bodily delights had become especially familiar to the emperor, to make the
accusation. He used bribery and promises, and he showed them the greater
influence which they would enjoy after the wife was brought down.

Next, Calpurnia – for that was the mistress' name – was given a private
audience with the emperor. She grovelled at his knees and cried out that
Messalina had married (*nupsisse*) Silius. In that moment she asked (the other
mistress) Cleopatra, who was standing nearby awaiting the question, whether
she had heard the same. When Cleopatra nodded, Calpurnia requested that
Narcissus be summoned. He begged pardon for his past actions, when he had
kept silent concerning people like Titius, Vettius, and Plautius,[5] and then
reiterated that not even now would he make allegations of adultery, nor would
he demand back the house, the slaves, and the remaining trappings of rank. On
the contrary, Silius might profit from these, only let him give back the wife and
void the wedding contract. 'Are you aware that you are divorced?' Narcissus
challenged. 'For the people, the Senate, and the soldiers saw Silius' wedding,
and unless you act quickly her husband holds the city.'

Then Claudius called together his most eminent friends (*potissimi amicorum*) and questioned first Turranius,[6] the prefect of the grain supply, and
then Lusius Geta,[7] the commander of the praetorians. Once they had confessed,

the rest erupted into a shouting match: Claudius must go to the camp, secure the praetorian cohorts, and safeguard his security before his revenge. It is well known that Claudius was so overwhelmed with terror that he asked again and again if he himself had control of the empire, and if Silius remained a private citizen. ... *(Tacitus then goes on to describe Messalina's Bacchic revelries with Silius before messengers arrive with the news that they have been discovered.)*

Although the desperate state of affairs precluded any planning, Messalina nevertheless directly resolved on a course which had often aided her: to meet and be seen by her husband,[8] and she sent word that Britannicus and Octavia were to hurry to their father's arms.[9] She also beseeched Vibidia, the senior Vestal Virgin, to approach the *pontifex maximus*[10] and plead for mercy. Meanwhile, with just three companions – for so suddenly was she left alone[11] – she covered the whole expanse of the city on foot, then took the road to Ostia in a vehicle used to collect garden waste. No one pitied her, for the horror of her shameful actions outweighed everything.

There was no less trepidation on Claudius' side, for they did not have much confidence in the praetorian prefect Geta, who was equally capricious whether something was honourable or corrupt. Narcissus, therefore, supported by others who shared the same fears, declared that there was no hope of saving the emperor, unless, for that day alone, Claudius transferred command of the troops to one of the freedmen, and he volunteered to take it on himself. What is more, so that Claudius would not be persuaded to regret his actions by L. Vitellius and Largus Caecina[12] as he was carried back to the city, Narcissus insisted on a seat in the same carriage and was added to their company. ... *(Tacitus then relates what Claudius was believed to have said during that fateful ride, and the reactions of his companions.)*

Now Messalina was in sight and crying out that he should listen to the mother of Octavia and Britannicus. Her accuser (Narcissus) railed against her, repeating the account of Silius and the wedding. At the same time, to turn Claudius' eyes away from her, he handed the emperor the documents which listed her debaucheries. Shortly afterwards, as Claudius was entering the city, the children from their marriage were in the process of being brought before him, but Narcissus ordered them to be removed. He was not able to deter Vibidia, nor dismiss her indignant demands that a wife not be sent to her death without a defence. Narcissus therefore replied that the emperor would hear her and she would have the opportunity to refute the charge. In the meantime, the Vestal Virgin would do well to withdraw and turn her attention to her sacred responsibilities.

During all of this Claudius kept oddly silent, while Vitellius appeared dumbfounded: all things were subject to the will of the freedman. Narcissus ordered the adulterer's house to be thrown open and the emperor to be escorted there. He first pointed out the statue of Silius' father in the vestibule – banned by senatorial decree; then he drew attention to the ancestral items of the Nerones and Drusi which had come to this household as the price of ignominy.[13] Next he led Claudius, enraged and blurting out threats, to the camp, where an assembly of the troops had been arranged. After Narcissus made a preliminary address, Claudius gave but a short speech; for although his resentment was justified, his shame prevented him from voicing it. Then came an unending cry from the cohorts demanding the names of the offenders and their punishment. When Silius was brought before the tribunal he sought neither to defend himself nor to delay, but asked only for a quick death. Several illustrious Roman equestrians exhibited the same steadfastness. ... *(Tacitus goes on to describe the fallout from the affair, and names nine men executed along with Silius, including the prefect of the watch, the procurator of the gladiatorial school, one senator, and the actor Mnester.)*

Meanwhile, in the Gardens of Lucullus, Messalina was trying to prolong her life. She was composing a plea, not without hope and with sparks of outrage – for she had retained so much of her conceit even during extreme circumstances. And if Narcissus had not hastened her death, ruin would have rebounded onto the accuser. For Claudius, after he had returned home and had been mollified by a well-timed dinner, grew warm from wine and gave orders for someone to go and inform 'the poor woman' – said to be the exact phrase that he used – that she must present herself the next day to plead her case. The words were noted: anger was dwindling, love was returning, and, if they hesitated now, the coming night with its memories of the marital bedchamber would be a reason for dread. Narcissus therefore rushed out and ordered the centurions and the tribune who was present to carry out the execution: it was – he said – the emperor's command. Euodus, one of the freedmen, was assigned to keep watch and ensure that the deed was done. He quickly went ahead to the gardens, where he found Messalina prostrate on the ground, with her mother, Lepida,[14] sitting beside her. She, estranged from her daughter while she prospered, had been won over by pity in her time of need and was now urging her not to wait for her killer. Her life was over, Lepida told her; there was nothing left but to seek out a death with dignity. But there was nothing virtuous in that soul, thoroughly corrupted by her lusts. Her tears and pointless wailing were dragging things out, when the doors were battered open by an assault from the new arrivals. The tribune stood before her in silence, but the freedman was excoriating her with a flood of invective better suited for slaves.

Then, for the first time, Messalina perceived her situation. She took up a blade but was so flustered that she was ineffectually placing it at her throat and her breast, when she was run through by a sword-thrust from the tribune. Her mother was granted custody of the body. The news that Messalina had died was brought to Claudius while he was dining; it was not specified whether by her own hand or someone else's. He did not ask, but only called for a cup and conducted the banquet in the usual way. Even in the days that followed he showed no sign of antipathy or joy, anger or grief, or, in fact, any other human emotion – not when he saw her accusers rejoicing, nor when he saw his children mourning. The Senate supported his forgetfulness, decreeing that Messalina's name and statues be removed from private and public settings.[15] The insignia of a quaestor were conferred upon Narcissus by decree, mere trinkets for one whose conceit meant he conducted himself as the superior of Pallas and Callistus . . .[16]

1 Mnester (*PIR*[2] M 646), a famous pantomime actor.

2 Caligula. Tacitus' account of his reign has not survived.

3 C. Appius Iunius Silanus (*cos.* 28; *PIR*[2] I 822). Messalina and Narcissus successfully plotted to have him executed in 42.

4 Rome's port, situated thirty kilometres west of the city.

5 Titius Proculus (*PIR*[2] T 268), Vettius Valens (a physician; *PIR*[2] V 492), and Plautius Lateranus (*PIR*[2] P 468) were other alleged lovers of Messalina. Proculus and Valens are named by Tacitus as executed with Silius: Tac. *Ann.* 11.35.3. Plautius Lateranus escaped death only to be executed in 65 as one of the Pisonian conspirators: Tac. *Ann.* 11.36.4, 15.49.3, 60.1.

6 C. Turranius Gracilis (*PIR*[2] T 410), who had held that office since at least AD 14; he was over ninety years old by this point.

7 L. Lusius Geta (*PIR*[2] L 435). He and his colleague Rufrius Crispinus were removed from their posts by Agrippina the Younger in 51, according to Tacitus because they would have supported Messalina's children over Nero: Tac. *Ann.* 12.42.

8 Tacitus repeatedly emphasizes the critical importance of Messalina being able to plead her case in person.

9 Messalina is here presented by Tacitus as savvy enough to recognize the emotional impact the appearance of her son and daughter by Claudius could cause.

10 Claudius, who was the head priest of the priestly college of *pontifices*. Note the assumption that Messalina had a pre-existing relationship with Vibidia.

11 The abandonment of an emperor in the hours before his fall is a frequent trope in the literary sources, e.g. Nero: [Sen.] *Oct.* 631; Joseph. *BJ* 4.493; Dio Cass. 63.27.2b–3 (Xiph.; Zonar.; cf. JA); *Epit. de Caes.* 5.7.

12 C. Caecina Largus (*PIR*[2] C 101), *cos. ord.* 42.

13 Messalina had allegedly been redistributing Claudius' family heirlooms to Silius: Tac. *Ann.* 11.12.3; Dio Cass. 61(60).31.3 (Xiph.; *EV*; Zonar. 11.10).

14 Domitia Lepida (*PIR*[2] D 180), the cousin of Agrippina the Younger. Her second husband was C. Appius Iunius Silanus, executed in 42 thanks to Messalina's machinations (see above, n. 3); presumably this either caused or contributed significantly to their estrangement.

15 For the epigraphic evidence supporting Tacitus' account of a condemnation of Messalina's memory (*damnatio memoriae*), see Fagan 2002: 573 n. 30.

16 The final sentence is corrupt in the manuscript tradition.

6.2 The fall of Agrippina the Younger

Agrippina the Younger married the emperor (her paternal uncle) Claudius in 49 and, according to the literary sources, quickly established herself as a powerful figure at the court: Tacitus (*Ann.* 12.7.3) claims that 'everything was subject to a woman'. In the narrative accounts of Claudius' reign, she is portrayed as a scheming, murderous harlot, consumed by her desire to secure the succession for her own son, Nero, in place of Britannicus, Claudius' son with Messalina. This obsession allegedly culminated in her murder of Claudius on 13 October 54, sparked, according to Cassius Dio, by fears he was about to name Britannicus his heir: Dio Cass. 61(60).34.1–2 (Xiph.; Zonar.; JA); cf. Suet. *Claud.* 43–4; Tac. *Ann.* 12.64–67 (see above, **3.38** [**b**]). At the point of transition, Agrippina is portrayed as wielding enormous power: she is able to conceal the truth of Claudius' death, command the imperial guards, and restrict the movement of other high-level courtiers: Tac. *Ann.* 12.68.2–3. The assumption in the literary accounts is that she maintained this outsized influence at the start of Nero's reign, and that Nero – only sixteen years old at the time of his accession – initially welcomed his mother's involvement: Tac. *Ann.* 13.1–3; Suet. *Nero* 9; Dio Cass. 61.3.2 (Xiph.; JA; Zonar.); cf. **4.21**. For the ill-defined role of imperial mothers at the court, see Hug, **Vol. 1, 67, 74–5**. For Agrippina, see Barrett 1996; Ginsburg 2006; Drinkwater 2019: 32–55, 174–187.

(a) Agrippina crowning Nero

The Sebasteion is a large temple complex at Aphrodisias in western Turkey, which was dedicated to Aphrodite, the deified Augustus, and his Julio-Claudian successors. The site underwent construction from the reign of Tiberius into the reign of Nero, and featured two three-storey buildings flanking a narrow processional approach to a temple. The upper two storeys of both buildings boasted marble relief panels – close to two hundred in total; see Smith 1987. This relief (**fig. 6.1.1**) is one of two featuring Agrippina; for discussion, see Ginsburg 2006: 85–91. On the south structure, Agrippina is shown next to the emperor Claudius, clasping his hand. In this relief, found on the north structure, Agrippina, associated with the goddess Demeter and wearing a diadem, places a crown upon Nero's head; her son is dressed as a general. Most scholars assign this relief to the beginning of Nero's reign, an acknowledgement by the local designers of the role Agrippina played in bringing Nero to power (e.g. Smith 1987: 130; Rose 1997: 47), but others have proposed an earlier, Claudian date (Drinkwater 2019: 40). The image of Agrippina crowning Nero is anything but subtle. Viewers did not need to be court insiders to draw conclusions – rightly or wrongly – about the power relationships between mother and son.

(b) AD 54: Equal partners?

The coin in **fig. 6.1.2**, a gold aureus, was minted at Rome in December of 54, in the first months of Nero's reign. The obverse shows busts of the emperor and his mother facing each other, with no discernible hierarchy between them (repeated with *RIC* 1^2 Nero 2, a silver denarius, and *RIC* 1^2 Nero 3, another aureus; cf. above, **5.22** for a similar motif on a coin of Severus Alexander). The obverse legend reads AGRIPP(ina) AVG(usta) DIVI CLAVD(ii) NERONIS CAES(aris) MATER ('Agrippina Augusta, (wife) of the deified Claudius, mother of Nero Caesar'). The reverse shows a very common motif on Nero's coinage in the first years of his reign: the *corona civica*. This oak-wreath encloses the letters EX S(enatus) C(onsulto) ('in accordance with a decree of the Senate'), and is surrounded by the legend NERONI CLAVD(ii) DIVI F(ilio) CAES(ari) AVG(usto) GERM(anico) IMP(eratori) TR(ibunicia) P(otestate) ('To Nero, son of the deified Claudius, Caesar Augustus Germanicus Imperator with Tribunician Power').

(c) Nero takes steps to curb Agrippina's influence

Tacitus, *Annals* 13.18.2–19.1

By AD 55, Nero allegedly had begun to grow tired of his mother's interference. She failed to dissuade him from his relationship with the freedwoman Acte (see above, **3.49**) and

Figure 6.1.1 Relief of Nero and Agrippina, from the Sebasteion at Aphrodisias.
Aphrodisias Museum.
Photo: funkyfood London - Paul Williams / Alamy Stock Photo.

Figure 6.1.2 Aureus of Nero, Roman mint, AD 54 (*RIC* 1² Nero 1). British Museum, 1864, 1128.252.
Photo: © The Trustees of the British Museum. All rights reserved.

her waning influence is contrasted in the literary accounts with Nero's reliance on his tutor, L. Annaeus Seneca, and the praetorian prefect Sex. Afranius Burrus. Sensing power slipping from her grasp, Agrippina, so it is claimed, made a bold gamble and threatened to throw her support behind Britannicus instead: Tac. *Ann.* 13.14. Nero responded by having Britannicus poisoned at dinner before her very eyes; see above, **4.26**. The threat to his mother's position did not, as the following passage shows, go unnoticed. Agrippina's frantic efforts to retain her position illustrate how the public loss of the emperor's favour could bring down even the most powerful courtier.

No munificence could soothe his mother's anger. She clung to Octavia;[1] she held frequent covert meetings with her friends, appropriating funds from all sources – beyond even her innate avarice – as a sort of emergency reserve. She welcomed tribunes and centurions, and the respect she showed regarding the names and virtues of the nobility – those who were still left – suggested she was seeking a leader and a party.

When Nero learned of this, he ordered the withdrawal of the military watch – assigned to her previously as the wife of the emperor, and now as the mother – as well as the German bodyguards lately added as a similar token of esteem.[2] In addition, so that she might not be called on by a crowd of morning visitors,[3] he broke up their home and moved his mother into the residence which had once been Antonia's. Whenever he came to visit her there, he arrived surrounded by a pack of centurions and left after a hasty kiss.

Nothing in human affairs is as fickle and fleeting as a reputation for power built on no strength of its own. Immediately Agrippina's threshold was deserted: no one comforted her; no one visited her, except for a few women,[4] and whether they did so out of love or hatred is unclear.

1 Claudia Octavia, daughter of Claudius and Messalina, Nero's wife, and not, prior to the murder of Britannicus, portrayed as one of Agrippina's usual allies at the court.
2 Cassius Dio records that even those outside court circles understood it would be prudent to avoid Agrippina once they saw her unattended by her bodyguards: Dio Cass. 61.8.6 (Xiph.); cf. Suet. *Ner.* 34.1. For the critical importance of these 'imperial trappings' in establishing and maintaining one's position at the court, see Hug, **Vol. 1, 65–6**.
3 Tacitus' evocation of the *salutatio* ritual is explicit: he uses the participle *salutantium* to describe the crowd; cf. Foubert 2016: 144–5. For the *salutatio* in general, see above, **4.1–8** and Davenport, **Vol. 1, 292–304**.
4 I.e. people of no political use whatsoever.

(d) AD 55: An assertion of hierarchy

The shift in power suggested by the literary sources appears to be reflected in the coinage. This gold aureus (**fig. 6.1.3**), dating from 55, still features busts of Nero and his mother on the obverse, but now they are jugate, with Nero's bust given precedence. Additionally, Nero's titulature now appears on the obverse, with the legend NERO CLAVD(ii) DIVI F(ilius) CAES(ar) AVG(ustus) GERM(anicus) IMP(erator) TR(ibunicia) P(otestate) CO(n)S(ul) ('Nero, son of the deified Claudius, Augustus Germanicus Imperator with Tribunician Power, Consul'). Agrippina is relegated to the reverse legend: AGRIPP(ina) AVG(usta) DIVI CLAVD(ii) NERONIS CAES(aris) MATER ('Agrippina Augusta, (wife) of the deified Claudius, mother of Nero Caesar'). The reverse image shows a *quadriga*

Figure 6.1.3 Aureus of Nero, Roman mint, AD 55 (*RIC* 1[2] Nero 6). British Museum, 1964, 1203.89.
Photo: © The Trustees of the British Museum. All rights reserved.

drawn by elephants carrying two chairs on which are seated figures of the divine Claudius and the divine Augustus. The letters EX S(enatus) C(onsulto) ('in accordance with a decree of the Senate') sit above the elephants. Agrippina does not appear on any coin of Nero's minted after 55, an absence which accords with the depictions in the historical narratives of Nero's efforts to curtail her influence at the court.

(e) Nero has Agrippina murdered

Tacitus, *Annals* 14.2.1–4.2, 7.1–6, 8.2–5

Against the odds, Agrippina succeeded in reconciling with her son after the murder of Britannicus in 55; she also survived an accusation of conspiracy orchestrated by her rival, Iunia Silana, that same year: Tac. *Ann.* 13.18–21. Tacitus (*Ann.* 13.21.6) underlines the importance of Agrippina discussing the matter with Nero in person, in a meeting where 'she secured vengeance against her accusers and rewards for her friends'. Matters came to a head, however, in 59, when, according to Tacitus, Nero abruptly resolved to murder his mother, egged on by his mistress, Poppaea Sabina. Tacitus (*Ann.* 14.1.3) claims that no one countered Poppaea's complaints, because 'everyone longed for the mother's influence (*potentia*) to be checked and none believed the son's hatred would crystallize so much as to murder her'. For other accounts, see Suet. *Ner.* 34.1–4; Dio Cass. 62(61).11–14 (Xiph.).

Cluvius[1] states that Agrippina was so driven by her desire to preserve her influence (*potentia*) that, in the middle of the day, at a time when Nero was growing warm with wine and rich food, she regularly presented herself before her intoxicated son, all dolled up and set for incest. Now those closest to them began taking notice of the lascivious kisses and the sweet nothings that were the harbinger of the unspeakable act, and Seneca, to circumvent feminine wiles, sought support from a woman. He brought in the freedwoman Acte,[2] who was worried about both her own vulnerable position and the damage to Nero's reputation. Acte was to report to Nero that the incest was common knowledge, since his mother bragged about it, and that the soldiers would not support the sovereignty (*imperium*) of an impious emperor. According to Fabius Rusticus,[3] the desire for such a relationship came not from Agrippina, but from Nero; it was foiled by the cunning of the same freedwoman. ... *(Tacitus then heaps more slurs upon Agrippina's character and sexual habits.)*

   Nero therefore avoided private meetings with her, and commended her for taking some leisure (*otium*) whenever she left for her gardens or her estate at Tusculum or Antium.[4] At last, calculating that she would remain a complete embarrassment wherever she was kept, he decided to kill her, debating only whether it should be done with poison, with the sword, or with some other kind of violence. He initially settled upon poison. If it were to be given at the emperor's table, however, the affair could not be ascribed to chance, since Britannicus had already met a similar fate. It seemed a tall order to corrupt the servants of a woman whose own criminal enterprises had honed her instincts for treachery, and besides, she had already enhanced her body's tolerance by taking antidotes in advance. As for cutting her down with a sword, no one could come up with a means of concealment, and he was afraid that whoever was chosen for such an atrocity might refuse to carry out his orders.

At that point the freedman Anicetus revealed his own genius; he was the prefect of the fleet at Misenum, tutor to the boy Nero,[5] and was absolutely loathed by Agrippina; the feeling was mutual. Anicetus explained that it was possible to construct a ship with a section designed to break apart once out at sea, washing the unsuspecting woman overboard. Nothing left so much room for accidents as the sea, he said, and, if she were to be carried off by shipwreck, who would be so unjust as to see foul play in the transgressions of the wind and waves? Of course the emperor would then grant the deceased a temple, altars, and the other trappings for demonstrating filial devotion.

The ingenuity (of the plan) attracted supporters and the date helped too, as Nero was accustomed to celebrating the festival of the Quinquatrus at Baiae.[6] He lured his mother there, repeatedly musing that parents' tantrums need to be endured and their emotions soothed; his intention was to spawn a rumour of their reconciliation, which Agrippina, easily made joyful – so typical of women – would fall for. When she arrived – she was coming from Antium – Nero went to the shore to meet her, welcomed her with open arms and an embrace, and led her to Bauli.[7] ... *(Tacitus then goes on to describe the infamous assassination attempt. According to his account, it was bungled from start to finish: Agrippina had been forewarned, the sea was too calm, the ship failed to disintegrate as advertised, and, when Agrippina finally did end up in the water, the ship was still close enough to shore that she simply swam to safety.)*

Meanwhile, as Nero was waiting for a message that the deed was done, there came the news that Agrippina had escaped with a minor injury and had been in just enough danger to leave no doubt as to who was responsible. Paralysed with fear, he insisted that she would be there at any moment, hungry for vengeance. Whether she armed her slaves or inflamed the soldiers, or got herself in front of the Senate and the people, and laid at his feet the shipwreck, her wound, and the murder of her friends – what counter-measures could he muster?[8] Unless Burrus and Seneca had any ideas. He had them summoned immediately; whether they had been ignorant of the plot up until this point is not clear.

Neither of them said anything for a long time. Either they did not want to waste their time trying to dissuade him, or they believed that matters had sunk so low that Nero was lost unless Agrippina were pre-empted. Eventually Seneca took the lead insofar as he looked at Burrus and asked whether the order to kill her should be given to the soldiers. Burrus replied that the praetorian guard had sworn an oath to the entire house of the Caesars and, still mindful of Germanicus,[9] would balk at any violent measures against his descendants: Anicetus would have to carry out what he promised.

Without hesitation, Anicetus asked to be put in charge of the crime. His response prompted Nero to declare that on this day an empire was given to him, and that the giver of so great a gift was his freedman. Anicetus should hurry, he added, and take with him the men most amenable to following orders. Then, upon hearing that

Agermus[10] had come with a message from Agrippina, Nero seized the initiative and set the scene for a counter-accusation. He threw a sword at Agermus' feet as he was carrying out Agrippina's instructions, then ordered him to be chained up, as if he were a conspirator caught in the act. The idea was that he would fabricate a story in which his mother plotted the destruction of the emperor, and then committed suicide from shame when the crime was discovered. ... (*At this point, Tacitus describes the actions of the people when they learned of the shipwreck and Agrippina's narrow escape. His account implies that those outside court circles still believed she was an important and influential figure at Nero's court.*)

Anicetus surrounded the villa with sentries, smashed the door open, and shoved aside all the slaves he encountered until he reached the entrance to the bedroom. A few slaves were milling around outside it; the rest had fled, terrified by the incursion. In the dimly lit bedroom was one of the maids and Agrippina, who was growing ever more worried because no one – not even Agermus – had come from her son. Had her plan come to fruition, the situation would have looked different – so she thought – but instead there was isolation, a sudden uproar, and the signs of great trouble.

At that point the maid began to leave. 'Are you also abandoning me?' she asked and then saw Anicetus behind her, accompanied by the trierarch Herculeius and by Obaritus, a centurion of the marines.[11] If Anicetus had come to look in on the patient, she said, he could report back that she felt rejuvenated. If he were here to commit a crime, she would give credence to nothing involving her son – he had not given the orders for the murder of his mother. The killers surrounded the bed and the trierarch struck the first blow, hitting her head with a club. Then, as the centurion was drawing his sword to make an end of it, Agrippina thrust her womb towards him. 'Strike me in the belly,' she cried and was felled with many wounds.

1   M. Cluvius Rufus (*PIR*^{2} C 1206), a contemporary of the later Julio-Claudian emperors, including Nero, whose work is now lost.
2   Nero had been involved with Acte since 55; for her position at his court, see above, **3.49**.
3   *PIR*^{2} F 62. Another contemporary of Nero, whose writings have been lost.
4   Both located south of Rome.
5   Anicetus (*PIR*^{2} A 589) had probably been Nero's *paedagogus* (cf. **3.14** [a], n. 1). His long history with Nero (and his established loyalty) presumably allowed him to secure the important naval position commanding the fleet stationed at Misenum. He reappears in the narrative in 62 to give evidence against Octavia (Tac. *Ann.* 14.62), another example of his willingness to do whatever Nero asked.
6   The Quinquatrus festival, in honour of the goddess Minerva, was celebrated from 19–23 March. Baiae was a popular holiday destination on the Bay of Naples.
7   A villa situated (according to Tacitus) between Misenum and Baiae.
8   Note the belief that these various power groups would all assume Agrippina's authority remained intact.
9   Agrippina was the daughter of Germanicus.
10 L. Agermus. *PIR*^{2} A 456; cf. Suet. *Ner.* 34.3.
11 The *trierarchus* and the *centurio classicus* were officers in the fleet. Both men would have served under Anicetus.

6.3 The murder of Domitian

The assassination of Domitian on 18 September 96 received extended narrative treatments in Suetonius and Cassius Dio; Dio's version survives in later epitomes. There are also briefer (and sometimes derivative) notices of the event in several other authors: Plin. *Pan.* 49.1–3 (= **2.16 [b]**); Philostr. *V A* 8.25–7; Aur. Vict. *Caes.* 11.7–8; Eutr. 7.23.6–8.1; *Epit. de Caes.* 11.11–14; Oros. 7.10; Zos. 1.6.4; Malalas 10.52. With one highly dubious exception (Malalas 10.52), the ancient sources all see the assassination as the result of a palace plot, in which members of the inner court took the lead in planning and carrying out the emperor's death; some modern scholars have accepted this picture in broad outline. On the other hand, some scholars have seen wider senatorial involvement; Collins (2009) outlines the debate and cites earlier literature. The extended narratives of the incident, as with many narratives of conspiracies against emperors, could well have fictional elements designed to turn the doubtful scraps of information at the disposal of our authors (or their sources) into gripping accounts: Ash 2016. For instance, Dio claims that a list of Domitian's intended victims was discovered on a limewood tablet by a boy favourite; Herodian recounts a near identical incident in the events leading to Commodus' assassination: see below, **6.4 (b)**. It has been suspected, therefore, that Dio (or one of his sources) added a detail from a later imperial assassination to add interest to the narrative; see Collins 2009: 84, citing earlier literature.

Rather than reading these narratives for information about what really happened in September 96, it is perhaps more profitable to probe them for Suetonius' and Dio's assumptions about the court as a social figuration. They illuminate the many categories of more intimate courtiers who were in close contact with the emperor, including astrologers, family members, *amici*, soldiers, nurses, practitioners of religious rites, and freedmen (including freedmen of other members of the imperial family). They also assume that cliques of courtiers of diverse social stations could form, and that there was enough mutual trust within these groupings to allow the planning of something so dangerous as the murder of the emperor. The narratives also evoke a pervading atmosphere of fear at the court of Domitian – something claimed of the courts of many emperors: Kelly Forthcoming. There may be some truth to the picture in this case: Suetonius apparently had access to eyewitness testimony that Domitian slept with a dagger under his pillow, which says something about how he perceived his own court.

(a) Suetonius, *Life of Domitian* 14.1, 16–17

Domitian was frightening and odious to everyone as a result of these things,[1] and he was at last destroyed by a conspiracy of his friends (*amici*) and his closest freedmen, together with his wife. Long before, he began to have a suspicion about the final year and day of his life – even about the hour and indeed the very mode of his death. When he was a youth, astrologers had foretold all these things. His father had also once made fun of him openly over dinner for abstaining from the mushrooms,[2] saying that he was ignorant of his fate, since he was not fearful of the sword instead. . . . *(Suetonius then recounts a series of anecdotes illustrating Domitian's timorous nature and obsession with personal security [cf. **2.16 (c)**], as well as describing various portents that supposedly foretold his death.)*

On the day before he died, Domitian had ordered that some fruit[3] that had been offered to him should be saved for the next day. He added, 'Provided that I am permitted to eat it.' Turning to his nearest dining companions, he asserted that on the next day the moon would stain itself with blood in Aquarius and some event would occur that people throughout the world would talk about. And then, around the middle of the night, he was so scared that he leapt out of bed. On the next morning, he heard the case of a diviner (*haruspex*) sent from Germany who was consulted about a flash of lightening and had foretold a change in political circumstances; Domitian condemned him. While he scratched an inflamed wart on his forehead too vigorously and drew blood, he said, 'I wish this were all!'

Then he asked about the hour and it was announced deliberately that it was the sixth, instead of the fifth, which he used to fear. He was delighted at this, as though the danger had now ended, and hurried to his ablutions. But Parthenius, his head bedroom attendant, diverted him, announcing that there was someone there to report on some important matter or other that should not be put off. Thus once all his attendants were dismissed, he retired to his bedroom and was killed there.

The following is more or less everything that was made public about the nature of the conspiracy and the murder. The conspirators were hesitating about when and how they should attack – should they do so while Domitian was bathing or while dining? – when Stephanus, a procurator of Domitilla[4] and at the time charged with embezzlement, offered advice and concrete action. For several days, he wrapped his left arm with wool and bandages as if it were injured, so as to ward off suspicion. Just before the critical time, he inserted a dagger between (the bandages). He then claimed to have information about a conspiracy and, when he had been admitted on the strength of this, he pierced the dumbfounded Domitian, who was reading a document that had been handed to him by Stephanus, in the groin. Domitian was wounded and fighting back when Clodianus, a *cornicularius*,[5] and Maximus, a freedman of Parthenius, and Satur, a manager of the bedroom attendants,[6] and somebody from the gladiatorial school attacked and slaughtered him with seven wounds.

A boy who was as usual tending to the Lares of the bedroom and was a witness to the murder used to recount this additional detail: that he was ordered by Domitian, as soon as he received the first wound, to hand him the dagger underneath his pillow and to call his attendants. But he found nothing at the bedhead except for the dagger's handle and, furthermore, he discovered that all the doors were barred. Meanwhile, Domitian struggled for a long time with Stephanus, whom he had grabbed and pulled down to the ground, trying now to wrench away the weapon and now to gouge out Stephanus' eyes with his fingers, even though they were gashed.

He was killed on the fourteenth day before the Kalends of October,[7] in the forty-fifth year of his life and the fifteenth year of his principate. His corpse was carried out on a common bier by paupers' undertakers and Phyllis his nurse conducted the funeral rites at her suburban villa on the via Latina.[8] However, she secretly took his remains to the Temple of the Gens Flavia and mixed them with the ashes of Julia, the daughter of Titus,[9] whom she herself had also brought up.

1 In the previous chapter, Suetonius has catalogued a series of Domitian's self-aggrandizing acts.

2 The emperor Claudius was rumoured to have been killed with poison smeared on mushrooms: Suet. *Claud.* 44.2; Tac. *Ann.* 12.67.1 (= **3.38 [b]**); Dio Cass. 61(60).34.2–3 (Xiph.; Zonar. 11.11).

3 *Tubures*, apparently a kind of exotic fruit: see *OLD* s.v. *tubur*.

4 A niece of Domitian (*PIR²* F 418). He had banished her in 95 and executed her husband, Flavius Clemens (*cos.* 95; *PIR²* F 240): Dio Cass. 67.14.1–2 (Xiph.); Euseb. *Hist. eccl.* 3.18.4; cf. Dolansky, **Vol. 1, 402**.

5 *Corniculariii* were assistants to senior officers; in this case, perhaps to a praetorian prefect or a military tribune in the praetorian guard: Grainger 2003: 4, 20.

6 *Decurio cubiculariorum*. Middle managers within the imperial household often carried the military title *decurio*: see Edmondson, **Vol. 1, 171**.

7 18 September 96.

8 Note the role of Nero's nurses in his funeral: Suet. *Ner.* 50. The nurses of Nero and Domitian evidently maintained a close relationship with them even in adulthood.

9 Domitian's relationship with his niece Julia (*PIR²* F 426) was close, to judge from the rumours of incest between the two: Plin. *Ep.* 4.11.6; Suet. *Dom.* 22; Juv. 2.29–33; Dio Cass. 67.3.2 (Xiph.; Zonar. 11.19), cf. 4.2 (Xiph.; *EV*).

(b) Cassius Dio 67.14.5–15.6, 17.1–2 (Xiph.; Zonar. 11.20)

Yet Domitian was not helped at all by this,[1] but was the target of a plot and died in the next year, in the consulship of C. Valens, who passed away as consul in his ninetieth year, and C. Antistius. The men who organized the deed and made the attack were Parthenius his bedroom attendant, even though he had been so honoured by Domitian that he even wore a sword,[2] and Sigeros, also a bedroom attendant himself, along with Entellus, the *a libellis*, and Stephanus, a freedman. Domitia, Domitian's wife, and Norbanus, the (praetorian) prefect, and his colleague Petronius Secundus were not ignorant of the plan – so it is said, at least. For Domitia was always detested by Domitian and for this reason used to fear death. The others did not love him anymore, some because they were charged with something, others because they were expecting to be.

I myself also heard this: that Domitian wanted to kill all of them at once, being suspicious of them. He wrote down their names on a two-leafed tablet of limewood and placed it under the pillow of the couch on which he used to sleep. A certain young slave boy, one of the naked 'whisperers',[3] took it away when Domitian was sleeping during the day and held onto it, without realizing what it contained. Domitia came across the tablet and read what was written. She informed the others, and they therefore hurried along the conspiracy that they had in mind anyhow.

Yet they did not attempt the deed until they had established who was going to be the successor to Domitian's office. So they had conversations with certain other men, but when none of them accepted – for they all feared that the conspirators were testing them – they went to Nerva, since he was both the most well-born and the most reasonable person. Besides, he was in danger, having been accused by astrologers, who said that he was going to be emperor. As a consequence of this above all, they convinced him easily to accept imperial power. Domitian had certainly examined closely the days and hours when the leading men had been born and was pre-emptively killing off a significant number of men who were not even hoping to obtain power. He would have slaughtered Nerva, had not one of the astrologers, who regarded Nerva with goodwill, said that the latter was going to die within a few days. Domitian believed that this was actually going to happen and did not want to be guilty of his murder also, since he was going to expire shortly at any rate. . . . *(Dio then relates a number of omens and predictions that supposedly surrounded Domitian's murder, including that of Larginus Proculus [PIR^2 L 109], who foretold the date of the murder and was therefore sent from Germany to be tried before Domitian.)*

As soon as Domitian got up to leave the law court and was about to have his customary daytime nap, Parthenius firstly took the blade out of the sword which always used to lie beneath Domitian's pillow, so that the emperor could not use it. Then, Parthenius sent in Stephanus, since he was physically stronger than the others. Stephanus struck Domitian, albeit not with a mortal blow, but the emperor was lying on the ground, laid out by him. Thus, Parthenius, fearing that Domitian could get away, leapt on him – or, as some people think, sent in the freedman Maximus. And so, not only was Domitian slain, but Stephanus also perished on the spot when those who were not part of the conspiracy came running together to attack him.

1 The execution of Nero's *ab epistulis*, Epaphroditus, who had assisted Nero's suicide, as a warning to Domitian's own freedmen.
2 On the grant of swords and daggers to imperial freedmen as a special privilege, see Krenn 2011: 182–3.
3 Perhaps so called because they had licence to say witty, slanderous things that others dared not articulate; cf. Dio Cass. 48.44.3.

6.4 The murder of Commodus

A relatively brief account of the murder of Commodus on the final day of 192 survives in Xiphilinus' epitome of Cassius Dio, and Herodian offers a more extended narrative. There are also short notices in later sources: SHA *Comm.* 17.1–2, cf. 9.3; Aur. Vict. *Caes.* 17.7–9; Eutr. 8.15; *Epit. de Caes.* 17.5–6; Oros. 7.16; Zos. 1.7.1; cf. Malalas 12.13. Herodian's account has significant consistencies with what survives of Dio's version, but there are also differences. For example, Herodian gives a greater role to Marcia in the initial stages of the plot, and attributes the plot to the conspirators' desire for self-preservation, whereas in Dio's version, disgust at Commodus' increasingly unbalanced behaviour is an additional motivation. The historicity of Herodian's version has been criticized (see especially Hohl 1932), not least because the account involves the discovery of a list of Commodus' intended victims – a detail suspiciously reminiscent of Dio's account of the murder of Domitian; see **6.3 (b)** above. On the other hand, Herodian's account has been defended: Grosso 1964: 399–405; Whittaker 1969: 1.109–10 n. 4.

Prosopographical research and a passage in the *Historia Augusta* (*Pert.* 4.4) have also given rise to the theory that the plot was the product of long-term planning, with the praetorian prefect Laetus putting men loyal to him in key military positions around the empire and recruiting Pertinax as a co-conspirator: Birley 1969, 1988: 81–8; cf. Hekster 2002: 80–3. But even if the accounts of Dio and Herodian are misleading or essentially works of historical fiction, their assumptions about the court are revealing. Imperial concubines, praetorian prefects, imperial freedmen, boy favourites, and athletic trainers interact with each other, and have overlapping interests; some of them form bonds of trust firm enough to execute murder plots. And as with the accounts of Domitian's murder, these narratives assume that fear pervaded the court and motivated violent action.

(a) Cassius Dio 73(72).22 (Xiph.; cf. *EV*; PP)

He certainly did die – or rather was killed – not long after. For Laetus[1] and Eclectus[2] conspired against him, vexed with him on account of what he was doing and also being afraid, since he kept threatening them because they were trying to stop him from doing these things. Commodus wanted to kill both of the consuls, Erucius Clarus and Sosius Falco, and on the first of the month[3] to come forth from the gladiatorial school as both a consul and a *secutor*[4] simultaneously. For he had the first cell in their school, just as if he were one of their number.

Moreover – may nobody disbelieve this! – he cut off the head of the Colossus and erected a sculpture of his own head in its place. Then, giving it a club and placing a bronze lion beneath it so that it would resemble Hercules, he inscribed on it, in addition to the extra names that I have already mentioned,[5] this also: '(Member of the) first rank of the *secutores*; the sole left-hander to be victorious over twelve times one thousand men' – I think this was the number.[6]

Because of these things, Laetus and Eclectus attacked Commodus, having communicated the plan to Marcia. On the last day of the year, indeed, at night, when people were occupied with the festival, they gave him poison in his beef through the agency of Marcia. He could not be killed immediately due to the wine and the baths, for which he always used to have an insatiable appetite,[7] but even vomited something up, and after this he made certain threats, suspecting that he had been poisoned. So they set a certain Narcissus,[8] a trainer of athletes, loose against him, and had this man strangle Commodus when he was bathing.

1 Q. Aemilius Laetus (*PIR*[2] A 358), Commodus' praetorian prefect.
2 Eclectus (*PIR*[2] E 3), Commodus' *a cubiculo*.
3 That is, on 1 January 193.
4 A category of gladiator.
5 Cf. Dio Cass. 73(72).15.3–16.1 (Xiph.).
6 On the Colossus and its inscription, see Hekster 2002: 122–5.
7 Precisely how Dio saw the wine and baths as preventing Commodus' swift demise is unclear; the epitomator has perhaps compressed the account here.
8 *PIR*[2] N 26.

(b) Herodian 1.16.1, 16.2–17.11

At length, then, it was necessary to put a stop to Commodus, since he was insane and the Roman empire was being ruled by a tyrant. . . . (*Herodian here digresses, outlining the origins of the Saturnalia in late December and of the cult of the god Janus, for which early January was especially important.*) When everyone was celebrating these festivities, Commodus wanted to come forth not from the imperial residence,[1] as was customary, but from the gladiators' quarters, and he wished to be seen by the Roman people not in a fine garment and imperial purple, but instead bearing arms himself and with the other gladiators going out with him.

He reported his intention to Marcia, his most favoured concubine, who was not so different from a duly married wife and had all the honours that belonged to an Augusta, except for the fire.[2] When she learnt of his bizarre and unseemly desire, in the first place she began to entreat him, and falling at his feet she begged him with tears not to dishonour the Roman empire or to endanger himself by delivering himself to gladiators and desperate men. But when she had beseeched him a great deal and had not prevailed upon him, Marcia went away crying.

Commodus sent for Laetus, the praetorian prefect, and Eclectus, the *a cubiculo*, and ordered them to make everything ready for him to pass the night in the gladiators' quarters and to come forth from there for the sacrifices of the festival, so that he could be seen armed by the Romans. They began entreating him and trying to persuade him not to do something unworthy of the position of emperor. But Commodus was annoyed, and sent them away and went back into his bedroom as if he was going to have a sleep, for he usually did this at midday. Taking a writing tablet – one of the sort made from limewood cut into thin sheets and folded from both sides in a continuous curve – he wrote down (the names of) those whom he needed to murder that night. Marcia was the first of them, and Laetus and Eclectus followed. In addition to them, there was a great number of the leading men of the Senate. For he wanted to do away with all the senior men and the remaining friends (*philoi*) inherited from his father, since he was ashamed to have eminent witnesses to his base deeds. He wanted to give away the property of the wealthy, and to allot it to the soldiers and the gladiators, so that the former would guard him and the latter delight him.

Once he had written on the tablet, he put it on his couch, supposing that nobody was going to come in there. But there was a certain slave boy – very much still a child – one of those without clothes but adorned with gold and very costly gemstones in whom luxurious Romans always delight. Commodus used to love him excessively, with the result that he used to sleep with him very often and call him 'Philocommodus'[3] – the name showing the emperor's affection towards the boy. This boy was playing without any particular purpose and, as he usually did, ran into the bedroom; Commodus had gone out for his customary baths and drinking binges. The boy picked up the tablet lying on the couch just to play with it, and left the room.

By chance, he met Marcia. Now, embracing and kissing the boy – for she too felt affection for him – she took the tablet away from him, fearing that he might destroy something important out of childishness, playing with it in ignorance. She discovered Commodus' handwriting on it, and for this reason became even more eager to read the writing. When she discovered that death-dealing document and found out that she was going to die before everyone else, that Laetus and Eclectus were going to be next, and that the others would also be murdered, she lamented to herself, saying, 'Well, Commodus! So these are the thanks that I get for my goodwill and love, and for the insulting and drunken behaviour from you that I put up with for so many years. But you yourself will not escape punishment from a sober woman, you drunkard!'

Marcia said these things and then summoned Eclectus. Since he was a bedroom attendant, he was in the habit of visiting her; moreover, she was also rumoured to be having sex with him. Giving him the tablet, she said, 'Look at the sort of festival we are going to celebrate tonight!' Eclectus read it and was panic-stricken – for he was an Egyptian by birth, and was inclined by nature to be at the same time daring and dynamic, and also a slave to emotion. He then sealed up the tablet and sent it with one of his trusted men to Laetus so he could read it. Laetus was also agitated and came before Marcia as if intending to consult them concerning what the emperor had ordered about the gladiators' quarters. While they pretended to be considering different issues relating to Commodus, they agreed to act pre-emptively rather than being the victims, and that it was not the time to delay or defer.

The decision was to give a noxious drug to Commodus, and Marcia promised that she could do this very easily. For she was in the habit of mixing the first drink and giving it to him, so he could have greater pleasure by drinking something from his beloved. Commodus returned from the baths and Marcia put the drug into the cup, mixed it with sweet-smelling wine, and gave it to him. Being thirsty after many baths and bouts against wild animals, he began drinking it just like the usual loving-cup without sensing anything. Immediately, a torpor fell upon him, and he drifted off to sleep, thinking he was worn out from exercise.

Eclectus and Marcia ordered everybody to depart and to go back to their own households; they, of course, were giving him the chance to rest (they claimed). Commodus often suffered this on other occasions because of drunkenness. Bathing and eating often, he did not set aside time for sleep, since he was engaged in a constant succession of different pleasures, to which he was enslaved at any given moment. For a short time he rested. But when the drug reached his stomach and intestines, he became dizzy, and a great deal of vomiting ensued. This happened either because the food that he had previously eaten along with all the drink flushed out the drug, or because of the antidote which he had taken beforehand – something emperors habitually do before every meal. Anyway, there was a great deal of vomiting, and the others feared that he might disgorge all the poison and recover – and then kill the lot of them. So they persuaded a certain Narcissus, who was valiant and in the full vigour of youth, to go in and strangle Commodus. They promised him big rewards. He ran in and murdered Commodus, who was weakened thanks to poison and intoxication, by throttling him.

1 Commodus was perhaps at this point living in the Villa Vectiliana on the Caelian Hill: SHA *Comm.* 16.3; Oros. 7.16.4.
2 On the ceremonial fire, an honour attested for the emperor and members of his family from the Antonine period onward, see Mommsen 1887–8: 1.423–4.
3 'Commodus-lover'.

Bibliography

Ancient Works

The following editions of ancient texts were used in preparing the translations contained in this sourcebook.

[Aelius Aristides], *To the King* = Keil, B. (1898) *Aelii Aristidis Smyrnaei quae supersunt omnia*. Volume 2: *Orationes XVII–LIII continens*. Berlin: Weidmann.

Ammianus Marcellinus = Seyfarth, W., Jacob-Karau, L., and Ulmann, I. (1978) *Ammiani Marcellini Rerum gestarum libri qui supersunt* (2 vols.). Bibliotheca Teubneriana. Leipzig: Teubner.

Arrian, *Discourses of Epictetus* = Schenkl, H. (1916) *Epicteti Dissertationes ab Arriano digestae*, 2nd ed. Bibliotheca Teubneriana. Leipzig: Teubner.

Athenaeus, *The Learned Banqueters* = Olson, S. D. (2006–12) *Athenaeus: The Learned Banqueters* (8 vols.). Loeb. Cambridge, Mass.: Harvard University Press.

Aulus Gellius, *Attic Nights* = Marshall, P. K. (1990) *A. Gellii Noctes Atticae* (2 vols.), 2nd ed. OCT. Oxford: Clarendon.

Aurelius Victor, *On the Caesars* = Pichlmayr, F. and Gruendel, R. (1970) *Sexti Aurelii Victoris Liber de Caesaribus*. Bibliotheca Teubneriana. Leipzig: Teubner.

Cassius Dio, *Roman History* = Boissevain, U. P. (1895–1931) *Cassii Dionis Cocceiani historiarum Romanarum quae supersunt* (5 vols.). Berlin: Weidmann.

Cicero, *On Duties* = Winterbottom, M. (1994) *M. Tulli Ciceronis De officiis*. OCT. Oxford: Clarendon.

Cicero, On Laws = Powell, J. G. F. (2006) *M. Tulli Ciceronis De re publica, De legibus, Cato maior de senectute, Laelius de amicitia*. OCT. Oxford and New York: Oxford University Press.

Code of Justinian = Krüger, P. (1914) *Corpus Iuris Civilis*. Volume 2: *Codex Iustinianus*, 9th ed. Berlin: Weidmann.

Corpus Inscriptionum Latinarum = Mommsen, T. et al. (eds.) (1869–) *Corpus Inscriptionum Latinarum* (17 vols.). Berlin: G. Reimer.

Digest = Krüger, P. and Mommsen, T. (1911) *Corpus Iuris Civilis*. Volume 1: *Institutiones; Digesta*, 12th ed. Berlin: Weidmann.

Donatus, *Life of Vergil* = Rolfe, J. C., Hurley, D. W., and Goold, G. P. (1997) *Suetonius* (2 vols.), rev. ed. Loeb. Cambridge, Mass.: Harvard University Press. 2.448–64.

Eutropius = Hellegouarc'h, J. (1999) *Eutrope: Abrégé d'histoire romaine*. Collection des universités de France, 356. Paris: Les Belles Lettres.

Fronto, *Letters* = van den Hout, M. P. J. (1988) *M. Cornelii Frontonis Epistulae*. Bibliotheca Teubneriana. Leipzig: Teubner.

Galen, *On My Own Books* = Boudon-Millot, V. (2007) *Galien,* Volume 1: *Introduction générale, Sur l'ordre de ses propres livres, Sur ses propres livres, Que l'excellent médecin est aussi philosophe.* Collection des universités de France. Paris: Les Belles Lettres.

[Galen], *On Theriac to Piso* = Boudon-Millot, V. (2016) *Galien,* Volume 6: *Thériaque à Pison.* Collection des universités de France. Paris: Les Belles Lettres.

Greek Constitutions = Oliver, J. H. and Clinton, K. (1989) *Greek Constitutions of Early Roman Emperors from Inscriptions and Papyri.* Memoirs of the American Philosophical Society, 178. Philadelphia, Pa.: American Philosophical Society.

Herodian = Lucarini, C. M. (2005) *Herodianus: Regnum post Marcum.* Bibliotheca Teubneriana. Munich and Leipzig: Saur.

Historia Augusta = Hohl, E., Samberger, C., and Seyfarth, W. (1971) *Scriptores historiae Augustae* (2 vols.), 5th ed. (vol. 1), 3rd ed. (vol. 2). Bibliotheca Teubneriana. Leipzig: Teubner.

Horace, *Odes* = Shackleton Bailey, D. R. (2001) *Q. Horati Flacci Opera,* 4th ed. Bibliotheca Teubneriana. Berlin and New York: de Gruyter.

Josephus, *Life*; *Jewish Antiquities* = Thackeray, H. et al. (1926–65) *Josephus* (10 vols.). Loeb. London: Heinemann; Cambridge, Mass.: Harvard University Press.

Juvenal, *Satires* = Clausen, W. V. (1992) *A. Persi Flacci et D. Iuni Iuvenalis saturae,* rev. ed. OCT. Oxford: Clarendon.

Lactantius, *On the Deaths of the Persecutors* = Creed, J. L. (1984) *De mortibus persecutorum.* Oxford Early Christian Texts. Oxford: Clarendon.

Latin Panegyrics = Mynors, R. A. B. (1964) *XII panegyrici Latini.* OCT. Oxford: Clarendon.

Lucan, *Pharsalia* = Shackleton Bailey, D. R. (1997) *M. Annaei Lucani De bello civili libri X,* 2nd ed. Bibliotheca Teubneriana. Stuttgart: Teubner.

***Marcus Aurelius,* Meditations** = Dalfen, J. (1987) *Marci Aurelii Antonini Ad se ipsum libri XII,* 2nd ed. Bibliotheca Teubneriana. Leipzig: Teubner.

Martial, *Epigrams* and *On the Spectacles* = Shackleton Bailey, D. R. (1990) *M. Valerii Martialis Epigrammata.* Bibliotheca Teubneriana. Stuttgart: Teubner.

Nicolaus of Damascus, *Life of Augustus* = Toher, M. (2017) *Nicolaus of Damascus: The Life of Augustus and the Autobiography,* with tr. and comm. Cambridge: Cambridge University Press.

Ovid, *Letters from Pontus* = Richmond, J. A. (1990) *P. Ovidi Nasonis Ex Ponto libri quattuor.* Bibliotheca Teubneriana. Leipzig: Teubner.

Ovid, *Tristia* = Luck, G. (1967–77) *Tristia* (2 vols.). Wissenschaftliche Kommentare zu griechischen und lateinischen Schriftstellern. Heidelberg: Carl Winter.

***Oxyrhynchus Papyri* 42** = Parsons, P. J. (1974) *The Oxyrhynchus Papyri XLII.* Graeco-Roman Memoirs, 58. London: Egypt Exploration Society.

Philo, *Embassy to Gaius* = Cohn, L. and Wendland, P. (1915) *Philonis Alexandrini opera quae supersunt,* Volume 6: *Quod omnis probus liber sit. De vita contemplativa. De aeternitate mundi. In Flaccum. Legatio ad Gaium.* Berlin: G. Reimer.

Philostratus, *Life of Apollonius* = Jones, C. P. (2005) *Philostratus: Life of Apollonius of Tyana* (3 vols.). Loeb. Cambridge, Mass.: Harvard University Press.

Philostratus, *Lives of the Sophists* = Stefec, R. S. (2016) *Flavii Philostrati vitas sophistarum.* OCT. Oxford: Clarendon.

Pliny the Elder, *Natural History* = König, R. and Winckler, G. (1973–2004) *C. Plinius Secundus der Ältere: Naturkunde* (38 vols.). Sammlung Tusculum. Munich: Heimeran.

Pliny the Younger, *Letters* = Mynors, R. A. B. (1963) *C. Plini Caecili Secundi epistularum libri decem*. OCT. Oxford: Clarendon.

Pliny the Younger, *Panegyric* = Mynors, R. A. B. (1964) *XII panegyrici Latini*. OCT. Oxford: Clarendon.

Plutarch, *Life of Lucullus* = Ziegler, K. and Gärtner, H. (2000) *Plutarchus: Vitae Parallelae*. Volume 1, fascicle 1, 5th ed. Munich and Leipzig: Saur.

Polybius, *Histories* = Pédech, P. et al. (1969–2004) *Polybe: Histoires* (10 vols.). Collection des universités de France. Paris: Les Belles Lettres.

Reynolds, *Aphrodisias* = Reynolds, J. (1982) *Aphrodisias and Rome: Documents from the Excavation of the Theatre at Aphrodisias*. Journal of Roman Studies Monographs, 1. London: Society for the Promotion of Roman Studies.

Roman Inscriptions of Britain = Collingwood, R. G., Wright, R. P, and Tomlin, R. (1995) *The Roman Inscriptions of Britain*. Volume 1: *Inscriptions on Stone*, rev. ed. Stroud: Sutton.

Senatorial Decree on Gnaeus Piso the Father = Eck, W., Caballos, A., and Fernández, F. (1996) *Das Senatus consultum de Cn. Pisone patre*. Vestigia, 48. Munich: Beck.

Seneca the Younger, *Letters* = Reynolds, L. D. (1965) *L. Annaei Senecae Ad Lucilium epistulae morales* (2 vols.). OCT. Oxford: Clarendon.

[Seneca the Younger], *Octavia* = Zwierlein, O. (1986) *L. Annaei Senecae Tragoediae*. OCT. Oxford: Clarendon.

Seneca the Younger, *On Anger, On Tranquillity of Mind,* and *To Polybius On Consolation* = Reynolds, L. D. (1977) *L. Annaei Senecae Dialogorum libri duodecim*. OCT. Oxford: Clarendon.

Seneca the Younger, *On Benefits* = Hosius, C. (1900) *L. Annaei Senecae opera quae supersunt*. Volume 1.2: *De beneficiis libri VII. De clementia libri II*. Bibliotheca Teubneriana. Leipzig: Teubner.

Statius, *Achilleid; Thebaid* = Hall, J. B., Ritchie, A. L., and Edwards, M. J. (2007) *P. Papinius Statius*. Volume 3: *Thebaid and Achilleid*. Cambridge: Cambridge Scholars.

Statius, *Silvae* = Courtney, E. (1990) *P. Papini Stati Silvae*. OCT. Oxford: Clarendon.

Strabo, *Geography* = Radt, S. (2002–11) *Strabons Geographika* (10 vols.). Göttingen: Vandenhoeck & Ruprecht.

Suetonius, *Lives of the Caesars* = Kaster, R. (2016) *C. Suetoni Tranquilli De vita Caesarum libros VIII et De grammaticis et rhetoribus liberum*. OCT. Oxford: Clarendon.

Suetonius, *Lives of the Poets* = Rolfe, J. C. (1914) *Suetonius with an English Translation* (2 vols.). London: Heinemann; Cambridge, Mass.: Harvard University Press. 2.452–506.

***Sylloge Inscriptionum Graecarum*³** = Dittenberger, W. and Hiller von Gaertringen, F. (eds.) (1915–24) *Sylloge Inscriptionum Graecarum*, 3rd ed. Leipzig: S. Hirzel.

Tacitus, *Agricola* = Woodman, A. J. and Kraus, C. S. (2014) *Tacitus: Agricola*. Cambridge: Cambridge University Press.

Tacitus, *Annals* = Heubner, H. (1994) *Cornelii Taciti libri qui supersunt*. Volume 1: *Annales*, rev. ed. Bibliotheca Teubneriana. Stuttgart and Leipzig: Teubner.

Tacitus, *Histories* = Heubner, H. (1978) *Cornelii Taciti libri qui supersunt*. Volume 2, fascicle 1: *Historiarum libri*. Bibliotheca Teubneriana. Stuttgart and Leipzig: Teubner.

Valerius Maximus, *Memorable Doings and Sayings* = Briscoe, J. (1998) *Valerius Maximus: Factorum et dictorum memorabilium libri IX* (2 vols.). Bibliotheca Teubneriana. Stuttgart and Leipzig: Teubner.

Velleius Paterculus, *Histories* = Watt, W. S. (1988) *Vellei Paterculi Historiarum ad M. Vinicium consulem libri duo*. Bibliotheca Teubneriana. Leipzig: Teubner.

Vitruvius, *On Architecture* = Krohn, F. (1912) *Vitruvii De architectura libri decem*. Bibliotheca Teubneriana. Leipzig: Teubner

Modern Works Cited

Absil, M. (1997) *Les préfets du prétoire d'Auguste à Commode: 2 avant Jésus-Christ–192 après Jésus-Christ. De l'archéologie à l'histoire*. Paris: de Boccard.

Acton, K. (2011) 'Vespasian and the Social World of the Roman Court', *AJPh* 132: 103–24.

Alföldi, A. (1970) *Die monarchische Repräsentation im römischen Kaiserreiche*. Darmstadt: Wissenschaftliche Buchgesellschaft. [Reprinted from *MDAI(R)* 49 (1934): 3–118, 50 (1935): 1–158.]

Allen, J. (2006) *Hostages and Hostage-Taking in the Roman Empire*. New York: Cambridge University Press.

Anagnostou-Laoutides, E. and Charles, M. B. (2015) 'Titus and Berenice: The Elegiac Aura of an Historical Affair', *Arethusa* 48: 17–46.

Ando, C. (2000) *Imperial Ideology and Provincial Loyalty in the Roman Empire*. Classics and Contemporary Thought, 6. Berkeley, Calif., Los Angeles, and London: University of California Press.

André, N. et al. (2004) 'Vom "schwebenden Garten" zum Tempelbezirk: Die Untersuchungen der École Française de Rome in der Vigna Barberini', in Hoffmann and Wulf 2004: 112–43.

Arnold, F. et al. (eds.) (2012) *Orte der Herrschaft: Charakteristika von antiken Machtzentren*. Menschen – Kulturen – Traditionen, 3. Rahden: Marie Leidorf.

Ash, R. (2007) *Tacitus: Histories, Book II*. Cambridge Greek and Latin Classics. Cambridge: Cambridge University Press.

(2016) '"Never Say Die!" Assassinating Emperors in Suetonius' *Lives of the Caesars*', in *Writing Biography in Greece and Rome: Narrative Technique and Fictionalization*, ed. K. de Temmerman and K. Demoen. Cambridge: Cambridge University Press. 200–16.

Avery, W. T. (1940) 'The *adoratio purpurae* and the Importance of the Imperial Purple in the Fourth Century of the Christian Era', *MAAR* 17: 66–80.

Aymard, J. (1951) *Essai sur les chasses romaines, des origines à la fin du siècle des Antonins (cynegetica)*. Bibl. Éc. Franc., 171. Paris: de Boccard.

Baldwin, B. (1979) 'Juvenal's Crispinus', *AClass* 22: 109–14.

Ball, L. F. (2003) *The Domus Aurea and the Roman Architectural Revolution*. Cambridge: Cambridge University Press.

Barrett, A. A. (1996) *Agrippina: Mother of Nero*. London: B. T. Batsford.

(2002) *Livia: First Lady of Imperial Rome*. New Haven, Conn. and London: Yale University Press.

(2015) *Caligula: The Abuse of Power*, 2nd ed. London and New York: Routledge.

Bartman, E. (1999) *Portraits of Livia: Imaging the Imperial Woman in Augustan Rome.* Cambridge and New York: Cambridge University Press.

Bartoli, A. (1929) 'Scavi del Palatino (Domus Augustana) 1926–28', *NSA* 5: 3–29.

(1938) *Domus Augustana.* Rome: Istituto di studi romani.

Barton, C. A. (2002) 'The Roman Blush: The Delicate Matter of Self-Control', in *Constructions of the Classical Body*, ed. J. I. Porter. Ann Arbor, Mich.: University of Michigan Press. 212–34.

Barton, T. (1994a) *Ancient Astrology.* Sciences of Antiquity. London: Routledge.

(1994b) 'Astrology and the State in Imperial Rome', in *Shamanism, History and the State*, ed. N. Thomas and C. Humphrey. Ann Arbor, Mich.: University of Michigan Press. 146–63.

(1994c) *Power and Knowledge: Astrology, Physiognomics, and Medicine under the Roman Empire.* The Body, in Theory. Ann Arbor, Mich.: University of Michigan Press.

Bartsch, S. (1994) *Actors in the Audience: Theatricality and Doublespeak from Nero to Hadrian.* Revealing Antiquity, 6. Cambridge, Mass. and London: Harvard University Press.

Bastet, F. L. (1970) 'Lucain et les arts', in *Lucain*, ed. M. Durry. Entretiens sur l'Antiquité classique, 15. Geneva: Fondation Hardt. 121–58.

Bastianini, G. (1975) 'Lista dei prefetti d'Egitto dal 30ᵃ al 299ᴾ', *ZPE* 17: 263–328.

(1988) 'Il prefetto d'Egitto (30 a.C.–297 d.C.): Addenda (1973–1985)', *ANRW* 2.10.1: 503–17.

Baughman, K. E. (2014) 'Poppaea Sabina, Jewish Sympathies, and the Fire of Rome', *Women in Judaism: A Multidisciplinary Journal* 11.2.

Baumer, L. E. (2007) 'Mehrschichtige Botschaften: Anmerkungen zu Komposition und Deutung der so genannten Cancelleriareliefs', *AK* 50: 93–107.

Beacham, R. (2007) 'Playing Places: The Temporary and the Permanent', in *The Cambridge Companion to Greek and Roman Theatre*, ed. M. McDonald and J. M. Walton. Cambridge: Cambridge University Press. 202–26.

Beck, H. (2009) 'From Poplicola to Augustus: Senatorial Houses in Roman Political Culture', *Phoenix* 63: 361–84.

Bek, L. (1980) *Towards Paradise on Earth: Modern Space Conception in Architecture: A Creation of Renaissance Humanism.* ARID Suppl., 9. Odense: Odense University Press.

Bell, C. (1992) *Ritual Theory, Ritual Practice.* New York and Oxford: Oxford University Press.

(1997) *Ritual: Perspectives and Dimensions.* New York and Oxford: Oxford University Press.

Belli, R. (2009) 'Il ninfeo di Punta Epitaffio: Antrum cyclopis e l'ideologia di un imperatore', in *Apolline Project. Volume 1: Studies on Vesuvius' North Slope and the Bay of Naples*, ed. G. F. De Simone and R. T. Macfarlane. Quaderni della ricerca scientifica, Serie Beni Culturali, 14. Naples: Università degli Studi Suor Orsola Benincasa; Provo, Utah: Brigham Young University. 49–63.

Bergmann, M. (1982) 'Zum Fries B der flavischen Cancelleriareliefs', *Marburger Winckelmann-Programm 1981*: 19–31.

Bertolazzi, R. (2013) 'From the *CIL* Archives: A New Statue Base of Julia Domna from *Mustis* (Tunisia)', *ZPE* 184: 304–8.

(2015) 'The Depiction of Livia and Julia Domna by Cassius Dio: Some Observations', *AAntHung* 55: 413–32.

Billows, R. (1993) 'The Religious Procession of the *Ara Pacis Augustae*: Augustus' *supplicatio* in 13 B.C.', *JRA* 6: 80–92.

Bingham, S. and Imrie, A. (2015) 'The Prefect and the Plot: A Reassessment of the Murder of Plautianus', *Journal of Ancient History* 3: 76–91.

Birley, A. R. (1969) 'The Coups d'Etat of the Year 193', *BJ* 169: 247–80.

(1988) *Septimius Severus: The African Emperor*, rev. ed. London: B. T. Batsford.

(1997) *Hadrian: The Restless Emperor*. London and New York: Routledge.

(2005) *The Roman Government of Britain*. Oxford: Oxford University Press.

(2007) 'Sejanus: His Fall', in *Corolla Cosmo Rodewald*, ed. N. Sekunda. Akanthina 2. Gdańsk: Foundation for the Development of Gdańsk University. 121–50.

de Blois, L. (1986) 'The Εἰς Βασιλέα of Ps.-Aelius Aristides', *GRBS* 27: 279–88.

Boatwright, M. T. (1987) *Hadrian and the City of Rome*. Princeton, N. J.: Princeton University Press.

Boëthius, A. (1960) *The Golden House of Nero: Some Aspects of Roman Architecture*. Jerome Lectures, 5. Ann Arbor, Mich.: University of Michigan Press.

Borg, B. (1995) 'Problems in the Dating of the Mummy Portraits', in *The Mysterious Fayum Portraits: Faces from Ancient Egypt*, ed. E. Doxiadis. London: Thames and Hudson. 229–33.

(1996) *Mumienporträts: Chronologie und kultureller Kontext*. Mainz: von Zabern.

(2012) 'Portraits', in *The Oxford Handbook of Roman Egypt*, ed. C. Riggs. Oxford: Oxford University Press. 613–29.

Boschung, D. (2002) *Gens Augusta: Untersuchungen zu Aufstellung, Wirkung und Bedeutung der Statuengruppen des julisch-claudischen Kaiserhauses*. Monumenta artis Romanae, 32. Mainz: von Zabern.

(2012) 'The Reliefs: Representation of Marcus Aurelius' Deeds', in *A Companion to Marcus Aurelius*, ed. M. van Ackeren. Malden, Mass., Oxford, and Chichester: Wiley-Blackwell. 305–14.

Boulvert, G. (1970) *Esclaves et affranchis impériaux sous le Haut-Empire romain: Rôle politique et administratif*. Biblioteca di Labeo, 4. Naples: Jovene.

(1974) *Domestique et fonctionnaire sous le Haut-Empire romain: La condition de l'affranchi et de l'esclave du prince*. Annales littéraires de l'Université de Besançon, 151; Centre de recherches d'histoire ancienne, 6. Paris: Les Belles Lettres.

(1981) 'La carrière de Tiberius Claudius Augusti libertus Classicus (AE 1972, 574)', *ZPE* 43: 31–41.

Bowditch, P. L. (2001) *Horace and the Gift Economy of Patronage*. Classics and Contemporary Thought, 7. Berkeley, Calif., Los Angeles, and London: University of California Press.

Bowersock, G. W. (1969) *Greek Sophists in the Roman Empire*. Oxford: Clarendon.

Bowman, A. K., Garnsey, P., and Rathbone, D. (eds.) (2000) *The Cambridge Ancient History*. Volume 11: *The High Empire, A.D. 70–192*, 2nd ed. Cambridge: Cambridge University Press.

Boyle, A. J. (2008) *Octavia: Attributed to Seneca,* with tr. and comm. Oxford: Oxford University Press.

Bradley, K. R. (1978) *Suetonius' Life of Nero: An Historical Commentary*. Collection Latomus, 157. Brussels: Latomus.

Braund, D. C. (1984) *Rome and the Friendly King: The Character of Client Kingship.* London: Croom Helm; New York: St. Martin's Press.

Braund, S. M. (1996) 'The Solitary Feast: A Contradiction in Terms?' *BICS* 41: 37–52.

Brunt, P. A. (1988a) '*Amicitia* in the Roman Republic', in *The Fall of the Roman Republic and Related Essays.* Oxford: Clarendon. 351–81.

(1988b) 'The Emperor's Choice of *amici*', in *Alte Geschichte und Wissenschaftsgeschichte: Festschrift für Karl Christ zum 65. Geburtstag*, ed. P. Kneissl and V. Losemann. Darmstadt: Wissenschaftliche Buchgesellschaft. 39–56.

Bruun, C. (1990) 'Some Comments on the Status of Imperial Freedmen (The Case of Ti. Claudius Aug. lib. Classicus)', *ZPE* 82: 271–85.

(2010) 'Matidia die Jüngere – Gesellschaftlicher Einfluss und dynastische Rolle', in *Augustae: Machtbewusste Frauen am römischen Kaiserhof? Herrschaftsstrukturen und Herrschaftspraxis II*, ed. A. Kolb. Berlin: Akademie Verlag. 211–33.

Bukowiecki, E. and Wulf-Rheidt, U. (2015) 'I bolli laterizi delle residenze imperiali sul Palatino a Roma', *MDAI(R)* 121: 311–482.

von Bülow, G. and Zabehlicky, H. (2011) *Bruckneudorf und Gamzigrad: Spätantike Paläste und Großvillen im Donau-Balkan-Raum. Akten des Internationalen Kolloquiums in Bruckneudorf vom 15. bis 18. Oktober 2008.* Kolloquien zur Vor- und Frühgeschichte, 15. Bonn: Habelt.

Buraselis, K. (2000) *Kos: Between Hellenism and Rome. Studies on the Political, Institutional and Social History of Kos from ca. the Middle Second Century B.C. until Late Antiquity.* TAPhS 90, part 4. Philadelphia, Pa.: American Philosophical Society.

Burrell, B. (2004) *Neokoroi: Greek Cities and Roman Emperors.* Cincinnati Classical Studies, 9. Leiden and Boston, Mass.: Brill.

Burzacchini, G. (2017) *Ateneo di Naucrati Deipnosofisti (Dotti a banchetto): Libro V.* Bologna: Pàtron.

Caballos Rufino, A., Eck, W., and Fernández Gómez, F. (eds.) (1996) *El Senadoconsulto de Gneo Pisón Padre*, with tr. and comm. Ediciones Especiales, 18. Seville: Universidad de Sevilla.

Calament, F. (2005) *La révélation d'Antinoé par Albert Gayet: Histoire, archéologie, muséographie* (2 vols.). Bibliothèque d'études coptes, 18.1–2. Cairo: Institut français d'archéologie orientale.

Caldelli, M. L. (2008) 'Un atleta dimenticato e gli amori di Elagabalo: Nota su un mosaico di Puteoli', *MEFRA* 120: 469–73.

Cameron, A. (1987) 'The Construction of Court Ritual: The Byzantine *Book of Ceremonies*', in *Rituals of Royalty: Power and Ceremonial in Traditional Societies*, ed. D. Cannadine and S. R. F. Price. Past and Present Publications. Cambridge: Cambridge University Press. 106–36.

Campbell, J. B. (1984) *The Emperor and the Roman Army, 31 BC–AD 235.* Oxford: Clarendon.

Canepa, M. P. (2009) *The Two Eyes of the Earth: Art and Ritual of Kingship between Rome and Sasanian Iran.* Transformation of the Classical Heritage, 45. Berkeley, Calif., Los Angeles, and London: University of California Press.

Carandini, A. and Bruno, D. (2008) *La casa di Augusto: Dai 'Lupercalia' al Natale.* Rome and Bari: Laterza.

Carettoni, G. (1983) *Das Haus des Augustus auf dem Palatin.* Mainz: von Zabern.

Caspari, F. (1916) 'Das Nilschiff Ptolemaios IV', *JDAI* 31: 1–74.

Champlin, E. (1980) *Fronto and Antonine Rome*. Cambridge, Mass.: Harvard University Press.

(2003) *Nero*. Cambridge, Mass. and London: Belknap Press of Harvard University Press.

(2005) 'Phaedrus the Fabulous', *JRS* 95: 97–123.

(2011) 'Sex on Capri', *TAPhA* 141: 315–32.

(2012) 'Seianus Augustus', *Chiron* 42: 361–88.

Charles, M. B. and Anagnostou-Laoutides, E. (2012) 'Vespasian, Caenis and Suetonius', in *Studies in Latin Literature and Roman History XVI*, ed. C. Deroux. Collection Latomus, 338. Brussels: Latomus. 530–47.

Chatr Aryamontri, D. and Renner, T. (2017) 'Investigating the "Villa degli Antonini" at Lanuvium', *JRA* 30: 372–86.

Chausson, F. (2008) 'Une dédicace monumentale provenant du théâtre de *Suessa Aurunca*, due à Matidie la jeune, belle-soeur de l'empereur Hadrien', *JS* 2: 233–59.

Cipollone, M. (2011) '*Senatus consultum de honoribus Germanici decernendis*: Contributo alla lettura della *Tabula Siarensis*, da un'iscrizione inedita del Museo Archeologico di Perugia', *Bollettino di Archeologia Online* 2: 3–18.

Claridge, A., Toms, J., and Cubberley, T. (2010) *Rome: An Oxford Archaeological Guide*, 2nd ed. Oxford Archaeological Guides. Oxford: Oxford University Press.

Clarke, J. R. (1991) *The Houses of Roman Italy: 100 B.C.–A.D. 250: Ritual, Space, and Decoration*. Berkeley, Calif., Los Angeles, and London: University of California Press.

Coarelli, F. (ed.) (2009) *Divus Vespasianus: Il bimillenario dei Flavi*. Rome: Electa.

(2012) *Palatium: Il Palatino dalle origini all'impero*. Rome: Edizioni Quasar.

Cogitore, I. (2002) *La légitimité dynastique d'Auguste à Néron à l'épreuve des conspirations*. Bibl. Éc. Franc., 313. Rome: École française de Rome.

Coleman, K. M. (2006) *M. Valerii Martialis Liber Spectaculorum*, with trans. and comm. Oxford: Oxford University Press.

Collins, A. W. (2009) 'The Palace Revolution: The Assassination of Domitian and the Accession of Nerva', *Phoenix* 63: 73–106.

Connolly, S. (2010) *Lives Behind the Laws: The World of the Codex Hermogenianus*. Bloomington, Ind. and Indianapolis, Ind.: Indiana University Press.

Corbier, M. (2001) '*Maiestas domus Augustae*', in *Varia epigraphica: Atti del Colloquio Internazionale di Epigrafia (Bertinoro, 8–10 giugno 2000)*, ed. M. G. Angeli Bertinelli and A. Donati. Faenza: Fratelli Lega. 155–99.

Corcoran, S. (2007) 'Galerius's Jigsaw Puzzle: The *Caesariani* Dossier', *AntTard* 15: 221–50.

Courrier, C. (2016) 'Mouvements et destructions de statues: Une lecture topographique de la répudiation d'Octavie', in *Faire parler et faire taire les statues: De l'invention de l'écriture à l'usage de l'explosif*, ed. C. M. D'Annoville and Y. Rivière. CÉFR, 520. Rome: École française de Rome. 297–350.

Courtney, E. (1980) *A Commentary on the Satires of Juvenal*. London: Athlone Press.

Cramer, F. H. (1954) *Astrology in Roman Law and Politics*. Memoirs of the American Philosophical Society, 37. Philadelphia, Pa.: American Philosophical Society.

Creed, J. L. (ed.) (1984) *Lactantius: De mortibus persecutorum*. Oxford: Clarendon.

Crook, J. A. (1955) *Consilium Principis: Imperial Councils and Counsellors from Augustus to Diocletian*. Cambridge: Cambridge University Press.

Dalfen, J. (1974) 'Einige Interpolationen im Text von Marc Aurels τὰ εἰς ἑαυτόν', *Hermes* 102: 47–57.

D'Arms, J. H. (1970) *Romans on the Bay of Naples: A Social and Cultural Study of the Villas and their Owners from 150 B.C. to A.D. 400*. Loeb Classical Monographs. Cambridge, Mass.: Harvard University Press.

Darwall-Smith, R. H. (1996) *Emperors and Architecture: A Study of Flavian Rome*. Collection Latomus, 231. Brussels: Latomus.

Davenport, C. (2012) 'Cassius Dio and Caracalla', *CQ* 62: 796–815.

  (2019) *A History of the Roman Equestrian Order*. Cambridge: Cambridge University Press.

Davenport, C. and Manley, J. (eds.) (2014) *Fronto: Selected Letters*. Classical Studies Series. London: Bloomsbury Academic.

De Caro, S. (2002) *I Campi Flegrei, Ischia, Vivara, storia e archeologia*. Naples: Electa.

Deckers, J. G. and Meyer-Graft, R. (1979) 'Die Wandmalerei im Kaiserkultraum von Luxor', *JDAI* 94: 600–52.

De Franceschini, M. (1991) *Villa Adriana: Mosaici, pavimenti, edifici*. Bibliotheca Archaeologica, 9. Rome: 'L'Erma' di Bretschneider.

Deppmeyer, K. (2008) *Kaisergruppen von Vespasian bis Konstantin: Eine Untersuchung zu Aufstellungskontexten und Intentionen der statuarischen Präsentation kaiserlicher Familien* (2 vols.). Schriftenreihe Antiquitates, 47. Hamburg: Kovač.

Derchain, P. (1991) 'Un projet d'empereur', in *Ägypten im afro-orientalischen Kontext: Aufsätze zur Archäologie, Geschichte und Sprache eines unbegrenzten Raumes: Gedenkschrift Peter Behrens*, ed. D. Mendel and U. Claudi. Afrikanistische Arbeitspapiere, Sondernummer 1991. Cologne: Institut für Afrikanistik, Universität Köln. 109–24.

DiLuzio, M. J. (2016) *A Place at the Altar: Priestesses in Republican Rome*. Princeton, N. J. and Oxford: Princeton University Press.

Dmitriev, S. (2005) *City Government in Hellenistic and Roman Asia Minor*. Oxford: Oxford University Press.

Dolansky, F. (2008) '*Togam virilem sumere*: Coming of Age in the Roman World', in *Roman Dress and the Fabrics of Roman Culture*, ed. J. Edmondson and A. Keith. Toronto and London: University of Toronto Press. 47–70.

  (2011) 'Celebrating the Saturnalia: Religious Ritual and Roman Domestic Life', in *A Companion to Families in the Greek and Roman Worlds*, ed. B. Rawson. Malden, Mass., Oxford, and Chichster: Wiley-Blackwell. 488–503.

von Domaszewski, A. (1909) *Abhandlungen zur römischen Religion*. Leipzig and Berlin: Georg Olms.

Dominik, W. J. (1994) *The Mythic Voice of Statius: Power and Politics in the Thebaid*. Mnemos. Suppl., 136. Leiden, New York, and Cologne: Brill.

Drerup, H. (1959) 'Bildraum und Realraum in der römischen Architektur', *MDAI(R)* 66: 145–74.

Driediger-Murphy, L. G. (2019) *Roman Republican Augury: Freedom and Control*. Oxford Classical Monographs. Oxford: Oxford University Press.

Drinkwater, J. F. (1987) *The Gallic Empire: Separatism and Continuity in the North-Western Provinces of the Roman Empire, A.D. 260–274.* Historia Einzelschriften, 52. Stuttgart: Franz Steiner.

(2019) *Nero: Emperor and Court.* Cambridge: Cambridge University Press.

Duindam, J. (1995) *Myths of Power: Norbert Elias and the Early Modern European Court.* Amsterdam: Amsterdam University Press.

(2003) *Vienna and Versailles: The Courts of Europe's Dynastic Rivals, 1550–1780.* Cambridge: Cambridge University Press.

(2016) *Dynasties: A Global History of Power, 1300–1800.* Cambridge: Cambridge University Press.

Dunbabin, K. (1986) 'Sic erimus cuncti . . .: The Skeleton in Graeco-Roman Art', *JDAI* 101: 185–255.

Dunkle, R. (2014) 'Overview of Roman Spectacle', in *A Companion to Sport and Spectacle in Greek and Roman Antiquity*, ed. P. Christesen and D. G. Kyle. Blackwell Companions to the Ancient World. Oxford: Wiley-Blackwell. 381–94.

Durry, M. (1938) *Les cohorts prétoriennes.* Paris: de Boccard.

Dyck, A. W. (1996) *A Commentary on Cicero, De Officiis.* Ann Arbor, Mich.: University of Michigan Press.

Eck, W. (1972) 'M. Pompeius Silvanus, *consul designatus tertium* – Ein Vertrauter Vespasians und Domitians', *ZPE* 9: 259–76.

(1995–8) *Die Verwaltung des römischen Reiches in der hohen Kaiserzeit: Ausgewählte und erweiterte Beiträge* (2 vols.). Arbeiten zur römischen Epigraphik und Altertumskunde, 1 and 3. Basel and Berlin: F. Reinhardt.

(2000a) 'The Emperor and his Advisers', in Bowman, Garnsey, and Rathbone 2000: 195–213. [Ger. version: Eck 1995–8: 2.3–29.]

(2000b) 'The Growth of Administrative Posts', in Bowman, Garnsey, and Rathbone 2000: 238–65. [Ger. version: Eck 1995–8: 2.67–106.]

(2006) 'Der Kaiser und seine Ratgeber: Überlegungen zum inneren Zusammenhang von *amici, comites* und *consiliarii* am römischen Kaiserhof', in Kolb 2006: 67–77.

Eck, W., Caballos Rufino, A., and Fernández Gómez, F. (eds.) (1996) *Das Senatus consultum de Cn. Pisone patre.* Vestigia, 48. Munich: Beck.

Edwards, C. (2007) *Death in Ancient Rome.* New Haven, Conn. and London: Yale University Press.

Ehrenberg, V., Jones, A. H. M., and Stockton, D. L. (eds.) (1976) *Documents Illustrating the Reigns of Augustus and Tiberius*, 2nd ed., reprinted with addenda. Oxford: Oxford University Press.

Elias, N. (1983) *The Court Society*, tr. E. Jephcott. Oxford: Blackwell. [Ger. orig. (1969) *Die höfische Gesellschaft.* Darmstadt: Hermann Luchterhand.]

Elkins, N. T. (2017) *The Image of Political Power in the Reign of Nerva, AD 96–98.* Oxford and New York: Oxford University Press.

Ellis, R. (1890) 'Owen's "Tristia"', *Hermathena* 7: 183–212.

Erman, A. (1917) *Römische Obelisken.* Abhandlungen der Königlich-Preussischen Akademie der Wissenschaften. Philosophisch-historische Klasse, 4. Berlin: G. Reimer.

Eshleman, K. (2012) *The Social World of Intellectuals in the Roman Empire: Sophists, Philosophers, and Christians.* Greek Culture in the Roman World. Cambridge: Cambridge University Press.

Fagan, G. (2002) 'Messalina's Folly', *CQ* 52: 566–79.

Fantham, E. (2011) 'A Controversial Life', in *Brill's Companion to Lucan*, ed. P. Asso. Leiden and Boston, Mass.: Brill. 3–20.

Faoro, D. (2016) 'Carriere parallele: Cn. Vergilius Capito e Ti. Claudius Balbillus', *ZPE* 199: 213–17.

Farquharson, A. S. L. (1944) *The Meditations of the Emperor Marcus Antoninus* (2 vols.), with tr. and comm. Oxford: Clarendon.

Faust, S. (2012) *Schlachtenbilder der römischen Kaiserzeit: Erzählerische Darstellungskonzepte in der Reliefkunst von Traian bis Septimius Severus.* Tübinger Archäologische Forschungen, 8. Rahden: Marie Leidorf.

Feissel, D. (1996) 'Deux constitutions tétrarchiques inscrites à Éphèse', *AntTard* 4: 273–89.

Fentress, E., Goodson, C., and Maiuro, M. (eds.) (2016) *Villa Magna: An Imperial Estate and its Legacies. Excavations 2006–10.* Archaeological Monographs of the British School at Rome, 23. London: British School at Rome.

Fentress, E. and Maiuro, M. (2011) 'Villa Magna near Anagni: The Emperor, his Winery and the Wine of Signia', *JRA* 24: 333–69.

Ferguson, J. (1979) *Juvenal: The Satires.* New York: St. Martin's Press.

Ferri, R. (2003) *Octavia: A Play Attributed to Seneca*, with comm. Cambridge Classical Texts and Commentaries, 41. Cambridge: Cambridge University Press.

Fishwick, D. (1987–2005) *The Imperial Cult in the Latin West: Studies in the Ruler Cult of the Western Provinces of the Roman Empire* (4 vols.). Etudes préliminaires aux religions orientales dans l'Empire romain, 108; Religions in the Graeco-Roman World, 145–7. Leiden, Boston, Mass., New York, Copenhagen, and Cologne: Brill.

Fittschen, K. (1976) 'Zur Herkunft und Entstehung des 2. Stils', in *Hellenismus in Mittelitalien: Kolloquium in Göttingen vom 5. bis 9. Juni 1974* (2 vols.), ed. P. Zanker. Abhandlungen der Akademie der Wissenschaften in Göttingen. Philologisch-Historische Klasse, 3.97. Gottingen: Vandenhoeck & Ruprecht. 2.539–63.

Fleury, P. (2006) *Lectures de Fronton: Un rhéteur latin à l'époque de la seconde sophistique.* Collection d'Études Anciennes, 64. Paris: Les Belles Lettres.

Flexsenhar, M. (2016) 'Marcia, Commodus' "Christian" Concubine and CIL X 5918', *Tyche* 31: 135–47.

Flory, M. B. (1995) 'The Symbolism of Laurel in Cameo Portraits of Livia', *MAAR* 40: 43–68.

Flower, H. I. (2006) *The Art of Forgetting: Disgrace and Oblivion in Roman Political Culture.* Studies in the History of Greece and Rome. Chapel Hill, N.C.: University of North Carolina Press.

Foubert, L. (2010) 'The Palatine Dwelling of the mater familias: Houses as Symbolic Space in the Julio-Claudian Period', *Klio* 92: 65–82.

(2016) 'Crowded and Emptied Houses as Status Markers of Aristocratic Women in Rome: The Literary Commonplace of the *domus frequentata*', *EuGeStA* 6: 129–50.

Frankfurter, D. (1998) *Religion in Roman Egypt: Assimilation and Resistance.* Princeton, N. J.: Princeton University Press.

Friedländer, L. (1886) *M. Valerii Martialis epigrammaton libri: Mit erklärenden Anmerkungen* (2 vols.). Leipzig: S. Hirzel.

Frighetto, R. (1977–8) 'La domus di Antonia Caenis e il Balineum Caenidianum', *RPAA* 50: 145–54.

Furneaux, H. (1891) *The Annals of Tacitus.* Volume 2: *Books XI–XVI.* Oxford: Clarendon.

Galimberti, A. (2017) '*P.Oxy.* 471: Hadrian, Alexandria, and the Antinous Cult', in *Empire and Religion: Religious Change in Greek Cities under Roman Rule,* ed. E. Muñiz Grijalvo, J. M. Cortés Copete, and F. Lozano Gómez. Impact of Empire, 25. Leiden and Boston, Mass.: Brill. 98–111.

Gasparri, C., Capaldi, C., and Spina, L. (2009) *Le sculture farnese.* Volume 2: *I ritratti.* Naples and Milan: Electa.

Gaudemet, J. (1982) 'Note sur les *amici principis*', in *Romanitas – Christianitas: Untersuchungen zur Geschichte und Literatur der römischen Kaiserzeit. Johannes Straub zum 70. Geburtstag,* ed. G. Wirth, K.-H. Schwarte, and J. Heinrichs. Berlin and New York: de Gruyter. 42–60.

Geertz, C. (1999) 'Centers, Kings, and Charisma: Reflections on the Symbolics of Power', in *Rites of Power: Symbolism, Ritual, and Politics since the Middle Ages,* ed. S. Wilentz. Philadelphia, Pa.: University of Pennsylvania Press. 13–38.

Giesey, R. E. (1987) 'The King Imagined', in *The French Revolution and the Creation of Modern Political Culture.* Volume 1: *The Political Culture of the Old Regime,* ed. K. M. Baker. Oxford: Pergamon Press. 41–59.

Ginsberg, L. D. (2017) *Staging Memory, Staging Strife: Empire and Civil War in the Octavia.* New York: Oxford University Press.

Ginsburg, J. (2006) *Representing Agrippina: Constructions of Female Power in the Early Roman Empire.* Oxford: Oxford University Press.

Goldbeck, F. (2010) *Salutationes: Die Morgenbegrüßungen in Rom in der Republik und der frühen Kaiserzeit.* Klio Suppl., 16. Berlin: Akademie Verlag.

Goodyear, F. R. D. (1981) *The Annals of Tacitus.* Volume 2: *Annals 1.55–81 and Annals 2.* Cambridge: Cambridge University Press.

Gowers, E. (1993) *The Loaded Table: Representations of Food in Roman Literature.* Oxford: Clarendon.

(2010) 'Augustus and "Syracuse"', *JRS* 100: 69–87.

Grainger, J. D. (2003) *Nerva and the Roman Succession Crisis of AD 96–99.* London and New York: Routledge.

Grenier, J.-C. (2008) *L'Osiris Antinoos.* Cahiers Égypte Nilotique et Méditerranéenne, 1. Montpellier: Université Paul Valéry.

Griffin, M. T. (1984) *Nero: The End of a Dynasty.* London: B. T. Batsford.

(1997) 'The Senate's Story', *JRS* 87: 249–63.

(2013) *Seneca on Society: A Guide to De Beneficiis.* Oxford: Oxford University Press.

Grosso, F. (1964) *La lotta politica al tempo di Commodo.* Memorie dell'Accademia delle Scienze di Torino: Classe di scienze morali, storiche e filologiche Ser. 4a, 7. Turin: Accademia delle scienze.

Grüner, A. (2013) 'Die kaiserlichen Villen in severischer Zeit: Eine Bestandsaufnahme', in Sojc, Winterling, and Wulf-Rheidt 2013: 231–86.

Gutsfeld, A. (2000) 'Hadrian als Jäger: Jagd als Mittel kaiserlicher Selbstdarstellung', in Martini 2000: 79–99.

Guyot, P. (1980) *Eunuchen als Sklaven und Freigelassene in der griechisch-römischen Antike.* Stuttgarter Beiträge zur Geschichte und Politik, 14. Stuttgart: Klett-Cotta.

Haensch, R. (2012) '*Arx imperii?* Der Palast auf dem Palatin als das politisch-administrative Zentrum in der Reichshauptstadt Rom nach dem Zeugnis der schriftlichen Quellen', in *Politische Räume in vormodernen Gesellschaften: Gestaltung, Wahrnehmung, Funktion. Internationale Tagung des DAI und des DFG-Exzellenzclusters TOPOI vom 18.–22. November 2009 in Berlin*, ed. O. Dally et al. Rahden: Marie Leidorf. 267–76.

(2018) 'Die Herausbildung von Stäben und Archiven bei zentralen Reichskanzleien einer verschleierten Monarchie: Das Beispiel des Imperium Romanum', in *Die Verwaltung der Stadt Rom in der hohen Kaiserzeit: Formen der Kommunikation, Interaktion und Vernetzung*, ed. K. Wojciech and P. Eich. Antike Imperien: Geschichte und Archäologie, 2. Paderborn: Ferdinand Schöningh. 287–306.

Hales, S. (2003) *The Roman House and Social Identity*. Cambridge: Cambridge University Press.

(2013) 'Republican Houses', in *A Companion to the Archaeology of the Roman Republic*, ed. J. D. Evans. Blackwell Companions to the Ancient World. Malden, Mass., Oxford, and Chichester: Wiley-Blackwell. 50–66.

Halfmann, H. (1986) *Itinera principum: Geschichte und Typologie der Kaiserreisen im römischen Reich*. Heidelberger althistorische Beiträge und epigraphische Studien, 2. Stuttgart: Franz Steiner.

(2001) *Städtebau und Bauherren im römischen Kleinasien: Ein Vergleich zwischen Pergamon und Ephesos*. Ist. Mitt. Beih., 43. Tübingen: Wasmuth.

Hall, J. M. (2014) *Artifact and Artifice: Classical Archaeology and the Ancient Historian*. Chicago and London: University of Chicago Press.

Hannestad, N. (1986) *Roman Art and Imperial Policy*. Jutland Archaeological Society Publications, 19. Aarhus: Jutland Archaeological Society.

Hardie, P. (2002) *Ovid's Poetics of Illusion*. Cambridge: Cambridge University Press.

Harker, A. (2008) *Loyalty and Dissidence in Roman Egypt: The Case of the Acta Alexandrinorum*. Cambridge: Cambridge University Press.

Harlow, M. (2004) 'Clothes Maketh the Man: Power Dressing and Elite Masculinity in the Later Roman World', in *Gender in the Early Medieval World: East and West, 300–900*, ed. L. Brubaker and J. M. H. Smith. Cambridge: Cambridge University Press. 44–69.

Harrison, G. W. M. (1987) 'Martial 1.41: Sulphur and Glass', *CQ* 37: 203–7.

Hart, G. (2005) *The Routledge Dictionary of Egyptian Gods and Goddesses*, 2nd ed. London: Routledge.

Hartnett, J. (2017) *The Roman Street: Urban Life and Society in Pompeii, Herculaneum, and Rome*. New York: Cambridge University Press.

Haynes, H. (2010) 'The Tyrant Lists: Tacitus' Obituary of Petronius', *AJPh* 131: 69–99.

Head, B. V. (1892) *Catalogue of the Greek Coins of Ionia*, ed. R. S. Poole. A Catalogue of the Greek Coins of the British Museum. London: Trustees of the British Museum.

Hekster, O. (2002) *Commodus: An Emperor at the Crossroads*. Dutch Monographs on Ancient History and Archaeology, 23. Amsterdam: J. C. Gieben.

(2010) 'Trophy Kings and Roman Power: A Roman Perspective on Client Kingdoms', in *Kingdoms and Principalities in the Roman Near East*, ed. T. Kaizer and M. Facella. Oriens et Occidens, 19. Stuttgart: Franz Steiner. 45–55.

(2015) *Emperors and Ancestors: Roman Rulers and the Constraints of Tradition*. Oxford Studies in Ancient Culture and Representation. Oxford: Oxford University Press.

Helzle, M. (2003) *Ovids Epistulae ex Ponto, Buch I–II: Kommentar.* Wissenschaftliche Kommentare zu griechischen und lateinischen Schriftstellern. Heidelberg: Carl Winter.

Hemelrijk, E. A. (2015) *Hidden Lives, Public Personae: Women and Civic Life in the Roman West.* Oxford: Oxford University Press.

Hennig, D. (1975) *L. Aelius Seianus: Untersuchungen zur Regierung des Tiberius.* Vestigia, 21. Munich: Beck.

Henriksén, C. (1998–9) *Martial, Book IX: A Commentary* (2 vols.). Acta Universitatis Upsaliensis: Studia Latina Upsaliensia, 24. Uppsala: S. Academiae Ubsaliensis.

Héron de Villefosse, A. (1899–1902) 'Le trésor de Boscoreale', *MMAI* 5: 1–290.

Hervey, J. (1931) *Some Materials towards Memoirs of the Reign of King George II* (3 vols.), ed. R. Sedgwick. London: Eyre and Spottiswoode.

Herz, P. (1978) 'Kaiserfeste der Prinzipatszeit', *ANRW* 2.16.2: 1135–1200.

Herzog, R. (1922) 'Nikias und Xenophon von Kos', *HZ* 125: 189–247.

Higginbotham, J. (1997) *Piscinae: Artificial Fishponds in Roman Italy.* Chapel Hill, N. C. and London: University of North Carolina Press.

Hoffmann, A. and Wulf, U. (eds.) (2004) *Die Kaiserpaläste auf dem Palatin in Rom: Das Zentrum der römischen Welt und seine Bauten.* Sonderbände der Antiken Welt; Zaberns Bildbände zur Archäologie. Mainz: von Zabern.

Hohl, E. (1932) 'Die Ermordung des Commodus: Ein Beitrag zur Beurteilung Herodians', *Philologische Wochenschrift* 52: 1135–44.

Hölbl, G. (2001) *A History of the Ptolemaic Empire*, tr. T. Saavedra. London and New York: Routledge.

Holford-Strevens, L. (2003) *Aulus Gellius: An Antonine Scholar and his Achievement*, rev. ed. Oxford: Oxford University Press.

Holloway, R. R. (2004) *Constantine and Rome.* New Haven, Conn. and London: Yale University Press.

Holloway, S. and Worsley, L. (2017) '"Every body took notice of the scene of the drawing room": Performing Emotions at the Early Georgian Court, 1714–60', *Journal for Eighteenth-Century Studies* 40: 443–64.

Holztrattner, F. (1995) *Poppaea Neronis potens: Die Gestalt der Poppaea Sabina in den Nerobüchern des Tacitus, mit einem Anhang zu Claudia Acte.* Grazer Beiträge Suppl., 6. Horn: Berger.

Hopkins, K. (1963) 'Eunuchs in Politics in the Later Roman Empire', *PCPhs* 189: 62–80.

  (1978) *Conquerors and Slaves.* Sociological Studies in Roman History, 1. Cambridge: Cambridge University Press.

van den Hout, M. P. J. (1999) *A Commentary on the Letters of M. Cornelius Fronto.* Mnemos. Suppl., 190. Leiden, Boston, Mass., and Cologne: Brill.

Hurlet, F. (2000) 'Les sénateurs dans l'entourage d'Auguste et de Tibère: Un complément à plusieurs synthèses récentes sur la cour impériale', *RPh* 74: 123–50.

  (2018) '*Interdicta aula:* Cour impériale et hiérarchie spatiale (Haut-Empire romain)', in *Statuts personnels et espaces sociaux: Questions grecques et romaines*, ed. C. Moatti and C. Müller. Travaux de la Maison Archéologie et Ethnologie René-Ginouvès, 25. Paris: de Boccard. 271–86.

Hurley, D. W. (2001) *Suetonius: Divus Claudius.* Cambridge Greek and Latin Classics. Cambridge: Cambridge University Press.

Huskey, S. J. (2006) 'Ovid's (Mis)guided Tour of Rome: Some Purposeful Omissions in *Tr.* 3.1', *CJ* 102: 17–39.

Iacopi, I. and Tedone, G. (2005–6) 'Bibliotheca e Porticus ad Apollinis', *MDAI(R)* 112: 351–78.

Iara, K. (2015) *Hippodromus Palatii: Die Bauornamentik des Gartenhippodroms im Kaiserpalast auf dem Palatin in Rom*. Palilia, 30. Wiesbaden: Reichert.

Imhof, A. (1867) *Emendata quaedam et observata in Statii Silvis*. Halle: Typis orphanotrophei.

Jaeger, M. (2008) *Archimedes and the Roman Imagination*. Ann Arbor, Mich.: University of Michigan Press.

Janni, P. (1996) *Il mare degli Antichi*. Storia e civiltà, 40. Bari: Dedalo.

Jeppesen, K. K. (1993) 'Grand camée de France: Sejanus Reconsidered and Confirmed', *MDAI(R)* 100: 141–75.

Jones, A. H. M. (1964) *The Later Roman Empire, 284–602: A Social, Economic, and Administrative Survey* (3 vols.). Oxford: Blackwell.

Jones, B. W. (1992) *The Emperor Domitian*. London: Routledge.

Jones, C. P. (1972) 'Aelius Aristides, Εἰς Βασιλέα', *JRS* 62: 134–52.

(1981) 'The Εἰς Βασιλέα Again', *CQ* 31: 224–5.

(2004) 'A Speech of the Emperor Hadrian', *CQ* 54: 266–73.

Jordan, H. (1860) *M. Catonis praeter librum De re rustica quae extant*. Leipzig: Teubner.

Jucker, H. (1976) 'Der grosse Pariser Kameo: Eine Huldigung an Agrippina, Claudius und Nero', *JDAI* 91: 211–50.

Kampen, N. (2009) *Family Fictions in Roman Art: Essays on the Representation of Powerful People*. New York: Cambridge University Press.

Kassel, R. and Austin, C. (eds.) (1986) *Poetae Comici Graeci*. Volume 5: *Damoxenus – Magnes*. Berlin and New York: de Gruyter.

(eds.) (1998) *Poetae Comici Graeci*. Volume 6.2: *Menander: Testimonia et fragmenta apud scriptores servata*. Berlin and New York: de Gruyter.

Kasulke, T. (2000) 'Hadrian und die Jagd im Spiegel der zeitgenössischen Literatur', in Martini 2000: 101–27.

Kelly, B. (2020) 'Court Politics and Imperial Imagery in the Roman Principate', in *The Social Dynamics of Roman Imperial Imagery*, ed. A. Russell and M. Hellström. Cambridge: Cambridge University Press. 128–58.

(Forthcoming) 'Was the Roman Imperial Court an "Emotional Community"?', in *The Roman Imperial Court in the Principate and Late Antiquity: Continuities, Changes, Connections*, ed. C. Davenport and M. McEvoy. Oxford: Oxford University Press.

Kemezis, A. M. (2016) 'The Fall of Elagabalus as Literary Narrative and Political Reality', *Historia* 65: 348–90.

Ker, J. (2009) *The Deaths of Seneca*. Oxford: Oxford University Press.

Kierdorf, W. (1987) 'Freundschaft und Freundschaftsaufkündigung von der Republik zum Prinzipat', in *Saeculum Augustum* (3 vols.), ed. G. Binder. Darmstadt: Wissenschaftliche Buchgesellschaft. 1.223–45.

Kiessel, M. (2011) 'Die Architektur des spätantiken Palastareals nordöstlich und östlich der spätantiken Aula in Trier', in *Untergang und Neuanfang: Tagungsbeiträge der Arbeitsgemeinschaft Spätantike und Frühmittelalter 3 (Siedlungsarchäologie) und 4 (Militaria und Verteidigungsanlagen)*, ed. J. Drauschke, R. Prien, and S. Ristow. Studien zu Spätantike und Frühmittelalter, 3. Hamburg: Kovač. 77–106.

(2012–13) 'Das spätantike Palastareal nordöstlich und östlich der "Basilika" in Trier', *TZ* 75/6: 85–199.

Kleiner, D. E. E. (1992) *Roman Sculpture*. Yale Publications in the History of Art. New Haven, Conn. and London: Yale University Press.

Kleiner, D. E. E. and Buxton, B. (2008) 'Pledges of Empire: The Ara Pacis and the Donations of Rome', *AJA* 112: 57–89.

Klodt, C. (2001) *Bescheidene Größe: Die Herrschergestalt, der Kaiserpalast und die Stadt Rom. Literarische Reflexionen monarchischer Selbstdarstellung.* Hypomnemata, 137. Göttingen: Vandenhoeck & Ruprecht.

Kolb, A. (ed.) (2006) *Herrschaftsstrukturen und Herrschaftspraxis: Konzepte, Prinzipien und Strategien der Administration im römischen Kaiserreich.* Berlin: Akademie Verlag.

Körner, C. (2002) 'Die Rede Εἰς Βασιλέα des Pseudo-Aelius Aristides', *MH* 59: 211–28.

Kosmetatou, E. (2002) 'The Public Image of Julia Mamaea: An Epigraphic and Numismatic Inquiry', *Latomus* 61: 398–414.

Kragelund, P. (2016) *Roman Historical Drama: The Octavia in Antiquity and Beyond.* Oxford: Oxford University Press.

Krause, C. (1995) 'Wo residierten die Flavier? Überlegungen zur flavischen Bautätigkeit auf dem Palatin', in *Arculiana: Recueil d'hommages offerts à Hans Bögli*, ed. F. E. König and S. Rebetez. Avenches: Ed. L.A.O.T.T. 459–68.

(2003) *Villa Iovis: Die Residenz des Tiberius auf Capri.* Sonderbände der Antiken Welt. Mainz: von Zabern.

(2004) 'Die Domus Tiberiana: Vom Wohnquartier zum Kaiserpalast', in Hoffmann and Wulf 2004: 32–58.

Krenn, K. (2011) 'Cleanders Stellung am Hof des Commodus: Zur Deutung des Titels *a pugione*', *Tyche* 26: 165–97.

Kühn, K. G. (1821–8) *Medicorum graecorum opera quae exstant* (28 vols.). Leipzig: Cnobloch.

Kühn, W. (1987) 'Der Kuss des Kaisers: Plinius *paneg.* 24.2', *WJA* 13: 263–71.

Kunst, C. (2008) *Livia: Macht und Intrigen am Hof des Augustus.* Stuttgart: Klett-Cotta.

Kushnir-Stein, A. (2003) 'Agrippa I in Josephus', *SCI* 22: 153–61.

Kuttner, A. L. (1995) *Dynasty and Empire in the Age of Augustus: The Case of the Boscoreale Cups.* Berkeley, Calif., Los Angeles, and Oxford: University of California Press.

Laes, C. (2009) 'What Could Marcus Aurelius Feel for Fronto?', *Studia Humaniora Tartuensia* 10.A.3.

Lahusen, G. (1999) 'Zu römischen Statuen und Bildnissen aus Gold und Silber', *ZPE* 128: 251–66.

Lauro, M. G. (1998) 'L'area archeologica di Tor Paterno: Campagne di scavo 1987–1991', in *Castelporziano III: Campagne di scavo e restauro 1987–1991*, ed. M. G. Lauro. Rome: Viella. 63–105.

Leary, T. J. (1996) *Martial Book XIV: The Apophoreta,* with comm. London: Duckworth.

Leigh, R. (2016) *On Theriac to Piso, Attributed to Galen: A Critical Edition with Translation and Commentary.* Studies in Ancient Medicine, 47. Leiden and Boston, Mass.: Brill.

Lembke, K. (1994) *Das Iseum Campense in Rom: Studie über den Isiskult unter Domitian.* Archäologie und Geschichte, 3. Heidelberg: Verlag Archäologie und Geschichte.

Lendon, J. E. (1997) *Empire of Honour: The Art of Government in the Roman World*. Oxford: Clarendon.

Leprohon, R. J. (2013) *The Great Name: Ancient Egyptian Royal Titulary*. Writings from the Ancient World, 33. Atlanta, Ga.: Society of Biblical Literature.

Le Roux, P. (2009) 'L'empereur romain et la chasse', in *Chasses antiques: Pratiques et représentations dans le monde gréco-romain (IIIe siècle av.–IVe siècle apr. J.-C.)*, ed. J. Trinquier and C. Vendries. Archéologie et culture. Rennes: Presses universitaires de Rennes. 23–35.

Levi, J. (2012) 'Melancholy and Mourning: Black Banquets and Funerary Feasts', *Gastronomica* 12: 96–103.

Levick, B. (2007) *Julia Domna, Syrian Empress*. Women of the Ancient World. London and New York: Routledge.

  (2014) *Faustina I and II: Imperial Women of the Golden Age*. Women in Antiquity. Oxford: Oxford University Press.

Lichtheim, M. (1980) *Ancient Egyptian Literature*. Volume 3: *The Late Period*. Berkeley, Calif., Los Angeles, and London: University of California Press.

Lifschitz, B. (1970) 'Notes d'épigraphie grecque', *ZPE* 6: 57–64.

Liverani, P. (1999) 'Il cosidetto monumento partico di Lucio Vero: Problemi di interpretazione e di cronologia', in *100 Jahre: Österreichische Forschungen in Ephesos. Akten des Symposions Wien 1995*, ed. H. Friesinger et al. Denkschriften der philosophisch-historischen Klasse, 260. Vienna: Verlag der Österreichischen Akademie der Wissenschaften. 639–45.

Loprieno, A. (1995) *Ancient Egyptian: A Linguistic Introduction*. Cambridge: Cambridge University Press.

Lugli, G. (1962) *Fontes ad topographiam veteris urbis Romae pertinentes*. Volume 8.1: *Mons Palatinus*. Rome: Università di Roma, Istituto di topografia antica.

MacCormack, S. (1981) *Art and Ceremony in Late Antiquity*. Berkeley, Calif., Los Angeles, and London: University of California Press.

MacDonald, W. L. and Pinto, J. A. (1995) *Hadrian's Villa and its Legacy*. New Haven, Conn.: Yale University Press.

Maiuri, A. (1925) *Nuova silloge epigrafica di Rodi e Cos*. Florence: Le Monnier.

Malloch, S. J. V. (2001) 'Gaius' Bridge at Baiae and Alexander-*Imitatio*', *CQ* 51: 206–17.

Maniscalco, F. (1997) *Ninfei ed edifice marittimi severiani del Palatium imperiale di Baia*. Naples: Massa.

Mar, R. (2009) 'La *Domus Flavia*, utilizzo e funzioni del palazzo di Domiziano', in Coarelli 2009: 250–63.

Mari, Z. and Sgalambro, S. (2007) 'The Antinoeion of Hadrian's Villa: Interpretation and Architectural Reconstruction', *AJA* 111: 83–104.

Marincola, J. (ed.) (2007a) *A Companion to Greek and Roman Historiography* (2 vols.). Oxford, Maldon, Mass., and Carlton: Blackwell.

  (2007b) 'Speeches in Classical Historiography', in Marincola 2007a: 101–15.

Marquardt, J. (1886) *Das Privatleben der Römer* (2 vols.), 2nd ed. Leipzig: S. Hirzel.

Martini, W. (ed.) (2000) *Die Jagd der Eliten in den Erinnerungskulturen von der Antike bis in die frühe Neuzeit*. Formen der Erinnerung, 3. Göttingen: Vandenhoeck & Ruprecht.

Martini, W. and Schernig, E. (2000) 'Das Jagdmotiv in der imperialen Kunst hadrianischer Zeit', in Martini 2000: 129–55.

Marzano, A. (2007) *Roman Villas in Central Italy: A Social and Economic History*. Columbia Studies in the Classical Tradition, 30. Leiden and Boston, Mass.: Brill.

Mastino, A. and Ruggeri, P. (1995) '*Claudia Augusti liberta Acte*, le liberta amata da Nerone ad Olbia', *Latomus* 54: 513–44.

Mattern, S. P. (2008) *Galen and the Rhetoric of Healing*. Baltimore, Md.: Johns Hopkins University Press.

Matthews, J. F. (1989) *The Roman Empire of Ammianus*. London: Duckworth.

(2007) 'The Emperor and his Historians', in Marincola 2007a: 269–82.

McCarter, S. (2015) *Horace between Freedom and Slavery: The First Book of Epistles*. Wisconsin Studies in Classics. Madison, Wis.: University of Wisconsin Press.

McFadden, S. (2015) 'The Luxor Temple Paintings in Context: Roman Visual Culture in Late Antiquity', in *Art of Empire: The Roman Frescoes and Imperial Cult Chamber in Luxor Temple*, ed. M. Jones and S. McFadden. New Haven, Conn. and London: Yale University Press. 105–33, 185–8.

McGill, S. (2013) 'The Plagiarized Virgil in Donatus, Servius, and the *Anthologia Latina*', *HSPh* 107: 365–83.

Meckler, M. L. (1999) 'Caracalla the Intellectual', in *Gli imperatori Severi: Storia, archeologia, religione*, ed. E. dal Covolo and G. Rinaldi. Biblioteca di Scienze Religiose, 138. Rome: LAS. 39–46.

Meeks, D. and Favard-Meeks, C. (1997) *Daily Life of the Egyptian Gods*, tr. G. M. Goshgarian. London: John Murray.

Megow, W.-R. (1987) *Kameen von Augustus bis Alexander Severus*. Antike Münzen und geschnittene Steine, 11. Berlin: de Gruyter.

Mellor, R. (1999) *The Roman Historians*. London and New York: Routledge.

Meyboom, P. G. P. (2005) 'The Creation of an Imperial Tradition: Ideological Aspects of the House of Augustus', in *The Manipulative Mode: Political Propaganda in Antiquity. A Collection of Case Studies*, ed. K. A. E. Enenkel and I. L. Pfeijffer. Mnemos. Suppl., 261. Leiden and Boston, Mass.: Brill. 219–74.

Meyer, H., Grimm, A., and Kessler, D. (1994) *Der Obelisk des Antinoos: Eine kommentierte Edition*. Munich: W. Fink.

Michel, A.-C. (2015) *La cour sous l'empereur Claude: Les enjeux d'un lieu de pouvoir*. Rennes: Presses universitaires de Rennes.

Michiels, J. (1902) 'Les *cubicularii* des empereurs romains d'Auguste à Diocletien', *Musée Belge* 6: 364–87.

Migliorati, G. (2003) *Cassio Dione e l'impero romano da Nerva ad Antonino Pio: Alla luce dei nuovi documenti*. Milan: Vita e Pensiero.

Millar, F. G. B. (1965) 'Epictetus and the Imperial Court', *JRS* 55: 141–8.

(1981) 'The World of the Golden Ass', *JRS* 71: 63–75.

(1992) *The Emperor in the Roman World (31 BC–AD 337)*, 2nd ed. London: Duckworth.

(1993) 'Ovid and the *domus Augusta*: Rome Seen from Tomoi', *JRS* 83: 1–17.

Miller, N. P. (1987) *Tacitus, Annals 14: A Companion to the Penguin Translation*. Bristol: Bristol Classical Press.

Moffatt, A. and Tall, M. (2012) *Constantine Porphyrogennetos: The Book of Ceremonies* (2 vols.), with tr. Byzantina Australiensia, 18. Canberra: Australian Association for Byzantine Studies.

Mommsen, T. (1887–8) *Römisches Staatsrecht* (3 vols.), 3rd ed. Leipzig: S. Hirzel.

Montet, P. (1961) *Géographie de l'Égypte ancienne. Deuxième partie: La Haute Égypte.* Paris: C. Klincksieck.

Moreau, P. (2005) 'La *domus Augusta* et les formations de parenté à Rome', *CCG* 16: 7–23.

Morel, W., Büchner, K., and Blänsdorf, J. (eds.) (2011) *Fragmenta Poetarum Latinorum epicorum et lyricorum praeter Ennium et Lucilium*, 4th ed. Berlin and New York: de Gruyter.

Morgan, F. P. (2018) *Dress and Personal Appearance in Late Antiquity: The Clothing of the Middle and Lower Classes.* Late Antique Archaeology, 1. Leiden and Boston, Mass.: Brill.

Morgan, J. (2017) 'At Home with Royalty: Re-viewing the Hellenistic "Palace"', in *The Hellenistic Court: Monarchic Power and Elite Society from Alexander to Cleopatra*, ed. A. Erskine, L. Llewellyn-Jones, and S. Wallace. Swansea: The Classical Press of Wales. 31–67.

Mowat, R. (1901) 'Martelage et abrasion des monnaies sous l'Empire romain: Leurs contremarques', *RN* 5: 443–71.

Muir, E. (1997) *Ritual in Early Modern Europe.* New Approaches to European History, 11. Cambridge: Cambridge University Press.

Müller, M. (2001) 'Re and Re-horakhty', in Redford 2001: 3.123–6.

Murgatroyd, P. (2017) *Juvenal's Tenth Satire.* Liverpool: Liverpool University Press.

Murgatroyd, T. (2013) 'Petronius' *Satyrica*', in *A Companion to the Neronian Age*, ed. E. Buckley and M. T. Dinter. Malden, Mass., Oxford, and Chichester: Wiley-Blackwell. 241–57.

Murison, C. L. (1999) *Rebellion and Reconstruction: Galba to Domitian. An Historical Commentary on Cassius Dio's Roman History Books 64–67 (A.D. 68–96).* Atlanta, Ga.: Scholars Press.

Murray, O. (1965) 'The "quinquennium Neronis" and the Stoics', *Historia* 14: 41–61.

Nadolny, S. (2016) *Die severischen Kaiserfrauen.* Palingenesia, 104. Stuttgart: Franz Steiner.

Nagle, B. R. (2004) *The Silvae of Statius*, with tr. Bloomington, Ind.: Indiana University Press.

Newlands, C. (2002) *Statius' Silvae and the Poetics of Empire.* Cambridge: Cambridge University Press.

Nielsen, I. (1999) *Hellenistic Palaces: Tradition and Renewal.* Studies in Hellenistic Civilization, 5. Aarhus: Aarhus University Press.

Nikšić, G. (2011) 'Diocletian's Palace: Design and Construction', in von Bülow and Zabehlicky 2011: 187–202.

Nixon, C. E. V. and Rodgers, B. S. (1994) *In Praise of Latin Roman Emperors: The Panegyrici Latini*, with tr. and comm. Transformation of the Classical Heritage, 21. Berkeley, Calif., Los Angeles, and Oxford: University of California Press.

Nonnis, D. (2009) 'Ara sepolcrale di *Antonia Caenis*, concubina di Vespasiano', in Coarelli 2009: 404–5.

North, J. A. (1990) 'Diviners and Divination at Rome', in *Pagan Priests: Religion and Power in the Ancient World*, ed. M. Beard and J. North. London: Duckworth. 51–71.

Olson, K. (2017) *Masculinity and Dress in Roman Antiquity*. Routledge Monographs in Classical Studies. London and New York: Routledge.

Pani, M. (2003) *La corte dei Cesari fra Augusto e Nerone*. Biblioteca essenziale Laterza, 54. Rome: Laterza.

Panov, M. (2020) 'Inscriptions on the Obelisk of Antinous', *Göttinger Miszellen* 260: 127–44.

Parani, M. (2007) 'Defining Personal Space: Dress and Accessories in Late Antiquity', in *Objects in Context, Objects in Use: Material Spatiality in Late Antiquity*, ed. L. Lavan, E. Swift, and T. Putzeys. Late Antique Archaeology, 5. Leiden and Boston, Mass.: Brill. 497–529.

Parkes, R. (2015) 'Reading Statius through a Biographical Lens', in *Brill's Companion to Statius*, ed. W. J. Dominik, C. E. Newlands, and K. Gervais. Leiden and Boston, Mass.: Brill. 465–80.

Paterson, J. (2007) 'Friends in High Places: The Creation of the Court of the Roman Emperor', in Spawforth 2007: 121–56.

Patterson, O. (1982) *Slavery and Social Death: A Comparative Study*. Cambridge, Mass. and London: Harvard University Press.

Peachin, M. (1989) 'The Office of Memory', in *Studien zur Geschichte der römischen Spätantike: Festgabe für Professor Johannes Straub*, ed. E. Chrysos. Athens: Pelasgos. 168–208.

 (1990) 'Prosopographic Notes from the Law Codes', *ZPE* 84: 105–12.

Peirce, P. (1989) 'The Arch of Constantine: Propaganda and Ideology in Late Roman Art', *Art History* 12: 387–418.

Pensabene, P. and Gallocchio, E. (2011) 'Contributo alla discussione sul complesso augusteo palatino', *ArchClass* 62: 475–87.

Peremans, W. and van't Dack, E. (1950–81) *Prosopographia Ptolemaica* (9 vols.). Studia Hellenistica, 6, 8, 11–13, 17, 20–1, 25. Leuven: Bibliotheca Universitatis.

Perrin, Y. (2003) 'Aux marches du palais: Les accès au Palatium de 54 à 70', in *The Representation and Perception of Roman Imperial Power*, ed. L. de Blois et al. Impact of Empire, 3. Amsterdam: J. C. Gieben. 358–75.

Pflug, J. (2013) 'Die bauliche Entwicklung der Domus Augustana im Kontext des südöstlichen Palatin bis in severische Zeit', in Sojc, Winterling, and Wulf-Rheidt 2013: 181–212.

Phillimore, J. S. (1918) *P. Papini Stati Silvae*, 2nd ed. Oxford: Clarendon.

Pollini, J. (2012) *From Republic to Empire: Rhetoric, Religion, and Power in the Visual Culture of Ancient Rome*. Oklahoma Series in Classical Culture, 48. Norman, Okla.: University of Oklahoma Press.

Potter, D. (1994) *Prophets and Emperors: Human and Divine Authority from Augustus to Theodosius*. Cambridge, Mass.: Harvard University Press.

 (1998) 'Senatus Consultum de Cn. Pisone', *JRA* 11: 437–57.

Pratt, M. L. (1991) 'Arts of the Contact Zone', *Profession* 91: 33–40.

 (1992) *Imperial Eyes: Travel Writing and Transculturation*. London and New York: Routledge.

Purcell, N. (1987) 'Town in Country and Country in Town', in *Ancient Roman Villa Gardens*, ed. E. B. MacDougall. Dumbarton Oaks Colloquia on the History of Landscape Architecture, 10. Washington, D.C.: Dumbarton Oaks. 187–203.

Quirke, S. T. G. (2001) 'Judgement of the Dead', in Redford 2001: 2.211–14.

Raimondi Cominesi, A. (2018) 'Augustus in the Making: A Reappraisal of the Ideology behind Octavian's Palatine Residence through its Interior Decoration and Topographical Context', *Latomus* 77: 704–35.

Ramsey, J. T. (2006) *A Descriptive Catalogue of Greco-Roman Comets from 500 B.C. to A.D. 400*. Syllecta Classica, 17. Iowa City, Iowa: The University of Iowa.

Redford, D. B. (ed.) (2001) *The Oxford Encyclopedia of Ancient Egypt* (3 vols.). Oxford: Oxford University Press.

Remijsen, S. (2015) *The End of Greek Athletics in Late Antiquity*. Greek Culture in the Roman World. Cambridge: Cambridge University Press.

Renberg, G. H. (2010) 'Hadrian and the Oracles of Antinous (SHA *Hadr.* 14.7); With an Appendix on the So-Called Antinoeion at Hadrian's Villa and Rome's Monte Pincio Obelisk', *MAAR* 55: 159–98.

Reynolds, J. M. (1962) '*Vota pro salute principis*', *PBSR* 30: 33–6.

(1982) *Aphrodisias and Rome: Documents from the Excavation of the Theatre at Aphrodisias Conducted by Professor Kenan T. Erim, Together with some Related Texts*. JRS Monographs, 1. London: Society for the Promotion of Roman Studies.

Reynolds, J. M. and Ward Perkins, J. B. (1952) *The Inscriptions of Roman Tripolitania*. Rome and London: British School at Rome.

Reynolds, L. D. and Wilson, N. G. (2013) *Scribes and Scholars: A Guide to the Transmission of Greek and Latin Literature*, 4th ed. Oxford: Oxford University Press.

Ribbeck, O. (1898) *Scaenicae Romanorum poesis fragmenta*. Volume 2: *Comicorum fragmenta*, 2nd ed. Leipzig: Teubner.

Richlin, A. (2006a) 'Fronto + Marcus: Love, Friendship, Letters', in *The Boswell Thesis: Essays on Christianity, Social Tolerance, and Homosexuality*, ed. M. Kuefler. Chicago: University of Chicago Press. 111–29.

(2006b) *Marcus Aurelius in Love: Marcus Aurelius and Marcus Cornelius Fronto,* with tr. and comm. Chicago and London: University of Chicago Press.

Riedel, A. (2008) 'Zwischen Villenluxus und Repräsentationsarchitektur: Neue Untersuchungen zum Gartenstadion auf dem Palatin', in *Bericht über die 44. Tagung für Ausgrabungswissenschaften und Bauforschung vom 24. bis 28. Mai 2006 in Breslau*, ed. K. Tragbar. Stuttgart: Koldewey-Gesellschaft. 135–43.

Riggs, C. (2010) 'Funerary Rituals (Ptolemaic and Roman Periods)', *UCLA Encyclopedia of Egyptology*, ed. W. Wendrich et al. Los Angeles. https://escholarship.org/uc/item/1n10x347 (accessed 21 May 2022).

Rilinger, R. (1997) '*Domus* und *res publica*: Die politisch-soziale Bedeutung des aristokratischen "Hauses" in der späten römischen Republik', in Winterling 1997: 73–90.

Ripat, P. (2011) 'Expelling Misconceptions: Astrologers at Rome', *CPh* 106: 115–54.

Robert, L. (1967) 'Sur des inscriptions d'Éphèse: Fêtes, athlètes, empereurs, épigrammes', *RPh* 41: 7–84.

Roche, P. (ed.) (2011) *Pliny's Praise: The Panegyricus in the Roman World*. Cambridge: Cambridge University Press.

Rogers, R. S. (1947) 'The Roman Emperors as Heirs and Legatees', *TAPhA* 78: 140–58.

(1959) 'The Emperor's Displeasure – *amicitiam renuntiare*', *TAPhA* 90: 224–37.

Roller, D. W. (2018) *Cleopatra's Daughter and Other Royal Women of the Augustan Era.* New York: Oxford University Press.

Roller, M. B. (2001) *Constructing Autocracy: Aristocrats and Emperors in Julio-Claudian Rome.* Princeton, N. J.: Princeton University Press.

(2006) *Dining Posture in Ancient Rome: Bodies, Values, and Status.* Princeton, N. J. and Oxford: Princeton University Press.

Rosa, J. (1994) 'A Constructed View', in *A Constructed View: The Architectural Photography of Julius Shulman*, ed. J. Rosa. New York: Rizzoli. 35–110.

Rose, C. B. (1990) '"Princes" and Barbarians on the Ara Pacis', *AJA* 94: 453–67.

(1997) *Dynastic Commemoration and Imperial Portraiture in the Julio-Claudian Period.* Cambridge Studies in Classical Art and Iconography. Cambridge: Cambridge University Press.

Rosenwein, B. H. (2006) *Emotional Communities in the Early Middle Ages.* Ithaca, N. Y. and London: Cornell University Press.

Ross, S. K. (2001) *Roman Edessa: Politics and Culture on the Eastern Fringes of the Roman Empire, 114–242 CE.* London and New York: Routledge.

Rüpke, J. (2007) *Religion of the Romans*, tr. and ed. R. Gordon. Cambridge and Malden, Mass.: Polity. [Ger. orig. (2001) *Die Religion der Römer.* Munich: Beck.]

(2008) *Fasti sacerdotum: A Prosopography of Pagan, Jewish, and Christian Religious Officials in the City of Rome, 300 BC to AD 499*, tr. D. M. B. Richardson. Oxford: Oxford University Press. [Ger. orig. (2005) *Fasti sacerdotum: Die Mitglieder der Priesterschaften und das sakrale Funktionspersonal römischer, griechischer, orientalischer und jüdisch-christlicher Kulte in der Stadt Rom von 300 v. Chr. bis 499 n. Chr.* Stuttgart: Franz Steiner.]

Ryberg, I. S. (1967) *Panel Reliefs of Marcus Aurelius.* Monographs on Archaeology and the Fine Arts, 14. New York: Archaeological Institute of America.

Sainte-Simon, L. de Rouvroy de (1983–8) *Mémoires* (8 vols.), ed. Y. Coirault. Bibliothèque de la Pléiade. Paris: Gallimard.

Saladino, V. (2008) 'Ara funeraria di Antonia Caenis', in *Augusta Fragmenta: Vitalità dei materiali dell'antico da Arnolfo di Cambio a Botticelli a Giambologna*, ed. M. Scalini. Milan: Silvana. 86–9.

Saller, R. P. (1980) 'Anecdotes as Historical Evidence for the Principate', *G&R* 27: 69–83.

(1982) *Personal Patronage under the Early Empire.* Cambridge: Cambridge University Press.

(1984) '*Familia, domus*, and the Roman Conception of the Family', *Phoenix* 38: 336–55.

(1994) '*Familia* and *domus*: Defining and Representing the Roman Family and Household', in R. P. Saller, *Patriarchy, Property and Death in the Roman Family.* Cambridge: Cambridge University Press. 74–101.

Salway, R. W. B. (2006) 'Equestrian Prefects and the Award of Senatorial Honours from the Severans to Constantine', in Kolb 2006: 115–35.

Salza Prina Ricotti, E. (2001) *Villa Adriana: Il sogno di un imperatore.* Bibliotheca Archaeologica, 29. Rome: 'L'Erma' di Bretschneider.

Schlinkert, D. (1996) 'Vom Haus zum Hof: Aspekte höfischer Herrschaft in der Spätantike,' *Klio* 78: 454–82.

Schmidt, M. G. (1986) *Caesar und Cleopatra: Philologischer und historischer Kommentar zu Lucan 10, 1–171.* Studien zur klassischen Philologie, 25. Frankfurt, Bern, and New York: Peter Lang.

Schöpe, B. (2014) *Der römische Kaiserhof in severischer Zeit (193–235 n. Chr.).* Historia Einzelschriften, 231. Stuttgart: Franz Steiner.

Schumacher, L. (2001) 'Hausgesinde – Hofgesinde: Terminologische Überlegungen zur Funktion der *familia Caesaris* im 1. Jh. n. Chr.', in *Fünfzig Jahre Forschungen zur antiken Sklaverei der Mainzer Akademie 1950–2000: Miscellanea zum Jubiläum*, ed. H. Bellen and H. Heinen. Forschungen zur antiken Sklaverei, 35. Stuttgart: Franz Steiner. 331–52. [Reprinted in *Historischer Realismus*, ed. F. Bernstein and L. Schumacher. Kleine Schriften zur Alten Geschichte, 26. Göttingen (2018): Antike.]

Scott, A. G. (2015) 'Cassius Dio, Caracalla, and the Senate', *Klio* 97: 157–75.

(2018) *Emperors and Usurpers: An Historical Commentary on Cassius Dio's Roman History Books 79(78)–80(80) (A.D. 217–229).* American Classical Studies, 58. New York: Oxford University Press.

Seager, R. (1977) '*Amicitia* in Tacitus and Juvenal', *AJAH* 2: 40–50.

(2005) *Tiberius*, 2nd ed. Malden, Mass. and Oxford: Blackwell.

Seston, W. and Euzennat, M. (1971) 'Un dossier de la chancellerie romaine: La *Tabula Banasitana*. Étude de diplomatique', *CRAI* 115: 468–90.

Sévigné, Marie de Rabutin-Chantal de (1972–8) *Correspondance* (3 vols.), ed. R. Duchêne. Paris: Gallimard.

Shackleton Bailey, D. R. (2015) *Statius: Silvae*, with tr., rev. by C. A. Parrott. Loeb. Cambridge, Mass. and London: Harvard University Press.

Shaw, I. (2000) 'Egypt and the Outside World', in *The Oxford History of Ancient Egypt*, ed. I. Shaw. Oxford: Oxford University Press. 308–23.

Sherwin-White, A. N. (1966) *The Letters of Pliny: A Historical and Social Commentary.* Oxford: Clarendon.

(1973) 'The *Tabula* of Banasa and the *Constitutio Antoniniana*', *JRS* 63: 86–98.

Sherwin-White, S. (1978) *Ancient Cos: An Historical Study from the Dorian Settlement to the Imperial Period.* Hypomnemata, 51. Göttingen: Vandenhoeck & Ruprecht.

Sidéris, G. (2000) 'La comédie des castrats: Ammien Marcellin et les eunuques, entre eunucophobie et admiration', *RBPh* 78: 618–717.

Simon, E. (1967–8) 'Beobachtungen zum Grand Camée de France', *KJ* 9: 16–22.

Smallwood, E. M. (1966) *Documents Illustrating the Principates of Nerva, Trajan and Hadrian.* Cambridge: Cambridge University Press.

(1976) *The Jews under Roman Rule: From Pompey to Diocletian.* Leiden: Brill.

Smith, M. (2009) *Traversing Eternity: Texts for the Afterlife from Ptolemaic and Roman Egypt.* Oxford: Oxford University Press.

Smith, R. (2007) 'The Imperial Court of the Late Roman Empire, c. AD 300–450', in Spawforth 2007: 157–232.

(2011) 'Measures of Difference: The Fourth-Century Transformation of the Roman Imperial Court', *AJPh* 132: 125–51.

Smith, R. R. R. (1987) 'The Imperial Reliefs from the Sebasteion at Aphrodisias', *JRS* 78: 88–138.

(2021) '*Maiestas Serena*: Roman Court Cameos and Early Imperial Poetry and Panegyric', *JRS* 111: 75–152.

Sojc, N. (ed.) (2012a) *Domus Augustana: Neue Forschungen zum 'Versenkten Peristyl' auf dem Palatin / Investigating the 'Sunken Peristyle' on the Palatine Hill*. Leiden: Sidestone.

Sojc, N. (2012b) 'Introduction: Research on the Sunken Peristyle of the Domus Augustana', in Sojc 2012a: 11–46.

Sojc, N. and Winterling, A. (2009) 'I banchetti nel palazzo imperiale in epoca flavia attraverso le testimonianze archeologiche e letterarie: Tentativo di un'interpretazione interdisciplinare', in Coarelli 2009: 294–301.

Sojc, N., Winterling, A., and Wulf-Rheidt, U. (eds.) (2013) *Palast und Stadt im severischen Rom*. Stuttgart: Franz Steiner.

Spawforth, A. J. S. (ed.) (2007) *The Court and Court Society in Ancient Monarchies*. Cambridge: Cambridge University Press.

Starr, C. G. (1949) 'Epictetus and the Tyrant', *CPh* 44: 20–9.

Stern, H. (1954) 'Remarks on the *adoratio* under Diocletian', *JWI* 17: 184–9.

Stevenson, W. (1995) 'The Rise of Eunuchs in Greco-Roman Antiquity', *JHSex* 5: 495–511.

Strocka, V. M. (1972) 'Beobachtungen an den Attikareliefs des severischen Quadrifons von Lepcis Magna', *AntAfr* 6: 147–72.

Strong, A. K. (2016) *Prostitutes and Matrons in the Roman World*. New York: Cambridge University Press.

Strootman, R. (2014) *Courts and Elites in the Hellenistic Empires: The Near East After the Achaemenids, c. 330 to 30 BCE*. Edinburgh Studies in Ancient Persia. Edinburgh: Edinburgh University Press.

Sullivan, J. P. (1991) *Martial: The Unexpected Classic. A Literary and Historical Study*. Cambridge: Cambridge University Press.

Swift, L. J. (1966) 'The Anonymous Encomium of Philip the Arab', *GRBS* 7: 267–89.

Syme, R. (1971) *Emperors and Biography: Studies in the Historia Augusta*. Oxford: Clarendon.

   (1979–91) *Roman Papers* (7 vols.), ed. E. Badian and A. R. Birley. Oxford: Clarendon.

   (1980a) 'Fiction about Roman Jurists', *ZRG* 97: 78–104. [Reprinted: Syme 1979–91: 3.1393–1414.]

   (1980b) 'Guard Prefects of Trajan and Hadrian', *JRS* 70: 64–80.

Talbert, R. J. A. (1984) *The Senate of Imperial Rome*. Princeton, N. J.: Princeton University Press.

Tamm, B. (1963) *Auditorium and Palatium: A Study on Assembly-Rooms in Roman Palaces during the 1st Century B.C. and the 1st Century A.D.* Stockholm Studies in Classical Archaeology, 12. Stockholm: Almqvist & Wiksell.

   (1968) '*Aula regia*, αὐλή and *aula*', in *Opuscula*, ed. G. Säflund. Acta Universitatis Stockholmiensis; Stockholm Studies in Classical Archaeology, 5. Stockholm: Almqvist & Wiksell. 135–243.

Thompson, D. J. (2013) 'Hellenistic Royal Barges', in *The Ptolemies, the Sea and the Nile: Studies in Waterborne Power*, ed. K. Buraselis, M. Stefanou, and D. J. Thompson. Cambridge: Cambridge University Press. 185–96.

Thomson, M. (2012) *Studies in the Historia Augusta*. Collection Latomus, 337. Brussels: Éditions Latomus.

Tomei, M. A. (2011a) 'Introduzione al Monumento e storia degli scavi', in Tomei and Filectici 2011: 12–37.

(2011b) 'Fronte settentrionale: Sintesi degli scavi. Storia e architettura dell'area', in Tomei and Filetici 2011: 59–85.

(2011c) 'Fronte verso il Velabro: Sintesi degli scavi. Storia e topografia dell'area', in Tomei and Filetici 2011: 155–75.

(2011d) 'Criptoportico: Sintesi degli scavi. Storia e topographica dell'area', in Tomei and Filetici 2011: 222–9.

Tomei, M. A. and Filetici, M. G. (eds.) (2011) *Domus Tiberiana: Scavi e restauri 1990–2011*. Milan: Electa.

Töpfer, K. (2011) *Signa militaria: Die römischen Feldzeichen in der Republik und im Prinzipat*. Monographien des Römisch-Germanischen Zentralmuseums, 91. Mainz: Verlag des Römisch-Germanischen Zentralmuseums.

Torelli, M. (1982) *Typology and Structure of Roman Historical Reliefs*. Ann Arbor, Mich.: University of Michigan Press.

Tougher, S. (1999) 'Ammianus and the Eunuchs', in *The Late Roman World and its Historian: Interpreting Ammianus Marcellinus*, ed. D. Hunt and J. W. Drijvers. London and New York: Routledge. 64–73.

(2008) *The Eunuch in Byzantine History and Society*. Routledge Monographs in Classical Studies. London and New York: Routledge.

Toynbee, J. M. C. (1944) *Roman Medallions*. Numismatic Studies, 5. New York: American Numismatic Society.

Treggiari, S. (1975) 'Jobs in the Household of Livia', *PBSR* 43: 48–77.

Turpin, W. (1981) '*Apokrimata, decreta*, and the Roman Legal Procedure', *BASP* 18: 145–60.

Uccelli, G. (1950) *Le navi di Nemi*, 2nd ed. Rome: La Libreria dello Stato.

Vale, M. (2001) *The Princely Court: Medieval Courts and Culture in North-West Europe, 1270–1380*. Oxford: Oxford University Press.

Varner, E. R. (2004) *Mutilation and Transformation: Damnatio Memoriae and Roman Imperial Portraiture*. Monumenta Graeca et Romana, 10. Leiden and Boston, Mass.: Brill.

Vassileiou, A. (1984) 'Crispinus et les conseillers du prince (Juvénal, *Satires*, IV)', *Latomus* 43: 27–68.

Villedieu, F. (2013) 'La Vigna Barberini à l'époque sévérienne', in Sojc, Winterling, and Wulf-Rheidt 2013: 157–80.

Vogt, J. (1978) '*Nomenclator*: Vom Lautsprecher zum Namenverarbeiter', *Gymnasium* 85: 327–38.

Voisin, J.-L. (2015) '*Exoriente sole* (Suétone, Ner. 6): D'Alexandrie à la *Domus Aurea*', in *L'Urbs: Espace urbain et histoire (Ier siècle av. J.-C.–IIIe siècle ap. J.-C)*, 2nd ed. Classiques École française de Rome. Rome: École française de Rome. 509–43.

Völker, T. and Rohmann, D. (2011) '*Praenomen Petronii*: The Date and Author of the *Satyricon* Reconsidered', *CQ* 61: 660–76.

Walbank, F. W. (1940) '*Licia telae addere* (Virgil, *Georg*. i. 284–6)', *CQ* 34: 93–104.

Walker, S. (1997) 'Mummy Portraits in their Roman Context', in *Portraits and Masks: Burial Customs in Roman Egypt*, ed. M. Bierbrier. London: British Museum Press. 1–6.

(ed.) (2000) *Ancient Faces: Mummy Portraits from Roman Egypt*. New York: Routledge and The Metropolitan Museum of Art.

Wallace-Hadrill, A. (1982) '*Civilis Princeps*: Between Citizen and King', *JRS* 72: 32–48.

(1994) *Houses and Society in Pompeii and Herculaneum*. Princeton, N. J.: Princeton University Press.

(1995) *Suetonius*, 2nd ed. London: Bristol Classical Press.

(1996) 'The Imperial Court', in *The Cambridge Ancient History. Volume 10: The Augustan Empire, 43 B.C.–A.D. 69*, 2nd ed., ed. A. K. Bowman, E. Champlin, and A. Lintott. Cambridge: Cambridge University Press. 283–308.

(2011) 'The Roman Imperial Court: Seen and Unseen in the Performance of Power', in *Royal Courts in Dynastic State and Empire: A Global Perspective*, ed. J. Duindam, T. Artan, and M. Kunt. Rulers & Elites, 1. Leiden and Boston, Mass.: Brill. 91–102.

Wardle, D. (1994) *Suetonius' Life of Caligula: A Commentary*. Collection Latomus, 225. Brussels: Latomus.

(2014) *Suetonius: Life of Augustus*, with tr. and comm. Clarendon Ancient History Series. Oxford: Oxford University Press.

Weaver, P. R. C. (1965) 'The Father of Claudius Etruscus: Statius *Silvae* 3.3', *CQ* 15: 145–54.

(1972) *Familia Caesaris: A Social Study of the Emperor's Freedmen and Slaves*. Cambridge: Cambridge University Press.

(1980) 'Two Freedman Careers', *Antichthon* 14: 143–56.

(1994) 'Epaphroditus, Josephus, and Epictetus', *CQ* 44: 468–79.

Welch, K. E. (2006) '*Domi militiaeque*: Roman Domestic Aesthetics and War Booty in the Republic', in *Representations of War in Ancient Rome*, ed. S. Dillon and K. E. Welch. New York: Cambridge University Press. 91–161.

Wellebrouck, G. (2017) 'Claudia Acte: Le destin d'une affranchie', *BAGB* 1: 97–122.

Wessner, P. (1931) *Scholia in Iuvenalem vetustiora*. Bibliotheca Teubneriana. Leipzig: Teubner.

Whittaker, C. R. (1969) *Herodian: History of the Empire* (2 vols.), with tr. Loeb Classical Library. Cambridge, Mass.: Harvard University Press.

Wightman, E. M. (1970) *Roman Trier and the Treveri*. London: Hart-Davis.

Wilkes, J. J. (1993) *Diocletian's Palace, Split: Residence of a Retired Roman Emperor*. Occasional Publication (Ian Sanders Memorial Fund), 1. Oxford: Oxbow Books.

Wilkinson, R. H. (1992) *Reading Egyptian Art: A Hieroglyphic Guide to Ancient Egyptian Painting and Sculpture*. London: Thames & Hudson.

Williams, M. H. (1988) 'θεοσεβὴς γὰρ ἦν: The Jewish Tendencies of Poppaea Sabina', *JThS* 39: 97–111.

Williams, W. (1975) 'Formal and Historical Aspects of Two New Documents of Marcus Aurelius', *ZPE* 17: 37–78.

Wilson, E. (2014) *The Greatest Empire: A Life of Seneca*. Oxford: Oxford University Press.

Wilson, N. G. (2017) *From Byzantium to Italy: Greek Studies in the Italian Renaissance*, 2nd ed. Bloomsbury Academic: London and New York.

Winterling, A. (ed.) (1997) *Zwischen 'Haus' und 'Staat': Antike Höfe im Vergleich*. HZ Beiheft, 23. Munich: Oldenbourg.

(1999) *Aula Caesaris: Studien zur Institutionalisierung des römischen Kaiserhofes in der Zeit von Augustus bis Commodus (31 v. Chr.–192 n. Chr.)*. Munich: Oldenbourg.

(2009a) 'A Court without "State": The *aula Caesaris*', in Winterling 2009c: 79–102. [Ger. orig. 'Hof ohne "Staat": Die *aula Caesaris* im 1. und 2. Jahrhundert n. Chr.', in Winterling 1997: 91–112.]

(2009b) 'Friendship and Patron-Client Relations', in Winterling 2009c: 34–57. [Ger. orig. (2008) 'Freundschaft und Klientel im kaiserzeitlichen Rom', *Historia* 57: 298–316.]

(2009c) *Politics and Society in Imperial Rome*, tr. K. Lüddecke. Malden, Mass., Oxford, and Chichester: Wiley-Blackwell.

Wiseman, T. P. (2009) Review of Carandini and Bruno 2008, *JRA* 22: 527–45.

(2013a) *The Death of Caligula: Josephus Ant. Iud. XIX 1–273*, with tr. and comm. Liverpool: Liverpool University Press.

(2013b) 'The Palatine, from Evander to Elagabalus', *JRS* 103: 234–68.

(2015) '*Conspicui postes tectaque digna deo*: The Public Image of Aristocratic and Imperial Houses in the Late Republic and Early Empire', in *L'Urbs: Espace urbain et histoire (Ier siècle av. J.-C.–IIIe siècle ap. J.-C.)*, 2nd ed. Classiques École française de Rome. Rome: École française de Rome. 393–413.

(2019) *The House of Augustus: A Historical Detective Story*. Princeton, N. J. and Oxford: Princeton University Press.

Wolters, R. (1999) 'C. Stertinius Xenophon von Kos und die Grabinschrift des Trimalchio', *Hermes* 127: 47–60.

Wood, S. E. (1995) 'Diva Drusilla Panthea and the Sisters of Caligula', *AJA* 99: 457–82.

(2001) *Imperial Women: A Study in Public Images, 40 B.C.–A.D. 68*, 2nd ed. Mnemos. Suppl., 194. Leiden and Boston, Mass.: Brill.

Woodhull, M. L. (2012) 'Imperial Mothers and Monuments in Rome', in *Mothering and Motherhood in Ancient Greece and Rome*, ed. L. Hackworth Petersen and P. Salzman-Mitchell. Austin, Tex.: University of Texas Press. 225–51.

Woodman, A. J. and Martin, R. H. (eds.) (1996) *The Annals of Tacitus: Book 3*, with comm. Cambridge Classical Texts and Commentaries, 32. Cambridge: Cambridge University Press.

Wulf-Rheidt, U. (2011) 'Die Entwicklung der Residenz der römischen Kaiser auf dem Palatin vom aristokratischen Wohnhaus zum Palast', in von Bülow and Zabehlicky 2011: 1–18.

(2012a) 'Augustus und das Gespür für den richtigen Ort – Die Situierung der ersten Kaiserresidenz auf dem Palatin in Rom', in Arnold et al. 2012: 33–40.

(2012b) 'Nutzungsbereiche des flavischen Palastes auf dem Palatin in Rom', in Arnold et al. 2012: 97–112.

(2013) 'Die Bedeutung der severischen Paläste für spätere Residenzbauten', in Sojc, Winterling, and Wulf-Rheidt 2013: 287–306.

(2014) '*Den Sternen und dem Himmel würdig*': *Kaiserliche Palastbauten in Rom und Trier*. Trierer Winkelmannsprogramm, 24. Wiesbaden: Harrassowitz.

(2015) 'The Palace of the Roman Emperors on the Palatine in Rome', in *The Emperor's House: Palaces from Augustus to the Age of Absolutism*, ed. M. Featherstone et al. Urban Spaces, 4. Berlin and Boston, Mass.: de Gruyter. 3–18.

Yegül, F. and Favro, D. (2019) *Roman Architecture and Urbanism: From the Origins to Late Antiquity*. Cambridge: Cambridge University Press.

Zanker, P. (1988) *The Power of Images in the Age of Augustus*, tr. A. Shapiro. Ann Arbor, Mich.: University of Michigan Press. [Ger. orig. (1987) *Augustus und die Macht der Bilder*. Munich: Beck.]

    (2002) 'Domitian's Palace on the Palatine and the Imperial Image', in *Representations of Empire: Rome and the Mediterranean World*, ed. A. K. Bowman et al. PBA, 114. Oxford: Oxford University Press. 105–30.

Zucca, R. (1993) 'La Tavola di Esterzili e la *controversia finium* tra *Vanacini* e *Mariani* in Corsica', in *La Tavola di Esterzili: Il conflitto tra pastori e contadini nella Barbaria sarda*, ed. A. Mastino. Sassari: Edizione Gallizzi. 185–205.

Index of Sources

The following sources are reproduced in this book. Numbers in bold are document numbers. For abbreviation conventions, see above, p. xvii.

4. PAPYRI

5. COINS

6. ARTEFACTS

Index of Personal Names

Numbers in bold are document numbers (or document cluster numbers).
Prominent individuals are indexed under the short form of their name commonly used in English-language scholarship. Their full name is also listed; in the case of emperors, this is the name at accession.

General Index

Numbers in bold are document numbers.
For emperors and other ancient individuals, see Index of Personal Names.